The Psychology of Nuclear Proliferation

D0797120

Dozens of states have long been capable of acquiring nuclear weapons, yet only a few have actually done so. Jacques E. C. Hymans finds that the key to this surprising historical pattern lies not in externally imposed constraints, but rather in state leaders' conceptions of national identity. Synthesizing a wide range of scholarship from the humanities and social sciences to experimental psychology and neuroscience, Hymans builds a rigorous model of decisionmaking that links identity to emotions and ultimately to nuclear policy choices. Exhaustively researched case studies of France, India, Argentina, and Australia – two countries that got the bomb and two that abstained – demonstrate the value of this model while debunking common myths. This book will be invaluable to policymakers and concerned citizens who are frustrated with the frequent misjudgments of states' nuclear ambitions, and to scholars who seek a better understanding of how leaders make big foreign policy decisions.

JACQUES E. C. HYMANS is Assistant Professor of Government at Smith College, Massachusetts.

The Psychology of Nuclear Proliferation

Identity, Emotions, and Foreign Policy

Jacques E. C. Hymans

CAMBRIDGE UNIVERSITY PRESS
Cambridge, New York, Melbourne, Madrid, Cape Town, Singapore, São Paulo

Cambridge University Press
The Edinburgh Building, Cambridge CB2 8RU, UK

Published in the United States of America by Cambridge University Press, New York

www.cambridge.org
Information on this title: www.cambridge.org/9780521616256

First published 2006
Reprinted 2007

Printed in the United Kingdom at the University Press, Cambridge

A catalogue record for this publication is available from the British Library

ISBN-13 978-0-521-85076-6 hardback
ISBN-13 978-0-521-61625-6 paperback

Contents

Figures

Tables

Preface

One southern winter evening in Buenos Aires, I met Dr. Conrado Varotto, father of Argentina's once-secret uranium enrichment program. "The bomb is in the human heart or it isn't," he told me. "We could have done it, but we didn't, because the bomb was not in our hearts." I was skeptical of Varotto's claim, but in the end, after a great deal of research and thought, I decided he was right. Indeed, in a sense this book is an extended elaboration on Dr. Varotto's basic point. It argues that decisions to go or not to go nuclear reflect the psychology of the leaders who make them. In particular, there are discrete decisionmaking pathways leading from different national identity conceptions, through emotions, to ultimate nuclear choices. This argument not only provides what I think is a powerful answer to the nuclear proliferation puzzle; it also provides a potentially fruitful basis for thinking about foreign policy decisionmaking more generally.

The project is nothing if not ambitious, and I am deeply grateful to the hundreds of people who have assisted and encouraged me to develop it. I owe a profound debt to the many politicians, scientists, civil servants, scholars, archivists, activists, and others who offered me their time and wisdom (and in some cases, their spare bedroom) as I struggled to discover the truth of their nations' nuclear histories. Some of these people are referenced directly in the text, but I am equally grateful to them all. Of course, their cooperation should not be taken to imply that they necessarily endorse the overall argument that I have tried to make here.

I had a dream dissertation committee in the Department of Government at Harvard University: Jorge I. Domínguez (chair), Yoshiko M. Herrera, Stanley Hoffmann, Alastair Iain Johnston, and Stephen P. Rosen. They opened new worlds to me. Professor Herrera was exceptionally helpful while I was preparing this book. My classmates in the Government Department also assisted me more than they can ever know. I particularly wish to thank Ted Brader, Kanchan Chandra, Christina Davis, Harumi Furuya, Anna Grzymala-Busse, Lawrence Hamlet, Aaron Lobel, Bonnie Meguid, Kathleen O'Neill, Andrew Rudalevige, Albino Santos,

Kenneth Scheve, Naunihal Singh, Oxana Shevel, Alvin Tillery, Michael Tomz, Joshua Tucker, and Maurits van der Veen for lending me their sharp minds and good hearts over the years.

During this project many people at institutions of research and higher learning gave me the resources and, more importantly, the confidence to continue. Special thanks to Abby Collins, Peter Hall, Charles Maier, and George Ross at the Minda de Gunzburg Center for European Studies at Harvard, from which I received a Krupp Foundation fellowship and remain an affiliate to this day; to John Coatsworth and Steven Reifenberg at the David Rockefeller Center for Latin American Studies at Harvard; to Christian Baudelot, Gilles Pécout, and Monique Trédé at the Ecole Normale Supérieure in Paris; to Christopher Chyba, Lynn Eden, and Scott Sagan at the Center for International Security and Cooperation at Stanford University; to Richard Herrmann and Richard Ned Lebow at the Mershon Center at the Ohio State University; and to Samuel Huntington, Stephen Rosen (again), Monica Duffy Toft, and Ann Townes at the Olin Institute for Strategic Studies at Harvard. Smith College took a chance on someone who had hardly ever faced students before, and I count myself lucky to be among the faculty here. Special thanks to Donald Baumer, Mlada Bukovansky, Susan Bourque, Donna Divine, Charles Staelin, and Greg White for their unfailing support. Thanks also to the Institute for the Study of World Politics and the Mellon Foundation for additional research and writing grants.

In addition to those listed above, a number of colleagues contributed mightily to the shaping of the book by reading draft chapters, sometimes more than once. I would be remiss if I did not express a particular debt of gratitude to Deborah Boucoyannis and Alexander George, colleagues and friends who have supported me and my project in extraordinary ways. I would also like to thank for their help James Alt, Kanti Bajpai, Michael Barletta, Bear Braumoeller, Marilynn Brewer, Wenceslao Bunge and the Bunge and Laulhé families, Pramit Pal Chaudhuri, Charles Cogan, Stephen P. Cohen, Ajin Choi, Michael Desch, Peter Edwards, Tanisha Fazal, Peter Feaver, Peter Furia, Sumit Ganguly, Betty Glad, Hein Goemans, Howard Gold, Mark Haas, Renée Haferkamp, Ron Hassner, Yinan He, Guy Hennebelle and the Hennebelle family, Ole Holsti, Herbert Hymans, Michael Jones-Correa, Devesh Kapur, Ronald Krebs, Peter Katzenstein, William Keller, Andy Kennedy, Michael Kenney, Andrew Kydd, Tomila Lankina, Steven Levitsky, Thomas Lienhard, Will Lowe, Isabela Mares, Andrew Martin, Ernest May, Rose McDermott, Dinshaw Mistry, Christopher Moore, Santiago Morales Rivera, Andrew Moravcsik, John Mueller, Kevin Narizny, Kim Neuendorf, Barry O'Neill, Eduardo and Susana Ortiz, T. V. Paul, Sylvain Perdigon, Daryl

Press, M. V. Ramana, Brian Rathbun, Georges Ripka, Jeremi Suri, Donald Sylvan, Maurice Vaïsse, Jonathan van Loo, Jeffrey Vanke, Ashutosh Varshney, Cynthia Verba, and Jim Walsh. Their input has been tremendous, but of course all errors, omissions, or illogical leaps are mine alone.

Thanks also to John Haslam, Ashlene Aylward, Elizabeth Davey, Sheila Kane and the entire team at Cambridge University Press for their sterling professionalism.

Early versions of some portions of the text were first published elsewhere. Thanks to the copyright holders for the permissions for my articles "Isotopes and Identity: Australia and the Nuclear Weapons Option, 1945–1999," *Nonproliferation Review*, Vol. 7, No. 1 (Spring 2000), pp. 1–23 (reproduced with permission of the *Nonproliferation Review*, Center for Nonproliferation Studies, Monterey Institute for Strategic Studies); "Of Gauchos and Gringos: Why Argentina Never Wanted the Bomb, and Why the United States Thought It Did," *Security Studies*, Vol. 10, No. 3 (Spring 2001), pp. 153–185 (reproduced with permission of Taylor and Francis and *Security Studies*); and "Why Do States Decide to Build Nuclear Weapons? Comparing the Cases of India and France," in Damodar Sardesai and Raju G. C. Thomas, eds, *Nuclear India in the 21st Century* (New York: Palgrave, 2002), pp. 139–160 (reproduced with permission of Palgrave Macmillan).

This book has been a labor of love for more people than just myself. Rieko Kage stuck with me through thick and thin and has now agreed to do so forever. I hope she knows what she is getting into. My mother, Myrna Hymans, taught me never to be satisfied with "good enough." My father, Jacques L. Hymans, read nearly every word I wrote in my life until his death in December 1999. I wish he could read these. This book is dedicated to him.

Acronyms and abbreviations

AAEC	Australian Atomic Energy Commission
AEC	Atomic Energy Commission (India)
ALP	Australian Labor Party
ANZUS	Australia, New Zealand, and United States Security Treaty
BJP	Bharatiya Janata Party (India)
CANDU	Canada Deuterium Uranium (nuclear reactor)
CEA	*Commissariat à l'Energie Atomique* (France)
CNEA	*Comisión Nacional de Energía Atómica* (Argentina)
CNIA	*Current Notes on International Affairs* (official Australian publication)
CTBT	Comprehensive Test Ban Treaty
DRDO	Defence Research and Development Organisation (India)
EDC	European Defense Community
EURATOM	European Atomic Community
IAEA	International Atomic Energy Agency
IMF	International Monetary Fund
INVAP	*Investigaciones Aplicadas, S.E.* (Argentine corporation)
KWU	*Kraftwerk Union* (German corporation)
NATO	North Atlantic Treaty Organization
NIC	National Identity Conception
NNPA	Nuclear Non-Proliferation Act (United States)
NPT	Treaty on the Non-Proliferation of Nuclear Weapons
PNE	Peaceful Nuclear Explosion
PTBT	Partial Test Ban Treaty
SNEPP	Study Nuclear Explosion for Peaceful Purposes (Indian project)

1   Introduction: life in a nuclear-capable crowd

This book is an analysis of why some – but only some – political leaders decide to endow their states with nuclear weapons. It finds that decisions to go or not to go nuclear result not from the international structure, but rather from individual hearts. Simply put, some political leaders hold a conception of their nation's identity that leads them to desire the bomb; and such leaders can be expected to turn that desire into state policy.

The book's focus on individual leaders is unusual in the social-scientific literature on proliferation and non-proliferation. Indeed, most authors on the subject hardly even bother to ask the question of how leaders come to desire nuclear weapons. Instead, they simply adopt a tragic sensibility, viewing nuclear weapons as a symptom of a fallen humanity's raw quest for power. More than a few even explicitly and unironically refer to nuclear weapons as "temptations," to those who succumb to those temptations as "nuclear sinners," and to the goal of non-proliferation efforts as the construction of an inevitably fragile "nuclear taboo." This book takes a different tack. It starts its analysis by pointing out the basic fact of the history of nuclear proliferation: the large and fast-growing number of nuclear-weapons capable states, contrasted with the small and slow-growing number of actual nuclear weapons states. This combination of widespread capability with widespread restraint, which has persisted despite numerous shocks, is baffling until one sheds the tragic sensibility. To do so need not mean adopting a blithe, sunny optimism about humankind. Rather, it means seeing political leaders for what they are – flesh-and-blood human beings – and the question of acquiring nuclear weapons for what it is – a revolutionary decision. Facing the unknown and unknowable nuclear future, burdened with the responsibility of protecting their nations from destruction, leaders can hardly do otherwise than look deep inside themselves for guidance. The answers they find via that process of introspection vary widely, but they can be systematically summarized and rigorously explained.

The leaders who have chosen to thrust their nations into the nuclear club include the democratic and the dictatorial, the religious and the secular, the rough and the refined, the Western and the Eastern, the Northern and the Southern. Very little unites them. Yet on the basis of case studies of leaders from France, Australia, Argentina, and India, this book does find something that sets those few leaders with definite nuclear weapons ambitions apart from the many who do not harbor such ambitions. What sets those few leaders apart is a deeply held conception of their nation's identity that I call "oppositional nationalist." Oppositional nationalists see their nation as both naturally at odds with an external enemy, and as naturally its equal if not its superior. Such a conception tends to generate the emotions of fear and pride – an explosive psychological cocktail. Driven by fear and pride, oppositional nationalists develop a desire for nuclear weapons that goes beyond calculation, to self-expression. Thus, in spite of the tremendous complexity of the nuclear choice, leaders who decide for the bomb tend not to back into it. For them, unlike the bulk of their peers, the choice for nuclear weapons is neither a close call nor a possible last resort but an absolute necessity.

In the process of making its case about the importance of oppositional nationalism for decisions to go nuclear, the book also develops a more general model of identity-driven foreign policy decisionmaking. In particular, the book carefully outlines the linkages from leaders' national identity conceptions, through emotions, to their ultimate foreign policy choices. This model holds the potential to improve our understanding not only of decisions on nuclear weapons, but also of other foreign policy decisions of revolutionary significance. The immediate task at hand, however, is to show the model's applicability to the issue of nuclear proliferation.

The puzzle

A sense of tragic foreboding hangs over debates about international security today. Contemporary academic, policy and popular writings now routinely warn of a coming "second nuclear age," as developing states and non-state actors obtain previously out of reach technologies and developed states begin stirring from a long, idealistic slumber.[1] In response to this apparently gathering storm, "non-proliferation" advocates in the

---

[1] See, for instance, Paul Bracken, *Fire in the East: The Rise of Asian Military Power and the Second Nuclear Age* (New York: HarperCollins, 1999); Colin S. Gray, *The Second Nuclear Age* (Boulder, CO: Lynne Rienner, 1999); Victor Cha, "The Second Nuclear Age: Proliferation Pessimism versus Sober Optimism in South Asia and East Asia," *Journal of Strategic Studies*, Vol. 24, No. 4 (December 2001), pp. 79–120; William J. Broad, "Chain Reaction: Facing a Second Nuclear Age," *New York Times*, August 3, 2003, "Week in Review," p. 1.

United States and elsewhere argue for tightened international systems of nuclear inspections and monitoring, "counter-proliferation" advocates promote preventive wars and great defensive shields, and "abolitionists" point to America's own fearsome arsenal as well as those of the other nuclear weapons states as the root cause of the worldwide danger.[2] It is important to have this debate. But, amid the consternation, few have paused to consider whether the much-feared flood of new nuclear weapons states may in fact be little more than a mirage.

For this is not the first time we have faced widespread projections of a coming "second nuclear age." The 1960s era US government and other estimates foresaw between fifteen and twenty-five nuclear weapons states by the end of the 1970s; 1970s era estimates foresaw as many as thirty-five nuclear weapons states by the end of the 1980s; the early 1990s betting line was that at least Germany and Japan and possibly many more states would soon join the nuclear weapons "club."[3] Such forecasts – even supposedly *optimistic* ones – have proved *too pessimistic*. In spite of the breathless reporting about new uranium enrichment or fuel reprocessing capacities, it must be emphasized that the basic pattern in the history of nuclear proliferation to this point is the small number of nuclear weapons states, as compared to the large number of states capable of building those weapons. The expansion of nuclear technological capacities that previous generations feared has indeed occurred, but the expected realization of their military potential has not followed. Today, although nuclear technology is decidedly old technology and ex-Soviet scientists and fissile material have been on the market for over a decade,[4] to the best of our knowledge fewer than ten states actually have the bomb. These are the United States (first nuclear weapons test 1945); Russia (1949); Great Britain (1952); France (1960); China (1964); India ("peaceful nuclear explosion" 1974; first official nuclear weapons test

---

[2] Leon Sloss, "The Current Nuclear Dialogue," *Strategic Forum*, 156 (January 1999); Jonathan Schell, "The Folly of Arms Control," *Foreign Affairs*, Vol. 79, No. 5 (September/October 2000), pp. 22–46.

[3] For examples of past estimates, see George Quester, "The Statistical 'N' of 'Nth' Nuclear Weapons States," *Journal of Conflict Resolution*, Vol. 27, No. 1 (March 1983), esp. pp. 166–167; John Mueller, "The Escalating Irrelevance of Nuclear Weapons," in T. V. Paul, Richard J. Harknett, and James J. Wirtz, eds., *The Absolute Weapon Revisited: Nuclear Arms and the Emerging International Order* (Ann Arbor, MI: University of Michigan Press, 1998), pp. 73–98. Two famous 1990s academic forecasts are the "pessimistic" John J. Mearsheimer, "Back to the Future: Instability in Europe after the Cold War," *International Security*, Vol. 15, No. 1 (Summer 1990), pp. 5–56 and the "optimistic" Stephen Van Evera, "Primed for Peace: Europe after the Cold War," *International Security*, Vol. 15, No. 3 (Winter 1990–91), pp. 7–57.

[4] Graham Allison *et al.*, *Avoiding Nuclear Anarchy: Containing the Threat of Loose Russian Nuclear Weapons and Fissile Material* (Cambridge, MA: MIT Press, 1996).

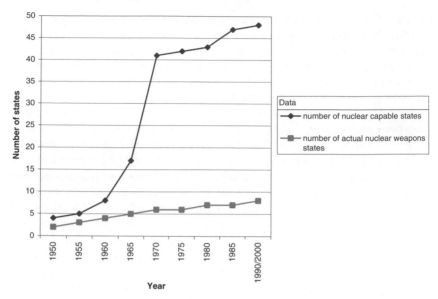

Figure 1.1 Potential *vs.* actual nuclear proliferation

1998); Pakistan (1998); plus almost certainly Israel (likely test 1979), and possibly North Korea (no test yet).[5]

Figure 1.1 offers a rough picture of the evolution in the numbers of actual and potential nuclear weapons states over time, adapted from work by Stephen Meyer and Richard Stoll on states' latent nuclear capabilities.[6] The figure reports their data at five-year intervals.[7]

This yawning gap between technical potential and military reality should have led to widespread rethinking of the phenomenon of nuclear

[5] It should also be noted that South Africa admitted production of a supply of "bombs in the basement" before their dismantlement in 1991. In addition, three Soviet successor states other than Russia briefly "inherited" some of the former superpower's nuclear stockpile, though they never had operational control of the weapons.

[6] To be considered nuclear-capable, states must satisfy the following conditions: indigenous uranium deposits (until 1970, when the international uranium market opened up); experience with mining and metallurgy; sufficient installed electrical capacity (200 megawatts); indigenous steel, nitric acid, electronic ignition production; a heavy construction industry; and a supply of chemists, physicists, chemical and nuclear engineers with three years' experience operating a nuclear reactor of any size. The original model of nuclear capability was developed in Stephen Meyer, *The Dynamics of Nuclear Proliferation* (Chicago: University of Chicago Press, 1984). For Stoll's updated data, see http://es.rice.edu/projects/Poli378/Nuclear/Proliferation/ model.html.

[7] Note that I have recoded the date of latent nuclear capacity for one country, Belgium, on the basis of my field research there. Stoll's data set misses the fact that Belgium had ample uranium reserves already in the 1940s in the Congo, which was its colony at the time.

weapons proliferation. To a surprising extent it has not. Much of the proliferation literature continues to focus its attention primarily on the "supply-side" issue of the growth of technical capacities. Volumes with titles like *How Nuclear Weapons Spread* are devoted entirely to analyses of the technological similarities between civilian and military nuclear programs.[8] Such a focus on technical capacity leads many proliferation specialists to persist in foretelling "life in a nuclear-armed crowd" a quarter-century after Albert Wohlstetter coined the phrase.[9] Indeed, William Arkin has aptly labeled the study of proliferation "the sky-is-still-falling profession."[10]

This is not to claim that all of the current literature is in denial about the gap between technical potential and military reality. Indeed, awareness of that gap has produced soaring evaluations of the past effectiveness of the "non-proliferation regime" and its centerpiece, the Non-Proliferation Treaty (NPT). The rising reputation of the regime over the past two decades has been especially noticeable in academic writing on international relations. Scholars working within all three major international relations paradigms – realists, institutionalists, and constructivists – have pointed to the regime as an essential dam holding back the tide of nuclear proliferation:

- Realists stress that the regime provides a framework for joint great power application of export controls, technical safeguards agreements, and other supply-side means of blocking states from acquiring and applying nuclear know-how.[11]
- Neo-liberal institutionalists stress that the regime offers states a functional means to escape the presumed proliferation "prisoner's dilemma" by giving them the assurance that their rivals are also keeping their nuclear powder dry.[12]
- Finally, constructivists stress that the regime has contributed to a "nuclear taboo," an international normative prohibition on the use of

[8] Frank Barnaby, *How Nuclear Weapons Spread: Nuclear Weapon Proliferation in the 1990s* (London: Routledge, 1994).

[9] Albert Wohlstetter *et al.*, *Moving Toward Life in a Nuclear Armed Crowd? Final Report to the US Arms Control and Disarmament Agency* (Los Angeles: Pan Heuristics, 1976).

[10] William M. Arkin, "The Sky-Is-Still-Falling Profession," *The Bulletin of Atomic Scientists*, Vol. 50, No. 2 (March/April 1994), p. 64.

[11] Zachary Davis, "The Realist Nuclear Regime," *Security Studies*, Vol. 2, Nos. 3–4 (Spring/Summer 1993), pp. 79–99; T. V. Paul, "Strengthening the Non-Proliferation Regime: The Role of Coercive Sanctions," *International Journal*, Vol. 51, No. 3 (Summer 1996), pp. 440–465.

[12] Roger K. Smith, "Explaining the Non-Proliferation Regime: Anomalies for Contemporary International Relations Theory," *International Organization*, Vol. 41, No. 2 (Spring 1987), pp. 253–281; Joseph S. Nye, "Maintaining the Non-Proliferation Regime," *International Organization*, Vol. 35, No. 1 (Winter 1981), pp. 15–38.

nuclear weapons, which has reduced their utility, tarnished their image, and thus diminished their attractiveness.[13]

The non-proliferation regime has made a difference. Careful case study research on various countries' nuclear histories has detailed the regime's role in easing many of them further down the nuclear weapons-free path.[14] Therefore, the mounting evidence that the regime today is encountering increasing political and technical difficulties is a matter of no little concern. But this begs the real question: has the regime caused states that *otherwise would have decided to acquire nuclear weapons* not to do so, or has it simply reinforced the non-proliferation commitments of *already abstaining states*? The chorus of praise for the regime implicitly suggests that without it the world would today be home to a "nuclear-armed crowd." But in fact there is much reason to doubt this counterfactual about the regime's impact.

First of all, if the regime were indeed the key to containing proliferation, then proliferation should have been rampant before the regime became a real factor in states' calculations, in the mid-1970s. Yet as Figure 1.1 shows, *already then* there was a wide gap between the numbers of nuclear-capable and nuclear weapons states. So, according to the very logic of those who take a "strong" view of the regime's success, by the time the regime was finally built, it should have been too late to prevent widespread proliferation.

Second, if the regime were so crucial, then recent proliferation should have been limited to "rogue states" that do not worry about their position in international society. Such states, not surprisingly, have been the focus of most policymakers' proliferation worries.[15] But, in fact, the list of nuclear weapons states is no rogues' gallery, and two of the youngest nuclear powers, India and Pakistan, are widely internationally recognized states whose ultimate choices for the bomb were even made by democratically elected leaders.

---

[13] Xinyuan Dai, "Information Systems in Treaty Regimes," *World Politics*, Vol. 54, No. 4 (July 2002), pp. 405–436; Patricia Hewitson, "Nonproliferation and Reduction of Nuclear Weapons: Risks of Weakening the Multilateral Nuclear Nonproliferation Norm," *Berkeley Journal of International Law*, Vol. 21, No. 3 (2003), pp. 405–494; Nina Tannenwald, "The Nuclear Taboo: the United States and the Normative Basis of Nuclear Non-Use," *International Organization*, Vol. 53, No. 3 (Summer 1999), pp. 433–468; Elizabeth Kier and Jonathan Mercer, "Setting Precedents in Anarchy: Military Intervention and Weapons of Mass Destruction," *International Security*, Vol. 20, No. 4 (Spring 1996), pp. 77–106.

[14] Mitchell Reiss, *Without the Bomb: The Politics of Nuclear Non-Proliferation* (New York: Columbia University Press, 1988). See also Mitchell Reiss, *Bridled Ambition: Why Countries Constrain their Nuclear Weapons Capabilities* (Baltimore, MD: Johns Hopkins University Press for the Woodrow Wilson Center, 1995).

[15] For a skeptical view of this development, see Raymond Tanter, *Rogue Regimes: Terrorism and Proliferation* (New York: St. Martin's Press, 1999).

Third, for the regime to play the key role that has been ascribed to it, it would have to have created stable expectations among states that it would last. But, in fact, the regime's survivability is regularly called into question, with the regime's proponents often the loudest doubters of all. Not only have they viewed all sorts of actions around the world, such as India's and Pakistan's 1998 tests, as potential mortal blows to the cause of non-proliferation; they also see various types of inaction, such as the continuing maintenance of large arsenals by the nuclear powers, as equally dangerous to the regime.[16] Given this generalized perception of the regime's weakness in the policy world (which stands in stark contrast to its glimmering academic reputation), it is hard to buy into the notion that it provides states with the stable expectations they crave.

Finally, if the regime is widely perceived as *brittle*, those who know it best equally perceive it as *hollow*. Close analysis of the regime's actual operation finds a set of ambiguous and erratically enforced rules, myriad technical loopholes, and underfunded international agencies. For one thing, until recently international inspections were only carried out at *declared* nuclear facilities.[17] The case of pre-1991 Iraq shows how easily a determined state could hide the true extent of its nuclear program.[18] Since the possibilities for cheating have been so wide open, the existence of the regime could hardly have reassured any states that were prone to doubt the good faith of their peers. Thus, *if* this really were a prisoner's dilemma type situation, they should have cheated and gone nuclear themselves. But instead, the vast majority of states have not "defected" from the regime.

In short, for all its utility, the non-proliferation regime simply cannot support the explanatory weight that it has been asked to bear. What, then, accounts for the slow pace of proliferation? This book suggests that the answer lies less in external efforts to stop states from going nuclear, and more in the hearts of state leaders themselves. It argues that, in fact, contrary to the conventional wisdom, most state leaders are not sorely tempted by the prospect of "going nuclear." Rather, state leaders tend to lack sufficient levels of motivation and/or certitude to catapult their states into a new and dangerous world of nuclear deterrence. In short, the

---

[16] See, for instance, Ambassador Thomas Graham, Jr. and Douglas B. Shaw, "Nearing a Fork in the Road: Proliferation or Nuclear Reversal?" *Nonproliferation Review*, Vol. 6, No. 1 (Fall 1998), pp. 70–76; Schell, "The Folly of Arms Control."

[17] Paul Leventhal, "IAEA Safeguards Shortcomings: A Critique," Nuclear Control Institute, Washington, DC, September 12, 1994, http://www.nci.org/p/plsgrds.htm.

[18] Moreover, even the unprecedented, intensive work of inspectors in post-Gulf War Iraq still *by their own admission* could produce only guesses about the true extent of Saddam's efforts. See Richard Butler, *The Greatest Threat: Iraq, Weapons of Mass Destruction, and the Growing Crisis of Global Security* (New York: Public Affairs, 2000).

non-proliferation regime has appeared to be a dramatic success because few state leaders have desired the things it prohibits.[19]

This argument turns the typical proliferation puzzle on its head. The typical puzzle has been, "Why are there *so few* nuclear weapons states?" This book asks instead, "Why are there *any at all?*" The book then answers this question in great detail, building both a theoretical model and a comparative empirical study of four nations' nuclear histories to show how some leaders do manage to generate enough will to grasp for the "absolute weapon," while most of their peers do not.

To solve the puzzle of proliferation, we need an explicit, theoretical account of the *demand* for nuclear weapons. Vague references to security dilemmas and the capacity for evil that lurks within all of us can no longer suffice. Recognizing the need, a small but growing number of political scientists have begun seriously to tackle it.[20] Most notably, in a brilliant theoretical synthesis drawing on the existing case study literature, Scott Sagan has suggested that proliferation can arise from one or more of three classic foreign policy motivations – the need to match power for power, the desire to reinforce national self-esteem, or the selfish demands of narrow domestic constituencies (usually atomic and military bureauracies and their supporters).[21] By attempting to develop systematically these three "models" of motivations, Sagan's article represents a major step forward for the field. On the other hand, Sagan's depiction of at least three separate and utterly quotidian motivations for the choice for the bomb does

---

[19] The general logic behind this point is elaborated in George W. Downs, David M. Rocke, and Peter N. Barsoom, "Is the Good News About Compliance Good News About Cooperation?" *International Organization*, Vol. 50, No. 3 (Summer 1996), pp. 379–406.

[20] This stands in contrast to the longstanding interest of historians in this question. See, on the US case, Richard Rhodes, *The Making of the Atomic Bomb* (New York: Touchstone, 1986); on the Soviet case, David Holloway, *Stalin and the Bomb: The Soviet Union and Atomic Energy, 1939–56* (New Haven, CT: Yale University Press, 1994); on the British case, Margaret Gowing, *Independence and Deterrence: Britain and Atomic Energy, 1945–1952* (London: Macmillan, 1974); on the French case, Dominique Mongin, *La bombe atomique française, 1945–1958* (Brussels: Bruylant, 1997); on the Chinese case, John Wilson Lewis and Xue Litai, *China Builds the Bomb* (Stanford, CA: Stanford University Press, 1988); and on the Israeli case, Avner Cohen, *Israel and the Bomb* (New York: Columbia University Press, 1998). Another seminal historical contribution of truly global sweep is Bertrand Goldschmidt, *The Atomic Complex: A Worldwide Political History of Nuclear Energy* (La Grange Park, IL: American Nuclear Society, 1982).

[21] Scott D. Sagan, "Why Do States Build Nuclear Weapons? Three Models in Search of a Bomb," *International Security*, Vol. 21, No. 3 (Winter 1996/7), pp. 54–86, also published in revised form as "Rethinking the Causes of Nuclear Proliferation: Three Models in Search of a Bomb," in Victor A. Utgoff, ed., *The Coming Crisis: Nuclear Proliferation, US Interests, and World Order* (Cambridge, MA: MIT Press, 2000), pp. 17–50. For other perspectives, see Richard Betts, "Paranoids, Pygmies, Pariahs and Non-Proliferation Revisited," *Security Studies*, Vol. 2, Nos. 3–4 (Spring/Summer 1993), pp. 100–123 and Gray, *The Second Nuclear Age*, esp. ch. 3.

not resolve the fundamental disconnect between the common expectation of widespread proliferation and the reality of limited proliferation – indeed, it deepens that puzzle. Most nuclear-weapons-capable states must deal with the presence of nuclear weapons in their wider regions, want to boost their self-esteem, and have domestic constituencies that would profit materially from an indigenous nuclear weapons effort. If, as Sagan suggests, any of these reasons on its own should be enough to motivate the choice for the bomb, it is hard to understand why more nuclear-weapons-capable states – including Germany, Japan, Sweden, and many others – never made that choice.

Pace Sagan, a closer focus on the demand side of proliferation in fact reveals not how many reasons state leaders have to "go nuclear," but rather how few. In the interconnected system that is the world, many foreign policy decisions are likely to have various direct and indirect effects, some intended and some unintended.[22] And the decision to go nuclear is a revolutionary decision.[23] As such, it is likely to disturb the system more than any other, inviting huge, multifarious, and unpredictable consequences.[24] Top decisionmakers, experienced as they are in the art of politics, cannot fail to recognize the enormity of the choice before them. For example, while on fieldwork in India in 1965, the political scientist Stephen P. Cohen typed up a list of thirty-four separate arguments over the bomb current among Indian elites at that time. The list gives us a sense of the difficult nature of the nuclear choice, not just in India but wherever the question comes up. A summary of Cohen's list is in Table 1.1.

Not only for India but for every state, this is a decision with potentially massive consequences on every level of politics and policy, including profound effects in the areas of military strategy, diplomacy, economics, domestic institutions, and ethical or normative self-image. It is difficult to determine the likely effects of the decision to go nuclear even on any one of these levels, and what is more, as Amartya Sen points out, the various prudential and normative levels are inextricably intertwined.[25]

---

[22] Robert Jervis, *System Effects: Complexity in Political and Social Life* (Princeton: Princeton University Press, 1997).

[23] Robert Jervis, *The Meaning of the Nuclear Revolution: Statecraft and the Prospect of Armageddon* (Ithaca, NY: Cornell University Press, 1989).

[24] Indeed, part of the unpredictability here is that there may not be many consequences at all; the attempted revolution may fizzle. This is the assessment of the nuclear "revolution" that is made by John Mueller, *Retreat from Doomsday: The Obsolescence of Major War* (New York: Basic Books, 1989), esp. ch. 5. But Mueller also notes that most people *believe* that there has been a nuclear revolution; and those beliefs are what interest us most here.

[25] Amartya Sen, "India and the Bomb," *Journal of Peace Economics, Peace Science and Public Policy*, Vol. 6, No. 4 (Fall 2000), pp. 16–34.

Table 1.1 *Cohen's "India and the bomb: a catalog of arguments"* *(abridged)*[a]

Issue-Area	Pro-Bomb Spin	Anti-Bomb Spin
Military-Strategic	• Bomb will deter attack • Bomb can be used tactically • Bomb makes up for conventional military deficits	• Bomb will invite attack • Any use of bomb risks escalation • Bomb is logistical nightmare and too big for most targets
Diplomatic-Reputational	• Bomb will raise national prestige • Others are going nuclear • We can easily break our commitment to a peaceful nuclear program	• Abstaining will raise national prestige • Others will only go nuclear if we do • Others will be alienated if we go back on our word
Economic	• Bombs are cheap • Bomb will give us more power in trade and aid talks	• Bombs are dear • Bomb will invite economic sanctions
Domestic-Institutional	• The people are demanding it • The military and scientists want it	• The people are not demanding it • Principle of civilian control of foreign and defense policy
Ethical-Normative	• Bomb would be a statement of independence from imperialists • We must avenge the deaths of our soldiers • Nehru built the basis for the bomb	• Bomb would be an admission that we are no better than the imperialists • Taking vengeance only produces new suffering • Nehru opposed the bomb in principle

Note: [a]Stephen P. Cohen private archive, Washington, DC.

In short, to go nuclear is an ideal-typical "big decision."[26] In light of this, the standard menu of "security," "prestige," or "domestic political" motivations for foreign policy choice is insufficient. The consequences of going nuclear are simply too vast to allow for a reasonable cost-benefit calculation. To be sure, various voices in society may sound strong pro- or anti-bomb notes; but the responsibility for choosing wisely is much

[26] See papers presented at "Making Big Choices: Individual Opinion Formation and Societal Choice," conference at the Weatherhead Center for International Affairs, Harvard University, May 25–26, 2000.

heavier for the top leader into whose hands the ultimate choice actually falls.

To go nuclear is to take a leap in the dark. The leader may certainly try to incorporate what is known about the contemporary strategic or political situation into decisionmaking on the bomb, but the relevance of such information is limited by the fact that the choice to go nuclear is likely to catapult the nation into a new era in which the old rules of thumb and ways of doing business will no longer apply. It is this high degree of general uncertainty that makes it so hard for most state leaders, even relatively risk-acceptant ones, to make a definitive decision to acquire nuclear weapons. For if you cannot calculate the risks involved, you cannot determine if you are willing to accept them.[27] Of course, the decision *not* to go nuclear also carries risks, but the stakes are generally lower because decisions (or non-decisions) to abstain from going nuclear are much more easily reversed.

Standard political science theory has trouble dealing with leaps in the dark. This book therefore builds a new theoretical model for explaining political decisions to acquire nuclear weapons.[28] I define the political decision to acquire nuclear weapons as an authoritative order to proceed with deliberate speed to the creation of a nuclear weapons arsenal. Why focus narrowly on the ultimate political decision? There are two reasons for this. First, the proliferation literature (and much of the policy debate as well) is overwhelmingly techno-centric, and it has allowed that techno-centrism to color its interpretation of the political will behind nuclear programs. This book will show that a narrow focus on political will complements the technical point of view, while allowing us to avoid the misinterpretations and misapprehensions of reality that techno-centric approaches have continually made. Second, even from a techno-centric perspective, without top-down political direction states do not acquire nuclear weapons in the full sense of the term. A nuclear weapon is not just a device that explodes with great force. It is a complex, integrated weapons *system* – including hardware, software, and human organizations.[29] Without top-down direction, the only states that could conceivably end up with full-fledged nuclear weapons "by accident" are those that inherit them from a failed regime, such as the post-Soviet states – and even those cases are far from clear-cut.

---

[27] See Yaacov Y. I. Vertzberger, "Rethinking and Reconceptualizing Risk in Foreign Policy Decision-Making: A Sociocognitive Approach," *Political Psychology*, Vol. 16, No. 2 (1995), pp. 347–380.

[28] The seminal text here is Richard Snyder, H. W. Bruck, and Burton Sapin, *Foreign Policy Decision Making* (New York: Free Press of Glencoe, 1962).

[29] Scott D. Sagan, *The Limits of Safety: Organizations, Accidents, and Nuclear Weapons* (Princeton: Princeton University Press, 1993).

Any full explanation of decisions to acquire the bomb must account not only for their ultimate *valence* but also their *timing* and the *manner* in which they are made. Political scientists have often neglected such issues, but they are of great real-world importance. Moreover, careful attention to timing and process can often help to sort out the real explanation for the ultimate outcome from the pretenders.

The goal of explaining not just the why, but also the when and the how of the ultimate decision to acquire the bomb necessitates a close focus on the motivations of individual leaders. In one sense, such a focus on leaders fits snugly within the growing movement in political science for greater attention to theoretical microfoundations and empirical process-tracing. But, in another sense, the stress placed here on the motivations of individual leaders is due to the observation that decisions to go nuclear are quite unlike most of the other decisions that political scientists investigate. As already argued, to go nuclear is an extraordinary step; and whatever the deep structural forces at work, to take such an extraordinary step will always require an extraordinary effort of will. The analysis of the choice for the bomb, therefore, requires a fundamentally different set of theoretical tools than the analysis of most other foreign policy choices. Meanwhile, on the empirical level, it requires what Barton Bernstein calls the "'empathetic reconstruction" of an individual leader's state of mind.[30]

Why have some – but only some – state leaders decided to endow their countries with the most terrible instruments of destruction ever created by human hands? The question does *not* answer itself.

The answer: a theoretical and empirical preview

Nuclear proliferation is a rare event in international politics. This introduction has suggested that it is rare because few state leaders may in fact need to be constrained from seeking the bomb. That suggestion turns the proliferation literature's typical starting assumption on its head.

The book proceeds in Chapter 2 to build a new model of foreign policy decisionmaking that is specifically tailored to explain revolutionary choices like the decision to go nuclear. The model begins with the contention that when relevant information about the likely consequences of a foreign policy decision is highly contradictory or unavailable, and a decisionmaker cannot simply wait for sufficient clarifying information to flow in – conditions that certainly apply to the case of nuclear proliferation – the resulting decisions will primarily reflect the decisionmaker's

[30] Barton Bernstein, "Understanding Decisionmaking, US Foreign Policy, and the Cuban Missile Crisis: A Review Essay," *International Security*, Vol. 25, No. 1 (Summer 2000), p. 163.

"national identity conception" (NIC). An NIC, as I define it, is an individual's understanding of the nation's identity – his or her sense of *what the nation naturally stands for* and of *how high it naturally stands*, in comparison to others in the international arena. This sense can be shared with most of the individual's compatriots, or it can be relatively idiosyncratic. But in either case, it is a set of deep-seated, essentially unfalsifiable beliefs about the "true" nature of the nation, which are developed through comparison and contrast with the "true" nature ascribed to certain external others. Sometimes an NIC may be generally shared throughout a society, for instance as the result of a traumatizing experience of war; but sometimes different members of the same society will hold strongly different NIC types, which then tilt against each other for political power.

The book identifies four ideal-typical NICs along the two dimensions of self–other comparison noted above. One of these NIC types, which I term "oppositional nationalist," turns out to be highly potent in sparking the choice to go nuclear. Oppositional nationalists define their nation as being both naturally at odds with and naturally equal (if not superior) to a particular external other. As a result, when facing the external other, oppositional nationalist leaders are uniquely predisposed to experience two highly volatile emotions: fear and pride. Indeed, one of the major efforts of this book is to show the value of studying emotions as mechanisms linking identities with foreign policy choice. The combination of fear and pride has a number of important effects not only on how the decisionmaker receives and processes information, but also on what basic desires the decisionmaker feels and tries to satisfy. Careful consideration of the impact of fear and pride leads to the proposition that for oppositional nationalist leaders, the decision to acquire nuclear weapons is not only a means to the end of getting them; it is also an end in itself, a matter of self-expression. This leads to a further proposition that decisions to go nuclear are likely not to be decisions of last resort, as many believe. Rather, such decisions are likely to be made hastily, without the considerable vetting process that political scientists typically assume precedes most important state choices. Indeed, one might say that this book pairs two kinds of uncontrolled reactions: the nuclear explosions created by the coming together of a critical mass of fissile material, and the explosive psychological cocktail of fear and pride that stems from oppositional nationalism.

The argument of this book, stripped to its barest essence, is that oppositional nationalist leaders push for the bomb, while others do not. But this is not to say that those other leaders are uninterested in all things nuclear. Some leaders, whom I term oppositional subalterns, cannot imagine actually getting nuclear weapons themselves but are desperate to secure the protection afforded by a superpower nuclear deterrent. Others, whom I term sportsmanlike nationalists, see no reason to build the bomb but also see much reason to build a significant nuclear technology base and even to oppose the international non-proliferation regime. The nuclear policy preferences of these sportsmanlike nationalists undermine the typical equation made by Western policymakers: if you are building up your nuclear infrastructure while opposing the NPT, you must want the bomb. The book shows that such assertions are neither theoretically nor empirically tenable.

The book tests its propositions against the nuclear histories of four very different countries: Argentina, Australia, France, and India. The first two did not go nuclear, while the second two did. Each case study combines rigorous analysis of the national identity conceptions of multiple leaders of these countries with original field research on their nuclear histories. Thus, the empirical chapters of this book are meant to offer not merely an interpretation of the available evidence, but a rigorous test of the theory on the basis of a greatly expanded information set. Each of the case studies in this book benefited from intensive field research, including substantial exploitation of state archival records, interviews with dozens of current and former top officials, and general cultural immersion. Time in the field amounted to over a full year in total, with at least one month spent in each of the four countries. I also consulted archives in Belgium, the United Kingdom, and the United States. I conducted interviews in English in India and Australia, generally in French in France, and generally in Spanish in Argentina.[31]

The case studies demonstrate the power of the variable of leaders' national identity conceptions. Of course, the narrow focus on one individual-level variable cannot in itself explain all of the twists and turns of these countries' nuclear histories. However, when one focuses especially on the precise question of political decisions to acquire nuclear weapons, it becomes clear that a leader's oppositional nationalism (or lack thereof) is crucial to the explanation.

The conclusions, in brief, from the four case studies are as follows:

• The French nuclear arsenal is often seen as an unquestioned object of national consensus, but in fact many French leaders during the first postwar decade were interested in *abdicating* the country's right to build the bomb in order to guarantee the same commitment by Germany. It took the 1954 rise to power of a political outsider, the oppositional nationalist prime minister Pierre Mendès France, to enact a policy U-turn and make the decision for a French nuclear arsenal.

---

[31] All quotations taken from the interviews were sent to the interview subjects for revision and comment before publication.

- Though enjoying one of the most formidable natural defenses in the world, Australian leaders in the 1950s and 1960s harbored grave fears for their national survival in the face of Communist encroachment. But since most of them lacked robust nationalism, they simply could not convince themselves that Australia on its own could ever develop an effective deterrent to counter the threat. One prime minister in the late 1960s and early 1970s, John Gorton, did harbor oppositional nationalism, and thus he tried to commit Australia to the nuclear weapons path. But then a Vietnam-war-induced sea change in attitudes about Communist China and Asia in general definitively ended the Australian dalliance with the idea of a homegrown bomb.

- Many experts are convinced that Argentina in the 1970s and 1980s was involved in a race with Brazil to acquire nuclear weapons. They point to Argentina's quest for an entirely indigenous nuclear fuel cycle and even a secret uranium enrichment facility. But, in fact, during that time Argentine leaders – military and civilian alike – shared a sportsmanlike nationalism that both attracted them to the idea of nuclear technology and repelled them from the idea of a nuclear arms race with Brazil. Argentina never even came close to a concrete determination in favor of building the bomb. Sometimes, where there is smoke there is no fire.

- Indian leaders from the Congress Party and other secularist parties long resisted making a definitive commitment to induct nuclear weapons into their arsenal, even while they did make halting efforts to develop India's nuclear weapons capability. It was only the 1998 rise to power of the Hindu nationalist Atal Behari Vajpayee and his Bharatiya Janata Party – ideal-typical oppositional nationalists – that produced the critical final Indian push across the nuclear threshold.

The book is organized as follows. Chapter 2 develops a general framework of national identity conceptions and foreign policy choice, concluding with specific hypotheses on choices on the nuclear issue. Chapter 3 explains the strategy for measuring national identity conceptions and implements it for the four country cases. Chapters 4 to 7 test the hypotheses developed in the earlier chapters on the nuclear histories of France, Australia, Argentina, and India in that order. Finally, Chapter 8 summarizes the findings of the study and sketches the policy implications.

2   Leaders' national identity conceptions and nuclear choices

In Chapter 1, I questioned why the nuclear proliferation literature generally takes state demand for nuclear weapons as practically a given, when in fact the acquisition of the bomb represents a leap in the dark on many dimensions. I argued that rather than asking, "Why are there *so few* nuclear weapons states?" we instead need to ask, "Why are there *any at all*?" But this is hardly a rhetorical question. Some leaders have indeed decided to endow their states with the bomb. What is more, in spite of the immense difficulties of making a clear cost–benefit calculation on this matter, leaders have often displayed breathtaking certitude in the rightness of their choices. How could this be? This chapter provides a detailed account of how, as indicated in Chapter 1, leaders' *conceptions of their nation's identity* (what I will call their "national identity conceptions" or NICs) drive their choices for or against the bomb. Most leaders' NICs do not lend themselves to embarking on such a perilous adventure. But others' NICs do produce a preference – and indeed, an emotional need – to reach for that instrument of unlimited destruction.

The chapter is organized as follows. The second part establishes the plausibility of the idea that "big decisions" such as the choice to go nuclear are likely to stem from leaders' NICs. The third part develops a more precise description of the NIC concept and lays out a typology of NICs. The fourth part first discusses the general process of NIC-driven decisionmaking, then identifies the emotional correlates of each NIC type and the behavioral consequences of those emotions, and finally connects these broad considerations to the particular case of nuclear decisions. The last part reviews some of the potential alternative hypotheses that were mentioned in the Introduction, explains the selection of country cases, and then places the specific question of this study in the context of the overall phenomenon of nuclear proliferation.

16

The decision to go nuclear: a big decision

The decision to acquire nuclear weapons is a big decision. This is to state the obvious – but it has some non-obvious ramifications. In particular, political scientists from various theoretical vantage points have found that big decisions are likely to stem from something other than a straightforward material cost–benefit calculation. Adopting a rational choice perspective, Dennis Chong argues that when relevant information is highly contradictory or unavailable, and a decisionmaker cannot simply wait for sufficient clarifying information to flow in – conditions that certainly apply to the case of nuclear proliferation – the resulting decisions will stem primarily from what Chong calls "dispositional" factors, such as the decisionmaker's core values.[1] Meanwhile, drawing on cognitive psychology, the "operational code" literature comes to a very similar conclusion. Ole Holsti lays out five "decisional settings" in which what he labels a decisionmaker's basic "beliefs" have been found to have the greatest direct impact on policy:

1. Situations that contain highly ambiguous components and are thus open to a variety of interpretations.
2. Non-routine situations that require more than the application of standard operating procedures and decision rules.
3. Situations that require decisions at the pinnacle of the government hierarchy by leaders who are relatively free from organizational and other constraints.
4. Responses to events that are unanticipated or contain an element of surprise.
5. Long-range policy planning, a task that inherently involves considerable uncertainty.[2]

The typical context of decisions to build nuclear weapons reflects at least *four* of the above "decisional settings" (the sometime exception being point number 4).

---

[1] Dennis Chong, *Rational Lives: Norms and Values in Politics and Society* (Chicago: University of Chicago Press, 2000). The rational choice theorist George Tsebelis has also noted that "actions taken in noniterative situations by individual decision makers (such as in crisis situations) are not necessarily well-suited for rational choice predictions." George Tsebelis, *Nested Games: Rational Choice in Comparative Politics* (Berkeley: University of California Press, 1990), p. 38, cited in Roger Petersen, *Understanding Ethnic Violence: Fear, Hatred, and Resentment in Twentieth-Century Eastern Europe* (Cambridge: Cambridge University Press, 2002), p. 34.

[2] Ole Holsti, "Foreign Policy Formation Viewed Cognitively," in Robert Axelrod, ed., *Structure of Decision* (Princeton: Princeton University Press, 1976, pp. 18–54). See also Alexander L. George, "The Causal Nexus between Cognitive Beliefs and Decision-Making Behavior: the 'Operational Code' Belief System," in Lawrence S. Falkowski, ed., *Psychological Models in International Politics* (Boulder, CO: Westview Press, 1979, pp. 95–124).

In short, the decision to acquire the bomb is almost an ideal-typical example of a big decision, one which – if it is taken at all – will be based in what Chong calls "dispositional factors" or what Holsti calls the "beliefs" of the decisionmaker. The precise dispositional factors/beliefs that are relevant to a particular big decision may differ according to the arena in which the decision is located. In the case of the decision to go nuclear, a decision clearly located in the arena of high international politics, the relevant factors are to be found in the leader's national identity conception (NIC).[3]

The national identity conception (NIC): definition and types

The concept of the "national identity conception"

As previously stated, the key independent variable in my causal argument about decisions to go nuclear is the leader's national identity conception, or NIC. The precise nature of the leader's NIC will largely determine whether or not he or she will favor the state's acquisition of nuclear weapons. What is more, the leader's NIC is not only seminal to his or her nuclear preference; it also produces an emotional process of nuclear decisionmaking that stands in stark contrast to the more typical process of cost–benefit calculation. So just what is an NIC? It is an individual's understanding of the nation's identity – his or her sense of *what the nation naturally stands for* and of *how high it naturally stands*, in comparison to others in the international arena. The paragraphs that follow elaborate on the key elements of this first-cut definition.

The NIC is an "individual" understanding. Most of the recent literature on nations and nationalism is dedicated to establishing that national identities are social facts, grounded in intersubjective understandings.[4] Since national identities are social-structural phenomena, constructivist applications of the national identity variable to foreign policy choice have rightly tended to focus on how it provides a "logic of appropriateness" that renders certain policy options simply "inconceivable" but

---

[3] Here I am admittedly skimming lightly over some difficult issues regarding metadecisions about what arena a specific decision is perceived to relate to. For a treatment of these issues, see Donald A. Sylvan and James F. Voss, eds., *Problem Representation in Foreign Policy Decision Making* (Cambridge: Cambridge University Press, 1998).

[4] See Anthony D. Smith, *Theories of Nationalism*, 2nd ed. (New York: Holmes and Meier Publishers, 1983).

leaves others open.[5] The insight that intersubjectively held national identities can render certain options inconceivable is an important one, but it is also limited. In particular, it does not allow us to use the identity variable to explain the specific policy choices that actually *are* made. To do this for the specific case of nuclear weapons decisions, I argue that we must drop down below the level of national identity as a social fact and instead look at what the leader has adopted as his or her specific interpretation, or "conception," of the national identity. What I am calling NICs are individual, or *subjective*, sets of choices about how to interpret the collective symbols and memories that are common to all in the nation, but often highly multivalenced in their potential meanings and significance.[6]

How do these NICs come about? Intellectuals and identity entrepreneurs are constantly developing new national identity conceptions and marketing them to the rest of society. The future national leader will probably be exposed to various such conceptions as a youth and, over time and for various motivations, will draw on these to develop a subjective conception of the nation's identity. Most often, the leader will simply have chosen from among the mainstream conceptions available in society. But sometimes the leader is in fact less an NIC consumer than an NIC producer. For instance, Chapter 3 discusses the ideas of the first Indian prime minister, Jawaharlal Nehru, whose "Nehruvian" conception about Indian identity remained dominant among the Indian leadership into the 1990s. In the end, precisely how the leader developed his or her NIC is not directly relevant to the primary goal of this book, which is to explain nuclear policy choices. What matters for the purposes of this study is that the leader arrives in power with a stable NIC upon which to draw when facing the big decision of going or not going nuclear.

The NIC is an "identity" conception as opposed to a mere perception of contemporary reality. There is a rich international relations literature on the important behavioral consequences of international perceptions.[7] This literature usefully confronts the standard political science narrative of perfectly rational calculators responding to objective contemporary reality. But even so, the threat perception literature often amounts to a simple tweaking of the standard narrative, replacing rational calculators with

---

[5] See Stephen Saideman, "Thinking Theoretically about Identity and Foreign Policy," in Shibley Telhami and Michael Barnett, eds., *Identity and Foreign Policy in the Middle East* (Ithaca, NY: Cornell University Press, 2002), esp. pp. 169–70.

[6] The importance of the subjective, as opposed to the intersubjective, level of identity is notably explored by in Jane Mansbridge and Aldon Morris, eds., *Oppositional Consciousness: The Subjective Roots of Social Protest* (Chicago: University of Chicago Press, 2001).

[7] The seminal work is Robert Jervis, *Perception and Misperception in International Politics* (Princeton: Princeton University Press, 1976).

cognitive misers, and perfect information with biased assessment. To explain big decisions where even a semblance of cost–benefit calculation is difficult if not impossible, we need to move beyond mere contemporary perception. As noted above, a leader's national identity conception does move beyond contemporary perception, though it may color such perceptions. It is a sense of what the nation *naturally* stands for and how high it *naturally* stands. The sense of what is natural for the nation allows the leader, even when calculation is difficult or impossible, to choose – as an act of self-expression.

The distinction being drawn here between an identity conception and a mere contemporary perception can be grasped through a consideration of the opening paragraph of Charles de Gaulle's *Mémoires de Guerre*, one of the most famous passages in autobiographical literature. De Gaulle writes: "Instinctively I have the feeling that Providence has created [France] either for complete successes or for exemplary misfortunes. If, in spite of this, mediocrity shows in her acts and deeds, it strikes me as an absurd anomaly, to be imputed to the faults of Frenchmen, not to the genius of the land. . . . In short, to my mind, France cannot be France without greatness."[8] The thought process here is subtle. De Gaulle claims he can certainly see it when France falls short, but this does not affect his "instinctive feeling" about France's true nature. In his inimitable words, France cannot *be France* without greatness. De Gaulle's NIC, therefore, helps him to set a metric for judging the nation's efforts today and for setting its goals for tomorrow.

The NIC reflects an ongoing process of "self–other comparison." How do we answer the basic questions of identity: what we stand for, and how high we stand? One way of doing so is to adopt a discrete "role" – a behavioral pattern that conforms to the expectations and needs of the overall social system.[9] Applying this notion to the domain of world politics, scholars have defined various "national role conceptions," all of which derive from the nation's perceived function in the international system.[10] Such an outside-in, deductive approach may be how some individuals provide

---

[8] Charles de Gaulle, *War Memoirs, Vol. 1: The Call to Honour 1940–1942*, trans. Jonathan Griffin (New York: The Viking Press, 1955), p. 3.

[9] Ralph Linton, "Status and Role," reprinted in Paul Bohannon and Mark Glazer, eds., *High Points in Anthropology*, 2nd ed. (New York: McGraw Hill, 1988), pp. 186–198.

[10] K. J. Holsti, "National Role Conceptions in the Study of Foreign Policy," *International Studies Quarterly*, Vol. 14 (1970), pp. 233–309. Note that this outside-in, deductive approach is also how IR scholars have defined many other important concepts on how "ideas" affect foreign policy, concepts such as "strategic culture," "foreign policy belief system," and "operational code." Seminal contributions to this wider literature include Alastair Iain Johnston, "Thinking about Strategic Culture," *International Security*, Vol. 19, No. 4 (Spring 1995), pp. 32–64; Deborah Larson, "The Role of Belief Systems and Schemas in Foreign Policy Making," *Political Psychology*, Vol. 15, No. 1 (1994); and

themselves with answers to the key questions of national identity. But in general, the international relations constructivist literature's tendency to conflate "identity" with "role" needs to be rethought.[11] Many people who develop a conception of national identity do so from the ground up, through a never-ending process of self-comparison that they make between their nation and others. The notion that self-comparison is crucial to identity has become standard in critical social theory, through the notion of "the Other," and in social psychology.[12] In social psychology, outgroups that serve as the primary basis for ingroup self-definition are termed "key comparison others."[13] It is the identification of similarities and differences (real or imagined) between "us" and "them" that clarifies the sense of who we are. It is important to emphasize that not all external actors are *key* others for the purpose of self-comparison. The psychological approach's appreciation of the specificity of the key comparison other explains why people can use self–other comparison to provide themselves with very clear answers to the basic questions of identity.

Having established in general what is meant by a "national identity conception" or NIC, we can now proceed to build a typology of specific NICs, because as we shall see, different NICs produce different impulses on the nuclear issue.

Typology of national identity conceptions

The previous section defined the NIC as an individual's understanding of the nation's identity – his or her sense of what the nation naturally stands for and of how high it naturally stands in comparison to others in the international arena. Those two dimensions, "what the nation naturally stands for" and "how high the nation naturally stands," correspond closely to what social psychologists have identified as the two primary

Alexander George, "The 'Operational Code': A Neglected Approach to the Study of Political Leaders and Decision Making," *International Studies Quarterly*, Vol. 13 (June 1969), pp. 190–222. Most works on "enemy images" are in this vein as well, but others come closer to a concept that parallels my notion of "identity." For an excellent example of the latter, see Richard K. Herrmann and Michael P. Fischerkeller, "Beyond the Enemy Image and Spiral Model: Cognitive-Strategic Research After the Cold War," *International Organization*, Vol. 49 (1995), pp. 415–450.

[11] For a parallel discussion of this point, see Ted Hopf, *Social Construction of International Politics: Identities and Foreign Policies, Moscow, 1955 and 1999* (Ithaca, NY: Cornell University Press, 2002).

[12] Bertrand Badie and Marc Sadoun, eds., *L'autre: Etudes réunies pour Alfred Grosser* (Paris: Presses de la fondation des sciences politiques, 1996); Roger Brown, *Social Psychology*, 2nd ed. (New York: The Free Press, 1985).

[13] Brown, *Social Psychology*, esp. p. 576. In my handling of the term, the "key comparison other" need not be another specific nation; it can be a set of other nations, such as the "Communist bloc," and it can even be the set of all other nations, the "foreigners."

dimensions of interpersonal social comparison: the dimension of "solidarity" and the dimension of "status."[14] (They also correspond more loosely to the two classic components of the analysis of foreign policy choice: "intentions" and "capabilities.") What sorts of basic positions along these two dimensions can an NIC exhibit?

The solidarity dimension. The key question for the first or "solidarity" dimension of self-definition is whether "we" and "they" naturally stand for similar or different interests and values. This can be conceived as a horizontal dimension of self–other comparison. Sometimes it is suggested that identity conceptions are *necessarily* built on black–white "us versus them" dichotomies. But, in fact, as Jane Mansbridge and other contributors to the social movements literature have noted, a division of the world into "us and them" should not be taken to be synonymous with a feeling of "us against them."[15] Indeed, what Mansbridge terms the "oppositional consciousness" of "us against them" is in fact a relatively rare phenomenon.[16] Social psychologists find that the sense of "us against them" is much less likely to emerge if both we and they are perceived to be nested within wider, "transcendent" identity groupings. Such a perception provides a sense of basic commonality that undercuts the tendency toward stark black–white dichotomization.[17]

So, along this first, "solidarity" dimension of national self-definition, I distinguish between "oppositional," or starkly dichotomizing identity

---

[14] Kenneth D. Locke, "Status and Solidarity in Social Comparison: Agentic and Communal Values and Vertical and Horizontal Directions," *Journal of Personality and Social Psychology*, Vol. 84, No. 3 (March 2003), pp. 619–631.

[15] Jane Mansbridge, "Complicating Oppositional Consciousness," in Mansbridge and Morris, eds., *Oppositional Consciousness*, p. 239. See also Joan Cocks, *The Oppositional Imagination: Feminism, Critique and Political Theory* (London: Routledge, 1989), esp. Introduction, "Things in Two's Are Sometimes, but Not Always, Dichotomies," pp. 1–22. A work of IR that strongly makes this point is Hopf, *Social Construction of International Politics*, esp. p. 263.

[16] Note that in highlighting the notion of "consciousness," Mansbridge is explicitly adopting an *individual* level of analysis – a choice parallel to the one made in this book. In her work, "consciousness" is defined as the "ideas and feelings of an individual," as opposed to "culture" which is defined as "the customs, habits, values, and focal concerns of a social group." While Mansbridge admits that an "oppositional culture" could in theory exist, she finds culture typically too variegated to produce clear signals about how individuals should behave. Therefore, though culture certainly forms the *backdrop* for consciousness, any explanation for group action must in the end focus – as the volume's subtitle suggests – on its *subjective* roots. Mansbridge, "Complicating Oppositional Consciousness," esp. pp. 242–243.

[17] The original insight here was developed in Muzafer Sherif, "Superordinate Goals in the Reduction of Intergroup Conflict," *American Journal of Sociology*, Vol. 63, No. 4 (1958), pp. 349–356. The specific notion of a "transcendent identity" has been most fully developed by Herbert Kelman; see for instance his "The Interdependence of Israeli and Palestinian Identities: The Role of the Other in Existential Conflicts," *Journal of Social Issues*, Vol. 55, No. 3 (1999), pp. 581–600.

conceptions on the one hand, and other identity conceptions that nest the us–them distinction within a broader, transcendent identity conception. This distinction should not be taken to be synonymous with a distinction between a "competitive" or "cooperative" spirit. A competitive spirit *vis-à-vis* the "other" can still flourish even when the existence of a transcendent identity is recognized. There is an analogy here to team sports, where the competitive spirit exists side by side with the spirit of "sportsmanlike" play.[18] This is why the international Olympic movement, for all its vigorous promotion of fierce competition between national representatives, can legitimately claim to be promoting international comity. To take another example, Liah Greenfeld has analyzed in depth how what one might term sportsmanlike national identities came to compete vigorously, and often mutually beneficially, on the terrain of wealth accumulation.[19] In sum, some leaders hold oppositional NICs, while others hold sportsmanlike NICs.

The status dimension. The key question for the second or "status" dimension of self-definition is how high "we" stand relative to "them" in the international pecking order: are we naturally their equal (if not their superior), or will we simply never measure up? This can be understood as the vertical dimension of self–other comparison, as opposed to the first, horizontal dimension. The vertical dimension of self–other comparison is surprisingly often ignored in IR writing on identity, for instance in the field's many half-baked applications of social psychology's social identity theory.[20] But it is central to other identity scholars' thinking. For instance, Mansbridge notes that oppositional consciousness is not sufficient to produce a predisposition toward conflict with the dominant group. She writes that for idle dreams of toppling the other to turn into concrete action toward that end, oppositional consciousness must also be complemented by a belief in the potential "efficacy" of taking on the other group in a trial of strength.[21] The sense of group efficacy, Mansbridge

---

[18] As Robert Simon writes, "After all . . . if victory is the primary goal, one need simply schedule vastly inferior opponents." Robert L. Simon, *Fair Play: The Ethics of Sport*, 2nd ed. (Boulder, CO: Westview Press, 2004), p. 53.

[19] Liah Greenfeld, *The Spirit of Capitalism: Nationalism and Economic Growth* (Cambridge, MA: Harvard University Press, 2001). Note that the term "sportsmanlike" is mine, not Greenfeld's.

[20] For more on the use and abuse of social identity theory in the international relations discipline, see Jacques E. C. Hymans, "Applying Social Identity Theory to the Study of International Politics: A Caution and an Agenda," paper presented to the International Studies Association conference, New Orleans, Louisiana, March 2002.

[21] Mansbridge, "Complicating Oppositional Consciousness," p. 241. The psychological literature on self-efficacy makes many quite parallel points – and indeed it served as my initial inspiration. But in that literature self-efficacy feelings are thought to vary widely depending on the particular task at hand, whereas here we are emphasizing overall efficacy

writes, comes not only from a perception of contemporary openings in the political opportunity structure, but more profoundly from a sense of group "history" – which is inextricable from its identity.[22]

I define an NIC that gives rise to a sense of international "efficacy" – the sense that the nation can hold its head high in dealings with its key comparison other(s) – as a "nationalist" NIC.[23] Some readers may find this assertion surprising: are not all national leaders "nationalist" by definition? Not if we accept the definition of nationalism offered by the *Routledge Dictionary of Politics*: "the political belief that some group of people represents a natural community which should live under one political system, be independent of others and, often, has the right to demand equal standing in the world order with others."[24] Those who would treat all national leaders as "nationalists," particularly with respect to foreign policy, are ignoring or denying the last part of the definition – the right to equal standing.[25] For in fact, not all national leaders are convinced that their nations could or even should hold equal status with their key comparison others. One of the primary contributions of postcolonial studies is the notion of the "subaltern," whose basic meaning can be grasped through a consideration of its etymology: *sub* + *alter*, "below + other." Most work in "subaltern studies" has been dedicated to giving voice to the speechless and powerless on the bottom of the social scale, but some scholars have usefully tweaked this concept to identify a class of "subaltern states" in the international system. Such states are not voiceless as

feelings. See Albert Bandura, "Exercise of Personal Agency Through the Self-Efficacy Mechanism," in Ralf Schwarzer, ed., *Self-Efficacy: Thought Control of Action* (Washington, DC: Hemisphere Publishing Corp., 1992), pp. 3–38.

22 Mansbridge, "Complicating Oppositional Consciousness," p. 241. Mansbridge's notions of "oppositional consciousness" and "efficacy" resemble Donald Horowitz's basic typology of interethnic competition, which places, on one axis, the degree of perceived identity conflict (akin to "opposition"), and on the other axis, the degree of perceived stability of rank ordering (akin to "efficacy"). Donald Horowitz, *Ethnic Groups in Conflict* (Berkeley: University of California Press, 1985).

23 As Benedict Anderson has commented, the term "nationalism" should not be confused with "xenophobia," even though the two sometimes go together (Anderson, *Imagined Communities: Reflections on the Origin and Spread of Nationlism*, London: Verso, 1991). The distinction between the two is made even clearer when one considers the model presented in this chapter. Nationalism is to be found along the dimension of status, while xenophobia (a rough parallel to what I am calling oppositional NICs) is to be found along the dimension of solidarity.

24 David Robertson, *The Routledge Dictionary of Politics* (London: Routledge, 2003), p. 331. Anthony Smith seconds this definition, writing that nationalism properly understood promotes not only affection for one's national community, but also *ambition* for it. Smith, *Theories of Nationalism*, pp. 169–174.

25 The relative downplaying of the international dimension of the definition of nationalism is even evident in the small international relations literature on the subject; see for instance Stephen Van Evera, "Hypotheses on Nationalism and War," *International Security*, Vol. 18, No. 4 (Spring 1994), pp. 5–39.

Table 2.1 *Four ideal-typical national identity conceptions (NICs)*

	Solidarity dimension	
Status dimension	Us and them (nested in transcendent identity)	Us against them (black–white dichotomy)
We are naturally their equals, if not their superiors	Sportsmanlike nationalist	Oppositional nationalist
We are naturally below them	Sportsmanlike subaltern	Oppositional subaltern

subaltern members of domestic society are, but they know their place all the same. Indeed, subaltern state leaders, while enjoying the trappings of independent statehood, typically still express a negative national self-image that in many cases is an internalization of the image ascribed to their nation by the dominant powers.[26] In short, some national leaders hold nationalist NICs, while others hold subaltern NICs.

Crossing the two dimensions   We have now covered the two primary dimensions of national self-definition. By crossing them, we can identify four ideal-typical NICs: *oppositional nationalist; sportsmanlike nationalist; oppositional subaltern;* and *sportsmanlike subaltern.* Table 2.1 shows how these four ideal-typical NICs stand in relation to each other. As the case studies will show, all four of these NIC types can actually exist in the real world. It is wrong to think that an identity conception that is nationalist, or that is subaltern, must also be oppositional.[27]

From NICs to nuclear decisions

The generic pathway from NICs to choice

Each of the four ideal-typical NICs produces distinct cognitive and emotional effects, which in turn generate particular action tendencies on the nuclear issue. But before we can look at the specific impacts of certain

---

[26] See, for instance, Fernando Coronil, "Listening to the Subaltern: Postcolonial Studies and the Poetics of Neocolonial States," in Laura Chrisman and Benita Parry, eds., *Postcolonial Theory and Criticism* (Cambridge: D. S. Brewer, 2000), pp. 37–55. For an earlier identification of the same basic phenomenon without the jargon, see Albert O. Hirschman, *A Bias for Hope: Essays on Development and Latin America* (Boulder, CO: Westview Press, 1985).

[27] See the deconstruction of the "subalterns are necessarily oppositional" assumption in Bob Hodge and Vijay Mishra, *Dark Side of the Dream: Australian Literature and the Postcolonial Mind* (Sydney: Allen and Unwin, 1991).

NICs, we must first tackle the broader question of how NICs *in general* can impact foreign policy choice, for the model of identity-driven decision-making developed in this book differs from other models. As previously noted, the tendency in other works on identity and foreign policy is to argue that identity takes certain policy options off the table by rendering them "inconceivable." But, drawing on a wide range of literatures on identity, memory, emotions, and choice – from neuroscience to psychology to the humanities – we can make much more robust claims for the power of individual leaders' national identity conceptions as drivers of their biggest foreign policy decisions.

Why should we expect an NIC to drive, as opposed to simply constraining, an individual leader's foreign policy decisionmaking? The first step to appreciating this possibility is to recognize the key contribution of "self-categorization theory" (which subsumes the findings of "social identity theory"): its discovery that individuals contain *multiple levels of self*.[28] In other words, individuals do not always and only proceed on the basis of their personal self-interest, as many recent political science studies assume. Rather, certain environmental contexts will activate different levels of self – e.g., the family level, the professional level, the national level – each of which is just as psychologically real and emotionally central for the individual as any other. This existence of multiple levels of self can explain some of the altruistic behavior that has been documented between parents and children, for instance, or among fellow soldiers on the battlefield. National leaders are likely often to find themselves in situations which will activate their national level of self, and in particular this is likely when they are engaged in significant interactions with the "key comparison others" that are central to national self-definition. In spite of the rampant contemporary cynicism about the motivations of national leaders, there is in fact ample evidence that they are indeed capable of thinking and acting in accordance with their perception of the national interest, which stems in turn from their NIC.[29]

NICs, when activated, drive choice via the *recall of emotional memories*. Ernest Renan was the first scholar to identify collective memory as the raw material for national identity.[30] As I have defined them here,

---

[28] The seminal text is John C. Turner with Michael A. Hogg, Penelope J. Oakes, Stephen D. Reicher, and Margaret S. Wetherell, *Rediscovering the Social Group: A Self-Categorization Theory* (Oxford: Basil Blackwell, 1987).

[29] Barton Bernstein, "Understanding Decisionmaking, US Foreign Policy, and the Cuban Missile Crisis: A Review Essay," *International Security*, Vol. 25, No. 1 (Summer 2000), esp. pp. 162. But note that while I am arguing that leaders are capable of thinking and acting in accordance with their NIC, I am not arguing that they always do so. The theory advanced in this chapter is most certainly not a "theory of everything."

[30] Ernest Renan, "Qu'est-ce qu'une nation?" reprinted in John Hutchinson and Anthony D. Smith, *Nationalism* (New York: Oxford University Press), 1994, pp. 17–29.

national identity conceptions are individuals' particular interpretations of the nation's identity, but these interpretations still rely on the raw material of collective memory, and that raw material is often emotionally very raw indeed. People do not have to have been present to be stirred by tales of national tragedy and triumph, and indeed the emotional impact can be even more powerful when the story is learned than when it has been lived.[31]

We can turn to the literature on the psychology of memory to understand the effects of emotional memories on political choice – a topic to whose importance the political science literature is beginning to reawaken.[32] First of all, when the leader perceives the nation to be interacting with the key comparison other that plays a central role in the identity narrative, and especially when those interactions concern core issues of national survival, NIC-linked emotional memories rush back into his or her consciousness. Once they have been recalled, there are two primary pathways via which these emotional memories can impact choice: a cognitive and an emotional pathway.[33] Along the cognitive pathway, NIC-linked emotional memories often warp the processing of new information to keep it in conformity with the individual's (unconscious) desire to maintain a stable identity conception.[34] Note that because NIC-linked emotional memories tend to be more salient and sharper than other memories, they are more important in shaping perceptions of the nation's contemporary prospects. Along the emotional pathway,

---

[31] See Stephen P. Rosen, *War and Human Nature* (Princeton: Princeton University Press, 2005), p. 52. See also Claude Digeon, *La crise allemande de la pensée française 1870–1914* (Paris: Presses Universitaires de France, 1959) which carefully demonstrates the *increasing* emotional impact of the war of 1870 on succeeding generations of French intellectual elites, an impact that was felt most of all by a generation that had hardly even been alive when the war occurred.

[32] See, for instance, Donald L. Horowitz, *The Deadly Ethnic Riot* (Berkeley: University of California Press, 2001); Roger D. Petersen, *Understanding Ethnic Violence: Fear, Hatred, and Resentment in Twentieth-Century Eastern Europe* (Cambridge: Cambridge University Press, 2002); Neta C. Crawford, "The Passion of World Politics: Propositions on Emotion and Emotional Relationships," *International Security*, Vol. 24, No. 4 (Spring 2000), pp. 116–156. Earlier works that considered emotions in the context of international politics include David A. Welch, *Justice and the Genesis of War* (Cambridge: Cambridge University Press, 1993), Ralph K. White, ed., *Psychology and the Prevention of Nuclear War: A Book of Readings* (New York: NYU Press, 1986), and Richard Ned Lebow, *Between Peace and War: The Nature of International Crisis* (Baltimore, MD: Johns Hopkins University Press, 1981).

[33] Though these two pathways can be held analytically distinct, in practice they are both occurring at the same time in the same brain, and each can have important reciprocal effects on the other. See Daniel L. Schacter, *Searching for Memory: The Brain, the Mind, and the Past* (New York: Basic Books, 1996).

[34] For more on this phenomenon of "motivated bias," see Richard K. Herrmann, *Perceptions and Behavior in Soviet Foreign Policy* (Pittsburgh: University of Pittsburgh Press, 1985).

one of the more significant findings of the recent neuroscientific literature on the brain is that the recall of emotional memories is accompanied by the *reactivation of past emotions*. In other words, it is not only more likely that an emotional memory will be recalled than other memories; it is also typical that when the memory returns, so too does the emotion. For instance, recalling the memory of a fearful event reignites the original feeling of fear, often with little or no decay over time.[35] Emotions can affect not only how people understand a situation, but also what they want to get out of the situation in the first place, as well as their willingness to act in pursuit of those desires without much prior calculation.[36] Given the above-noted basic unpredictability of the effects of nuclear weapons acquisition, it makes sense that this emotional pathway should loom especially large in the explanatory theory of this book.

Note that because the emotions we are referring to are rooted in the NIC they have a stable source, and therefore the model here avoids some of the typical problems with using emotions to predict political choice – namely their presumed unpredictability and short duration. We all experience many stray emotions and memories throughout each day, but it is the persistence and recurrence of NIC-linked emotional memories that makes them particularly relevant to understanding decisionmaking.[37] Indeed, this scientific discovery of the reactivation of past emotions may hold the key to unlocking the puzzle of the special intensity of much intergroup conflict.

In conclusion, *when the leader perceives the nation to be interacting with a key comparison other over something significant, a set of NIC-linked emotional memories will flood back into the leader's mind, producing new emotions and cognitions that in turn generate a certain action tendency.* The next logical step, therefore, is to determine the emotional correlates of specific types of NICs, and what these mean for choice.

NIC-linked emotions and their behavioral tendencies

We can now specify the emotional correlates of the four ideal-typical NICs and the effects they have on choice. The basic claims made here are that fear is the emotional correlate of both types of oppositional NICs and that pride is the emotional correlate of both types of nationalist NICs.

---

[35] Joseph LeDoux, *The Emotional Brain: The Mysterious Underpinnings of Emotional Life* (New York: Touchstone, 1998), esp. p. 203.

[36] This is a modest appropriation of the much wider critique of traditional rationalist models in Antonio Damasio, *Descartes' Error: Emotion, Reason, and the Human Brain* (New York: G. P. Putnam, 1994).

[37] Thanks to Barry O'Neill for suggesting this point.

As we shall see, the activation of fear and/or pride in the decisionmaker has substantial consequences for his or her behavior, not only via effects on information and beliefs, but also via effects on the more fundamental level of desires.[38]

In developing the links between specific types of NICs and behavior, the theory presented here aspires to cross-cultural generalizability. An increasing body of literature from across the social sciences has made the point that "culture matters" to the nature of group goals, values, and interpretations of external reality.[39] The theoretical framework of this book is compatible with the less extreme versions of the cultural-ist strand. It admits that different cultures may be more or less conge-nial environments for the development of certain types of NICs; but it insists that each particular type of NIC, once established in an individual, will have essentially the same emotional and ultimate behavioral conse-quences. This stance finds strong empirical support from mainstream psychological research.[40]

Oppositional NICs and fear   I have defined "oppositional" NICs as being based on a stark black–white dichotomization of "us against them." It is reasonable to expect that an individual holding an opposi-tional type of NIC would feel *fear* when involved in significant interactions with "them." Like all emotions, the precise definition of fear is the subject of debate, but one could do worse than the basic dictionary definition: fear is a feeling of agitation and anxiety caused by the (perceived) presence or imminence of danger.[41] "Danger" here must be interpreted broadly to mean the possibility not only of physical but also emotional or psycho-logical harm. Indeed, much identity literature has found that fear of the other is not limited to expectations of physical harm.[42]

What are the consequences of fear for cognition and ultimately behavior? The IR literature often uses the word "fear" to dramatic effect, but it has rarely attempted to delineate precisely what fear is or what it

---

[38] Thanks to Roger Petersen for his insights on this point.

[39] Gert Hofstede, *Culture's Consequences: International Differences in Work-Related Values* (Beverly Hills, CA: Sage Publications, 1980); Lawrence E. Harrison and Samuel P. Huntington, eds., *Culture Matters: How Values Shape Human Progress* (New York: Basic Books, 2000).

[40] Klaus R. Scherer, "The Role of Culture in Emotion-Antecedent Appraisal," *Journal of Personality and Social Psychology*, Vol. 73, No. 5 (November 1997), pp. 902–22.

[41] This definition fits with the appraisal theory of emotions. See Klaus R. Scherer *et al.*, eds., *Appraisal Processes in Emotion: Theory, Methods, Research* (New York: Oxford University Press, 2001).

[42] This has been a theme in the literature ever since the pioneering work of Simmel on the notion of the "Stranger." See Kurt Wolff, ed., *The Sociology of Georg Simmel* (New York: Free Press, 1950).

does.[43] The implicit tendency in some of the IR literature has been to argue that fear and anxiety, for instance in a crisis situation, focus the mind and thus actually produce better-calculated responses to external stimuli than if they had not been present.[44] Some research in the field of American politics has shown that the very moderate levels of fear induced by campaign advertising can increase the decisionmaker's alertness, thus leading to higher decisionmaking performance.[45] But contemporary work in neuroscience and psychology has found that any substantial amount of fear will have more drawbacks than benefits for cognitive processing performance. Moreover, once they are activated, even completely unfounded fears are devilishly persistent.[46]

In particular, fear has several effects on the decisionmaker: on the *perception of the level of threat*, on the *level of cognitive complexity* with which the decisionmaker operates, on the *felt urgency to act*, and on the *ultimate goal* sought by that action. I consider each of these points in turn; later I will explicitly draw the links between these general points and the specific matter of nuclear decisionmaking.

Higher threat assessment.[47] Fear tends to create, on the cognitive level, a predisposition toward high threat perception, whose effects are well known in the IR literature.[48] There can be many mechanisms by which fear leads to higher threat estimates, and indeed often exaggeratedly high ones. One such mechanism is that the fearing individual has a tendency to

---

[43] For instance, Barry Buzan's *People, States, and Fear: The National Security Problem in International Relations* (Brighton, UK: Wheatsheaf, 1983) never defines the word "fear." One recent work that offers an interesting exploration of the consequences of fear is Neta C. Crawford, *Argument and Change in World Politics: Ethics, Decolonization, and Humanitarian Intervention* (Cambridge: Cambridge University Press, 2002), esp. pp. 26–7.

[44] An argument like this one can be found in Barry Posen, *The Sources of Military Doctrine: France, Britain and Germany between the World Wars* (Ithaca, NY: Cornell University Press, 1984). Crawford, "The Passion of Politics" also mentions these arguments.

[45] Ted A. Brader, "Campaigning for Hearts and Minds: How Campaign Ads Use Emotion and Information to Sway the Electorate," Ph.D. dissertation, Harvard University, 1999.

[46] "Telling an acrophobic that no one has ever accidentally fallen off the Empire State Building and that he will be just fine if he goes to the top, or forcing him to go up there to prove the point, does not help, and can even make the fear of heights worse rather than better" (LeDoux, *The Emotional Brain*, p. 236).

[47] I use this term as it is used in the policymaking world: a "threat assessment" is an estimate of the other side's capacity to do us harm, if we do nothing. Such threat assessments are then *followed* by recommendations of measures to take in order to counter the threat, thus producing a "net assessment."

[48] See, for instance, Ole Holsti, "Crisis Decision Making," in Philip Tetlock *et al.*, eds., *Behavior, Society, and Nuclear War*, Vol. I (New York: Oxford University Press, 1989), pp. 8–84; Raymond Cohen, "Threat Perception in International Crisis," *Political Science Quarterly*, Vol. 93, No. 1 (Spring 1978), pp. 93–107. For more on the fear–threat connection, see Carroll Izard, *The Psychology of Emotions* (New York: Plenum Press, 1991), p. 284.

develop a sort of tunnel vision *vis-à-vis* the threatening stimulus. By narrowly focusing on the perceived source of the threat, there is a tendency to ascribe to it overwhelming significance and to react in kind.[49]

Lower cognitive complexity. "Cognitive complexity" is the ability to make new or subtle distinctions when confronted with new information – an ability that in turn makes the individual more receptive to new information.[50] Fear has been shown to lead to lower cognitive complexity.[51] Concrete effects of lower cognitive complexity include a further inflation in threat assessments (because of an inability to see ambiguity or nuance in the other's actions and pronouncements); a conflation of different types of threat, lumping threats to status together with threats to life and limb; and simplistic ideas about the utility of different instruments for dealing with the perceived threat.[52] For instance, a leader operating under lowered cognitive complexity may consider military power to be a universally fungible resource like money, leading to the erroneous conclusion that the more destructive power the state amasses, the more secure it will be.[53]

Greater urgency to act.[54] The psychologist Kim Witte writes that a "heightened level of fear and threat motivates people to take some kind of action – any action."[55] This demand for action leads to haste in the decisionmaking *process*. A hasty process in turn tends to produce an even heavier reliance on stereotypes, and failures to complete the search for relevant information about the situation or to digest the relevant information that is at hand, in addition to producing quick final action.

---

[49] Crawford, "The Passion of World Politics" makes this point in relation to how fear might affect nuclear deterrence stability on p. 147. For the scientific basis for my claims, see Izard, *The Psychology of Emotions*, p. 312. See also Edward J. Lawler and Shane R. Thye, "Bringing Emotions into Social Exchange Theory," *Annual Review of Sociology*, Vol. 25 (1999), p. 232.

[50] The definition is borrowed from Janice Gross Stein, "Political Learning by Doing: Gorbachev as Uncommitted Thinker and Motivated Learner," *International Organization*, Vol. 48, No. 2 (Spring 1994), p. 165.

[51] One reason for this is that the experience of fear diverts mental energy that would otherwise have been available for cognition. The relevant literature is cited in Lawler and Thye, "Bringing Emotions into Social Exchange Theory," p. 230.

[52] See Richard W. Cottam, *Foreign Policy Motivation: A General Theory and a Case Study* (Pittsburgh: University of Pittsburgh Press, 1977).

[53] A careful consideration of the various simplifications that power analysis is subject to is David A. Baldwin, "Power Analysis and World Politics: New Trends versus Old Tendencies," *World Politics*, Vol. 31, No. 2 (January 1979), pp. 161–194. For the ambiguities of "power" and nuclear weapons, see Robert Jervis, "International Primacy: Is the Game Worth the Candle?" *International Security*, Vol. 17, No. 4 (Spring 1993), pp. 52–67.

[54] I would like to thank Stephen P. Rosen for pointing out this dimension.

[55] Kim Witte, "Fear as Motivator, Fear as Inhibitor: Using the Extended Parallel Process Model to Explain Fear Appeal Successes and Failures," in Peter A. Andersen and Laura K. Guerrero, eds., *Handbook of Communication and Emotion: Research, Theory, Applications, and Contexts* (San Diego: Academic Press, 1998), p. 428.

Ultimate goals: decreasing the danger or decreasing the fear? As the experience of fear is physically uncomfortable and mentally oppressive, the urge to decrease the fear – in other words, trying to calm down – can become as important to the individual as the urge to decrease the danger.[56] This is the most significant of all the behavioral consequences of the fear emotion, for the behaviors that decrease fear are not always danger-decreasing as well. The urge to decrease the fear can be seen at the root of many seemingly irrational responses to threat, from the "ostrich" approach of simply sticking one's head in the sand, to witch hunts and the appeal to protective deities, or to the acquisition of totems of power.[57]

The examples in the preceding sentence give just a hint of the incredible diversity of the potential behavioral responses to the experience of fear. In the past, psychologists believed that a standard type of fearful behavior would occur involuntarily in response to a conditioned stimulus. But today, the psychological consensus is that although fear creates an *urge* to act defensively, that urge might be expressed in myriad ways.[58] The well-known basic distinction in fear responses is between "fight" and "flight." In other words, some choose to defy the fear-producing object while others try simply to hide from or evade it. What explains these different choices? To understand this, we need to turn to intervening variables. As Kim Witte and others have argued, the crucial intervening step between fear and behavior is pride.[59] In a nutshell, pride in the face of fear leads to defiance, while a lack of pride in the face of fear leads to avoidance. This two-step model of fear and then pride is akin to the bureaucratic process of intelligence analysis: first, a "threat assessment" is developed, which identifies the dangers if we do nothing; then, a "net assessment" is developed, which identifies the degree to which we can do something to forestall the dangers. But pride even in the absence of fear has significant behavioral consequences, which can be termed self-assertion.

Nationalist NICs and pride   The importance of pride as a switching mechanism between two very different responses to fear naturally

---

[56] Witte, "Fear as Motivator," p. 430.

[57] For many examples of fear-driven "irrational" behavior, see Jean Delumeau, *Rassurer et protéger: le sentiment de sécurité dans l'Occident d'autrefois* (Paris: Fayard, 1989).

[58] Jerome Kagan, *Three Seductive Ideas* (Cambridge, MA: Harvard University Press, 1998), p. 22.

[59] Witte, "Fear as Motivator"; Jervis, *Perception and Misperception in International Politics*, esp. pp. 372–378, and Richard Nadeau, Richard G. Niemi, and Timothy Amato, "Emotions, Issue Importance and Political Learning," *American Journal of Political Science*, Vol. 39, No. 3 (August 1995), pp. 558–574. Note that because the literature on pride *per se* is rather thin, in this section I am also relying on the literatures on related phenomena such as "self-efficacy" and "self-esteem."

leads to a consideration of the second, status dimension of NICs. Along this dimension, I have defined "nationalist" NICs as being based on a basic sense of international efficacy, or in other words, faith in the nation's natural ability to hold its head high in relation to its key comparison other(s). Given this definition, it is hardly a stretch to expect that the nationalist would feel *pride* when involved in significant interactions with those others. Indeed, the linkage of nationalism with pride is almost a truism, but, as in the case of fear, the IR literature has tended to use the word more than it has investigated its true meaning.

The dictionary definition of pride has two key elements: it is both a general sense of one's proper dignity and value, and a specific pleasure or satisfaction taken from (actual or expected) achievement or possession.[60] The feeling of national pride has several effects on the decisionmaker: on perceptions of the nation's *relative potential power*; on perceptions of the nation's *ability to avoid mistakes or accidents*; on the *felt importance of autonomous action*; and on the *ultimate goals* sought by that action. I consider each of these in turn.

Higher relative potential power perceptions. Feelings of pride enhance the nationalist's sense of the nation's "natural" capability, *if it exerts itself*, to affect others' behavior.[61] Pride may lead to "exaggerated" perceptions of how high in power and status the nation can hope to rise, but the extra effort these perceptions encourage can often turn such "exaggerated" self-perceptions into self-fulfilling prophecies. Indeed, it is important to note that pride is generally associated with greater effort, not with standing pat.[62]

Illusions of control. Feelings of pride also give rise to a sense that we are not mistake- or accident-prone. This is what psychologists call "illusions of control."[63] Such illusions short-circuit searches for information about potential unintended consequences of a given decision, and they also produce inattention to the details of policy implementation. These points are pithily summarized in the biblical phrase, "Pride goeth before a fall." (Such illusions are crucially important for understanding decisions

---

[60] Jon Elster prefers to separate "pride," a feeling derived from a specific action, from "pridefulness," a generalized sense of self-worth. Jon Elster, *Strong Feelings: Emotion, Addiction, and Human Behavior* (Cambridge, MA: MIT Press, 1999), p. 22. For another discussion of definitions, see also Donald L. Nathanson, *Shame and Pride: Affect, Sex, and the Birth of the Self* (New York: Norton, 1992), pp. 83–86.

[61] By contrast, the extreme lack of pride produces "depression," a condition in which people do not believe that they can do anything to change others' behavior toward them.

[62] Here I am extrapolating from findings on the effects of personal pride to group pride.

[63] Julie K. Norem and Nancy Canto, "Cognitive Strategies, Coping, and Perceptions of Competence," in Robert J. Sternberg and John Kolligan, Jr., eds., *Competence Considered* (New Haven: Yale University Press, 1990), pp. 192–193.

to build nuclear weapons, given the catastrophic potential of nuclear "normal accidents.")[64]

The need to act autonomously. High pride also affects preferences over strategies by making people *want* to do on their own what they think they *can* do on their own. In other words, it produces positive utility from the *act* of "standing alone," even if the ultimate material objective of that act could be more easily or more fully achieved by cooperation. Indeed, for the prideful, to receive assistance can even be a worse blow than whatever harm that assistance averted. As the great African-American abolitionist Frederick Douglass put it:

> The American people have always been anxious to know what they shall do with us. . . . Do nothing with us! If the apples will not remain on the tree of their own strength, if they are worm-eaten at the core, if they are early ripe and disposed to fall, let them fall! I am not for tying or fastening them on the tree in any way, except by nature's plan, and if they will not stay there, let them fall. And if the negro cannot stand on his own legs, let him fall also. All I ask is give him a chance to stand on his own legs![65]

Douglass' acute sense of racial pride led him to desire the experience of autonomy, even if there turned out to be some material price to pay for it.

Ultimate goals: impressing others or ourselves? Pride is addictive. It feels good, and yet such feelings are hard to sustain and therefore require constant reinforcement.[66] This desire is all the more acute in many nationalists, who often proceed from a conviction about the nation's "natural" place in the sun as opposed to its perceived actual place in the gutter. The nationalist's quest to prove himself right can thus be as much directed inward, to reinforce his own ideas, as outward, to impress others. Indeed, Robert Jervis has suggested that weapons procurement decisions may often result as much from the desire to bolster self-confidence as from any other motivation.[67]

---

[64] For a catalogue of these dangers, see Scott D. Sagan, *The Limits of Safety: Organizations, Accidents, and Nuclear Weapons* (Princeton: Princeton University Press, 1993).

[65] Frederick Douglass, "What the Black Man Wants: Speech at the Annual Meeting of the Massachusetts Anti-Slavery Society at Boston (April 1865)," in Carlos E. Cortés, Arlin I. Ginsburg, Alan W. F. Green, and James A. Joseph, eds., *Three Perspectives on Ethnicity: Blacks, Chicanos, and Native Americans* (New York: G. P. Putnam's Sons, 1976), p. 93.

[66] Michael Lewis argues that global feelings of pride (which he terms "hubris") are difficult to sustain and therefore require constant reinforcement. Michael Lewis, "Self-conscious Emotions: Pride, Shame, and Guilt," in M. Lewis and J. Haviland, eds., *Handbook of Emotions* (New York: Guilford, 1993), pp. 623–636.

[67] Robert Jervis, *The Meaning of the Nuclear Revolution* (Ithaca, NY: Cornell University Press, 1989), p. 214.

Hypotheses on NICs and nuclear choices

What nuclear decisions are likely to arise out of the cauldron of NIC-driven emotions? Here, I first show why oppositional nationalist leaders – who experience the combined emotions of fear and pride – are likely to be highly motivated for nuclear weapons acquisition, while leaders with other types of NICs are not likely to be so motivated. I then spell out each NIC type's likely preferences on ancillary nuclear policy choices.

NICs and the choice on the bomb   Why are oppositional nationalist leaders likely to seek nuclear weapons? All of the psychological mechanisms mentioned above combine to produce this result. The "opposition" in oppositional nationalism generates feelings of fear in confrontations with the key comparison other (no *other* "other" will do). Fear produces a higher threat assessment, which motivates a serious commitment to enhance the nation's defenses. It also produces a greater urgency to act, to do something significant to improve the security situation. Fear also lowers cognitive complexity, blurring the perceived lines between destructive force and political-military power, and therefore making having the bomb seem more advantageous. Finally, to the goal of decreasing the danger it adds the goal of decreasing the fear, which can be achieved through acquisition of symbols of power – and there is no symbol of power more powerful than a nuclear bomb. Then, in the two-step process of threat assessment followed by net assessment, after the "opposition"-generated fear comes "nationalism"-generated pride. Pride produces higher potential capability perceptions, which lead to the sense that we can in fact build our own credible nuclear deterrent. It produces "illusions of control," which dissolve anxieties about unintended consequences such as nuclear accidents. Pride also creates a preference for undertaking autonomous action, such as self-help through nuclear proliferation, even if other solutions to the nation's security problems are available. And, finally, to the goal of cowing others it adds the goal of impressing ourselves – a goal that can hardly be better achieved than through the terrible beauty of a homemade mushroom cloud.

In short, the operations of fear and pride together point the oppositional nationalist leader strongly in the direction of seeking the bomb. Indeed, as I have stressed, the action of these emotions produces more than mere *ceteris paribus* policy preferences. The argument of this book is not only about decisional outcomes; it is also about decisionmaking *processes*. The oppositional nationalist leader, operating under the emotional impulsions of fear and pride, is not likely to tarry long before taking the nuclear leap in the dark. For the oppositional nationalist leader, the decision to acquire nuclear weapons is not only a means to the end of getting them; it is also an end in itself, a matter of self-expression. This decision, as the product of a rush of emotions, is likely also to be a *hasty* decision – in other words, a decision that comes without serious prior calculation.[68] In the leader's haste to choose for the bomb, other policy alternatives are likely to have been simply brushed aside, as are questions about how to prepare to manage the additional technical hurdles, political storms and bureaucratic headaches that inevitably come in the bomb's wake.

The oppositional nationalist's emotional impulsions in this direction are so strong that the mere arrival in power of such a leader is practically a sufficient condition to spark a decision to build the bomb, assuming a few other basic conditions apply. These conditions are the following. First, the state should have at least some experience in the nuclear field. This experience, however, need not have been extensive; a leader's decision certainly need not wait for a stockpile of plutonium or enriched uranium sufficient for a bomb to be accumulated. Second, the state should be engaged in reasonably intense interactions with the key comparison other. These interactions are what sets off the activation of the NIC, emotional memories, and so forth. Third, the leader should have a fair degree of control over the state apparatus. Interestingly, this condition does not tend to be as restrictive as one might assume. Domestic nuclear institutions have tended to be centralized under the control of the top leader, even in generally relatively decentralized polities. This gives a degree of latitude even to those leaders who might normally find themselves quite constrained by a Cabinet or a Congress, for instance. However, this and the other conditions do suggest that we should see more oppositional nationalist leaders than nuclear weapons states.

Other NICs, lacking the mixture of fear and pride, are not likely to motivate leaders to seek the "absolute weapon." Leaders holding oppositional subaltern NICs would certainly deeply desire the protection they consider the bomb to provide, but they would lack the self-assurance required to "go nuclear" themselves: they would worry about whether their state could actually develop a secure second-strike capability, whether they could rule out the possibility of "normal accidents," whether moving down this path would cause their allies to abandon them, and so on. Meanwhile, leaders holding sportsmanlike nationalist NICs might feel supremely confident that they could ride out the storm that acquiring the bomb would create, but they would see no need to brew that storm. And while they might perceive some potential international status benefits from the acquisition of nuclear weapons, they should choose to forgo

---

[68] For more on decisions without calculations, see Rosen, *War and Human Nature*.

those benefits in light of the potential provocation that acquisition would represent to their rivals.[69] Indeed, they might even argue that the nation would reap greater status benefits from nuclear abstention. Finally, leaders holding sportsmanlike subaltern NICs would lack either the motivation or the certitude required to take such a dramatic step as building the bomb.

It is important to reiterate that the distinction I am making here is not between "crazy" oppositional nationalists and "sensible" others. Everyone is operating in the same informational vacuum and is therefore reduced to turning this issue into a matter of individual self-expression. Indeed, it is necessary to recall that leaders' NICs may take different shapes *vis-à-vis* different key comparison others. Oppositional nationalism is not generally a character trait; it is an individual's understanding of the nation in comparison to a certain key comparison other. This raises the question, which of these self–other relationships is more likely to matter most to a leader's nuclear policy choices? The answer stems from the relative level of psychological motivation that each NIC creates. The basic rule of thumb here is that fear creates more motivation than pride, which in turn produces more motivation than the lack of fear or the lack of pride. So in the case where an individual has various NICs toward different external actors, the order of importance of these self-definitions for nuclear policy is as follows: oppositional nationalism (fear + pride) > oppositional subaltern (fear alone) > sportsmanlike nationalism (pride alone) > sportsmanlike subaltern (neither emotion).

Implications of NICs for ancillary nuclear policy questions   What of ancillary nuclear policy questions, such as whether or not to seek nuclear technological autonomy for the nation, whether or not to resist the discriminatory international non-proliferation regime, and whether or not to seek a nuclear "umbrella" from a superpower? The theoretical framework presented in this chapter can speak to these issues as well, with one important caveat. Ancillary nuclear decisions are less revolutionary – less "big" – than the decision to acquire the bomb itself. Therefore the policies states adopt on these matters are probably more apt to be understood through conventional political science analysis. For instance, they may be downstream results of the basic choice of whether or not to get the bomb; or they can result from run-of-the-mill political considerations; or they

---

[69] One can cook up hypothetical situations in which a sportsmanlike nationalist state leader is confronted with an overwhelming objective threat, a combination that produces a kind of counterfeit of the emotional effects of oppositional nationalism. But it is very rare to find threats that are so overwhelming that they brook literally no debate about their nature.

Table 2.2 *Leaders' NICs and likely nuclear policy preferences*

NIC type	Go for bomb?	Pursue nuclear technological autonomy?	Resist non-proliferation regime?	Seek superpower nuclear guarantees?
Oppositional nationalist	Likely	Likely	Likely	Ambiguous to likely
Oppositional subaltern	Unlikely	Unlikely	Unlikely	Likely
Sportsmanlike nationalist	Unlikely	Likely	Likely	Unlikely
Sportsmanlike subaltern	Unlikely	Unlikely	Unlikely	Ambiguous to unlikely

can simply result from good old-fashioned cost–benefit analysis. Still, it is worthwhile listing the basic tendencies to which different NICs give rise on these ancillary nuclear policy questions, and Table 2.2 does so.

Below I explain the origins of these basic tendencies one NIC at a time.

Oppositional nationalist NICs. Oppositional nationalists want the bomb. In line with this overall goal, they should generally promote advancement of indigenous nuclear technology and reject the nuclear non-proliferation regime. However, some oppositional nationalists might see taking other steps on these ancillary matters as better promoting the overall goal of getting the bomb. For instance, they may view joining the international non-proliferation regime as the quickest way to acquire the relevant technology necessary for an indigenous bomb effort. In that case, they will indeed want to join the regime. The oppositional nationalist's likely stance on the matter of nuclear guarantees is even more ambiguous. On the one hand, oppositional nationalists are likely to be desperate for some protection against the perceived threat, but on the other hand, they are likely to want to avoid falling under a superpower's tutelage. This simultaneous *demand for* and *resentment of* a superpower's assistance is plainly in evidence, for instance, in Maoist China's relationship with the Soviet Union in the late 1950s.[70] In the final analysis, as fear is a stronger motivator than pride, the oppositional nationalist will probably accept the umbrella as a quick fix to pressing security problems, while still continuing work on the long-term preferred solution of an independently held nuclear deterrent. Indeed, if the leader plays his cards right (as Mao did), the period

[70] See John Wilson Lewis and Xue Litai, *China Builds the Bomb* (Stanford: Stanford University Press, 1988), esp. p. 221.

of superpower tutelage may in fact hasten the development of indigenous technical capabilities.[71]

Sportsmanlike nationalist NICs. Given their tendency not to fear their key comparison others, sportsmanlike nationalists should not seek nuclear weapons. They should also reject accepting a superpower "nuclear umbrella," seeing no great security need for one and fearing that accepting it would cause them to fall under the superpower's tutelage. But at the same time, sportsmanlike nationalists may well be interested in building a significant nuclear technology infrastructure, for both the "productive" goal of boosting national development and the "self-expressive" goal of increasing their nation's international prestige. For these same reasons of self-expression, they may well also resist the non-proliferation regime because of its discriminatory character of dividing the world into nuclear "haves" and "have-nots" (they could, however, probably swallow non-discriminatory, universal nuclear disarmament measures).[72] When inflamed by heavy-handed international pressures, sportsmanlike nationalists' pride should lead to a particular emphasis on the self-expressive elements of their nuclear policy stance.

The above hypotheses for sportsmanlike nationalists are quite novel in the proliferation literature. They provide a theoretical justification for the oft-heard (and oft-mocked) claim by various states that their rejection of the NPT and/or buildup of nuclear technology does not indicate that they harbor nuclear weapons ambitions. Such choices, of course, leave the door open to an eventual nuclear weapons drive, and sportsmanlike nationalists will be aware of that fact. But the awareness that the door is open should not be equated with a desire to walk through it. As stressed in Chapter 1, the proliferation literature has time and again been mistaken to extrapolate nuclear postures from technical potential. Indeed, *if* sportsmanlike nationalists believe that their stances on the NPT or on building up nuclear technology are in fact seriously threatening to trap them in a conflict spiral that ultimately leads to nuclear proliferation, they will likely moderate those stances.

Oppositional subaltern NICs. Given their lack of belief in their nation's capacity to muster a credible deterrent, oppositional subaltern leaders

---

[71] The fact that the nuclear umbrella can potentially serve as a proliferation incubator again tips the scales slightly in favor of the oppositional nationalist's acceptance of superpower tutelage. But it need not serve this function. Thanks to Andy Kennedy for this insight.

[72] The strength with which such policies are maintained, however, may vary according to the overall historical context. In the first decades of the "nuclear era," nuclear energy was seen as the key to the future, so the discriminatory provisions of the NPT were felt much more keenly than they are today, when nuclear energy is increasingly becoming tarred as a technological dead end.

should not seek to acquire nuclear weapons. However, oppositional sub-alterns will certainly be motivated to find some solution to their sense of insecurity. The most seductive policy in their eyes is likely to be the option of hiding underneath someone else's nuclear umbrella. Indeed, even having received a superpower nuclear guarantee, they are likely to be perennially unsatisfied by what they see as its low credibility, and so they will be constantly pleading for a renewed and tightened guarantee.[73] Meanwhile, oppositional subaltern leaders should consider rejecting the NPT or to developing such nuclear technology on their own as bold stances that are simply beyond their nation's capacities. In any case they will subject their stances on such issues to the overriding priority of main-taining the good relations with the superpower that provides them with the nuclear guarantee.[74]

Sportsmanlike subaltern NICs. Lacking either sufficient motivation or gumption, sportsmanlike subaltern NICs should make no decision to acquire nuclear weapons. Moreover, they should not go out of their way to seek a nuclear umbrella, and if they happen to enjoy the protection of one they should be satisfied by a low level of credibility – indeed, they may worry that its credibility is too high. They should also see no reason to develop a level of nuclear technology beyond what would be economically efficient or to stay outside the NPT. Indeed, they will strongly favor the creation of formal international institutions like the NPT regime that provide them with certain rights that are perhaps incommensurate with their perceived material power potential.

Theory-testing and contextualization

The theory has been advanced and the hypotheses enumerated. There remain two unanswered theoretical questions. First, the question of

---

[73] This phenomenon was very much in evidence among many Western European states during the Cold War, but it is not the straight realist behavior that it is often portrayed to be. For just as acquisition of nuclear weapons can provoke as well as deter, so too does increasing the credibility of extended deterrence over a certain threshold. By seeking the umbrella, a state can end up increasing its importance as a target. For instance, French governments in the 1950s clearly understood that they could have too much of a good thing. They accepted the US nuclear umbrella against the Soviets but did not want to become a priority target of Soviet nuclear attack, so they never allowed US nuclear weapons to be placed on French soil. See Olivier Pottier, "Les armes nucléaires américaines en France," *Cahiers du Centre d'Etudes d'Histoire de la Défense*, No. 8 (1998), pp. 35–60, and Chapter 4 of this book.

[74] As a small caveat to this general rule, one could imagine that oppositional subaltern states might on occasion indulge in some fear-driven paroxysm of self-defeating behavior, akin to the peasant riots that the parallel mentality in the domestic context sometimes produces. See James C. Scott, *Weapons of the Weak: Everyday Forms of Peasant Resistance* (New Haven: Yale University Press, 1985).

theory testing: how can we know if the theory advanced here is right? Second, the question of the theory's relevance: even if the theory were proven right, how much would this help us to understand the overall issue of nuclear proliferation? This section tackles these questions in turn.

Testing the theory

Any serious effort at understanding nuclear proliferation soon confronts the unfortunate fact that our basic information set on the nuclear histories of countries other than the United States and the United Kingdom is generally very poor. There are many books on proliferation around the world, but as stated earlier, most tend to focus on nuclear capacities instead of on nuclear intentions – and then confuse the two. The literature is also notorious for exhibiting a double standard in its treatments of "Northern" and "Southern" states.[75] Most tellingly, given the objectives of this project, the literature tends to rely heavily on outsiders' assessments – often by US government agencies – rather than on careful study of internal state documents or in-depth interviews with those who were directly involved. Such an arm's length approach to data-gathering is a sure formula for recycling the old conventional wisdom in perpetuity. The only way to break the cycle is to select a few country cases and to do intensive field research there. That is what I have done. Moreover, it should be noted that the nature of the theory being tested here – its focus on leaders as individuals and on their nuclear decisionmaking processes rather than merely on the decisional outcomes – also recommends such an in-depth research approach.

This study focuses on four country cases – Argentina, Australia, France, and India. The hope is that the theory could eventually be applied to many other cases of proliferation and non-proliferation, but with a careful selection of four cases it can nevertheless be subjected to a serious test.[76] The cases were selected according to three considerations. First, for the purpose of ensuring variation on the dependent variable, it was necessary to select a mix of nuclear and non-nuclear (but

---

[75] The Northern bias of works on proliferation has been often noted, especially by scholars from other world regions. The point is strongly made in Martin Van Creveld, *Nuclear Proliferation and the Future of Conflict* (New York: The Free Press, 1993).

[76] Peter Hall has noted that the in-depth, process-tracing strategy utilized in this book is typically at its most effective with a small-*n* comparative research design of three or four cases, while the marginal returns of having more than four cases are generally small. Peter A. Hall, "Aligning Ontology and Methodology in Comparative Research," in James Mahoney and Dietrich Rueschemeyer, eds., *Comparative Historical Analysis in the Social Sciences* (Cambridge: Cambridge University Press, 2003), pp. 373–404.

Table 2.3 *Case selection criteria (overall criterion: possibility of adequate access to inside information)*

	Built the bomb	Did not build the bomb
"Northern" state	France (first reactor online: 1940s; decision for bomb: 1950s)	Australia (first reactor online: 1950s; no decision for bomb)
"Southern" state	India (first reactor online: 1950s; decision for bomb: 1990s)	Argentina (first reactor online: 1950s; no decision for bomb)

evidently nuclear-capable) states.[77] Second, for the purpose of testing the theory's claims to generality, it was necessary to select a mix of countries from both the North and the South, and countries whose moments of truth on nuclear weapons occurred at different junctures of the nuclear era. Finally, for the purpose of adequate access to information, it was necessary to select countries whose nuclear moments of truth lay somewhat in the past, and whose societies are open enough today to maximize the chances that the facts of the case could be ascertained.[78] How the four selected cases selected respond to these criteria can be visualized in Table 2.3.

The mix of selected cases also turns out to be valuable from the perspective of *competitive* theory testing. As mentioned in Chapter 1, until now the proliferation literature has, broadly speaking, offered four general hypotheses on why states might choose to acquire nuclear weapons. These are the following:

- Techno-centrism: the gradual advancement of a state's technical nuclear capacities inexorably leads to the eventual production of nuclear weapons.
- Defensive realism: a state facing a more powerful regional adversary will seek to "equalize" the security situation through the acquisition of nuclear weapons.[79]

---

[77] Note, however, that only in-depth field research could determine whether or not the non-nuclear states had actually witnessed a decision to go nuclear that had simply never been implemented.

[78] This stricture tends to weight the case selection away from the "rogue regimes" that are the typical focus of the proliferation literature. This is not necessarily a bad thing. Indeed, more open societies represent "hard tests" for the leader-centric theory developed here; if it works on those cases, we may reasonably assume that it would also work on the tyrannies like North Korea or Libya that garner the lion's share of the literature's attention.

[79] Some variants of defensive realism would claim that proliferation would occur unless the state could procure a credible nuclear guarantee from a superpower protector; others would claim that this would occur regardless of the availability of a guarantee. I disagree

Table 2.4 *The cases* vs. *commonly asserted explanations for the bomb*

Country	Technocentric hypothesis: State has developed latent nuclear capacity?[a]	Realist hypothesis: State is facing a superior regional power?	Norms hypothesis: State is a pretender for regional or great power status?	Bureaucratic politics hypothesis: State has well-placed nuclear bureaucracy?	Year of decision to go nuclear
Argentina	Yes: 1961	Yes (Brazil, UK)	Yes	Yes (until 1990s)	None
Australia	Yes: 1961	Yes (China)	No	Yes (until 1970s)	None
France	Yes: 1950	Yes (USSR)	Yes	Yes	1954
India	Yes: 1958	Yes (China)	Yes	Yes	1998[b]

Notes: estimates of the variables are drawn from the book's case study chapters.
[a] As estimated by the latent capacity model used in Figure 1.1.
[b] The coding of 1998 as the definitive Indian decision for the bomb is not unquestionable (see Chapter 7).

- International norms: a state seeking international prestige, for instance one that pretends to regional leadership or great power status, will seek nuclear weapons as a membership ticket to the most exclusive international club.
- Bureaucratic politics: a self-interested nuclear bureaucracy with sufficient political clout and direct access to the top leader will impose its preference for nuclear weapons on the rest of the state.

None of these traditional perspectives easily explains the pattern of proliferation outcomes of the four cases, as Table 2.4 demonstrates.

As the table shows, all four countries had ample means and – if we buy in to the standard perspectives – plenty of reasons to "go nuclear." Therefore, not surprisingly, US government documents reveal significant, longstanding suspicions about each country's nuclear intentions. For instance, as early as the late 1940s the US government accused Argentina of seeking nuclear weapons.[80] Moreover, a secret 1963 study by Secretary of Defense Robert S. McNamara listed Australia among eight states likely to acquire nuclear weapons in the next decade in the absence of a global

with both variants. For instance, the four country cases reviewed in this book show no correlation between having a strong alliance partner and nuclear abstention. For instance, even though it was non-aligned, indeed diplomatically isolated in the 1970s and 1980s, Argentina did not go nuclear; meanwhile, even though France was a very close US ally in the 1950s, it did go nuclear.

[80] Regis Cabral, "The Interaction of Science and Diplomacy: The United States, Latin America and Nuclear Energy, 1945–1955," Ph.D. dissertation, University of Chicago, 1986.

test ban (which in fact never materialized).[81] Yet of the four country cases selected, only France and India did end up building the bomb. Moreover, as the case studies will demonstrate, even the French and Indian stories do not conform well to the conventional models. For one thing, neither state saw decisions to acquire nuclear weapons occurring quickly after it reached an adequate level of technical capacity: France waited several years, and India waited several decades before finally taking the ultimate nuclear plunge. Overall, the closer one gets to these cases, and the more one focuses on the questions of why, when, and how decisions on the bomb were made, the less one finds traditional explanatory variables such as those listed in Table 2.4 to be satisfactory. The case study chapters demonstrate that the theory introduced in this book performs far better than the alternatives, although it, too, does not anticipate all the twists and turns in the four countries' nuclear histories.

Placing decisions for nuclear weapons in context

This study is primarily geared to explain decisions by top political leaders to acquire nuclear weapons. It is important to reiterate that such decisions are not synonymous with the actual acquisition of the bomb itself. Depending on how far the state has come technically, such acquisition may occur between a few days and several years after the political decision has been taken. Indeed, the state may never get its bomb. Dedicated efforts to acquire nuclear weapons may founder at the stage of implementation for various reasons. To take the most obvious example, a political decision may never be realized because of technical failure on the part of nuclear scientists and engineers. But other variables on the levels of bureaucratic, domestic, and international politics may well also intervene to knock a nuclear weapons program off the course on which a top leader originally set it. Nevertheless, the top-down political decision to go nuclear is the most significant, and indeed unavoidable, step along the way to the acquisition of nuclear weapons.

Such top-down political decisions are significant in no small measure because of the tremendous momentum they create toward actual acquisition. One can identify both a psychological and institutional rationale for the power of top-down political decisions to spawn actual nuclear weapons. The psychological rationale is based in "escalation of commitment" theory. This theory sees decisionmakers as eager to protect their

---

[81] The others were China, Sweden, India, Japan, South Africa, West Germany, and Israel. Robert S. McNamara, secret memorandum to President John F. Kennedy, "The Diffusion of Nuclear Weapons With and Without a Test Ban Agreement," February 12, 1963, accessed through National Security Archive, document no. NP00941.

self-esteem and therefore likely to become ever more certain of the correctness of their decisions on complex, consequential questions after they make them – even in the face of mounting evidence to the contrary.[82] Therefore they become determined to finish what they started. Moreover, given that this type of decision engages the entire "national self," other decisionmakers and the public at large should also be subject to the forces of escalation of commitment – a kind of "rally round the flag" effect. Meanwhile, the institutional rationale for the power of the initial nuclear decision is a straightforward bureaucratic momentum argument. Although bureaucracies require initial direction, once they are given that direction they tend to move of their own accord. This momentum can be understood either from a classical Weberian perspective on bureaucracies as almost pathologically devoted to the implementation of political will, or from a more modern perspective on bureaucracies as stakeholders. The bureaucratic head of steam generated by the initial decision may often prove strong enough even to overpower later political leaders who wish to undo their predecessors' choice. In short, it may be hard to make a nuclear decision, but once that decision has been made, for both institutional and psychological reasons it is also hard – though not impossible – to unmake it.

Top-down nuclear decisions may have a good chance of ending up bearing fruit, but are they really necessary for nuclear weapons proliferation? The answer to this question depends to some extent on one's definition of proliferation. Few would contest the notion that top-down political direction is necessary to endow a state with a bona fide nuclear weapons arsenal – the traditional definition of nuclear proliferation.[83] But a sizeable portion of the proliferation literature in recent years has begun to

---

[82] For a balanced assessment of this theory as against the alternative "control theory," which is related to more conventional ideas about policy "learning," see Charles F. Hermann, Robert S. Billings, and Robert Litchfield, "Escalation or Modification: Responding to Negative Feedback in Sequential Decision Making," paper presented to the Fifth National Conference on Public Management Research, George Bush School of Government and Public Service, December 3–4, 1999, http://www-bushschool.tamu.edu/pubman/papers/1999/ Hermann99.pdf.

[83] Why? Because, although we colloquially speak of nuclear "bombs," in fact what we are discussing here are highly complex weapons *systems*, which integrate a nuclear explosive device with other technologies such as missiles. Moreover, these weapons systems, if they are ever to be employed in battle, require extensive testing and training by those charged with firing them. The combination of technologies, plus the element of human familiarity with those technologies, simply cannot be achieved without top-down direction. Without such efforts, even a fully fabricated bomb core is not an "instrument of attack or defense in combat" (the dictionary definition of a weapon) – it is simply a menace to those in its vicinity. My thinking on this issue has been aided by Christopher S. Parker, "New Weapons for Old Problems: Conventional Proliferation and Military Effectiveness in Developing States," *International Security*, Vol. 23, No. 4 (1999), pp. 119–147.

contend that this traditional definition of proliferation is too restrictive. For Benjamin Frankel and Avner Cohen, for instance, a state that has developed the various pieces of the nuclear puzzle, *even if it has not put them all together yet*, can be considered to have a virtual or "opaque" nuclear arsenal, which carries with it some of the same strategic consequences as an actual one (an example would be the case of Israel).[84] Cohen and Frankel's argument is a provocative one. But, in fact, keeping one's arsenal virtual is not just a "stylistic" choice, as Cohen and Frankel assert.[85] For instance, two of Cohen and Frankel's examples of opaque or virtual nuclear arsenals in the 1980s and 1990s were India and Pakistan. If moving from virtual to actual nuclear arsenals were truly a mere stylistic choice, then the 1998 decisions by both countries to "come out" as nuclear powers should not have rocked the South Asian region nearly as much as they clearly did (see Chapter 7 for more on this). To take another example, one of the more radical arms control proposals bandied about in Washington today is for the existing nuclear powers to unmake their arsenals and to retain them only in a virtual state.[86] No one doubts that this would represent an enormous strategic revolution. But if going from actual to virtual arsenals is such a big step, then going from virtual to actual arsenals must also be a big step, not a mere stylistic choice. In short, the simple fact is that whether or not we admit the strategic relevance of virtual or opaque nuclear arsenals, the distinction between "having" and "not having" nuclear weapons still stands, and therefore the dichotomous "yes–no" decision on nuclear weapons still remains a crucially important one for us to understand. And as this chapter has argued, the key variable for understanding why some say "yes" and others say "no" is the nature of the leader's NIC.

---

[84] Avner Cohen and Benjamin Frankel, "Opaque Nuclear Proliferation," in Benjamin Frankel, ed., *Opaque Nuclear Proliferation: Methodological and Policy Implications* (London: Frank Cass, 1991), pp. 14–44. For a generally positive summary and critique see Michel Fortmann, "The Other Side of Midnight: Opaque Proliferation Revisited," *International Journal*, Vol. 48 (Winter 1992–93), pp. 151–175.

[85] Cohen and Frankel, "Opaque Nuclear Proliferation," p. 23. For more on the South Asian case, see Chapter 7.

[86] Michael J. Mazarr, *Nuclear Weapons in a Transformed World: The Challenge of Virtual Nuclear Arsenals* (New York: St. Martin's Press, 1997).

3   Measuring leaders' national identity conceptions

Methodological considerations

Chapter 2 introduced the notion of leaders' national identity conceptions, or NICs, as the critical variable for understanding why some leaders choose to endow their states with nuclear weapons while others do not. But how can we measure leaders' NICs? The matter of measurement is a major stumbling block that the political science literature on identity is just beginning to tackle.[1] This chapter presents my answer to the question of NIC measurement and then applies that answer to state leaders from the four country case studies of France, Australia, Argentina, and India. The reader should be advised that this is a relatively technical chapter, important for the purposes of social-scientific testing but not required for an adequate comprehension of the chapters that follow.

Operationalizing identity: concept streamlining

One of the primary difficulties for operationalizing identity is that it is often highly complex and capacious in its conceptualization.[2] To deal with this problem, Chapter 2 presented a much more focused approach to identity as a variable. It claimed that we do not need to understand the national group's identity in all its complexity in order to explain nuclear policy decisions. Rather, we can focus on NICs, which are held by *individual leaders* – and indeed we can focus on a precise *aspect* of the NIC: how the leader understands the natural positioning of the nation with respect to its key comparison other(s). This aspect of positioning can be

---

[1] Rawi Abdelal, Yoshiko M. Herrera, Alastair Iain Johnston, and Rose McDermott, "Identity as a Variable," paper presented to the conference on The Measurement of Identity, Harvard University, December 2004.

[2] See Kimberly A. Neuendorf, "Quantitative Content Analysis Options for the Measurement of Identity," paper presented at the conference on The Measurement of Identity, Harvard University, December 2004. Special thanks are in order for her probing comments on this chapter as well.

conceptualized along two basic dimensions, which Chapter 2 labeled the dimensions of "solidarity" and "status."[3]

First, on the dimension of *solidarity*, the key question is whether, according to the leader's NIC, "our" and "their" interests and values stand naturally in a black–white dichotomy. When the answer is affirmative, I call the NIC "oppositional"; when the answer is negative, I call the NIC "sportsmanlike." Chapter 2 suggested that this matter of dichotomization is more important than the precise content of the interests and values we ascribe to each side. In other words, the model's predictions are the same whether the leader perceives his nation's values as "communist" in black–white opposition to those of the "capitalists," or as "capitalist" in black–white opposition to those of the "communists." Moreover, Chapter 2 further simplified the measurement task on this dimension by pointing to the seminal importance of transcendent identities that contain both "us" and "them." Simply put, the presence of a transcendent identity should prevent the emergence of an oppositional NIC, while the absence of a transcendent identity permits – though it does not necessitate – that emergence.[4]

Second, on the dimension of *status*, the key question is how high, according to the leader's NIC, "we" naturally stand relative to "them" in the international pecking order. In other words, are we naturally their equal if not their superior, or their inferior? In the former case, I call the NIC "nationalist"; in the latter case, I call the NIC "subaltern." Chapter 2 suggested that this *overall* perception of relative natural status should impact perceptions of what is natural in many specific domains of competition – for instance, economic, military, or athletic pursuits. Therefore, statements on all these subjects provide useful information for interpreting a leader's nuclear policy tendencies. This greatly simplifies the measurement task in two ways. First, it allows the researcher to avoid developing decision rules for "relevant" versus "irrelevant" domains of self–other comparison: all domains are relevant. Second, it allows the researcher to avoid problems of circularity, for while statements on the nuclear issue might well be influenced by previously determined nuclear intentions, statements on other issues are unlikely to be so contaminated, yet the theory suggests that they are just as relevant for interpreting those ultimate nuclear intentions.[5]

---

[3] What I am calling the "positioning" aspect of identity content is a subset of what Abdelal *et al.* term "relational content." The term "positioning" clearly suggests the *basic* perceived natural relationship between "us" and "them," as opposed to the particular symbols, memories, and narratives that adumbrate that basic idea.

[4] The assumption that a transcendent identity blocks the emergence of an oppositional NIC is, however, challenged by the French case discussed below.

[5] Note that discussion of nuclear issues comprises a miniscule portion of the overall data from the four country cases.

In sum, the theory introduced in Chapter 2 greatly telescopes the bewilderingly complex overall question of how to assess national identity content into the much more tractable question of how leaders view their nations *vis-à-vis* their key comparison other(s) along merely two dimensions of relative positioning. But still, a major measurement challenge remains.

A multimethod approach

The typical approach to identity measurement that has been employed in the literature can be described as "interpretivist." The interpretivist methodology involves the study of a wide selection of "speech acts" with careful attention to nuance, pregnant silences, Freudian slips, and other seemingly small things that might in fact hold the key to the entire puzzle. There is great merit to the interpretivist approach, but particularly because this approach often does not produce consensus interpretations, it makes sense also to utilize a quantitative content analysis to provide additional indicators on the quantities of interest.[6]

The major benefits of a quantitative content analysis approach to identity measurement are threefold. First, and most crucially, quantitative content analysis offers us a different way of reading, one that tends to highlight certain preponderant objects or themes in the text, as opposed to the interpretivist approach's tendency to highlight its more picturesque aspects.[7] Quantitative content analysis is therefore a good complement to the interpretivist approach. Second, quantitative content analysis, if done well, offers us a transparent and reliable measurement option – transparent in the sense that the objectives and procedures of the analysis are explicitly delineated, and reliable in the sense that if we take these objectives and procedures as given, the results are not heavily dependent on the personality or private knowledge of the analyst. This allows the reader to accept (or dismiss) findings more easily. Third, quantitative content analysis, being quantitative, opens up the possibility of utilizing the power of statistical techniques, something that the interpretivist approach cannot. For instance, if we assume that the coded materials provide a reasonable sample of the leader's entire set of thoughts, we can draw 95 percent confidence intervals around the quantitative scores along the two dimensions of solidarity and status. This can help determine, for instance, whether a divergence that is discovered between the rhetorics of different leaders may in fact likely be simply the result of random chance.

[6] See Yoshiko M. Herrera and Bear Braumoeller, eds., "Symposium: Discourse and Content Analysis," *Qualitative Methods*, Vol. 2, No. 1 (Spring 2004), pp. 15–39.
[7] I owe this distinction between the "preponderant" and the "picturesque" to the historian Charles Maier.

It is important to reiterate that, in general, the best way to use quantitative content analysis to study identity is as a complement to the interpretivist approach and not as a replacement for it. Many interpretivist critiques of quantitative content analysis are well founded, for instance its tendency to rub out subtle textual nuances in pursuit of sufficient quantities of data. Given that this book covers different countries and time periods, it is necessary to devote attention to context and nuance at a level unreachable through a purely quantitative content analysis – if such a thing can even be said to exist at all. Indeed, if there exists a strong interpretivist literature that has come to a rough consensus about the NIC of some leader or leaders, it would be foolish to view a single quantitative result as falsifying that consensus interpretation. However, that result could lead to a more profound reexamination of the bases for the interpretive consensus.

Therefore, this book relies on a systematic, *multimethod* approach that involves three major steps. The first step in the approach is to review extant interpretivist analyses to create a certain set of *priors* about what might reasonably be said about the NICs of the leaders investigated. The second step in the approach is to obtain quantitative content analysis results as an *additional indicator*, one that, as noted above, can be especially important for cases where there are significant competing interpretations. The third step in the approach is to make an *overall judgment* about the leaders' NICs on the basis of both the existing interpretations and the quantitative evidence. In certain cases, where it is necessary to "break a tie," this step can also involve further qualitative analysis of the texts. The following sections describe in more detail the procedures undertaken for the quantitative content analysis, as it is the more unusual element of this multi-method approach.

Source material

The first step in any exercise in content analysis is to identify and select texts that are likely to contain clues about what one is trying to measure.[8] The quantitative measurement procedure utilized in this book relies entirely on clearly delineated sets of leaders' major public speeches. The best texts for understanding a leader's NIC are likely to be major, regularly scheduled speeches such as "state of the union" addresses, which are explicitly concerned with the overall nature and direction of the nation

---

[8] Martin W. Bauer, "Classical Content Analysis: A Review," in Martin W. Bauer and George Gaskell, eds., *Qualitative Researching With Text, Image, and Sound: A Practical Handbook* (Thousand Oaks, CA: Sage Publications, 2000), p. 149.

at home and in the world, and are addressed to a broad national audience. A second-best option is to use broad foreign affairs addresses made to a nationally representative audience, such as a national parliament. The least-best option is to use topical speeches on specific issues, especially if these speeches are made to specific audiences, because here the content is likely to provide a skewed picture of the leader's overall thinking. However, if enough such speeches could be located and coded, even this option might provide a true, albeit noisy signal of the leader's NIC.

The advantages of using major public speeches to analyze leaders' NICs are several. First, such speeches are often explicitly concerned with outlining the NIC that the leader has embraced; second, they are not tailored to the concerns of narrow audiences with specific agendas; and third, in most cases the universe of speeches to be sampled from can be well delimited and assembled. On the other hand, political scientists as well as ordinary citizens have understandably learned to view politicians' statements with skepticism. Clearly, political speech is very often "instrumental." But, if done right, a content analysis can often get beneath speakers' strategic purposes to elucidate their deeper structure of beliefs.[9] For instance, it is certainly true that politicians often hide their low motivations for taking various decisions, falsely "explaining" those decisions as the result of their consideration of the "national interest." But what is necessary to understand is that in these statements the "lie" is typically not the depiction of the politician's notion of the national interest, it is rather the claim that the political decision was in fact taken on that basis. Thus, the *dissembling* "national interest" justification offered for, say, an economic policy choice can actually shine a *true* light on the politician's NIC, which is what we need to understand in order to predict *nuclear* choices. It is of course always possible that someone will develop the pathological need – and also have enough sheer brainpower – to maintain two completely separate basic understandings of the nation in relation to others, using one to determine preferences on issues and the other to make those preferences palatable for public consumption. If a leader were indeed that two-faced, the historical process-tracing methodology employed in the case study chapters would easily uncover it.

The quantitative coding frame

The goal of the quantitative content analysis is to generate new data on three main issues: (1) the key comparison other(s) in each leader's

---

[9] Ithiel de Sola Pool, "Trends in Content Analysis Today: A Summary," in Ithiel de Sola Pool, ed., *Trends in Content Analysis* (Urbana: University of Illinois Press, 1959), esp. p. 206.

NIC; (2) the leader's understanding of the natural relationship with the other(s) on the dimension of solidarity; (3) the leader's understanding of the natural relationship with the other(s) on the dimension of status. To this end, I have developed a simple and coherent quantitative coding frame.

The first step is to collect the raw data for the quantitative content analysis. In this case, the raw data consists of lists of any *external actors* that are mentioned in a given paragraph in a speech.[10] An external actor is defined as any human community (or collection of human communities) that is not primarily based inside the territory we claim as our national boundaries. Thus, references by French leaders to "France" are not counted, but references to "Germany" or "the Palestinians" are, as well as references to groupings of states (e.g., "The Free World"), wider geographical entities (e.g., "Europe"), wider cultural or civilizational entities (e.g., "The Arab World"), and the world community as a whole (e.g., "the United Nations"). Note that communities that are *in part* based in our territory are counted as external actors e.g., if the French leader makes reference to "the Free World" or to "Europe." Indeed, as will be explained below, a good part of the analysis rests on the crucial distinction between, on the one hand, "truly foreign others," and on the other hand, "wider communities" of which our nation forms a part. The precise coding rules are given in the Appendix.

Having collected the raw data, we then proceed to the three content analysis tasks. *Task 1: Identification of the key comparison other(s).* As mentioned above, the first dimension of analysis is to identify the key comparison other(s) in a leader's NIC. The more paragraphs in which the leader refers to one or another "truly foreign other," the more claim it has to be the key comparison other. Note the assumption that only "truly foreign others" (as opposed to those wider communities of which our nation forms a part) can be key comparison others. For example, I accept that a French leader may employ Germany or the Communist bloc as a key comparison other, but not Europe.[11]

The assumption of the meaningfulness of frequency counts is typical of quantitative content analysis, but it can be questioned. For instance, in

---

[10] This choice of the paragraph as unit of analysis differs from much of the quantitative content analysis literature that tends to look at texts sentence-by-sentence or even word-by-word. In my view, to take as the unit of analysis anything smaller than the paragraph in this case would trade too much contextual understanding for only a minor increase in replicability of results. In addition, the reader will see below that the third quantitative measure is impossible without a unit of analysis that is bigger than a word or a sentence.

[11] There is clearly a judgment call here, however. British leaders, for instance, might well view "Europe" as a truly foreign other. This example underscores the crucial importance of beginning the analysis with a review of the interpretivist literature.

some cultures or political contexts there could be a taboo about invoking the name of a key comparison other, especially a feared one. But generally, if a certain foreign other really did loom that large in a leader's imagination, the leader would find some ways to invoke it which could be captured with quantitative content analysis. The key is simply to know when and how to look for indirect references to the other – another advantage to starting the analysis with a review of the interpretivist literature, as well as doing the quantitative content analysis by hand (as has been done here). Moreover, as this example suggests, the quantitative measure proposed here does not purport to be a strictly mechanical one. The results on the quantitative measure inevitably depend on certain qualitative choices that emerge from a close reading of the text. For instance, in the case of the Australian Liberal prime ministers, on the strength of the existing interpretive literature I chose to group references to different members of the Communist bloc together under the umbrella heading "the Communists." Such qualitative choices are inevitable; the key is simply for all such choices to be well justified.[12]

Task 2: Measurement along the dimension of solidarity. Having identified the key comparison other, the next step is to measure the relationship with the key comparison other on the dimension of solidarity: that is, whether the leader's NIC is "oppositional" or "sportsmanlike" *vis-à-vis* the key comparison other. As previously noted, an oppositional NIC is highly unlikely to emerge if we and they are perceived to be nested within a wider, transcendent identity. Therefore, the more the balance of references between the key comparison other and the wider communities favors the wider communities, the harder it is for an oppositional NIC to emerge. (Recall that an NIC is defined specifically with respect to the key comparison other, not with respect to all others.)

Quantitatively, the scale on this dimension goes from 0 (sportsmanlike NIC) to 1 (oppositional NIC). For heuristic purposes only, we can think of the rough boundary between sportsmanlike and oppositional NICs as 0.5. For instance, in the speeches coded for the Australian case, the Labor leader Joseph Chifley mentioned the Communists quite frequently (in 44 different paragraphs), but he mentioned the United Nations and the world in general much more frequently (in 75 different paragraphs).

---

[12] A further complication is that in rare cases the most-referenced other may not be the one that produces the most psychological motivation to act. As noted in Chapter 2, an NIC of oppositional nationalism *vis-à-vis* a certain foreign other will produce more motivation than, for instance, an NIC of sportsmanlike nationalism *vis-à-vis* a different foreign other. It would be credible to claim that the object of oppositional nationalism is the key comparison other even though it received somewhat fewer references than the object of sportsmanlike nationalism. But, in general, it would be surprising if a key comparison other did not receive the most references.

Chifley's score on this dimension was thus $44/(44 + 75) = 0.37$. By contrast, his successor, the Liberal leader Robert Menzies, mentioned the Communists far more frequently (in 122 paragraphs) than he mentioned the UN or the world in general (in 45 paragraphs). So Menzies' score on this dimension was $122/(122 + 45) = 0.73$, far higher than Chifley's. Moreover, the 95 percent confidence intervals around these scores did not overlap. In conclusion, the quantitative indicator suggests that Menzies' NIC was oppositional while Chifley's NIC was sportsmanlike *vis-à-vis* the Communists.[13]

Again, this quantitative indicator merely does what it says – it provides an indication. Importantly, recall that the absence (or weakness) of a transcendent identity *permits* but does not *necessitate* the emergence of an oppositional NIC *vis-à-vis* the key comparison other. A qualitative assessment is therefore necessary to determine whether a black–white dichotomization that helped inform the speaker's overall definition of the national self did in fact emerge. The existing interpretive literature, as well as additional qualitative analysis, can perform a crucial function here.

Task 3: Measurement along the dimension of status. The second dimension to measure is the dimension of status; in other words, one needs to answer the key question of how high, according to the leader's NIC, "we" naturally stand relative to "them" in the international pecking order. If we are perceived to be their equals if not their superiors, then the leader can be said to have a "nationalist" NIC; if not, then the leader can be said to have a "subaltern" NIC. Here again, quantitative content analysis can help. In particular, information on the speaker's perception of relative natural status can be detected in whether a paragraph *only* refers to a truly foreign other, or whether it *also* refers to a wider community in which we play a part.[14] A tendency to bundle references to a truly foreign other along with references to a wider community of which we form a part suggests a defensive desire to shield the nation from a direct, head-to-head relationship or comparison with its other. For instance, Menzies very rarely discussed Australia's relations with the Communist bloc (or with the USSR or Communist China in particular) without simultaneously also invoking some broader grouping of which Australia was a part – e.g., the "Free World," the "British Commonwealth," or sometimes the

[13] This example is presented for heuristic purposes. In fact, given Chifley's score *vis-à-vis* the Communists and the weight of the interpretive literature, it made more sense to define his key comparison other more broadly, as the "great powers" including both Communist and non-Communist states.

[14] Whether or not *they* also play a part in the wider community is immaterial for this measure, and indeed this is a crucial point for ensuring that the measures along the two dimensions remain independent of each other.

"United Nations." This rhetorical pattern was clearly driven by Menzies' desire to avoid the demoralizing direct comparison between Australia and its Communist enemy.

Quantitatively, the scale on this dimension also runs from 0 (subaltern NIC) to 1 (nationalist NIC). Again, for heuristic purposes, the rough boundary between subaltern and nationalist NICs can be seen as 0.5. In Menzies' case, he made only 25 "naked" references to the Communist world, versus 66 "screened" references to the Communists (that is, mentioning not only the Communists but also the "Free World," for instance).[15] Menzies' score on this dimension is thus $25/(25 + 66) = 0.27$. By contrast, the later prime minister, John Gorton, who held the top job from 1968 to 1971, was much more apt to talk about the Communist world without the screen of these wider groupings (69 "naked" references versus 16 "screened" references). Gorton's score on this dimension is thus $69/(69 + 16) = 0.81$. Moreover, the 95 percent confidence intervals that were calculated around these two points do not overlap. In sum, the evidence from the quantitative indicator on this dimension suggests Gorton's NIC *vis-à-vis* the Communists to be nationalist and Menzies' to be subaltern.

But again, for both of these interpretations to stick, we must proceed to the stage of qualitative verification and clarification. Qualitative analysis is particularly crucial on this measure because of the greater level of theoretical assumption involved in producing the quantitative results. For instance, the quantitative coding scheme does not anticipate "screened" references that reflect less a desire for protection *from* the other, than an offer of protection *to* others. For instance, the word "Free World" in the mouth of an American president has a much different connotation than it does in the mouth of an Australian prime minister. The existing interpretive literature, as well as additional qualitative analysis, can perform a crucial function here as well.

The reader should note that the coding frame presented in the above paragraphs has been carefully developed in order to ensure that the three quantitative measures are truly independent of each other. It is possible to have a low score on the dimension of solidarity and a high score on the dimension of status, or vice versa, or a high or low score on both axes. Moreover, this independence of the two dimensions of measurement is not merely a logical possibility – it also occurs in practice. For instance, again in the Australian case, the analysis finds different leaders' NICs

---

[15] Note that Menzies made more than one reference to *different* Communist bloc countries in 31 paragraphs. These different references are counted separately in the previous measure but combined in this one. This is why the total *n* here is 91 references, rather than the 122 references cited in the previous measure.

to be sportsmanlike subaltern, oppositional subaltern, and oppositional nationalist toward their key comparison others.

Reliability and validity

As noted above, one of the advantages of the quantitative content analysis technique is that it is transparent, in the sense that the objectives and procedures of the analysis are explicitly delineated. These procedures have been discussed briefly in the foregoing pages; a more complete description of the coding rules is available in the Appendix. Because of the method's transparency, we can also test its intercoder reliability: the degree to which the results obtained depend on the personality or private knowledge of the original coder. In November 2004, Rieko Kage, a fellow political scientist, was given the written coding rules and a practice test, a speech by Indian Prime Minister Jawaharlal Nehru. We then compared our coding results, and I gave some additional pointers on how to interpret the written rules, as well as some contextual information about Indian politics. This training phase was much shorter than is typical to teach new coders a coding scheme. We then proceeded to the formal test, on another speech by Nehru. This speech was chosen as a particularly hard test, given its large number of references to the world community on the one hand and to generic foreign others on the other. This is a distinction that is relatively subtle and therefore hard to code accurately, yet crucial to the coding scheme. The coding scheme passed this hard intercoder reliability test. Overall, the simple level of agreement between the lists of external actors was 0.82, which is generally taken to represent a good level of reliability.[16] Using the PRAM (Program for Reliability Assessment with Multiple Coders) program, I also performed the more sophisticated tests, Cohen's *kappa* and Scott's *pi*, which take into account the degree of expected agreement due to randomness. These both gave scores of 0.79, also indicating good reliability.[17]

The good reliability of the coding scheme is in large part due to its simplicity. That very simplicity, however, might lead some to wonder about the coding scheme's validity. In other words, do the measures as operationalized actually reflect the underlying quantities of interest? This question can be answered with reference to an earlier, more complex coding

---

[16] In 19 of the 22 paragraphs by both Kage and Hymans, 32 references to external others were found, and they also agreed that 3 paragraphs contained no external references. Meanwhile, Kage found 2 references to external others that Hymans had not found, and she did not find 6 references to external others that Hymans had found.

[17] The program is available for free from Skymeg Software. It is available on the web at http://www.geocities.com/skymegsoftware/pram.html.

scheme that I implemented on the entire data set. In that earlier scheme, I developed an extensive set of coding rules to directly measure levels of opposition and nationalism. For instance, I counted references to natural zero-sum conflict with a truly foreign other as indicating an oppositional NIC, while I counted references to natural harmony as counter-evidence. *With just a few exceptions, the indications of leaders' NICs that emerged from the simpler content analysis procedure were parallel to those that emerged from the more complex procedure.* This is strong evidence in favor of the validity of both procedures, while the simpler procedure has the added advantage of greater intercoder reliability.

Having introduced the coding procedures in broad-brush form, the chapter now employs the procedures for the leaders of the four country case studies of this work. I begin with Australia, the subject of Chapter 5, then move to Argentina, the subject of Chapter 6, then to India, the subject of Chapter 7. I leave France, the subject of Chapter 4, for last because that case presents some particularly difficult problems for the application of the coding strategy explicated above. The interested reader may turn to the book's Appendix for a more detailed report of the quantitative coding results summarized below, as well as for the complete set of quantitative coding rules.

Australia

As Chapter 5 will demonstrate, soon after the start of the Cold War Australia became heavily invested in both the theory and the practice of the West's nuclear deterrence posture against the Communist bloc. This major commitment was accompanied by frequent interrogation about the potential logic and the feasibility of acquiring a sovereign nuclear deterrent as well – an interrogation that, in the late 1960s, nearly produced an affirmative response. Then, in the early 1970s, discussions of the idea of an Australian bomb essentially came to an end. How can we explain the magnetic hold of nuclear weapons on Australian leaders during the 1950s and 1960s, and then the sudden dropping of that attraction in the 1970s? Following the theoretical framework presented in Chapter 2, the key element for hypothesis-building on this question is the measurement of the NICs of the Australian prime ministers during that period.

Existing perspectives on Australian identity conceptions

According to the standard interpretation of Australian NICs, the Labor prime ministers of the 1940s saw Australia as a minor power within the British Commonwealth and, no less important, the new United

Nations – where their colleague Herbert Evatt notably served as the first president of the General Assembly.[18] Then, the Liberal prime ministers from 1949 to 1972 saw Australia as a thinly populated nation of primarily British stock facing the "red-yellow peril" of Communism spreading throughout Asia. The evocative titles of some of the more prominent analyses of the foreign policy of this era include *In Fear of China, The Frightened Country*, and *Harvest of Fear*.[19] Finally, in 1972 a new Labor government led by Gough Whitlam offered a new conception of Australia as a vigorous, independent, yet cooperative participant in Asia-Pacific and world affairs, and this conception was to be embraced by later prime ministers of both parties.[20]

The standard interpretation of Australian NICs has, however, been challenged by two broad efforts at historical revisionism that locate their attacks primarily along the "status" dimension that runs from the subaltern to the nationalist. Some authors argue that the post-Menzies Liberals actually anticipated Whitlam's nationalism with their own increasingly independent-minded thinking about foreign affairs. These authors have most success with Prime Minister John Gorton (1968–71).[21] But other authors argue exactly the opposite point: not only were the Liberals subaltern, but also Whitlam basically proved to be one, too, despite his launch of a few random verbal salvoes at broad international targets.[22]

Table 3.1 presents a summary of the foregoing discussion, translated into the theoretical terminology of this book. An original content analysis of the leaders' speeches will provide an important additional indicator to help us resolve these issues.

---

[18] Alan Watt, *The Evolution of Australian Foreign Policy 1938–1965* (Cambridge: Cambridge University Press, 1967). See also H. V. Evatt, *Australia in World Affairs* (Sydney: Angus and Robertson, 1946).

[19] Gregory Clark, *In Fear of China* (Melbourne: Lansdowne, 1967); Alan Renouf, *The Frightened Country* (Melbourne: Macmillan, 1979); John Murphy, *Harvest of Fear: A History of Australia's Vietnam War* (St. Leonards, NSW: Allen & Unwin, 1993). See also David Lowe, *Menzies and the "Great World Struggle": Australia's Cold War 1948–1954* (Sydney: UNSW Press, 1999).

[20] Renouf, *The Frightened Country*; James A. Walter, *The Leader: A Political Biography of Gough Whitlam* (St. Lucia: University of Queensland Press, 1980), esp. pp. 117–126. Note, however, that Walter also gives some credit to the alternative position on Whitlam's NIC that will be elaborated below.

[21] Ian Hancock, *John Gorton: He Did It His Way* (Sydney: Hodder, 2002); Justus M. van der Kroef, "The Gorton Manner: Australia, Southeast Asia, and the US," *Pacific Affairs* Vol. 42, No. 3 (Autumn, 1969), 311–333. For a well-documented broader claim about changing Liberal NICs, see Alan Dupont, "Australia's Threat Perceptions: A Search for Security," *Canberra Papers on Strategy and Defence* No. 82 (Canberra: Strategy and Defence Studies Centre of Australian National University, 1991).

[22] See the discussion of Humphrey McQueen and other leftist historians in Rob Pascoe, *The Manufacture of Australian History* (Melbourne: Oxford University Press, 1979), esp. p. 146.

Table 3.1 *Possible interpretations of Australian prime ministers' NICs*

Prime ministers (grouped)	Standard NIC interpretation	Alternative NIC interpretation
Early Labor, 1945–49 (Joseph Chifley)	Sportsmanlike subaltern *vs.* great powers	
Early Liberals, 1949–67 (Robert Menzies, Harold Holt)	Oppositional subaltern *vs.* Communist bloc	
Later Liberals, 1968–72 (John Gorton, William McMahon)	Oppositional subaltern *vs.* Communist bloc	Oppositional nationalist *vs.* Communist bloc
Later Labor, 1972–75 (Gough Whitlam)	Sportsmanlike nationalist *vs.* Asian states, great powers	Sportsmanlike subaltern *vs.* great powers

Note: Interpretations are derived from the literature cited in the previous paragraphs.

The data sources

The Australian prime ministers from 1945 to 1975 unfortunately did not make the regular "state of the union"-type addresses that are ideal for coding NICs. A second-best alternative are general foreign affairs addresses to Parliament or on the radio or television, which were featured in the Australian Department of Foreign Affairs and Trade publication *Current Notes on International Affairs* (*CNIA*, later renamed the *Australian Foreign Affairs Record*).[23] In the case of the two later Liberal prime ministers, John Gorton (1968–71) and William McMahon (1971–72), they did not even make general foreign affairs addresses. This meant that I had to rely on a third-best alternative: important foreign policy speeches to Parliament on specific topical issues. These, too, were featured in the *CNIA*. The breakdown of the data and its quality is indicated by Table 3.2.

The content analysis

The first step in the content analysis is to make frequency counts of references to external actors that occur in the speeches. These counts, complemented by a qualitative reading, strongly support the standard interpretation that the Australian Liberals focused primarily on the Communists and on the Cold War division of the world. Menzies' total number of references to the Communists was more than double the number of references he made to other Asian powers or to Asia more generally. By contrast, the frequency counts show, again in line with the standard

[23] Because of Menzies' very long and verbose tenure, I used a stratified sample (approximately half) of his general foreign affairs addresses.

Table 3.2 *Summary of raw data quality for content analysis (Australia)*

Prime Minister (Name, dates in office)	NIC-relevance of speeches (Low–Med.–High)	Total data amount (Low–Med.–High)
Chifley, 1945–49	Medium (General)	Medium (363 refs.)
Menzies, 1949–66	Medium (General)	Medium (458 refs.)
Holt, 1966–67	Medium (General)	Medium (240 refs.)
Gorton, 1968–71	Low (Topical)	Medium (442 refs.)
McMahon, 1971–72	Low (Topical)	Medium (221 refs.)
Whitlam, 1972–75	Medium (General)	Medium (295 refs.)

interpretation, that the Labor Prime Minister Gough Whitlam (1972–75) primarily focused on Asian states – as neighbors, not as Cold War partners or enemies. Whitlam's rhetoric was even clearer in its repudiation of the Cold War categories than his Labor forebear Joseph Chifley had been. Even if one – wrongly, in my judgment – interprets Whitlam's references to the various Communist states and movements as references to a monolithic "Communist bloc," the total does not rise even to half of the references he made to other Asian powers or to Asia more generally. In sum, it seems clear that Whitlam's NIC did represent a significant break from that of the Liberals.

Having now identified the key comparison others for the various prime ministers, Figure 3.1 provides evidence on how those prime ministers depicted Australia's relationship with their key comparison other.

The story suggested by the figure is reinforced by 95 percent confidence intervals calculated around each data point (see Appendix for precise numbers). Along the X axis, the scores clearly suggest that the Labor prime ministers were sportsmanlike while the Liberals were oppositional *vis-à-vis* their respective key comparison others. Along the Y axis, the scores clearly suggest that the early Liberal and both early and later Labor prime ministers were subaltern, but that the later Liberals were nationalist *vis-à-vis* their respective key comparison others.

Overall judgments

The final step in the analysis is to come to overall judgments on the NICs of the Australian prime ministers. To do this, we need to consider the content analysis results together with the existing interpretations from the literature. For the first three prime ministers, the results perfectly mirror the standard interpretation of their NICs. Chifley's NIC was sportsmanlike subaltern *vis-à-vis* the great powers, while the

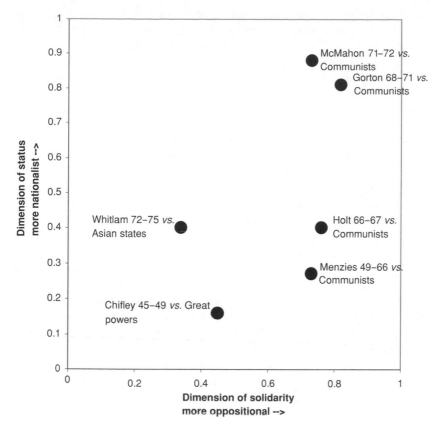

Figure 3.1 Quantitative results on Australian prime ministers' NICs, 1945–75

major Liberal prime minister, Menzies, and his successor Holt's NICs were oppositional subaltern *vis-à-vis* the Communist bloc. However, for the last three prime ministers the quantitative results generally support the *alternative* interpretations in the literature. It is advisable to take a closer look at these results before deciding against the standard interpretation.

First, whereas the standard interpretation in the literature is that all the Liberals held oppositional *subaltern* NICs, the quantitative results support the alternative interpretation that the later Liberals Gorton and McMahon held oppositional *nationalist* NICs. As noted previously, the alternative interpretation in the literature is especially strong with respect to Gorton.[24] My own qualitative analysis of Gorton's speeches reinforces this alternative interpretation; for instance, while visiting London, Gorton expressed his opinion that Australia would be a great power within thirty to sixty years – which he said was "but a blinking of the eyelid in the life of a nation."[25] Therefore, although the raw data quality in the content analysis is far from ideal, it does seem reasonable to endorse the alternative interpretation of Gorton as an oppositional nationalist.

By contrast, the case for interpreting McMahon as an oppositional nationalist is rather weak.[26] The much more common view in the literature is that McMahon peddled the traditional Liberal approach to foreign policy – indeed "in its crudest form."[27] Moreover, it is necessary to recall the raw data available for the content analysis of McMahon's NIC was sparse and of low quality. So it seems unwarranted to overturn the standard interpretation that McMahon held an oppositional subaltern NIC.

Finally, whereas the standard interpretation is that Whitlam brought in a new NIC of sportsmanlike nationalism, the content analysis indicates that he was more of a sportsmanlike subaltern, which again is more in line with the alternative interpretation.[28] My own qualitative analysis of Whitlam's speeches also suggests that the alternative interpretation may have a point.[29] Certainly, Whitlam made some nationalist noises; in his first press conference after the election, he famously called for "a more independent Australian stance in international affairs."[30] But as numerous commentators have pointed out, Whitlam seemed reticent to apply this general rhetoric of independence to concrete issues. For instance, discussing the opportunities for peace in Southeast Asia after the end of American military intervention, Whitlam stated, "The West threw away

---

[24] Hancock, *John Gorton*; van der Kroef, "The Gorton Manner"; Dupont, "Australia's Threat Perceptions."

[25] John G. Gorton, "Address to the Australia Club in London," *CNIA*, Vol. 40, No. 1 (January 1969), pp. 25–8. Note that this speech was not included in the quantitative data because it was not delivered to Parliament.

[26] Even Dupont, *Australia's Threat Perceptions*, p. 67, credits Gorton rather than McMahon as the main instigator of what he depicts as the Liberals' movement toward a more nationalist NIC.

[27] J. D. B. Miller, "Australian Foreign Policy – Constraints and Opportunities: I," *International Affairs*, Vol. 50, No. 2 (April 1974), p. 231.

[28] There is a significant difference, though, in that while the alternative interpretation would expect Whitlam's key comparison other to be the great powers, in fact it is the states of Asia. Note in this regard, however, that Whitlam registers an even lower score on the Y axis *vis-à-vis* the US and UK than *vis-à-vis* the Asians. "Sportsmanlike subaltern" characterizes Whitlam's approach to most of the outside world.

[29] This represents a change from my previous interpretation of Whitlam as a sportsmanlike nationalist. Thanks to Jim Green for pushing me on this.

[30] "The Prime Minister's Press Conference," *CNIA*, Vol. 43, No. 12 (December 1972), p. 619.

Table 3.3 *Global assessment of Australian leaders' NICs*

Sportsmanlike nationalist	Oppositional nationalist
None	Gorton (1968–71) *vs.* Communist bloc
Sportsmanlike subaltern	**Oppositional subaltern**
Chifley (1945–49) *vs.* Great powers	Menzies (1949–66) *vs.* Communist bloc
Whitlam (1972–75) *vs.* Asian states	Holt (1966–67) *vs.* Communist bloc
	McMahon (1971–72) *vs.* Communist bloc

an opportunity for a settlement in 1954 after Korea, after Geneva. I believe the United States, the Soviet Union, Japan, and China are determined not to let the second opportunity slip away because assuredly it will not be offered a third time."[31] That was essentially all he could offer – his "belief" that the big powers would be sensible this time around. This hope that others will solve the problem hardly reflects a nationalist sense of self-efficacy. In sum, though Whitlam clearly did introduce Australia to a new way of imagining the regional and world map, it does seem reasonable to conclude that when it came to concrete foreign policy questions he displayed sportsmanlike subaltern tendencies just as the earlier generation of Labor politicians had done.

The overall assessment of the Australian prime ministers is summarized in Table 3.3. This assessment will serve as the basis for the analysis of their nuclear policy preferences and actions in Chapter 5.

Argentina

As Chapter 6 recounts, from the mid-1960s to the late 1980s many observers believed that Argentina was working toward the acquisition of nuclear weapons. Northern anxieties about Argentina's nuclear intentions only abated after President Carlos Menem's (1989–99) major effort to increase international transparency and decrease civilian nuclear funding. Even today, if Argentina renews its lapsed commitment to the nuclear sector, external worries are likely to rebound, as they have about Brazil.[32] The central question for the case study in Chapter 6 is why a quarter-century's worth of Argentine leaders pursued the nuclear policies they did when in fact they had *no interest* in the bomb. The key element for

---

[31] Gough Whitlam, "Australia's Foreign Policy," *Australian Foreign Affairs Record*, Vol. 44, No. 1 (January 1973), p. 32.

[32] Larry Rohter, "If Brazil Wants to Scare the World, It's Succeeding," *New York Times*, October 31, 2004, "Week in Review" section p. 3.

hypothesis-building on this question is the measurement of the NICs of the Argentine presidents.

Existing perspectives on Argentine identity conceptions

The majority tendency in the literature on Argentine NICs is to argue that Argentine leaders as a group long considered their nation to be in structural conflict with the outside world – or otherwise put, with generic foreign others.[33] Within the overall rubric of oppositional nationalism, different regimes distinguished themselves by adopting different "favorite" enemies; for instance, military regimes, inspired by "geopolitical" thinking, tended to focus their animus on Argentina's neighbors and particularly Brazil,[34] while the Peronists, inspired by "dependencia" thinking, tended to focus their animus on the North and particularly the US.[35] Then, again according to the standard interpretation, in 1989 the newly elected Peronist President Carlos Menem repudiated Argentina's long oppositional nationalist tradition in favor of a radical neo-liberal experiment that the brilliant Argentine scholar Carlos Escudé labels "the realism of weak states."[36] In short, the standard interpretation depicts Argentine leaders as holding a string of oppositional nationalist NICs until 1989, and then a sportsmanlike subaltern NIC after that date.

The standard interpretation has, however, been contested by significant pieces of scholarship. Some authors cast doubt on the characterization of Argentine leaders' NICs as having traditionally been oppositional in nature. The Argentine scholar and journalist Mariano Grondona, for instance, finds the key to Argentine elites' national identity conception in their sense of distance from the centers of world power. The sense of distance, Grondona writes, leads to feelings both of external security – which Argentine leaders appreciate – and of international marginality – which

---

[33] Carlos Escudé, *Patología del nacionalismo: el caso argentino* (Buenos Aires: Editorial Tesis, 1987); Joseph S. Tulchin, *Argentina and the United States: A Conflicted Relationship* (Boston: Twayne, 1990).

[34] Jack Child, *Geopolitics and Conflict in South America: Quarrels among Neighbors* (New York: Praeger, 1985); see also his "Geopolitical Thinking in Latin America," *Latin American Research Review* Vol. 14, No. 2 (Summer 1979), esp. pp. 95–102. Note that the Argentine military conceived its "war" against subversion as directed against a largely internal enemy, albeit one with some transnational aspects. "Anti-communism" at home did not translate into anti-communism abroad. Therefore it falls outside the bounds of this study. See Mark J. Osiel, "Constructing Subversion in Argentina's Dirty War," *Representations*, No. 75 (Summer, 2001), pp. 119–158.

[35] An early version of this argument can be found in Juan José Hernández Arregui, *La formación de la conciencia nacional, 1930–1960* (Buenos Aires: Ediciones Hachea, 1970).

[36] Carlos Escudé, *El realismo de los estados débiles: la política exterior del primer Gobierno Menem frente a la teoría de las relaciones internacionales* (Buenos Aires: Grupo Editor Latinoamericano, 1995).

Table 3.4 *Possible interpretations of Argentine presidents' NICs*

Presidents (grouped)	Standard NIC interpretation	Alternative NIC interpretation
Pre-1989 presidents (*Revolución Argentina* 1966–73, Peronist restoration 1973–76, *Proceso* regime 1976–83, Raúl Alfonsín 1983–89)	Oppositional nationalist *vs.* neighbors, North, and generic foreign others	Sportsmanlike nationalist *vs.* generic foreign others
Post-1989 presidents (Carlos Menem 1989–99 and subsequent presidents)	Sportsmanlike subaltern *vs.* the North and generic foreign others	Sportsmanlike nationalist *vs.* generic foreign others

Note: Interpretations are derived from the literature cited in the previous paragraphs.

Argentine leaders hate. They react to their position by trying to get noticed by the outside world, through dramatic – but utterly sportsmanlike – assertions of national greatness.[37] Finally, some authors cast doubt on the degree to which Carlos Menem actually abandoned the nationalism of his predecessors. In a careful quantitative content analysis of the speeches of both Menem and his immediate predecessor Raúl Alfonsín, Victor Armony concludes that Menem actually merely updated the basic Argentine NIC of sportsmanlike nationalism for the new, neoliberal international climate.[38]

Table 3.4 presents a summary of the foregoing discussion using the theoretical terminology of this book. Rather than list all the presidents by name at this point, I group them according to the regimes in which they served: the *Revolución Argentina* from 1966 to 1973 (a military regime); the Peronist restoration from 1973 to 1976 (the product of democratic elections); and the *Proceso de Reorganización Nacional* from 1976 to 1983 (another military regime). The (shaky) current democratic regime was founded in 1983.

An original content analysis of the leaders' speeches will provide an important additional indicator to help us resolve these issues.

[37] Mariano Grondona, *Argentina en el tiempo y en el mundo* (Buenos Aires: Editorial Primera Plana, 1967). See also Grondona's more recent *La Argentina como vocación* (Buenos Aires: Planeta, 1995), and Edward S. Milenky, "Arms Production and National Security in Argentina," *Journal of Interamerican Studies and World Affairs*, Vol. 22, No. 3 (August 1980), pp. 267–288. Even the supposedly arch-oppositional nationalist Juan Perón himself is undergoing a reevaluation: see Laura Ruiz Jimenez, "Peronism and Anti-Imperialism in the Argentine Press: 'Braden or Perón' was also 'Perón is Roosevelt,'" *Journal of Latin American Studies*, Vol. 30, No. 3 (October 1998), pp. 551–571.

[38] Victor Armony, *Représenter la nation: Le discours présidentiel de la transition démocratique en Argentine 1983–1999* (Montreal: L'Univers des discours, 2000).

Table 3.5 *Summary of raw data quality for content analysis (Argentina)*

President (Name, dates in office)[a]	NIC-relevance of speeches (low–med.–high)	Total data amount (low–med.–high)
Onganía, 1966–70	High (State of Union)	Medium (102 refs.)
Levingston, 1970–71	High (State of Union)	Low (27 refs.)
Lanusse, 1971–73	High (State of Union)	Low (42 refs.)
Cámpora, 1973	High (State of Union)	Medium (277 refs.)
Juan Perón, 1973–74	High (State of Union)	Medium (112 refs.)
Isabel M. E. Perón, 1974–76	High (State of Union)	Low (67 refs.)
Videla, 1976–81	Low (Topical)	High (2098 refs.)
Viola, 1981	Low (Topical)	Medium (192 refs.)
Alfonsín, 1983–89	High (State of Union)	High (660 refs.)
Menem, 1989–99	High (State of Union)	High (690 refs.)
De la Rúa, 1999–2001	High (State of Union)	Medium (167 refs.)
Duhalde, 2002–3	High (State of Union)	Low (94 refs.)
Kirchner, 2003–current	High (State of Union)	Medium (132 refs.)

[a]*Notes:* No data for Presidents Galtieri and Bignone from 1981–83, as well as a few minor acting presidents

The data sources

Most of the Argentine presidents made the regular "state of the union"-type addresses that are ideal for coding NICs. For the Argentine presidents of the democratic periods 1973–76 and 1983–2004, I coded their yearly speeches at the opening of new sessions of Congress, plus their inaugural addresses if they made one. For the military presidents of the *Revolución Argentina*, the period of military rule, 1966–73, I coded their broadly publicized, yearly speeches to the *Comida de Camaradería de las Fuerzas Armadas* (Armed Forces Comradeship Dinner), held annually on or around July 9, Argentine Independence Day. Unfortunately, during the *Proceso de Reorganización Nacional*, the later period of military rule, 1976–83, the presidents no longer regularly addressed the *Comida*. In this case the only option available was the third-best route of coding speeches on topical foreign policy issues. I located a large number of such speeches by Generals Jorge Videla and Roberto Viola (1976–81; 1981) but unfortunately not for their successors Leopoldo Galtieri and Reynaldo Bignone (1981–83). Therefore the latter two presidents are unfortunately excluded from the data set. Note that all speeches were read in the original Spanish, in their officially published form. The breakdown of the data and its quality is indicated by Table 3.5.

Because of the low amount of data in some cases, in the content analysis below I group some of the presidents together with their colleagues, but only where this seems qualitatively justified.

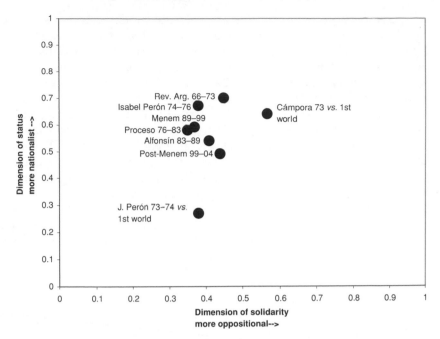

Figure 3.2 Quantitative results on Argentine presidents' NICs, 1966–2004
Note: unless otherwise noted, the presidents' key comparison others were "generic foreign others."

The content analysis

The quantitative data provides overwhelming evidence that generic others, rather any specific country, consistently served as Argentine leaders' top key comparison others. Almost every president's references to generic foreign others far outnumbered references either to Latin American neighbors or the North. Menem, for instance, made reference to generic foreign others over *six times* more frequently than he made reference specifically to the United States. The only two exceptions to this rule were the early 1970s Peronists, Héctor Cámpora and Juan Perón, who focused more of their attention on the North.[39]

Having identified the key comparison others for the various presidents, Figure 3.2 provides evidence on how the presidents depicted Argentina's relationship with their key comparison other.

[39] These two exceptions are evidence that the content analysis procedures were not simply "fooled" by seemingly generic statements that actually were coded references to a specific external other.

The story suggested by the figure is generally reinforced by 95 percent confidence intervals calculated around each data point (see Appendix for precise numbers). Along the X axis, the scores clearly suggest that the Argentine presidents were sportsmanlike, except for the Peronist oppositional interim president, Héctor Cámpora. Along the Y axis, the scores clearly suggest that all the presidents were nationalist, except for Juan Perón himself, who surprisingly appears subaltern. This odd latter result is due to a limitation in the quantitative coding that was noted earlier: the coding scheme is unable to tell the difference between a subaltern and what can be called a "super-nationalist" leader who sees himself less as president of his nation than as president of the world. A qualitative reading of Juan Perón's speeches reveals such a grandiose tendency, for instance in his declaration that his doctrine of *justicialismo* "can be applied as a humane solution to the majority of the problems of the world."[40] In short, Perón was in fact a nationalist after all – and indeed, that is an understatement.

Overall judgments

The final step in the analysis is to come to overall judgments on the NICs of the Argentine presidents. To do this, we need to consider the quantitative results together with the existing interpretations from the literature. Given the high quality of the raw data available in the Argentine case, the content analysis should be taken quite seriously. Interestingly, the content analysis largely supports the *alternative* interpretations in the literature. Rather than finding a set of oppositional nationalists followed by a set of sportsmanlike subalterns as the standard interpretation would expect, the content analysis found a long line of sportsmanlike nationalists with only one exception – and even he was merely an interim president whose historical importance is close to zero.

But in fact a qualitative reading of the 1973 speech by that interim president, Héctor Cámpora, is quite revealing because in it he uses the kind of oppositional nationalist rhetoric that the standard interpretation in the literature would have expected from the others. Cámpora built his speech around the dichotomy "dependency or liberation" and explicitly labeled the developed states of the North as Argentina's "enemies."[41] Even the Organization of American States was tarred as an instrument

---

[40] Juan Perón, "Discurso pronunciado ante los diputados y senadores nacionales reunidos en Asamblea Legislativa, al inaugurar el 99o período de sesiones ordinarias del Congreso nacional," in *Juan Perón 1973–1974: Todos sus discursos, mensajes, y conferencias*, Vol. II (Buenos Aires: Editorial de la Reconstrucción, 1974), p. 184. Available at http://lanic.utexas.edu/project/arl/pm/sample2/.

[41] President Héctor Cámpora speech in Congreso de la Nación, Cámara de Diputados, *Diario de Sesiones*, Sesión de Asamblea May 25, 1973, p. 55.

of "dependency and underdevelopment."[42] But besides Cámpora, only the presidents of the late 1960s military regime and Cámpora's Peronist colleagues even leaned in this direction.[43]

The fact that the content analysis found all presidents other than Cámpora to be sportsmanlike nationalist is particularly surprising in the case of Carlos Menem, who ruled from 1989 to 1999. In my own qualitative reading of Menem's speeches, I saw how the majority of authors could have been struck by his adoption – increasingly over time – of the language of neo-liberalism: openness, transparency, flexibility, reform, human rights. But I also saw the validity of Victor Armony's point that Menem found a way to embrace neo-liberalism without abandoning the language of Argentine nationalism. Even at the depths of Argentina's hyperinflation crisis in 1989, Menem was capable of stating: "The world is calling Argentina to carry out the protagonism that our best historical tradition maps for us, and that our necessities of development and integration demand of us."[44] And as Argentina recovered, Menem's breast-beating became even more blatant. By 1999 he was speaking casually of his agenda for "my next meetings with the leaders of the world" and crowing that Argentina was "among the 10 top countries in the world in the communications area," "one of the top countries in the world in fiber optic cable laid per inhabitant," "the fifth largest food producer," that its alliance relationship with the United States was of a special sort "boasted by few countries," that the country had had "the lowest levels of inflation in the world since 1995" and had been chosen by the IMF, "along with Germany and England . . . [as] leaders in financial, fiscal and monetary transparency," and above all that Argentina was a "young and glorious nation" committed to being at "the vanguard of the world of the future."[45] These are the words of the supposed first leader of a new era of Argentine self-effacement!

The overall assessment of the Argentine presidents is summarized in Table 3.6. This assessment will serve as the basis for the analysis of their nuclear policy preferences and actions in Chapter 6.

---

[42] Ibid., p. 35.

[43] Again, note that the military dictators from 1976 to 1983 also adopted a very tough rhetoric of war against subversion, but as noted earlier, that rhetoric was not outwardly directed and therefore falls outside the concerns of this study.

[44] Carlos Menem, "Hacia la conquista del país soñado" (address to the Asamblea Legislativa, May 1, 1990), in Carlos Menem: La esperanza y la acción (Buenos Aires: Emecé Editores, 1990), pp. 29–64. Available at http://lanic.utexas.edu/project/arl/pm/sample2/argentin/menem/.

[45] Carlos Menem, "Mensaje Presidencial del Doctor Carlos Saúl Menem a la Honorable Asamblea Legislativa en la Aperture del 117o Período de Sesiones Ordinarias," March 1, 1999, at http://www.presidencia.gov.ar/2ADD5.html (accessed October 17, 2000; link no longer active).

Table 3.6 *Global assessment of Argentine leaders' NICs*

Sportsmanlike nationalist	Oppositional nationalist
Most presidents (1966–present) *vs.* generic foreign others	Héctor Cámpora (interim president 1973) *vs.* North
Sportsmanlike subaltern	Oppositional subaltern
None	None

India

The story of India's self-interrogation about whether or not to build the bomb covers nearly its entire history as an independent state since 1947. As Chapter 7 will demonstrate, it was not until 1998 that a prime minister would make a straightforward decision to make India a nuclear weapons state. The key question for the Indian case study, therefore, is why the definitive decision to go nuclear occurred in 1998 and not before; and the key element for hypothesis-building is the measurement of the NICs of the Indian prime ministers over that entire period.

Existing perspectives on Indian identity conceptions

There is broad consensus in the literature over the proper interpretation of some Indian leaders' NICs. The first point of agreement in the literature is that India's first prime minister, Jawaharlal Nehru, offered a unique and powerful understanding of India's place in world history. According to the "Nehruvian" view, as an ancient civilization encompassing one-sixth of the world's population, India had both a right and a duty to seek great power status. But India could not act as a normal great power. Rather, it had a world-historical duty to tame the anarchy of international politics by effecting a change in the hearts of the superpowers – just as the non-violent "freedom struggle" had done to the British imperial overlord.[46] The second point of agreement in the literature is that at the end of the 1990s, India's traditional "secularist" political class, which owed so much to Nehru's original vision, lost power to a political movement with very different intellectual forebears: the Hindu nationalist Bharatiya Janata Party (BJP). The BJP, led by Prime Minister Atal Behari Vajpayee, came

---

[46] See, for instance, Jawaharlal Nehru, *The Discovery of India*, centenary ed. (Delhi: Oxford University Press, 1989); Stephen P. Cohen, *India: Emerging Power* (Washington, DC: Brookings Institution Press, 2002), esp. ch. 2; Balkrishna Govind Gokhale, "Nehru and History," *History and Theory*, Vol. 17, No. 3 (October 1978), pp. 311–322; and Surjit Mansingh, ed., *Nehru's Foreign Policy: Fifty Years On* (Delhi: Vedams Books, 1998).

into office in 1998 determined to rewrite the history books – literally – to reflect its idea of Hindus and Muslims (and by extension, of India and Pakistan) as engaged in an epic, centuries-old struggle for control of the subcontinent.[47]

The main debate in the literature is over the degree to which Nehru's NIC actually maintained its hold over subsequent secularist Indian prime ministers before Vajpayee and the BJP came to power. One reading is that Nehru's death led to his "retrospective deification" and to a "canonical standing" for his ideas about India and the world.[48] Authors taking this position argue that a reconsideration of India's traditional Nehruvian foreign policy only began in earnest when the end of the Cold War brusquely removed its foundations.[49]

On the other hand, some authors contend that as the gap between Nehruvian ideals and Indian reality grew ever wider, it was the continuing struggle with Pakistan that came to dominate even secularist Indians' vision of their nation's international mission.[50] Indeed, the identity ramifications of the bloody partition of British India into two states, and its continuing sequels in the contested territory of Kashmir, are hard to miss. Stephen P. Cohen, for instance, speaks of the Indo-Pakistani relationship as a classic "paired minority conflict" similar to the Israeli–Arab dispute, producing wars that resemble "communal riots with armor."[51] The fact that Indian leaders defined the Kashmir problem in terms of secular versus religious instead of Hindu versus Muslim hardly lessens its identity relevance.[52] But the notion that Pakistan gradually but ineluctably took hold as the secularist Indian leaders' key comparison other is hotly disputed. The secularists found frankly demeaning the comparison between

---

[47] Christophe Jaffrelot, *The Hindu Nationalist Movement in India* (New York: Columbia University Press, 1996); Stuart Corbridge and John Harriss, *Reinventing India: Liberalization, Hindu Nationalism and Popular Democracy* (Cambridge: Polity Press, 2000); Kai Friese, "Hijacking India's History," *New York Times*, December 30, 2002, p. A17.

[48] Michael Edwardes, "Illusion and Reality in India's Foreign Policy," *International Affairs*, Vol. 41, No. 1 (January 1965), p. 53.

[49] Sumit Ganguly, "India's Foreign Policy Grows Up," *World Policy Journal*, Vol. 20, No. 4 (Winter 2003–4), pp. 41–47.

[50] Surjit Mansingh, *India's Search for Power: Indira Gandhi's Foreign Policy, 1966–1982* (New Delhi: Sage Publications, 1984). Other interpretations suggest even deeper cultural roots for a focus on Pakistan. George Tanham, for instance, argues that Indian strategic culture has for millennia viewed the world as a series of geographic concentric circles, with the closest neighbors looming largest. This way of seeing the world naturally places Pakistan front and center in India's sights. George Tanham, *Indian Strategic Thought: An Interpretive Essay* (Santa Monica, CA: RAND, 1992).

[51] Stephen P. Cohen, "South Asia: The Origins of War and the Conditions for Peace," *South Asian Survey*, Vol. 4, No. 1 (1997), pp. 25–46. See also Cohen, *India: Emerging Power*, ch. 7.

[52] Ashutosh Varshney, "India, Pakistan, and Kashmir: Antinomies of Nationalism," *Asian Survey*, Vol. 31, No. 11 (November 1991), pp. 997–1019.

Table 3.7 *Possible interpretations of Indian prime ministers' NICs*

Prime ministers (grouped)	Standard NIC interpretation	Alternative NIC interpretation
Jawaharlal Nehru, 1947–64	Sportsmanlike nationalist *vs.* great powers and generic foreign others	
Later "Nehruvians," 1964–89	Sportsmanlike nationalist *vs.* great powers and generic foreign others	Oppositional nationalist *vs.* Pakistan
Post-Cold War secularists, 1989–98	Sportsmanlike nationalist *vs.* great powers and generic foreign others	Oppositional nationalist *vs.* Pakistan
Atal Behari Vajpayee 1998–2004	Oppositional nationalist *vs.* Pakistan	

Note: Interpretations are derived from the literature cited in the previous paragraphs.

India and such a backward ex-province one-tenth its size. In the long run, they firmly believed that the very idea of Pakistan was a feudal remnant that was destined to be eclipsed by the progressive march of history.[53] Meanwhile, the major BJP foreign policy architect Jaswant Singh turns the secularists' ideas against them, bemoaning the lack of "territorial consciousness" that led, in his eyes, to a substantial underestimation of the seriousness of the Pakistan threat.[54] Table 3.7 presents a summary of the foregoing discussion, in the theoretical terminology of this book.

An original content analysis of the leaders' speeches will provide an important additional indicator to help us resolve these issues.

The data sources

Indian prime ministers make yearly "state of the union"-type addresses at the Red Fort in Delhi on August 15, Independence Day.[55] This data is perfectly suited to the purpose of measuring NICs. I was able to locate speeches from 1947–49, 1963–64, and 1966–2003.[56] The gaps in the

---

[53] Shashi Tharoor, *Reasons of State: Political Development and India's Foreign Policy under Indira Gandhi, 1966–1977* (New Delhi: Vikas Publishing House, 1982).

[54] Jaswant Singh, *Defending India* (Basingstoke: Macmillan, 1999), p. 16.

[55] For an analysis of the symbolic significance of such national ceremonial occasions focusing on the January 26 Republic Day celebrations, see Srirupa Roy, "Divided We Stand: Diversity and National Identity in India," Ph.D. dissertation, University of Pennsylvania, 1999, UMI Microform 9953588.

[56] Note that these public addresses were given in Hindi; I used official Indian government translations wherever possible; where I could not locate these I used the translations of the Foreign Broadcast Information Service (FBIS) *Daily Report*.

Table 3.8 *Summary of raw data quality for content analysis (India)*

Prime minister (Name, dates in office)[a]	NIC-relevance of speeches (Low–Med.–High)	Total data amount (Low–Med.–High)
Nehru, 1947–64	High (State of the Union)	Medium (111 refs.)
Shastri, 1964–66	High (State of the Union)	Low (16 refs.)
I. Gandhi, 1966–77; 1980–84	High (State of the Union)	Medium (377 refs.)
Desai, 1977–79	High (State of the Union)	Low (35 refs.)
C. Singh, 1979–80	High (State of the Union)	Low (19 refs.)
R. Gandhi, 1984–89	High (State of the Union)	Medium (176 refs.)
V. P. Singh, 1989–90	High (State of the Union)	Low (32 refs.)
Rao, 1991–96	High (State of the Union)	Medium (144 refs.)
Gowda, 1996–97	High (State of the Union)	Low (25 refs.)
Gujral, 1997–98	High (State of the Union)	Low (61 refs.)
Vajpayee, 1998–2004	High (State of the Union)	Medium (243 refs.)

Note: [a]No data for Chandra Shekhar, prime minister 1990–91.

earlier years are puzzling, but with one exception these are contained within Nehru's premiership for which ample data exist (and about whose NIC there is little controversy). The breakdown of the data and its quality is indicated by Table 3.8.

The content analysis

Perhaps the core question raised by the debates in the literature is whether generic foreign "others" or Pakistan was the key comparison other for the Indian secularists. The frequency counts of references provide clear evidence on this question. In the speeches of the secularist prime ministers, references to generic foreign others were far more numerous than references to Pakistan. Taking the pre-1998 prime ministers as a group, there are about three references to generic foreign others for every two references to Pakistan.[57] This pattern was relatively constant across different prime ministers from Nehru, to his daughter Indira Gandhi, to his grandson Rajiv Gandhi. There was certainly no gradual increase in attention to Pakistan up to 1989, and there was only a slight increase after it (the secularist prime ministers of the 1990s made 51 references to generic

[57] It should be noted that there are also a large number of references to Great Britain, but the overwhelming majority of these are simply ritual invocations of the "freedom struggle" at the outset of the addresses, which after all are taking place on Independence Day. The British are rarely even mentioned by name. It is therefore debatable whether these are in fact references to the UK at all, and certainly the addresses do not tarry to elaborate the perceived differences between India and Britain. In short, India seems to have buried the British quite rapidly.

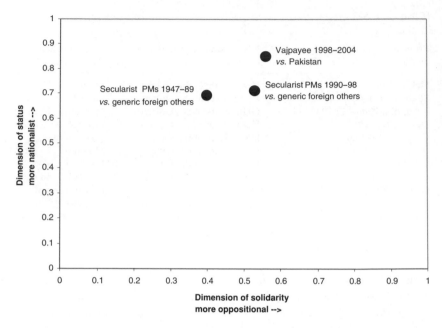

Figure 3.3 Quantitative results on Indian prime ministers' NICs, 1947–2004

foreign others versus 37 to Pakistan). By contrast, with the ascension of the BJP's Atal Behari Vajpayee, a dramatic rhetorical shift occurred. In Vajpayee's rhetoric, for every reference to generic others, there were more than two references to Pakistan (40 references to generic others, versus 85 to Pakistan). On this dimension, then, *Vajpayee represented a complete reversal* from the pattern of the previous five decades. In sum, the key comparison others for Indian prime ministers before 1998 were generic foreign others; for Vajpayee, it was Pakistan. Later on I will discuss the qualitative evidence that reinforces this conclusion.

Having identified the key comparison others for the various prime ministers, Figure 3.3 provides evidence on how those prime ministers depicted India's relationship with their key comparison other. I report results for the prime ministers grouped together for heuristic purposes with their colleagues from three different eras – the Cold War period, the post-Cold War period, and the Hindu nationalists.

The story suggested by Figure 3.3 is generally reinforced by the 95 percent confidence intervals. Along the Y axis, the scores for all the prime ministers evidently mark them as nationalists. Along the X axis, the scores clearly suggest that the pre-1990s secularists were sportsmanlike while Vajpayee was oppositional *vis-à-vis* their respective key comparison others. Meanwhile, the confidence intervals of the secularist 1990s prime ministers overlap with those of both Vajpayee and the earlier group. This could be taken to imply that the 1990s prime ministers were "transitional" figures between the Nehruvians and the Hindu nationalists. But recall the key point that the 1990s prime ministers continued to focus primarily on generic foreign others, not on Pakistan, as Vajpayee did. Moreover, Vajpayee's *own* take on generic foreign others was solidly sportsmanlike (0.38 along the X axis). So it does not make sense to portray the 1990s prime ministers as transitioning toward Vajpayee's oppositional nationalist NIC. It might be closer to the truth to conclude that they were transitioning to nowhere.

Overall judgments

The final step in the analysis is to come to overall judgments on the NICs of the Indian prime ministers. To do this, we need to consider the quantitative results together with the existing interpretations from the literature. Given the high quality of the raw data available in the Indian case, the content analysis performed here should be taken quite seriously. The quantitative findings support the standard interpretation in the literature, which sees a long line of Nehruvians who were sportsmanlike nationalist *vis-à-vis* generic foreign others, a weakening of the Nehruvian NIC in the 1990s, and then a sharp break when the Hindu nationalists arrived in power in 1998. Do these findings stand up to further qualitative scrutiny?

The case for this interpretation indeed seems quite strong. In addition to the evidence reported above, my own qualitative analysis reveals striking parallels between the rhetoric of Jawaharlal Nehru and his grandson Rajiv Gandhi a quarter-century later. For instance, both explicitly reminded their audience of Mahatma Gandhi's teaching that fear leads to hatred, as such is incompatible with a true spirit of independence, and therefore has no place in the Indian heart.[58] That is not the kind of statement that one would expect from an oppositional nationalist.

[58] Jawaharlal Nehru, "The Task Ahead" (radio broadcast from New Delhi, August 15, 1948), in *Jawaharlal Nehru's Speeches*, Vol. I (Delhi: Ministry of Information and Broadcasting, 1958), p. 80; and Rajiv Gandhi, "Forty Years of Independence" (speech at the Red Fort, August 15, 1987), in *Rajiv Gandhi: Selected Speeches and Writings*, Vol. III (Delhi: Ministry of Information and Broadcasting, 1988), p. 75. Indira Gandhi did not make such a specific reference, but she did speak glowingly of the importance of the teachings of Gandhi and Nehru in shaping her understanding of the world.

The evidence on the 1990s prime ministers is much weaker all around. Apart from the ambiguous quantitative results, my qualitative analysis found them to have dropped much of the traditional Nehruvian rhetoric of independence and national greatness. But, at the same time, my qualitative reading of the speeches reinforces the quantitative finding that Pakistan had not become the key comparison other. For instance, the 1990s prime minister, P. V. Narasimha Rao, devoted more of his total external references to Pakistan than the average secularist: 18 percent versus 11 percent for the secularists overall. But, when discussing Pakistan, Rao reflected the same mixture of sentiments that were evidenced by his predecessors: confusion, frustration, and above all the cold shoulder of contempt. Even in his most sustained treatment of Pakistan, during his 1995 Independence Day speech, Rao did not present a clear picture of Pakistan's broad interests and values that could be contrasted with those of India. He appeared simply dumbfounded at Pakistan's behavior: "Why are they doing this? It is beyond everybody's comprehension."[59] You cannot build a national self-definition against a foreign other that you do not even claim to understand.

Finally, all the evidence points to the BJP prime minister, Atal Behari Vajpayee, as oppositional nationalist toward Pakistan. Vajpayee's discussions of Pakistan revealed that in his eyes Pakistan was not merely an important foreign adversary; it was the foil for his definition of Indian nationhood. For instance, Vajpayee tried to extract a deeper meaning from India's 1999 Kargil war with Pakistan:

All of us remember the talisman Gandhiji gave us: when in doubt about what to do, he taught us, think of the least, of the most helpless man you have seen, ask yourself "Will this step be in his interest?" he said, and you will see all your doubts melt away.

Kargil gives us a second talisman. As we contemplate a step, let us ask ourselves, "Is it worthy of the soldier who gave his life on those mountains? Does the impulse which lies behind it measure up to the spirit which filled that soldier as he fought to protect our Motherland?"[60]

This was a remarkable statement, a repudiation on several levels of the traditional ideology of the Indian state. Notably, in contrast to the Gandhian focus on the weak in society, Vajpayee placed a new focus on the strong – and, in particular, on the soldier. In addition, he pushed aside

---

[59] P. V. Narasimha Rao, 1995 Independence Day address, translated and printed in *FBIS Daily Report: South Asia*, August 16, 1995, p. 58.

[60] Atal Behari Vajpayee, "Prime Minister Vajpayee's Independence Day Address to the Nation," August 15, 1999. Available at http://www.indiagov.org/special/cabinet/Primeminister/1999ID PM Speech.html.

Table 3.9 *Global assessment of Indian leaders' NICs*

Sportsmanlike nationalist	**Oppositional nationalist**
"Secularist" prime ministers (1947–98) *vs.* generic foreign "others"	Vajpayee (1998–2004) *vs.* Pakistan
Sportsmanlike subaltern	**Oppositional subaltern**
None	None

the old dream of creating a new and better world in favor of the much narrower dream of defending the Motherland – and, notably, of defending it against Pakistan.

The overall assessment of the Indian prime ministers is summarized in Table 3.9. This assessment will serve as the basis for the analysis of their nuclear policy preferences and actions in Chapter 7.

France

As Chapter 4 will show, the crucial political decision to build a French nuclear arsenal was taken in December 1954. From a number of perspectives, however, it is surprising that the crucial decision was not taken earlier. The central question for Chapter 4, therefore, is why the French waited so long; and the key element for hypothesis-building on this question is the measurement of the NICs of the French prime ministers during the first postwar decade.

First, however, it must be noted that the French case features some peculiarities that reduce the validity of the measurement techniques outlined earlier. There are two interlinked problems. First, the French Fourth Republic featured a series of weak governing coalitions with even weaker prime ministers. The prime ministers therefore tended to make highly topical and short-term-oriented statements, and moreover they usually fell before making too many of them. Only two exceptional prime ministers during this period, Charles de Gaulle and Pierre Mendès France, decided to try to speak and act as if they had a mandate to lead (they, too, soon learned that they did not). Second, compounding the problem of short-term orientation is the subtle foreign policy strategy that the standard interpretation claims the majority of French postwar leaders adopted. That strategy, which will be elucidated below, essentially contradicted a key assumption of the quantitative coding scheme. This does not make the quantitative analysis unimportant, but it does increase the importance of doing a solid qualitative analysis.

Existing perspectives on French identity conceptions

The standard interpretation argues that postwar French leaders were obsessed with their nation's position *vis-à-vis* Germany in the great power hierarchy, as indeed they had been since the late nineteenth century.[61] Because of this continued obsession with Germany, French leaders displayed much less worry about the looming Soviet threat – to the exasperation of France's Western allies.[62] In this interpretation, the profound differences between French "nationalists" and French "Europeans" – differences that emerged most strikingly in the debate over the country's proposed integration with a rearmed Germany in the supranational European Defense Community (EDC) – reflected differences in their NICs along the dimension of status. For the French "nationalists" such as Charles de Gaulle and Pierre Mendès France, a France that was shackled to a supranational Europe would no longer be France. Germany was a mortal threat, but if France preserved its great power status it could successfully deal with that threat.[63] By contrast, the French "Europeans" differed from the "nationalists" because they raised, in Lawrence Scheinman's words, the "question of feasibility" in addition to the "problem of fear."[64] In other words, after the German triumph of 1940 the bulk of the Fourth Republic political establishment had lost the sense of France's natural power and greatness that de Gaulle and Mendès France still retained. Since the Fourth Republic establishment prime ministers were resigned to an inevitable German victory in any head-to-head competition, they

---

[61] The classic work on the growth of the French obsession with Germany is Claude Digeon, *La crise allemande de la pensée française, 1870–1914* (Paris: Presses Universitaires de France, 1959). See also Stanley Hoffmann, "France: Two Obsessions for One Century," in Robert Pastor, ed., *A Century's Journey: How the Great Powers Shape the World* (New York: Basic Books, 1999).

[62] See, for instance, Pierre Gerbet, *Le relèvement 1944–1949* (Paris: Imprimerie Nationale, 1991); Mark S. Sheetz, "France and the German Question: Avant-garde or Rearguard? Comment on Creswell and Trachtenberg," *Journal of Cold War Studies*, Vol. 5, No. 3 (Summer 2003), pp. 37–45.

[63] Despite the political differences that separated de Gaulle and Mendès France, their similar conceptions of French identity have been widely noted. See, for instance, Lawrence Scheinman, "The Politics of Nationalism in Contemporary France," *International Organization*, Vol. 23, No. 4 (Autumn 1969), p. 837; F. Roy Willis, *France, Germany and the New Europe 1945–1967*, rev. ed. (Stanford, CA: Stanford University Press, 1968), p. 298.

[64] Scheinman, "The Politics of Nationalism in Contemporary France," p. 845. For a parallel interpretation, see Jean-Baptiste Duroselle, "Les changements dans la politique extérieure de la France depuis 1945," in Stanley Hoffmann, ed., *A la recherche de la France* (Paris: Editions du Seuil, 1963), pp. 347–400. The continuing interplay of fear of Germany with doubts about the feasibility of going it alone is well documented in Georges-Henri Soutou, *L'Alliance incertaine: Les rapports politico-stratégiques franco-allemands, 1954–1996* (Paris: Fayard, 1996).

felt that France's only hope was to lash its neighbor tightly to it in a constraining institutional embrace. Thus the French initiative for European integration was born.[65] This subtle foreign policy strategy causes difficulties for the quantitative coding rules, because they assume that the growth of a wider community identity that includes both us and the key comparison other practically rules out the potential for an oppositional NIC. In the French case, the standard interpretation holds that an oppositional subaltern NIC *vis-à-vis* Germany in fact propelled the French "Europeans" into Germany's arms. This is not only paradoxical from the perspective of the theory presented here; most scholars find it paradoxical as well and often note how "spectacular" a leap the French establishment was able to make in the early 1950s.[66] In short, the exceptional French case tends to confirm the reasonableness of the general rule that oppositional NICs and transcendent identities are strange bedfellows; though it also shows that they are not altogether incompatible.

In contrast to the standard interpretation, an alternative interpretation of postwar French elites' NICs has also emerged in recent years. According to the alternative interpretation, the French establishment in fact did see the advent of the superpower conflict as having eclipsed the old Franco-German dichotomy. Concerned not only about the Soviet menace but also about the domestic threat posed by the French Communist Party, French elites supported the development of the Western alliance as much as their still anti-German public would let them.[67] Meanwhile, the European project was not the symptom of a loss of national self-confidence on the part of the Fourth Republic establishment, but rather a means of restoring France's historic greatness in the new context of continental superpowers.[68] French "nationalists" like de Gaulle and Mendès France also did not oppose the principle of a united Europe under French leadership, but merely the specific institutional form that this principle took under the auspices of "Europeans" like Robert Schuman and Jean Monnet. When they got the institutions they wanted, they, too, joined the project.[69]

---

[65] A. W. Lovett, "The United States and the Schuman Plan: A Study in French Diplomacy 1950–1952," *Historical Journal*, Vol. 39, No. 2 (June 1996), pp. 425–455.

[66] See, e.g., Raymond Aron, "Historical Sketch of the Great Debate," in Raymond Aron and Daniel Lerner, eds., *France Defeats EDC* (New York: Frederick A. Praeger, 1957), pp. 2–4.

[67] Michael Creswell and Marc Trachtenberg, "France and the German Question, 1945–1955," *Journal of Cold War Studies*, Vol. 5, No. 3 (Summer 2003), pp. 5–28.

[68] William I. Hitchcock, *France Restored: Cold War Diplomacy and the Quest for Leadership in Europe, 1944–1954* (Chapel Hill: University of North Carolina Press, 1998).

[69] Creswell and Trachtenberg, "France and the German Question." For an earlier statement along these lines, see Daniel Lerner, "Reflections on France in the World Arena," in Lerner and Aron, eds., *France Defeats EDC*.

Table 3.10 *Possible interpretations of French prime ministers' NICs*

Prime ministers (grouped)	Standard NIC interpretation	Alternative NIC interpretation
Charles de Gaulle 1944–46	Oppositional nationalist *vs.* Germany	(Later became oppositional nationalist *vs.* USSR)
Fourth Republic "establishment" 1946–54	Oppositional subaltern *vs.* Germany	Oppositional nationalist *vs.* USSR
Pierre Mendès France 1954–55	Oppositional nationalist *vs.* Germany	Oppositional nationalist *vs.* USSR

Note: Interpretations are derived from the literature cited in the previous paragraphs.

Table 3.10 presents a summary of the foregoing discussion, translated into the theoretical terminology of this book.

An original content analysis of the leaders' speeches will provide an important additional indicator to help us resolve these issues.

The data sources

As noted above, unfortunately the French Fourth Republic prime ministers generally did not make the "state of the union"-type addresses that are the ideal data for our purposes. Indeed, given their weak political position they generally tried to avoid providing any insight into their thinking at all. Nevertheless, they did talk. I coded all inaugural and parliamentary foreign policy addresses by French prime ministers that were printed verbatim in the non-partisan annual reference publication *L'Année politique* from the 1944 Liberation to the 1955 fall from power of Pierre Mendès France.[70] In addition, because of Mendès France's importance to the French nuclear story and his self-conscious attempt to explain his thinking to the French people, I also coded the entire set of his weekly radio addresses to the nation and other addresses that were later published as compilations.[71] Note that all speeches were read in the original French. The breakdown of the data and its quality are indicated by Table 3.11. Note that the number of references by most individual Fourth Republic "establishment" prime ministers is so low that the only reasonable way to

---

[70] André Siegfried, ed., *L'Année politique* (Paris: Editions du Grand Siècle, annual).

[71] No other prime minister gave weekly radio addresses or saw his speeches compiled as Mendès France did. The radio addresses are compiled in Pierre Mendès France, *Dire la vérité: Causeries du samedi, juin 1954–février 1955* (Paris: René Julliard, 1955). The public addresses are compiled in Pierre Mendès France, *Gouverner, c'est choisir, t. 2: Sept mois et dix-sept jours, juin 1954–février 1955* (Paris: René Julliard, 1955).

Table 3.11 *Summary of raw data quality for content analysis (France)*

Prime minister (Name, dates in office)	NIC-relevance of speeches (Low–med.–high)	Total data amount (Low–med.–high)
De Gaulle, 1944–46	Low (topical)	Medium (152 refs.)
"Establishment," 1946–49 (Bidault, Blum, Gouin, Marie, Queuille, Ramadier, Schuman)	Low (topical)	Medium (168 refs.)
"Establishment," 1950–54 (Bidault, Faure, Laniel, Mayer, Pinay, Pleven, Queuille)	Low (topical)	High (805 refs.)
Mendès France, 1954–55	Low (topical)	High (1,908 refs.)

proceed is to interpret their NICs collectively. I place them in two clumps corresponding to the two phases of post-war French foreign policy.

The content analysis

The frequency counts of references to external actors, complemented by a qualitative reading of the speeches, support the standard interpretation that the French prime ministers focused much more on Germany than on the Communist bloc. Looking at this question narrowly, in the coded speeches the words "German" or "Germany" appear with twice the frequency of the words "Communist," "Soviet," "Russia," or "East" put together. The only prime minister who devoted most of his attention to the Communists was Joseph Laniel, which is understandable since he was serving at the height of the Indochina conflict.[72] In short, the priority of the German problem over the Communist menace for French leaders seems relatively clear. Claims that French leaders might have intentionally avoided bringing up the Communist threat even though it indeed was topmost in their minds are hard to fathom. The French Communist Party was electorally strong, of course, but after the early months of Liberation it was shunned by all prospective governing parties. As the domestic Communists had been thoroughly alienated, it is hard to see what the mainstream politicians had to gain by holding their tongues.

---

[72] In general, references to the Indochina conflict should not be seen as automatically referring to the "Communist bloc," as French leaders were often at pains to distinguish the two. But in my more elaborate coding I did include a large number of those references as references to the Communists, while including references to World War II, for instance, as references to Germany. In this more elaborate coding, too, Germany easily came out on top.

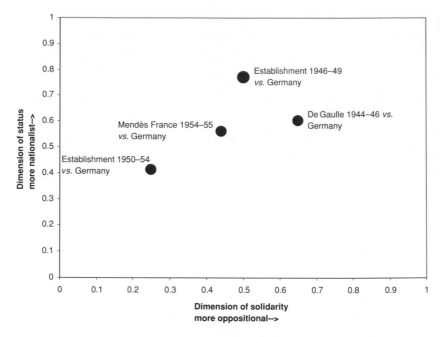

Figure 3.4 Quantitative results on French prime ministers' NICs, 1944–55

Having identified Germany as the key comparison other for the various prime ministers, Figure 3.4 provides evidence on how those prime ministers depicted France's relationship with its neighbor.

The story suggested by Figure 3.4 is generally reinforced by the 95 percent confidence intervals (see Appendix). Along the X axis, the scores clearly suggest that de Gaulle and the 1946–49 establishment prime ministers were oppositional, the 1950–54 establishment prime ministers were sportsmanlike, and Pierre Mendès France was solidly lodged in between them. Along the Y axis, the scores suggest that the 1950–54 establishment prime ministers were subaltern while the others were nationalist.[73]

Overall judgments

To arrive at overall judgments, as in the other cases we need to relate the quantitative data to the existing interpretations in the literature. The

---

[73] However, de Gaulle's confidence interval on the Y axis overlaps with that of the 1950–54 prime ministers.

quantitative results find De Gaulle to have been clearly oppositional nationalist and Mendès France to have been marginally so, and these are in line with the standard interpretation. The assessment that these two were oppositional nationalists is supported by my own qualitative reading of the texts as well. Perhaps only a de Gaulle could have the temerity to claim, in the ruined France of March 1945, that the as-yet-unrealized Allied victory over Germany would be "impossible without us."[74] But Mendès France had his own way of expressing great national self-confidence:

France is a good and solid vessel. And if the captain, the officers and all the crew are united by the same will, do not doubt that it will avoid the reefs, it will make it through the dangerous straits and it will attain the open sea.[75]

Coming after years of "European" rhetoric about interdependence, integration, and supranationalism, Mendès France's simple, even hackneyed reference to the self-contained French "ship of state" represented anything but rhetorical boilerplate. And needless to say, for Mendès France many of the "reefs" and "dangerous straits" were to be found along the Rhine.

The other quantitative codings are confusing until we recognize the limitations of the raw data and of the quantitative coding rules. Until 1949, Germany was an occupied country, prostrated under the boot of a military occupation. Many French still hoped that it would be permanently demilitarized. As Prime Minister Paul Ramadier declared in 1947, France's basic policy was that "Germany, which fouled [France's] soil and menaced its existence must no longer constitute a danger for her."[76] It is not surprising that in such circumstances an actually subaltern French establishment would sound nationalist – indeed, even more nationalist than Charles de Gaulle himself. Then, in 1949 Germany received its Basic Law and appeared headed for full sovereignty. The Fourth Republic establishment opted for European integration, and this choice practically guaranteed that Germany would henceforth be referred to in the context of the growing European institutional framework. This inevitably leads to a quantitative coding of the "Europeans" as sportsmanlike subaltern.

---

[74] Charles de Gaulle, "Discours à l'assemblée consultative sur le programme de la reconstruction française," 2 March 1945, in *L'Année politique 1945*, pp. 442–451. Note also that in the more complex content analysis procedure that was previously applied to this data set, the post-de Gaulle prime ministers of the 1940s showed up as oppositional subaltern toward Germany.

[75] Pierre Mendès France, "La France est un bon et solide navire," radio address of 3 July 1954, in Mendès France, *Dire la vérité*, p. 7.

[76] "Déclaration à l'Assemblée Nationale de M. Paul Ramadier, président du Conseil désigné le 21 janvier 1947," *L'Année politique 1947*, p. 322.

Table 3.12 *Global assessment of French prime ministers' NICs, 1944–55*

Sportsmanlike nationalist	Oppositional nationalist
None	Charles de Gaulle (1944–46) *vs.* Germany
	Pierre Mendès France (1954–55) *vs.* Germany
Sportsmanlike subaltern	**Oppositional subaltern**
None	Fourth Republic establishment (1946–54) *vs.* Germany

But as explained above, this points out a limitation of the coding rules, which do not anticipate the subtle logic of supranational integration from the oppositional subaltern perspective. My qualitative reading found the establishment prime ministers to be making it clear enough why they were doing what they were doing. In February 1952, for instance, Prime Minister Edgar Faure pithily summarized the establishment's inner conflict: "While we consider that there is no accursed people, that there are no men who cannot be brought to liberty, to democracy, to conscience, we also know what has happened during the painful years."[77]

In sum, although it has not greatly reinforced our confidence in the standard interpretation, the content analysis has helped us to dismiss the alternative interpretation that the Soviets were the French prime ministers' key comparison other. Therefore, the best option in this case is to accept the standard interpretation. The overall assessment of the French prime ministers is summarized in Table 3.12. This assessment will serve as the basis for the analysis of their nuclear policy preferences and actions reported in Chapter 4.

Having measured the independent variable in each of the four country cases, we can now proceed to test the theory that was developed in Chapter 2 on the respective nuclear histories of those countries.

---

[77] Edgar Faure, "Discours d'Edgar Faure, president du Conseil, prononcé devant l'Assemblée Nationale au cours du débat sur l'armée européenne," 13 February 1952, in *L'Année politique 1952*, p. 484.

4   The struggle over the bomb in the French Fourth Republic

Introduction

"Hurray for France! From this morning she is stronger and prouder!" Such was the February 13, 1960 reaction of President Charles de Gaulle to the news of the first French nuclear explosion.[1] Since that day, it has been hard to dissociate the French nuclear arsenal from de Gaulle's foreign policy of *grandeur*, from the "monarchical" presidential system he introduced in 1958, and indeed from overall French national identity.[2] But in fact, the coming of the French nuclear arsenal was far from foreordained. Indeed, on several occasions the French Fourth Republic establishment almost succeeded in *signing away* France's rights to nuclear weapons.

This chapter details the struggle over the bomb in the French Fourth Republic. It argues that this struggle reflected the very different conceptions of French national identity that were held by French "Europeans" and by French "nationalists." As detailed in Chapter 3, the "Europeans," who dominated the French Fourth Republic establishment, held an oppositional subaltern NIC *vis-à-vis* Germany. This NIC led them to be hostile to the idea of a French nuclear weapons drive. By contrast, the "nationalists," including de Gaulle and Pierre Mendès France, held an oppositional nationalist NIC *vis-à-vis* Germany. This NIC led them to embrace the idea of a French nuclear weapons drive, a drive that Mendès France jumpstarted with his dramatic nuclear decision of December 26, 1954.

While offering strong confirmation of the theoretical perspective adopted in this book, the chapter demonstrates the particularly glaring problems the French case poses for conventional theoretical perspectives on proliferation:

---

[1] Marcel Duval and Dominique Mongin, *Histoire des forces nucléaires françaises depuis 1945* (Paris: Presses Universitaires de France, 1993), p. 46.

[2] See, for instance, Beatrice Heuser, *Nuclear Mentalities? Strategies and Beliefs in Britain, France, and the FRG* (London: Macmillan, 1998), ch. 3.

- Realists generally view the French nuclear effort as a classic confirmation of the poor credibility of US extended deterrence once the Soviets had developed the wherewithal to threaten the American homeland.[3] But as this chapter will show, the French bomb decision took place at a moment when the credibility of the American nuclear deterrent was still high. Even more problematically, the chapter shows that the French bomb project was more a response to the perceived *German* challenge than to the Soviet menace.

- Meanwhile, institutionalists generally portray early instances of nuclear proliferation, such as the French case, as having occurred because the international non-proliferation regime and "nuclear taboo" had not yet been constructed. But this chapter finds that, faced with the absence of an existing non-proliferation regime, the French "Europeans" invented one – only to see a later French leader scuttle it. Moreover, it shows that the "nuclear taboo" was well internalized by many French leaders as early as 1946. Thus, the French case of proliferation cannot be seen as a product of supposedly benighted early years of the nuclear age, but rather poses as much a puzzle for the institutionalist approach as contemporary cases of proliferation.

- Finally, bureaucratic and domestic politics models generally have a field day with the French Fourth Republic, which was not a place where the head of government could typically have his way.[4] This chapter finds that in spite of the complex institutional context, the choice to go nuclear indeed was made by a single prime minister over the objections of most of his normal political and bureaucratic allies. But the chapter does also find that once the initial top-down decision was made, domestic institutions and actors other than the prime minister greatly mattered for the continued progress of the weapons drive.

The rest of the chapter presents a detailed look at French nuclear policymaking from 1945 to July 1956, the date after which the construction of a French nuclear bomb became essentially inevitable. The second part documents the efforts of the French "Europeans" to tie France's hands in the nuclear arena up to 1954. The third part covers the crucial year of decision, 1954. And the fourth explains how the December 1954 bomb

---

[3] Avery Goldstein, *Deterrence and Security in the 21st Century: China, Britain, France, and the Enduring Legacy of the Nuclear Revolution* (Stanford, CA: Stanford University Press, 2000).

[4] Not surprisingly, this general model is a popular one for describing the French case. An important early study was Lawrence Scheinman, *Atomic Energy Policy in France under the Fourth Republic* (Princeton: Princeton University Press, 1965). See also Gabrielle Hecht, *The Radiance of France: Nuclear Power and National Identity after World War II* (Cambridge, MA: MIT Press, 1998) and Alain Peyrefitte, *Le mal français* (Paris: Plon, 1976), pp. 283–290.

decision established a firm direction toward French nuclear weapons, which persisted in spite of subsequent attempts to reverse it.

Nuclear France before 1954

De Gaulle in the immediate postwar period: "We have time."

The French nuclear program was born soon after the destruction of Hiroshima. On October 18, 1945 Charles de Gaulle, as head of the Provisional Government, signed a decree creating the *Commissariat à l'énergie atomique* (CEA). The CEA was to be an entirely civilian atomic energy commission – the first of its kind in the world – while at the same time holding the monopoly on any future defense projects.[5] This defense mission is best understood in terms of de Gaulle's desire to maintain political control over nuclear affairs – and, in particular, to keep the atom out of the hands of the French military. The CEA's unusual organizational structure, which featured an administrative and a scientific chief who were coequal in power, was also designed in order to ensure political control – in no small part because Frédéric Joliot-Curie, the obvious choice for scientific chief, was a card-carrying Communist.[6]

De Gaulle neither ruled in nor ruled out a French bomb drive during his first, brief stint in power. As he told the press on October 13, a week before forming the CEA, "As to the atomic bomb, we have time. I am not convinced that atomic bombs will be used in the short run. At any rate, the French government will not lose sight of this question, which is most serious for the entire world, and whose consequences are clearly immense."[7] Why did de Gaulle not immediately declare that the CEA's purpose was to build nuclear weapons? For one thing, war-ravaged France was technically in no position to achieve that goal. Indeed, given the circumstances, that de Gaulle created the CEA at all is a rather remarkable tribute to his deep-rooted nationalism. But, in addition, in 1945 Germany – the object of de Gaulle's oppositional nationalism – was an occupied country that de Gaulle still hoped would be permanently divided and deindustrialized. Germany's prostrate condition in 1945 is presumably a significant part of why de Gaulle felt that "we have time." As the chapter demonstrates below, once Germany's return to sovereignty and rearmament became

---

[5] The civilian US Atomic Energy Commission was created two years later, in 1947. Dominique Mongin, *La bombe atomique française* (Bruxelles: Bruylant, 1997), p. 42.

[6] Ibid., p. 39.

[7] De Gaulle, cited in Bertrand Goldschmidt, *Atomic Rivals: A Candid Memoir of Rivalries among the Allies over the Bomb*, translated from the French by Georges M. Temmer (New Brunswick, NJ: Rutgers University Press, 1990).

a certainty, de Gaulle's position in favor of a French bomb hardened quickly.

The early years of the Fourth Republic: an "absence of nuclear-mindedness"

After de Gaulle resigned in January 1946, the early hints of a military direction for French nuclear activities vanished. Joliot-Curie focused the CEA's early work on pure scientific research and on peaceful applications of nuclear energy.[8] The pacific orientation of the CEA's research took on the character of official policy when France's ambassador to the United Nations, Alexandre Parodi, announced to the UN disarmament committee in June 1946,

I am authorized to state that the goals that the French government has assigned to the research of its scientists and engineers are purely peaceful. Our wish is that all nations do the same as soon as possible and it is with determination to reach this goal that France will submit itself to the rules that will be judged best to assure the control of atomic energy in the entire world.[9]

The Parodi declaration certainly was not a contractual obligation to abstain from building the bomb, but it did reflect the considered judgment of the French government that a significant French nuclear arsenal was neither feasible nor necessary. Such was the gist of a secret 1946 note by CEA executive committee member Pierre Auger for Foreign Affairs Minister Georges Bidault.[10] The note argued that France could perhaps muster the technical and mineral resources to build the bomb, but that strategically such an effort would be nonsensical. Auger projected the "probable attitude" of the six contemporary nuclear-weapons-capable states (Belgium, Canada, France, UK, US, and USSR) as follows: while the USSR and the US would definitely become nuclear powers, the other four would "honestly renounce the construction of destructive atomic weapons, for these cannot bring them any advantage." Moreover, the US and USSR themselves would not be able to use their arsenals at least in the near to medium term because of the restraints imposed both by "public opinion" – an indication that a "nuclear taboo" was already in place in 1946 – and by the "insufficiency" of available delivery systems.

---

[8] Ibid., p. 290.

[9] Alexandre Parodi, cited in Bertrand Goldschmidt, "La genèse et l'héritage," in *L'Aventure de la bombe: De Gaulle et la dissuasion nucléaire 1958–1969*, actes du colloque organisé par l'Université de France-Comté et l'Institut Charles de Gaulle (Paris: Plon, 1985), p. 27.

[10] "Note on the Atomic Bomb" marked "Very Important" from Pierre Auger to Georges Bidault, dated 1946. Georges Bidault papers, 457 AP 4, Archives Nationales, Paris.

The French military in these years generally shared the diplomats' and scientists' lack of enthusiasm for a French bomb. The military's lack of interest in the bomb was based on two major elements. First, it saw the bomb as essentially an arm for the superpower confrontation taking place above France's head, and besides, it viewed the American fear of a Soviet "bolt from the blue" as exaggerated. Second, it saw the bomb as essentially unusable for any rational military purpose – a comforting thought for an institution intent on maintaining its traditions. The military top brass would later consider these points of view confirmed by the non-use of nuclear weapons in the Korean War.[11]

In sum, the French Fourth Republic in the late 1940s displayed, as others have put it, a nearly "total absence of nuclear-mindedness."[12] To some extent, this lack of interest can be attributed to the priority the French accorded to the massive task of economic and social reconstruction. But it would not have cost any additional economic resources simply to list the creation of a nuclear arsenal as one of the CEA's long-term goals. That this did not happen shows the fallacy of the widespread assumption that states in the early years of the nuclear age simply assumed that they would eventually acquire the bomb. The French of the 1940s already understood the momentousness of going nuclear, and for the most part their strong inclination was to abstain from doing so.

Then, in 1950, a shock occurred – intense US pressure for German rearmament. France's "eternal enemy" was to be revived. This immediately raised the profile of the nuclear question. The prospect of German rearmament pushed the reigning Fourth Republic establishment not to reverse, but instead to *codify* France's abstention from the bomb.

1950–52: Discussions of German rearmament and the first attempted renunciation

With the dawning of the Cold War, the US began pressuring for the rearmament of the western portions of Germany. It officially proposed (West) German rearmament and membership in NATO in September 1950.[13] The issue of German rearmament was to divide French society profoundly in the next years. That debate was not over the value of

---

[11] Jean-Christophe Sauvage, "La perception des questions nucléaires dans les premières années de l'Institut des Hautes Etudes de Défense Nationale 1948–1955," in Maurice Vaïsse, ed., *La France et l'atome* (Brussels: Bruylant, 1994), esp. pp. 77–78.

[12] Christian De la Malène and Constantin Melnik, "Attitudes of the French Parliament and Government toward Atomic Weapons," RAND Research Memorandum RM-2170-RC (Santa Monica, CA: RAND Corporation, 1958), p. 1.

[13] From now on, I will use the word "Germany" to refer to West Germany. This was the way in which the French debate was framed.

German rearmament – practically all French elites agreed it was a disaster for France. Rather, the debate was over how best to respond to this frightening new military, political, and status threat.[14]

As noted in Chapter 3, the French Fourth Republic establishment held an oppositional subaltern NIC *vis-à-vis* Germany. Its natural reaction to the pressure for German rearmament was therefore not to increase French capabilities, but rather to seek a "European" solution that kept Germany down while mollifying the American big brother. In October 1950, France's ambassador to the United States, Henri Bonnet, wrote a long memorandum to the Foreign Ministry stating that the US was serious about its goal of recreating a German national army. But this, Bonnet wrote, would produce the "historical inevitability" of a German "reconquest by arms, or the recuperation by an alliance with the East [Soviet bloc], of the lost eastern provinces."[15] To head off that "inevitability" while avoiding a lessening of the American military commitment to Europe, Bonnet suggested the integration of German troops into a supranational European army.[16] Most of the rest of the French Fourth Republic establishment had the same fearful reaction, and on October 24, Prime Minister René Pleven presented his proposal for a supranational European Defense Community (EDC) to Parliament. The Pleven Plan quickly found support among France's less-German-phobic alliance partners, and negotiations over the precise form of the EDC soon began in earnest. The initial fears sparked by the sudden prospect of a renaissance of German military power were only to grow with time. As the French ambassador to Bonn, André François-Poncet, wrote to Robert Schuman in December 1952, "Since their military help was asked for and their liberation from their last chains promised, they are returning so naturally to the ways of thinking and of acting of the Hitlerian Reich, that distrust of them is justly reawakening."[17] François-Poncet argued that this

---

[14] Jacques Bariéty, "La décision de réarmer l'Allemagne, l'échec de la Communauté Européenne de Défense et les accords de Paris du 23 octobre 1954 vus du côté français," *Revue Belge de Philologie et d'Histoire*, Vol. 71, No. 2 (1993), pp. 354–383.

[15] Henri Bonnet, "Projet de memorandum sur la politique européenne de la France et le réarmement allemand," October 4, 1950, Henri Bonnet papers on microfilm, PA-AP, Vol. I, p. 179, archives du Ministère des Affaires Etrangères (henceforth MAE), Paris.

[16] Ibid. The reason why the French were so eager to keep the United States in Europe again had more to do with the goal of suppressing Germany's resurgence than it had to do with the goal of defending against an eventual Soviet attack. Indeed, during that period there were significant worries that the Americans were *too* willing to fight the Soviets (and with nuclear weapons, no less). These attitudes only changed during the 1960s. Alfred Grosser, "France and Germany in the Atlantic Community," *International Organization*, Vol. 17, No. 3 (Summer, 1963), p. 564.

[17] Telegram from André François-Poncet to Robert Schuman, December 22, 1952, in Cabinet du Ministre Robert Schuman dossier No. 43, MAE, Paris.

reawakening was all the more reason to persist in the "edification of the European–Atlantic Community."

If German rearmament with *conventional* forces was France's worst nightmare, German *nuclear* armament was simply "not conceivable."[18] Germany at the time had essentially no activities in the nuclear field, and the French aimed to keep things that way. But according to the "European" principle of non-discrimination, any restrictions placed on Germany had to be placed equally on all EDC partners.[19] Therefore, the parties agreed on Article 107 of the EDC treaty, which specified that all fissile material produced or acquired by any EDC state had to be devoted to non-military purposes. Moreover, this general principle was given teeth: the supranational EDC authorities had to approve any member state's production, importation, or exportation in one year of more than 500 grams of fissile material – far less than is necessary for a nuclear explosion. Supranational inspectors would verify compliance with these strictures.[20] The EDC treaty was signed on May 27, 1952 by Robert Schuman for France and by five other European states (Germany, Italy, and the Benelux nations). In short, *the French had signed away the right to sovereign nuclear weapons in exchange for the certainty that Germany could never have them either.*[21]

The Article 107 commitment is hardly surprising in the context of EDC, for the notion of a supranational European army made no sense if states were also building national nuclear weapons stockpiles. But that commitment is entirely at odds with the usual picture of a unitary French state inexorably lured by the power and prestige benefits of a nuclear arsenal. The French "Europeans" were not lured by those so-called temptations. The fact that the US, USSR, and Britain all had or would soon have nuclear weapons did not faze the French "Europeans" in their willingness to give up France's right to them.[22] From the point of view of the French "Europeans," France could do without the bomb if that was the price of keeping Germany non-nuclear. Indeed, their oppositional subaltern NIC

---

[18] For example, letter, marked "Very Secret," from Cabinet du Ministre, Ministère de la Défense Nationale et des Forces Armées to the Ministre des Affaires Etrangères, September 1954, Papiers Wormser 25, MAE, Paris. One finds the words "*inconcevable*" or "*pas concevable*" again and again in records of the time, with respect to this possibility.

[19] France did get a major exception for its armed forces stationed outside of Europe.

[20] "Note pour le Secrétaire Général, a.s. lettre du Commissariat à l'Energie atomique relative au traité instituant une Communauté européenne de defense," le jurisconsulte, Ministère des Affairs Etrangères, March 15, 1954, in Secrétariat Général, dossier CED, 70: dossier général 1er janvier–18 juin 1954, MAE, Paris.

[21] Though, in theory, the door was still open to a "European" bomb. This option would in fact attract some "Europeans" in subsequent years.

[22] Britain exploded its first bomb, in Australia, in October 1952. For more on that episode, see Chapter 5.

led them not merely to submit to a non-proliferation treaty regime, but actually to *invent* such a regime as a means of containing Germany.

The French "European" nuclear stance was not resisted by the important bureaucracies of the French state. The Foreign Ministry was highly in favor, and the military generally assented as well. It is true that CEA officials *later* objected to Article 107, arguing that during the EDC negotiations they had not been apprised of its content.[23] But the text was certainly available to an important organ of the state if it had cared to look for it.[24] Indeed, before the CEA chiefs finally contacted the Foreign Ministry on the issue in March 1954, Article 107 had already been clarified by a further protocol of March 1953. This protocol essentially guaranteed that the European authorities would grant the French the right to produce fissile material for peaceful purposes over the 500 gram limit – a step made necessary by the major nuclear plan passed by the French Parliament in July 1952.[25] So the EDC negotiators were certainly paying attention to the progress of the CEA. Why did the CEA not pay attention to the progress of the EDC negotiations? The most reasonable hypothesis is that the CEA at that time did not see itself as the guardian of the French bomb option.

EDC could have been the end of the French nuclear weapons story, but the French "Europeans" were to fail in their effort to convince Parliament to ratify the treaty. Therefore, when the oppositional nationalist

---

[23] Note from L'administrateur Général, délégué du gouvernement, et le Haut-Commissaire [du CEA] à Monsieur le Ministre des Affaires Etrangères, March 1, 1954, in Secrétariat Général, Dossier CED, 70: "Dossier Général 1er janvier–18 juin 1954," MAE, Paris.

[24] As Goldschmidt reports CEA administrative chief Pierre Guillaumat later admitted to him. Goldschmidt, in "Débats," in Georges-Henri Soutou and Alain Beltran, eds., *Pierre Guillaumat: la passion des grands projets industriels* (Paris: Editions Rive Droite, 1995), p. 71.

[25] Such a big civilian nuclear effort is something that my characterization of the French "European" establishment's NIC does not anticipate, and therefore it is a missed prediction for the theory. But the 1952 plan was not a fig leaf for a weapons drive. The government's internal discussions over the plan were entirely devoted to its economic utility – plutonium was at the time considered to be a new "black gold" (see Mongin, *La bombe atomique française*, pp. 168–169). Moreover, one of the original members of the CEA, Bertrand Goldschmidt, noted to me that the prime mover behind the 1952 plan, Secretary of State for Atomic Energy Félix Gaillard, was "not very interested [in the bomb] and slightly anti-military" (interview with Bertrand Goldschmidt, French atomic scientist and diplomat, Paris, September 29, 1998). My interpretation here is somewhat complicated by the fact that *after* the 1952 plan was passed, the CEA's pro-bomb faction led by Pierre Guillaumat actually optimized the new reactors for the production of weapons-grade plutonium. This technical choice did indeed bring France "closer" to the bomb (see Hecht, *The Radiance of France*). It is thus a caveat to the general story of French lack of interest in preparing military applications in the pre-1954 period. However, this was a technical development that pushed the limits of the settled policy; for various reasons outlined below, Guillaumat would find that he could not build the bomb without political assent.

Pierre Mendès France came to power in 1954, he was able to undo the restrictions on proliferation that his predecessors had fashioned.

The year of decision: 1954

Under the EDC treaty, France had signed away its right to acquire nuclear weapons. But in August 1954, Parliament rejected the EDC treaty. Then, on December 26, 1954, Prime Minister Pierre Mendès France secretly informed his government of his determination for France to have nuclear weapons. What explains this dramatic turnabout?

Various scholarly analyses have argued that the triggering factor was one of the following three events: the April–May 1954 military disaster of Dien Bien Phu; the new massive retaliation strategy of NATO codified in the summer of 1954 in the New Look policy; and/or the reality that German rearmament was going to go forward even though EDC had been voted down.[26] We must consider all three of these hypotheses carefully. Given Mendès France's oppositional nationalism toward Germany, the theory developed in this book would expect the third trigger to have been the determinant one, and as we shall see, indeed it was.

Dien Bien Phu

The Indochina war had not been going well for France. The Eisenhower administration, impatient to see positive results as it increasingly shouldered the financial burden for the war, pushed the French to launch a knockout blow. As a result, at the end of 1953 the French found themselves in a heavily fortified but isolated position in Northwest Vietnam, near a village named Dien Bien Phu.[27] That taking up this position was a mistake soon became apparent. It was not the French but the Viet-Minh who launched the knockout blow in March 1954.

Through early April the French fortress was still holding, but the situation looked very bleak. In a mission to Washington, Foreign Minister Georges Bidault and General Paul Ely secretly asked for a massive American air intervention, including the use of atomic bombs if necessary. President Eisenhower determined – though not without hesitation – that

---

[26] Others have pointed to the crushing political defeat in the Suez Crisis as a trigger. But clearly this could not have been so, for the decision occurred two years before Suez.

[27] The Americans had not precisely counseled taking this position, but this situation did result from the Americans' pressure on the French to be more bold. George C. Herring and Richard H. Immerman, "Eisenhower, Dulles, and Dienbienphu: 'The Day We Didn't Go to War' Revisited," *Journal of American History*, Vol. 71, No. 2 (September 1984), esp. pp. 344–345.

the French proposition was seriously flawed from a military point of view and potentially disastrous from a diplomatic point of view.[28] The Americans refused the French request, and Dien Bien Phu fell soon thereafter.

Avery Goldstein and others have argued that the refusal to assist the French at Dien Bien Phu led French leaders to doubt the credibility of the American nuclear security guarantee, even in the case of a Soviet attack on Western Europe.[29] The perceived decrease in the credibility of the guarantee, Goldstein writes, explains the decision later that same year to build the bomb. This deduction has some intellectual plausibility but is flatly contradicted by the historical record.

First, the French establishment's pleading with the Americans to save them from disaster at Dien Bien Phu was simply the end of their gradual process of submission to American strategic advice and support – not merely in Indochina, but globally. Bidault, for instance, did not view the American assistance as a substitute for French efforts; rather, he saw it as France's *only hope*. These men, with their subaltern NICs, did not have the gumption to jumpstart the French bomb program.

Second, the American refusal to internationalize the Indochina war was not a blow to "France," but only to the French supporters of the war. The man who actually would decide to build the bomb, Pierre Mendès France, actually strongly opposed the Indochina war and wanted it to end as swiftly as possible. In fact, Mendès France *caused the government to fall* by revealing its attempt to bring the Americans and atomic weapons into the conflict.[30] As he put it on June 9, 1954:

In the absence of [peace] talks or negotiations, you had a plan . . . that involved the massive intervention of American air power, risking Chinese intervention and general war. For facing disasters that one can no longer hide, the temptation is great to integrate them into a world conflict without pausing to consider the danger of major catastrophes, a sort of unconscious raising of the stakes in this infernal poker game where the fate of millions of human lives hangs in the balance . . . I do not know myself of any other case in which a French government has taken such responsibilities in such secrecy, and in such scorn of Parliament.[31]

In sum, Dien Bien Phu hardly convinced Mendès France that henceforth the Americans should not be trusted. Indeed, he was relieved that on this

---

[28] Ibid. On the atomic dimension, see esp. pp. 357–358.
[29] Goldstein, *Deterrence and Security in the 21st Century*, pp. 189–191.
[30] Jacques Nantet, *Pierre Mendès France* (Paris: Editions du Centurion, 1967), p. 135.
[31] Speech of Pierre Mendès France of June 9, 1954, *Journal Officiel de la République Française, Débats de l'Assemblée Nationale, 2e legislature, Vol. 25, session de 1954, tome IV, du 4 mai 1954 au 9 juin 1954* (Paris: Imprimerie des Journaux Officiels, 1956), p. 2851. Note that Mendès France specifically mentioned the Bidault request for the US *atomic* intervention elsewhere in his speech.

occasion France's ally had shown more sense than its own government. Much of the country was similarly relieved as well, and soon thereafter Mendès France was elevated to the post of prime minister.

New Look and the nuclearization of the Cold War

Some scholars have argued that the trigger for the French nuclear program was not a loss of confidence in extended deterrence, but just the reverse. In mid-1954, NATO adopted the New Look policy of automatic, instantaneous, and massive atomic reprisals against any Soviet incursion into the West. As part of this policy, the US asked the French and other European states to host American nuclear installations. The French perceived this as a major increase in the credibility of the US commitment – indeed, they feared that the policy was so robust that it might provoke the Soviets instead of deterring them.[32] But, so the argument goes, the nuclearization of the Cold War represented by New Look made the French reconsider their nuclear option not on military grounds, but in order to retain their great power status.[33]

In the past, NATO planning had essentially been based on the notion of conventional defense against a Soviet attack. Thus the French, who provided the bulk of the troops on the continent, had a major voice in NATO decisionmaking. The 1954 doctrinal shift toward an early and massive nuclear riposte led many French military officials such as General Valluy, the permanent French military representative to NATO, to worry about the complete loss of French influence in the alliance. Valluy expressed this worry in a letter to new Prime Minister Pierre Mendès France in August 1954.[34]

One way of rectifying the situation was clearly to embark on a nuclear weapons program. This option began to make headway in some political circles, and especially in Charles de Gaulle's entourage. The notion of a bomb program even made some sense to the army's General Staff. But the General Staff, a stronghold of support for the EDC, did not want to do anything that would imperil the prospect of a supranational integration that contained Germany. Therefore, even after EDC was voted down at the end of August, in September the General Staff produced an important paper that pronounced in favor of *an integrated,*

---

[32] Olivier Pottier, "Les armes nucléaires américaines en France," *Cahiers du Centre d'études d'histoire de la défense*, No. 8 (1998), pp. 35–60. See also Alphonse Juin, *Mémoires*, Vol. II (Paris: Fayard, 1960), pp. 254–255.

[33] For instance, Georges-Henri Soutou, "La politique nucléaire de Pierre Mendès France," *Relations Internationales*, No. 59 (Autumn 1989), esp. pp. 319–320.

[34] Ibid., pp. 319–320.

"European" bomb program. It justified the notion of a supranational bomb program on the basis of France's limited technological and financial capacity to mount an independent nuclear deterrent. But this supposedly "technical" argument was clearly a fig leaf for the top brass' strong "European" inclinations.[35] Indeed, at the time that Mendès France eventually did decide on a sovereign bomb program, as the then-chief of the CEA's Chemistry Division (later nuclear historian) Bertrand Goldschmidt comments, "the strongest force against the bomb was in the army itself."[36]

Thus the still dominant "Europeans," even in the face of New Look, demonstrated a continuing desire to subordinate French nuclear policy choices to their objective of European integration. Even, so, New Look clearly helped to shift the French nuclear debate into a higher gear. But the causal linkage here requires nuance. The effects of New Look were more pronounced because it coincided with the epic battle over the EDC Treaty and German rearmament. The pure prestige factor of being part of the "Big Three" may have warmed the "nationalists" up to the idea of going nuclear, but what really convinced them was that a French bomb seemed a means of keeping a newly rearming Germany out of that exalted grouping. It is well to remember that previous challenges to France's international status, such as Britain's 1952 entry into the nuclear club, did not produce any significant momentum toward a French bomb. As the influential Marshal Alphonse Juin (a strong voice against EDC) wrote in a personal 1956 letter to Senator Edgar Pisani, "Though we still figure at the side of the two Anglo-Saxon atomic powers in the military directorate of NATO, we risk to be supplanted there one day by West Germany if we limit ourselves merely to conventional weapons."[37]

As we will see below, Pierre Mendès France, with his NIC of oppositional nationalism toward Germany, shared these sentiments and indeed was even clearer about the central role of the German threat in his nuclear policy.

---

[35] Mongin, *La bombe atomique française*, pp. 251–252.

[36] Tape-recorded interview with Bertrand Goldschmidt by Dominique Franche, Jan. 13, 1998, Institut Pierre Mendès France, Paris. Part of the reason for this was concern about turf. The army's main bomb advocate, General Paul Bergeron, devoted most of his time and energy to attacking the atomic monopoly of the supposedly "Communist-infiltrated" CEA. See, for instance, Note by General Bergeron, "Eléments de décision pour un Programme Atomique Militaire," November 18, 1954, Fonds Blanc (145 K5), Service des Archives Privées, Service Historique de l'Armée de Terre, Château de Vincennes.

[37] Alphonse Juin, letter to Edgar Pisani, April 14, 1956, Fonds Juin (238 K5 Dossier 2), Service des Archives Privées, Service Historique de l'Armée de Terre, Château de Vincennes.

Pierre Mendès France and the attempt to contain German rearmament

Mendès France became prime minister in June 1954, in the wake of Dien Bien Phu. He first moved to sign a peace agreement with the Viet-Minh, and then he turned to the matter of the EDC. After being signed in 1952, the EDC had been twisting in the wind waiting for ratification, as the "nationalists" assaulted it on a number of fronts and the French "Europeans" dared not bring it to a vote. Though his government was divided on the issue, Mendès France decided to liquidate the treaty. In an electric atmosphere, Parliament voted down the treaty on August 30, 1954 by a 319–264 vote, with the bulk of the anti-EDC votes coming from the Communists and the Gaullists. Those who had defeated EDC triumphantly sang *La Marseillaise*. The Communist Jean Nocher yelled out, "We now ask that the partisans of the EDC sing us *Deutschland über alles!*"[38]

Having driven the last nail into EDC's coffin, Mendès France now had to wrestle with the prospect of a German national rearmament. His preference ordering was clear: even in a world of nuclear powers, Mendès France *preferred a non-nuclear France facing a disarmed Germany to a nuclear France facing a conventionally armed Germany*. In short, it was not keeping up with the "Big Three," but keeping ahead of Germany that fundamentally drove Mendès France's stance. And he believed that given Germany's status as an occupied country and France's status as a great power, he could have his first preference. The means of doing so, primarily, was to generate a Cold War *détente*.[39] When his diplomatic gambit failed, however, Mendès France issued his political decision in favor of a French nuclear arsenal. This section describes those crucial days in some detail, with particular attention to the relevance of Mendès France's NIC of oppositional nationalism toward Germany for understanding both his nuclear decisionmaking process and his ultimate choice.

Mendès France's first effort to cool down the arms race, and thus obviate the need for German rearmament, involved an opening to the Soviets before the French Parliament's ratification debate over EDC. But a July 1954 meeting Mendès France arranged with the Soviet Foreign Minister Molotov bore no fruit. As Mendès France told the historian Georgette Elgey, "It was not absurd to think that the signature by France of peace in Indochina and the rejection of the European army could

---

[38] Jean Nocher in *Journal Officiel de la République Française, Débats Parlementaires – Assemblée Nationale*, 2e séance du 30 Août 1954, p. 4471.

[39] This logic was initially laid out in the article by the historian Jacques Bariéty, "La décision de réarmer l'Allemagne."

have brought the Russians to a modification, at least a technical one [of their position]. They could have attempted to dissuade the West [from rearming Germany]; they did nothing."[40]

Mendès France knew that his was a dangerous game that risked complete diplomatic isolation. The Americans – not to mention many Frenchmen – viewed his actions with great suspicion. As he told Elgey:

We justly feared bilateral US–German accords and that German rearmament be made against us. I was dominated by that fear . . . When the EDC was rejected, Foster Dulles had the immediate reflex to go to Bonn. He avoided Paris and refused to see me. The catastrophic situation of a German–American accord was spared us by Churchill and Adenauer, who preferred all the same that we be included.[41]

A Nine-Power Conference thus commenced in London in late September.

Mendès France's main proposal at London was to maintain the principle of national armies and to place strict limits on German national rearmament in terms of production and acquisition of heavy or advanced weapons. His diplomatic trick was that the restriction on German heavy weapons and atomic, biological, and chemical weapons would not legally be the result of any "discrimination" against it, but rather simply because it was a "strategically exposed area" with borders on the Soviet bloc.[42] German Chancellor Konrad Adenauer understandably objected to this concept, but Mendès France held fast. The issue was sent to a working group that eventually produced a compromise in a late-night session.[43]

Mendès France was in for a surprise. The French Foreign Ministry was one of the bastions of Europeanism. As they had done in 1952, French diplomats that night again dropped the discriminatory provisions against Germany in favor of a binding commitment by all the continental European states (France, Germany, Italy, and the Benelux) not to produce atomic, biological, or chemical weapons. The agreement made the only way of escaping the commitment a decision of the North Atlantic Council of NATO – in other words, if the French wanted the bomb, the Americans would have to give them permission.[44] In short, French "European" negotiators, eager to bind Germany, had once again bound France on the

[40] Transcript of Mendès France interview with Georgette Elgey, corrected in Mendès France's hand, October 27, 1965, fonds Elgey, Archives Nationales, Paris.
[41] Ibid.
[42] Verbatim record (in English) marked Secret, "Conférence des Neuf: Londres 1954," Belgian Ministry of Foreign Affairs archives, carton 15.419, Brussels.
[43] Interviews with Jean-Marc Boegner, then *ministre plénipotentiaire* in the Ministre des Affaires Etrangères, later head of the Service des Pactes, Paris, January 27 and 30, 1998.
[44] Ibid.

issue of nuclear proliferation, this time right under the nose of their prime minister.

The next morning Mendès France, alerted by the diplomat Jean-Marc Boegner, resolved to fight this concession tooth and nail.[45] His efforts were fiercely resisted by all the delegations. The Belgian Premier Paul-Henri Spaak led the resistance, saying that although "we must give guarantees to France against excessive rearmament by Germany . . . I presume it is necessary also to give to Germany guarantees against an excessive rearmament by France."[46] The real heart of the issue, according to Spaak, was the question of production of atomic, biological, and chemical weapons. The best way to satisfy France without discrimination against Germany was for all the continental powers to renounce the production of such weapons. He asked pointedly:

Is it really in the intention of one of the Brussels powers to start building or producing atomic, biological or chemical weapons? And as we are always speaking of the presentation and the effect on public opinion, would it not be good if the continental partners of the Brussels Treaty should undertake not to produce on the continent any weapons of an atomic, biological, or chemical kind?[47]

Such an agreement, according to Spaak, would once and for all allow the West to "organize a common defence, and not armies which might be able to fight each other."[48]

---

[45] Ibid. See also Mongin, *La bombe atomique française*, p. 321.

[46] "Conférence des Neuf" verbatim transcript.

[47] Ibid. Note Spaak's clear allusion to a non-proliferation norm that was already very significant in the minds of Western leaders.

[48] Ibid. The isolation of France at the London talks and in general at that moment in history is quite significant for theory testing. Two possible arguments against the perspective I am advancing are (1) what I am calling France's "oppositional" consensus against Germany was actually just an objective assessment of the reality of the German threat; and (2) the other European states, if they had not been so small, would also have built nuclear weapons to counter that threat, but since they could not, they encouraged France to do so. These arguments add up to a quasi-Realist critique of my theory. This critique notably overlooks the important division between French nationalists and French "Europeans" on how to deal with the German threat, but of course many Realists pride themselves on resolutely ignoring domestic politics. Thus, in order to consider this critique on the international plane, I embarked on a "shadow case" study of Belgium, which had every "objective" reason to share French attitudes toward Germany in the early 1950s. The main finding of this study is that *the strategic debate in France differed markedly from that of its neighbor, Belgium*. This demonstrates the value of this book's focus on identity, as opposed to the Realist alternative. The debate differed especially in two aspects. First, *Belgian leaders on all sides feared the Soviet threat more than the German threat*. This mental flexibility differs markedly from France's continuing rigid focus on Germany. As Spaak told the Council of Europe in Strasbourg in September 1954, "Today, your famous longtime Franco-German quarrel has not much importance – excuse me for saying so – in the great conflict in which France and Germany are on the same side of the barricade, in the great conflict that today opposes East and West, in the

Mendès France's response was firmly negative: France would not accept any restrictions and Germany must accept significant ones. The following day, as the debate dragged on, German Chancellor Konrad Adenauer, who had been silent throughout the entire discussion, finally made a stunning statement, seemingly out of the blue: "I do not like to feel fractious or quarrel, therefore, I am prepared to declare, on behalf of the Federal Republic that we will voluntarily renounce the manufacture of A B C [atomic, biological, and chemical] weapons, not on the reasons of strategically exposed zones, but quite voluntarily!"[49] In the face of this, the conference adjourned.

When the conference reconvened for the 10th plenary session, also on October 2, the various powers attempted to shame Mendès France into agreeing to the same restriction as Adenauer had previously done. The Belgian Spaak led off by stating his willingness to follow Adenauer and renounce nuclear weapons unilaterally and without condition; then came the Italian Martino and the Dutch Beyen with similar pronouncements. All eyes turned to Mendès France. He disappointed them by repeating, this time more bluntly than ever before, his mantra: no renunciations by France and much more than a merely verbal renunciation of ABC weapons by Germany:

Rightly or wrongly the French parliament refused to ratify the EDC for various reasons; one of these – if the Chancellor will allow me to say it in his presence – is

---

great conflict that is no longer about defending a sacred territory but great ideas, a common civilization, moral rules and common policies and the same honorable conception of man" (Paul-Henri Spaak, "Pour l'Europe, la lutte continue!" Address September 18, 1954 to the Assembly of the Council of Europe, Strasbourg, in folder 12.486 "France 1954," Belgian Ministry of Foreign Affairs archives, Brussels). Second, *an important segment of Belgian opinion actually preferred a national German army to EDC*. Their thinking was that German direct participation in NATO would be more efficient for the purpose of protecting Western Europe against the Soviets. For instance, Spaak's main political rival, Paul van Zeeland (who was prime minister in 1950) sent off this telegram to his representative to the NATO discussions on German rearmament: "Would like to see the discussion end in compromise. However if you were confronted by absolute necessity to pronounce for a European army or NATO army my preferences go to NATO army" ("Projet de telegramme" from Van Zeeland to London, November 28, 1950, in folder 15.397 "CED 1948–Oct. 1951," archives du Ministère des Affaires Etrangères, Brussels). Apart from Raymond Aron, it is difficult to find any French elites taking such a position at any point during the EDC debate. Finally, it is worth repeating that *the Belgians were anything but favorable to the French nuclear adventure*, as is shown by Spaak's attempt to isolate Mendès France at London.

49 "Conférence des Neuf" verbatim transcript. This transcript strongly supports the interpretation in Spaak's memoirs that Adenauer voluntarily renounced the bomb, and at the same time it casts strong doubt on the recollections of French officials, reported in Elgey, *La république des tourmentes*, p. 250, that they had defeated an Adenauer who insisted that Germany needed atomic weapons. It would appear that the French misunderstood Adenauer's demands.

the French fears about German rearmament. How can I imagine that tomorrow I would present myself in front of the French parliament with a new text which would give to the Federal Republic the possibility of manufacturing arms in categories 4, 5, and 6 [various types of heavy weapons] which were previously prohibited.[50]

The UK representative, Anthony Eden, then criticized Mendès France strongly for his stubbornness: "Frankly what I cannot see is how we can expect to get at this table the whole of what was obtained under the EDC system when the EDC system is no longer there." Mendès France replied that he merely wanted to hear Adenauer "extend the engagement which he has just said to the whole of Annex II" (the list of heavy weapons). Adenauer replied with yet another stunning declaration, "I have before this meeting spoken to Mr. Mendès France. We recognize that he is faced with psychological difficulties *vis-à-vis* the Federal Republic and I would also be prepared to say that we would not manufacture any teledirected missiles." He also offered to accept some restrictions on other types of weapons.[51]

By the time the 11th plenary meeting convened, later that same day, Chancellor Adenauer was trying to some degree to wriggle out of the restrictions he had just accepted. He wanted to make all of his and other countries' engagements – including on the atomic/biological/chemical renunciation – subject to revision by decision of NATO. In this he was supported by the other delegations. Mendès France, knowing he had been victorious in the previous meeting, opposed the possibility of changes by anything but unanimous assent. Mendès France again pointed to the "psychological impact" of the issue of German rearmament, noting that if Adenauer had his way, "Tomorrow I will see in the press articles saying that in two or three years we will see atomic bombs and heaven knows what being produced [by Germany], and you know to what point public opinion will use this." Now, for the first time in the entire conference, Adenauer lost his patience with Mendès France, saying:

I think you are not looking at this in the right psychological light. You said that you could not accept the prohibition of A B C for France . . . If NATO proposes to review these renunciations, that is really not reducing your demands. You have completely achieved your demands today. France alone retains the right to produce A, B, and C weapons.

There followed a pause as the various delegations attempted to come to agreement. Finally they did reach a compromise: all of Germany's engagements would be subject to revision by 2/3 majority vote except

---

[50] "Conférence des Neuf" verbatim transcript.   [51] Ibid.

for its renunciation of atomic, biological, and chemical weapons, which would be for all time.[52]

At the London Conference, Mendès France was fighting for the *right* to build the bomb and for a restriction on Germany from doing the same. But at the same time, he was also warming up to the idea of *actually* building the bomb. In the light of the verbatim transcript of the conference, Mendès France's rationale appears clear. French military power must remain at least one order of magnitude superior to Germany's; thus, the fewer the restrictions on German conventional weapons, the greater the need for a French atomic force. As he later told Elgey:

At London, there was a rather theoretical discussion [among the French delegation]: should France have an atomic bomb or not? Certain scientists, like Francis Perrin, were against it; many military men were for it; others, who were against it, said, "We should maintain this negotiating leverage." Personally, it was disagreeable to me to see France on the same footing as Germany. I fought for the right to the atomic bomb because it was intolerable that France suffer discriminatory treatment by the Americans and English and find itself reduced to the rank of Germany. My idea was to keep the atomic bomb as a negotiating tool.[53]

On October 26, 1954, three days after the London and Paris accords were signed, Mendès France signed a secret decree which created the *Commission Supérieure des Applications Militaires de l'Energie Atomique*. He also formally requested a precise budget projection for a French bomb without delay.[54] This represented a crucial green light for formal contacts between the military and the CEA, in order to study the questions of nuclear bombs and submarines. In fact the full *Commission* never met, because the military top brass was still opposed to giving the CEA a lead role in the production of the atomic bomb. But a sub-committee headed by the more amenable General Jean Crépin, dubbed the *Comité des Explosifs Nucléaires*, met for the first time on November 4 and began working on the technical question of just what it would take to build

---

[52] Ibid. In fact, Germany's renunciation was greatly watered down compared to what it had agreed to in the EDC Treaty, for there was to be no supranational inspection system, and the door was implicitly left open to its getting nuclear weapons from other states or even to producing nuclear weapons outside of its own soil. It does not appear, however, that any of these eventualities were seriously considered by anyone at the time. But, later on in the 1950s, they were. See Georges-Henri Soutou, *L'Alliance incertaine: les rapports politico-stratégiques franco-allemands, 1954–1996* (Paris: Fayard, 1996).

[53] Transcript of Mendès France interview with Georgette Elgey, corrected in Mendès France's hand, August 20, 1969, fonds Elgey, Archives Nationales, Paris. This quote also appears in Elgey, *La république des tourmentes 1954–1959*, pp. 256–257.

[54] Aline Coutrot, "La politique atomique sous le gouvernement de Mendès France," in François Bédarida et Jean-Pierre Rioux, eds., *Pierre Mendès France et le mendésisme: L'expérience gouvernementale (1954–1955) et sa postérité* (Paris: Fayard, 1985), p. 312.

a plutonium bomb.[55] All of this work was in deep secrecy; as Mendès France and several of his ministers discussed in an early November meeting, if public opinion learned of these preparations the government would likely fall.[56]

But as he noted in his interview with Elgey, even though Mendès France was now actively preparing the bomb option, he had not yet given up his hopes of realizing his first preference: a Four-Power Conference that would cool down the arms race, reducing the need for a major German rearmament and thus for a French bomb. In pursuit of this goal, Mendès France planned a major surprise for an upcoming speech he would be making at the United Nations in New York. He wanted to propose not only a Four-Power Conference, but also an international ban on atomic tests.[57] If Mendès France's hoped-for test ban were to materialize, this would of course block France from acquiring nuclear weapons. But Mendès France was willing to trade France's right to go nuclear to keep the global nuclear arms race in check and therefore, not coincidentally, to render German rearmament unnecessary. Mendès France believed that the Soviets had been responsible for the failure of Indian Prime Minister Jawaharlal Nehru's earlier call for a test ban.[58] He believed that he could do better than Nehru and better than his own previous fruitless approaches to the USSR, now that the threat of German rearmament was hanging in the background. German rearmament had been accepted in principle but still awaited ratification by the French Parliament. This was the moment at which Mendès France considered his bargaining leverage with the Soviets to be at its peak.[59]

Mendès France asked his friend and political ally Jean-Jacques Servan-Schreiber and his CEA scientific chief Francis Perrin to develop the test ban proposal for him. They did so with enthusiasm.[60] On November 16, the text was ready.[61] But after arriving in the US, Mendès France decided to drop the proposal from his address. He had developed his strategy on

---

[55] Jean Crépin, "Histoire du Comité des Explosifs Nucléaires," in *L'Aventure de la bombe*, p. 80.

[56] The meeting was originally called to discuss the Algerian insurrection. Interviews with Henri Caillavet, French politician (Mendès France's secretary of the navy), January 28 and 30, 1998 and May 15, 1999, as well as written communication on May 11, 1999.

[57] Jean-Jacques Servan-Schreiber, *Passions* (Paris: Fixot, 1991), esp. pp. 297–306.

[58] Pierre Mendès France, *Choisir: conversations avec Jean Bothorel* (Paris: Stock, 1974), p. 78.

[59] Bariéty cites a note from Mendès France to Parodi on August 8 outlining this very strategy. See Bariéty, "La décision de réarmer l'Allemagne," pp. 374–375.

[60] Servan-Schreiber, *Passions*, p. 299.

[61] Letter marked "Very Urgent" from Jean-Jacques Servan-Schreiber "for the President," November 16, 1954, Carton "Voyage du Président en Amérique," Institut Pierre Mendès France, Paris.

the theory that the Soviets were the main stumbling block to a test ban treaty; but he learned in Washington that the Americans were no more interested in a test ban than were the Soviets. Especially because Dulles still suspected him of disloyalty to the Western alliance, Mendès France felt he could not push his luck.[62] Servan-Schreiber felt betrayed:

For the first time, I find myself in *moral* disaccord with him . . . I have begun to sense the approach of the end of our beautiful and productive adventure, the end of this epic of a France led by a just man [*un juste*], dragging the rest of the world by his vision to institute a human order founded not on the balance of terror, but on education and creative intelligence . . . For me, a life ends.[63]

Mendès France returned from his American tour in late November. It was probably then that a second informal meeting in his Quai d'Orsay office was held on the subject of the bomb.[64] Present were Minister of the Interior François Mitterrand, Minister of Defense Emmanuel Temple, and Mendès France's chief of staff Jacques Pelabon, plus the secretaries of the Army, Air Force, and the Navy, Jacques Chevallier, Diomède Catroux, and Henri Caillavet, respectively. In this quite long meeting, the men discussed in depth the question of a French atomic bomb from all sides – "political, cultural, ethical, military."[65] But, interestingly, the main topic of discussion was the opposition to the bomb among French socialists and intellectuals such as the biologist Jean Rostand, who argued that use of the bomb would affect the human gene pool and thereby extinguish the human race. Those at the meeting felt that in the face of such widespread public resistance, it would be impossible to declare openly for the bomb. Mendès France thus requested that Caillavet, as secretary of the Navy, look into the possibility of doing bomb research under the cover of ongoing research on nuclear propulsion for a submarine.[66] But also they were not entirely certain that anti-nuclear activists such as Rostand were wrong, and Temple in particular voiced reservations that building the bomb might lead to an unforeseen catastrophe. This was a great responsibility to assume, he repeated several times. Mendès France finally became impatient with Temple's indecision. That is why we are here, he told Temple, to choose and to take responsibility. Caillavet came away from the meeting with the definite impression that Mendès France had decided for a secret program to build the bomb. And in fact, Mendès France would not disappoint him.

---

[62] Pierre Mendès France, *Choisir*, p. 78.   [63] Servan-Schreiber, *Passions*, pp. 305–306.

[64] Interviews with Caillavet. Note that Caillavet is not certain if this meeting occurred before or after Mendès France's New York trip.

[65] Interviews with Caillavet.

[66] On Mendès France's orders, Caillavet prepared a budget proposition for Navy research, in which credits for the bomb were hidden. Interviews with Caillavet.

On December 26, 1954, an unusually large group of approximately forty high officials were summoned to Mendès France's office for a secret meeting.[67] They were presented with a draft decision whose first sentence read simply, "The making of atomic bombs is decided."[68] A separate paper prepared for the meeting, entitled "Strategic Conceptions," argued that while a French atomic bomb was "not necessary" for purely military purposes, since the "USA builds the bomb at an industrial rhythm," possession by France *did* "present a double interest: political [and] technical."[69] The initial cost estimate was 80 billion francs for the bomb and 45 billion for two submarines, spread out over five or six years.[70]

In the meeting, for which unfortunately no transcripts have surfaced, the prime minister asked anyone who wished to do so to make the case for or against a French atomic bomb. He listened patiently as various colleagues one by one took the floor to voice their opposition or support. The meeting was stiffly formal, and there was very little discussion or give-and-take. The meeting ended with Mendès France apparently taking a final decision. Bertrand Goldschmidt recounts that Mendès France argued:

It was a good idea to start fabricating prototypes of nuclear submarines and bombs, because it was capital for France's international influence, because even in disarmament discussions we would have more of a say if we had the bomb, and thirdly, and he insisted on this point, this would be what would differentiate us from the Germans, since the recent signature of the Paris Accords.[71]

Mendès France then turned to Finance Minister Edgar Faure, who had been reading his newspaper for the entire meeting (!), and said "And, *Monsieur le Ministre des Finances*, you will have to manage somehow!"[72]

[67] The information in this paragraph, in large measure, comes from the tape of Dominique Franche's interview with Bertrand Goldschmidt, held at the Institut Pierre Mendès France, Paris, and my own interviews with Goldschmidt. Caillavet, who was also present at the meeting, confirmed the veracity of Goldschmidt's remarks. Others present included the following – from the military: Bergeron, Vernoux, Lardin, Crépin, Combeaux, Guntzberger, Briard, Argoux. From Mendès France's Cabinet: Maignon, Jobert, Neurisse, Juillet, Binoche, Boris, Pelabon. Ministers or secretaries of state: Faure, Moch, Longchambon, Temple (plus Widmer from Temple's Cabinet), Caillavet, Catroux, Chevallier. From the CEA: Perrin, Goldschmidt, Guillaumat. "Réunion 26.12" file, Carton "Energie Atomique," Institut Pierre Mendès France, Paris.)

[68] Note "Projet de Décision," Dec. 26, 1954, Carton "Energie Atomique," Institut Pierre Mendès France, Paris.

[69] The note was vague on these points, especially on the precise political utility of the bomb. The only elaboration was as follows: "Political: toward our allies, toward our eventual enemies, toward Germany, toward the Union Française. Technical: military utilization implies a sufficient development of the civil infrastructure of the atomic industry." Note "Conceptions Stratégiques," December 26, 1954, in folder "Réunion Dimanche 26.12," Carton "Energie Atomique," Institut Pierre Mendès France, Paris.

[70] Ibid.

[71] Hymans interview with Goldschmidt. Substantially confirmed in interview with Caillavet.

[72] Hymans interview with Goldschmidt.

After the meeting, opponents of the bomb attempted to get Mendès France to retreat from his decision. Jules Moch sent the prime minister a letter on December 28 in which he reiterated his opposition to the conclusions to which Mendès France had come at the end of the meeting.[73] Perrin also did so, stressing the practical tradeoffs between industrial and military applications of atomic energy and the "attitude of the CEA personnel" in favor of keeping the French atomic effort "peaceful." Perrin argued finally that the initial steps toward the bomb were in any case indistinguishable from the next steps needed for the civil program, and thus it made no sense to hurry into a decision for the bomb.[74]

Mendès France would later claim in public that he never did make the ultimate decision to go nuclear, using Moch and Perrin's arguments as his own.[75] Privately, however, he made the more subtle argument that although he did make the decision, he subsequently never authorized the money to implement it.[76] This is true, but only because at the January 23 Council of Ministers meeting, Minister of Finance Edgar Faure objected to Mendès France's pressure to devote large resources to the nuclear program (three times the 1952 nuclear Five-Year Plan), on the basis of a flimsy and vague budget request concocted in the wee hours of the morning. As Faure later recalled, "The subject was brought up between 1 and 2 AM, while the meeting had begun at 6 PM. I opposed not the principle, but that a decision was to be taken in such hurried conditions."[77] They therefore agreed to take up the matter at their next meeting; but there was no next time, for the Mendès France government fell two weeks later. Thus Mendès France was *unable* to follow up his political decision with enough funding to ensure its implementation, but the initial political decision stood. Furthermore, the crucial indication that Mendès France had not changed his mind was that while he was trying to pass the bomb program through the normal channels, simultaneously he had Caillavet busily working on finding a way to sneak funding for the bomb program into the Navy's research budget.[78] Mendès France was not hesitating; he knew what he wanted and was willing to do just about anything to get

[73] Jules Moch, letter to Pierre Mendès France, December 28, 1954, Carton "Energie Atomique," Institut Pierre Mendès France, Paris.

[74] Francis Perrin, letter to Pierre Mendès France, apparently December 29, 1954, Carton "Energie Atomique," Institut Pierre Mendès France, Paris.

[75] Mongin, *La bombe atomique française*, pp. 340–1.

[76] This was how he explained himself to Bertrand Goldschmidt (Hymans interview with Goldschmidt). The ex-premier's motive for disowning parentage is clear enough: after 1958 he became a vociferous opponent of Charles de Gaulle and of de Gaulle's plans for the *force de frappe*.

[77] Edgar Faure, "Témoignage," in *L'Aventure de la bombe*, p. 87.

[78] Interviews with Caillavet. Caillavet emphasizes that since the government fell, the Navy budget never was used for these purposes.

it. In the end, in spite of Mendès France's failure to secure funding for the decision, it was his political decision for the bomb that served as the crucial catalyst for the march to the French bomb.

Mendès France's oppositional nationalism and the bomb decision

Before showing the effects of Mendès France's decision, it is necessary to conclude this longest and most crucial section of the chapter with a review of the performance of this book's theoretical perspective as an explanation for the French bomb decision.

In spite of the major upheavals on the world stage, the democratic nature of the regime, the rickety governmental coalition, and the play of powerful bureaucratic interests, the story of the decision for the French bomb is above all the story of a single oppositional nationalist prime minister's quest to do what he felt to be in the best interests of France.

Nuclear weapons, for Mendès France, were not like other weapons. As he had vociferously attacked the previous government for endangering the world over Dien Bien Phu, so he agonized over the choice to endanger the world by bringing into being another nuclear weapons state. He and his close associates together worried about contributing to the end of life on earth. And yet, in the end, in full cognizance of the moral and political responsibility he was placing on his shoulders, he took the fateful decision to go nuclear. In making that choice, he explicitly pointed to his hope that a French bomb would fundamentally reverse the dual trends of German resurgence and French decline. As noted previously, in the December 26 meeting, "Mendès France portrayed the bomb as capital for France's international influence," and "this would be what would differentiate us from the Germans."

It was Mendès France's oppositional nationalism *vis-à-vis* Germany that gave him the motivation and the certitude necessary to cross what was quite clearly an enormous psychological hurdle. As the theory developed in this book would expect, the fundamental driving factor in Mendès France's thinking on the bomb was Germany's resurgence on the international scene. The word that we find again and again in Mendès France's discourse on the issue of German rearmament, whether in his interviews with Elgey or in his statements at the London conference, is "fear": "We justly feared bilateral US–German accords"; "I was dominated by that fear"; "The French fears about German rearmament." This fear of Germany was nothing unique for a French leader. But Mendès France also had a strong nationalist pride. He liquidated EDC, refused to be "reduced to the rank of Germany," and truly believed even that he could bring the great powers together to head off German rearmament.

His desire for a test ban in particular shows that he could even accept some degree of lesser status *within* the great power club in order to keep Germany *out* of it and at the same time militarily inoffensive.[79]

Indeed, as Mendès France's reiteration of the word "fear" implies, this was an emotional decision for him.[80] Mendès France's desperation over the resurgence of Germany produced the same hasty and undemocratic decisionmaking process that he had so harshly criticized in the previous government's request for American intervention at Dien Bien Phu. While he did inform certain members of his government of his decision, he did not inform Parliament – much less put his decision to a vote. He tried to force through a vague but massive budgetary request in the middle of the night. In case that did not work, he told his Navy Secretary Henri Caillavet to prepare a way to sneak funding for the bomb into the naval research program. All of this effort to circumvent normal processes came in the service of what can only be described as a half-baked project. The decision to build nuclear weapons in 1954 came years before France was technically ready to implement it. Mendès France could only rely on some very preliminary analyses of the budgetary and technical requirements for building the bomb, and he had essentially no idea of France's requirements in terms of delivery systems. The nuclear submarine program he launched at the same time as the bomb program may have been hazily conceived as a potential delivery system, but if so this would have piled technical unknown upon technical unknown and, in any case, for it to serve this purpose there would also have to have been a major effort to develop submarine-launched missile technology, which there was not. In the end, France began developing a strategic bomber, the Mirage 4B, in 1957 but then gave it up for technical and cost reasons. As a consequence, France was "the first nation to go into atomic weapons without a clear plan for a strategic nuclear delivery system against her major potential enemy."[81] All of these examples demonstrate the great and indeed untoward haste with which Mendès France launched France into the nuclear weapons game.

---

[79] As stated in Chapter 2, the idea of the test ban – a non-discriminatory accord – is compatible with nationalist sentiments, whereas the idea of an accord that binds only non-nuclear weapons states is not. In parallel to this, as documented in Chapter 7, Indian nationalists long supported a CTBT while opposing the NPT.

[80] Bertrand Goldschmidt seconds this interpretation: "From 1954 on, it was the [establishing the] difference with Germany that counted . . . You see, we had just been occupied by Germany. We had to have, it was a kind of revenge, if you want, from this humiliating occupation. We had to have . . . differentiation." Transcript of Bertrand Goldschmidt interview for WGBH Boston television series "The Nuclear Age," Liddell Hart archives, King's College, London.

[81] Leonard Beaton and John Maddox, *The Spread of Nuclear Weapons* (New York: Frederick A. Praeger, 1962), p. 89.

Oppositional nationalism, nuclear symbolism, fear, pride, and haste, all coming together to produce a determination to build the bomb: the theory finds its clear echo in the case of Pierre Mendès France. But do decisions to build nuclear weapons matter? Was his decision truly responsible for the French acquisition of the bomb?

After 1954: the road to the bomb

Mendès France alone did not bring the French bomb into being, and indeed, the decision by Mendès France to build the bomb was not the end of the struggle over France's nuclear fate. But as this section will show, Mendès France's decision had a rapid, catalytic effect. Mendès France's decision was crucial for creating substantial, and as it turned out, unstoppable momentum toward a French nuclear arsenal on at least three levels: intra-bureaucratic (within the CEA), inter-bureaucratic (notably between the CEA and the military), and political.

First, Mendès France's decision had important ramifications inside the CEA itself. This was in no small part because Mendès France had enormous prestige with the CEA's leftist scientists. Notably, since it was Mendès France who had made the choice, the previously anti-bomb CEA scientific chief, Francis Perrin, came to accept the project.[82] The conversion of Perrin gave the CEA's pro-bomb administrative chief, Pierre Guillaumat, free rein to pursue his longstanding desire for a bomb.[83] As Yves Rocard, a rare pro-bomb scientist, writes in his memoirs:

At this juncture, a miracle happened: the policy brusquely changed. In 1954, Mendès France gave what everyone took for his orders, and Guillaumat found himself then strong enough to free himself of the hindrances that he had endured until then. He called on me: "I'm going to keep your land [that the CEA had offered Rocard for some unrelated experiments]. That's where we're going to make the bomb!"[84]

Indeed, merely three days after Mendès France's bomb decision, Guillaumat set up the *Bureau d'Etudes Générales*, which managed the bomb project, as "an increasingly autonomous unit within the CEA, with its own rules and management."[85] The existence of the Bureau was still hidden from most of the CEA, with much of its work taking place outside the main CEA campus in front corporations.[86] But it could not be

---

[82] Hymans interview with Goldschmidt.
[83] Georges-Henri Soutou and Alain Beltran, eds., *Pierre Guillaumat: la passion des grands projets industriels* (Paris: Editions Rive Droite, 1995).
[84] Rocard, *Mémoires sans concessions* (Paris: Grasset, 1988), pp. 175–176.
[85] Albert Buchalet, "Les premières étapes (1955–1960)," in *L'Aventure de la bombe*.
[86] Rocard, *Mémoires sans concessions* covers this in detail.

hidden from Perrin, so his conversion was crucial to the creation of real bureaucratic and technical momentum toward the bomb. There can be no doubt, therefore, that Mendès France's decision jumpstarted the French bomb program.

Second, on the inter-bureaucratic level, Mendès France's decision also had immediate and lasting effects. I previously noted the importance of Mendès France's initial October nuclear decision, which led to the initial contacts between the CEA and military officials. After Mendès France's definitive December decision, those contacts deepened quickly. Indeed, Guillaumat placed the *Bureau d'Etudes Générales* under the direction of a general, Albert Buchalet.[87] Without the political cover provided by Mendès France's decision, Guillaumat and Buchalet could not have set up the *Bureau*. Buchalet came to play an important bridging role between the military and CEA. As a result, an inter-ministerial protocol was signed in March 1955 that – finally – gave the CEA the clear leading role in the study and development program for the bomb.[88] This cleared the way for fast progress toward the objective of building the bomb.

Finally, on the political level, Mendès France's secret decision that France should obtain nuclear weapons was seminal. Buchalet recounts, "From then on, with each new government, the Prime Minister designate was informed of the verbal accord given by his predecessor, for him to confirm verbally."[89] Edgar Faure – who took over the top job after Mendès France's fall – writes that his "anxieties" about the bomb were vastly calmed by the idea that he was not responsible for making the fateful choice.[90] This peace of mind clinched Faure's approval of a huge, 85.5 billion franc budget request for nuclear bomb research (increased to 100 billion later that year).[91] Faure also gave *carte blanche* (again his words) to two Gaullist ministers, Pierre Billotte at Defense and Gaston Palewski, the state secretary for atomic energy, to arrange the bureaucratic modalities of the bomb program.[92] It is true, however, that some of Faure's successors, notably the solidly "European" Guy Mollet, felt angered rather than relieved to learn of Mendès France's decision and resolved to fight it tooth and nail.

Last gasp of the "Europeans": the near-renunciation of 1956

Despite the defeat of EDC and the secret development of a national atomic bomb program, some of France's "Europeans" were not yet

---

[87] Mongin, *La bombe atomique française*, p. 348.
[88] Buchalet, "Les premières étapes (1955–60)," p. 45.
[89] Ibid., p. 45. See also Guillaumat's comments in the same volume, p. 70.
[90] Faure argues however that the real choice for the French bomb was put off until de Gaulle. Faure, "Témoignage," pp. 87–88.
[91] Ibid.   [92] Ibid.

willing to quit. Still holding on to their oppositional subaltern NIC *vis-à-vis* Germany, they still felt as they had in 1954: that European integration was the only conceivable method for France to keep Germany under control, and that a French bomb would derail the integration process. In January 1955, the idea of a European atomic energy community as a means of preventing proliferation was first broached to the paradigmatic "European," Jean Monnet, by Max Isenbergh of the US Atomic Energy Commission. Monnet was immediately taken by the idea and was soon holding day-long sessions with Isenbergh. Monnet's proposal for a European Atomic Energy Community or EURATOM became one of the key proposals of the Conference of Messina's relaunch of the European integration process in May of that year.[93]

In January 1956, Guy Mollet of the Socialist Party became prime minister of France. Mollet was an outspoken proponent of European integration, an ally of Monnet's, and a fierce opponent of a French atomic bomb. Before his investiture, he signed the Monnet Declaration which declared not only that EURATOM must be dedicated exclusively to civil applications, but also that it must control all fissile materials – so that, in other words, national bomb programs would be impossible.[94] In his investiture speech before the French Parliament, Mollet reiterated this commitment.[95] This strongly felt and also politically popular anti-bomb stance could potentially have represented a serious, or even mortal blow to the nascent French bomb effort. Mollet the "European" meant it to be just that.

Needless to say, the "nationalists" who were the bomb's proponents reacted vigorously against the threat. This redux of the anti-EDC coalition included such political heavyweights as Marshal Juin; the CEA's Pierre Guillaumat; Charles de Gaulle and his parliamentary allies led by Michel Debré; and also Mendès France himself, who was serving as a minister without portfolio in Mollet's government.[96] As Debré wrote to Mendès France, under EURATOM if France ever wished "to liberate itself from the bonds that will have been imposed on it, however provisional or light they are, it will only be able to do so to the extent that, at the same time, Germany will be liberated."[97] Mendès France replied that he was in agreement: "This revenge [by the French "Europeans"]

[93] François Duchêne, *Jean Monnet: The First Statesman of Interdependence* (New York: W. W. Norton and Co., 1994), p. 264.

[94] Mongin, *La bombe atomique française*, p. 400.   [95] Ibid., p. 398.

[96] Michel Debré, *Trois républiques pour une France: Mémoires, 1946–1958 "Agir"* (Paris: Albin Michel, 1988), p. 236.

[97] Exchange of letters between Michel Debré and Pierre Mendès France, in Pierre Mendès France, *Oeuvres complètes IV: Pour une république moderne 1955–1962* (Paris: Gallimard, 1987), pp. 202–203.

has gone very far, since it has even consisted in the *de facto* renunciation of the controls on German rearmament."[98]

Faced with Mollet's challenge, the French "nationalists" threatened to rip the country apart in a replay of EDC.[99] Mollet and his allies could not afford another EDC-style political train wreck, which would definitively bury any hopes for European integration. They therefore had to swallow the bitter pill of allowing the nuclear weapons program to continue. Indeed, Mollet ended up having to agree to *accelerate* the bomb program. As Georges Guille, state secretary for atomic affairs (who was himself anti-bomb), explained to the prime minister, "If, parallel to the ratification of the Common Market and EURATOM treaties, you do not devote funds for an uranium isotope separation plant, the EURATOM treaty will not pass."[100] Mollet would later write that although his government had pushed for a different nuclear policy outcome, "parliamentary opinion did not follow it."[101]

It was a disheartened and beaten Mollet who appeared before the French Assembly on July 11, 1956 to defend the much watered-down EURATOM plan. For the first time, a French prime minister admitted the existence of a bomb program from the tribune of the Assemblée Nationale and said that it would continue. He implied that plans for the uranium isotope separation (enrichment) plant were also being elaborated. The only bone he could throw to his anti-bomb allies was that France would not conduct a test explosion before 1961, which he admitted was not much, since the CEA did not believe it could do it any sooner.[102] Having been offered these concessions, the Parliament passed the EURATOM motion.[103]

It was a great day for the bomb advocates. As General Charles Ailleret – the man who would eventually push the button on the first French nuclear test – writes in his autobiography:

---

[98] Ibid.

[99] Debré, *Trois républiques*, p. 233.

[100] Pierre Guillaumat, cited in Mongin, *La bombe atomique française*, p. 402. The plant was another part of the French drive for an independent nuclear bomb capacity. See Goldschmidt, "La genèse."

[101] Guy Mollet, Report on EURATOM, Sept. 1956, cited in Pierre Guillen, "La France et la négociation du traité d'Euratom," in Michel Dumoulin, Pierre Guillen, and Maurice Vaïsse, eds., *L'Energie nucléaire en Europe: Des origins à Euratom* (Bern: Peter Lang, 1994), p. 121.

[102] Guy Mollet speech before the Assemblée Nationale, July 11, 1956, cited in Mongin, *La bombe atomique française*, p. 432.

[103] This was not the final vote on the EURATOM treaty, which would not come until a year later; but it did consolidate the position of the pro-bomb side.

One could deduce from this that the battle for the French nuclear bomb had been won. Effectively, it was. Not only did the text passed by the *Assemblée* hardly constrain the action of France, but the Parliament had become conscious of the need and of the possibility to fabricate nuclear weapons in France. It would subsequently create no difficulties, in discussions over *loi-programmes* or annual budgets, to the idea that a French national defense with a real degree of independence required a national nuclear armament.[104]

Even after July 1956 there were important decisions on the bomb, including a new infusion of funds after the Suez crisis, the 1958 green light to prepare for the test in the Sahara, and the ultimate 1960 decision to test.[105] But these decisions were essentially mere ratifications of a bomb program whose existence and ultimate objective had already been accepted by all sides of the political mainstream.

In time, the anti-German rationale for the French bomb disappeared. The French nuclear arsenal would find new justifications under de Gaulle's regime. The transition, however, was slower than it outwardly appeared. Bertrand Goldschmidt recounts that whenever de Gaulle, as president of the Fifth Republic, would come to the CEA, he would ask "each time the same question: he wanted to know when, how, how fast and in how much time the Germans could in turn build themselves the bomb, if, repudiating their international engagements, they decided to make it. Despite a uniting Europe and the newly created links [between France and Germany], the General had never forgotten."[106]

---

[104] Charles Ailleret, *L'Aventure atomique française* (Paris: Grasset, 1968).

[105] Though no longer attempting to quash the bomb effort, the French "Europeans" did make one more foray into the question, with an attempt to "Europeanize" it along the lines suggested by the General Staff's recommendations of September 1954. Guy Mollet took the initiative in November 1956 and the negotiations with the Germans and Italians continued until de Gaulle stopped them upon his return to power in 1958. See Colette Barbier, "Les négociations franco-germano-italiennes en vue de l'établissement d'une coopération militaire nucléaire au cours des années 1956–1958," *Revue d'Histoire Diplomatique*, Vol. 104, Nos. 1–2 (1990), esp. pp. 86–87. This episode, though interesting, was of little historical consequence. Pierre Guillaumat wrote that since the CEA was not involved in the negotiations, legally "an engagement of the Ministry of National Defense represented a bad check. The German interlocutor became fully conscious of this fact in 1958; I do not know if he was surprised." (Pierre Guillaumat, letter to Maurice Vaïsse, Feb. 13, 1991, held at Institut Pierre Mendès France, Paris).

[106] Bertrand Goldschmidt, *Pionniers de l'atome* (Paris: Stock, 1987), p. 267.

5   Australia's search for security: nuclear umbrella, armament, or abolition?

Introduction

Most analysts surmise that Australia abstained from building the bomb because of, in T. V. Paul's words, "the low-conflict environment and the lack of credible security threats from Asia."[1] But, in fact, the story of Australia's nuclear stance is far more complicated than the country's basic material position would suggest. Far from lolling about "on the beach," the long succession of Liberal Party governments during the first quarter-century of the Cold War invested Australia heavily in the Free World's nuclear deterrence plans against the Communist threat. They eagerly offered their territory to host British nuclear weapons tests and important pieces of the worldwide American nuclear deterrence system. At the same time, they purchased nuclear-capable aircraft and actively sought "key to the cupboard" nuclear transfer arrangements with their British and American protectors. And in the late 1960s, a Liberal prime minister even tried to foment an Australian nuclear weapons program. It was only in 1972 – in a context of objectively greater strategic uncertainty than had existed a decade earlier – that Australia finally became satisfied with its strategic situation and developed a broader diplomatic agenda in support of international efforts to rein in the global nuclear arms race.

What explains Australia's long fascination with nuclear deterrence, its brief flirtation with the idea of a sovereign deterrent, and then the sudden chilling of those passions? The argument of this chapter is that the changes in Australia's nuclear policies were largely a function of the different NICs of the prime ministers who governed the country from 1945 to 1975. Australia's nuclear stance reflected first the oppositional subaltern NIC of Robert Menzies (1949–66), then the oppositional nationalist NIC of John Gorton (1968–71), and finally the sportsmanlike subaltern NIC of Gough Whitlam (1972–75).

[1] T. V. Paul, *Power versus Prudence: Why States Forgo Nuclear Weapons* (Montreal and Kingston: McGill/Queen's University Press, 2000), p. 79.

The Australian case poses significant problems for the conventional theoretical perspectives on proliferation.

- First, the case poses a particularly acute challenge to the realist hypothesis that objective threats drive nuclear policies. For instance, as noted above, realism has trouble explaining Prime Minister Menzies' high threat perceptions and desire for ever-higher deterrence credibility. It has even more trouble explaining his lack of interest in an independent deterrent in spite of those perceptions.
- Second, according to institutionalist logic, the birth of the Non-Proliferation Treaty should have come as a great relief to Australian policymakers eager to escape the proliferation prisoners' dilemma. But in fact, Prime Minister Gorton resented the treaty and was intent on staying out of it in order to protect his cherished nuclear weapons ambitions.
- Finally, bureaucratic politics models shine some light on the motivations of important actors in the Australian nuclear story.[2] But such models obscure as much as they clarify. For instance, the Australian Atomic Energy Commission housed both the strongest bureaucratic proponents of a nascent nuclear weapons program, *and* the sticklers for technical probity who snuffed it out.

The chapter is organized as follows. The second part covers the nuclear policies of the oppositional subaltern Menzies and his successor, Harold Holt. The third part discusses the nuclear policies of the oppositional nationalist Gorton and his successor, William McMahon. Finally, the transformation in Australian nuclear policies undertaken by the sportsmanlike subaltern Whitlam and the Labor Party government he led from 1972 to 1975 is explained.

The traditional Liberals, 1949–67: participation in free world defenses

During the first two decades of the Cold War, Australian foreign policy was subject to the outlook and actions of one man, the long-serving Liberal prime minister Sir Robert Menzies.[3] As Chapter 3 demonstrated,

---

[2] See Jim Walsh, "Surprise Down Under: The Secret History of Australia's Nuclear Ambitions," *Nonproliferation Review*, Vol. 5 (Fall 1997), pp. 1–20. I am profoundly grateful to Jim Walsh for allowing me to photocopy nearly all of the copious documentation he collected on his field research in Australia. Walsh's generous sharing of his archival treasure trove allowed me to spend relatively less time at the National Archives of Australia and relatively more time at other archives in Canberra and Sydney, which were heretofore unexploited but very revealing about Australia's nuclear past.

[3] The fact that Menzies was in control, especially in foreign policy matters where he sometimes even served as his own foreign minister, is widely accepted by scholars.

Menzies held an almost ideal-typical oppositional subaltern NIC *vis-à-vis* the Communists, and his foreign and nuclear policy choices reflect that NIC.

Menzies' first major foray into the nuclear field was his 1950 offer to host British nuclear tests.[4] Menzies made this offer without consulting his Cabinet and without requesting any *quid pro quo* from the British – not even access to the technical data necessary to assess the effects of the tests on Australia's citizens and environment.[5] The first British bomb exploded in 1952 on the Monte Bello islands off the Western Australian coast; subsequent tests were held at Emu Field and Maralinga in South Australia. The British would conduct major nuclear weapons tests on these sites through 1957, and they continued to perform minor trials, assessment tests, and experimental programs in the country until they completed their move to Nevada in 1963. Why did Menzies unilaterally make this rarest of decisions by a significant non-nuclear state, to offer up its own national territory to be used for someone else's nuclear explosions? And why did he make it so readily, while posing no conditions?

The Royal Commission into British Nuclear Tests in Australia (a high-level 1980s inquiry) concluded that Menzies' decision was due fundamentally to his tendency to "embrace British interests as being synonymous with those of Australia."[6] Menzies was indeed enamored of the British "Motherland," but he also viewed his choice as furthering Australia's national self-interest. In 1950, with China having just fallen to the Communists and with the North Korean attack on the South, Australian threat perceptions had reached a peak. The next battle for freedom, Menzies thought, would be fought on Australia's doorstep.[7] Meanwhile, Menzies felt that Australia was incapable of defending itself against encroaching Communism. Hosting the nuclear tests was a way of binding Britain and the West – Australia's "great and powerful friends," in Menzies' famous phrase – fully to the nation's defense. Nuclear explosions in Australia would serve not only to warn the Communists of Australia's

This is not however to imply that Menzies was a tyrant who could not be swayed by serious argument in Cabinet. See T. B. Millar, *Australia in Peace and War: External Relations 1788–1977* (Canberra: Australian National University Press, 1978), esp. pp. 26–27.

[4] This and subsequent information in this paragraph comes from the *Royal Commission into British Nuclear Tests in Australia* ("McClelland Report"), Parliamentary Paper No. 482/1985 (Canberra: Australian Government Publishing Office, 1985).

[5] Ibid., p. 447.

[6] Ibid., p. 11. To underscore Menzies' "Anglophilia," the Commission recalls Menzies' 1939 announcement as prime minister that "as Britain was at war with Germany, Australia was automatically at war with the same enemy" (p. 11).

[7] Peter G. Edwards with Gregory Pemberton, *Crises and Commitments: The Politics and Diplomacy of Australia's Involvement in Southeast Asian Conflicts, 1948–1965* (North Sydney: Allen & Unwin in association with the Australian War Memorial, 1992), pp. 70–71.

importance to Western defense, but also to increase that importance in the eyes of its Western allies, and most particularly Britain.[8] The stratagem worked; in 1952 the chief scientist in the British bomb effort, William Penney, remarked, "If the Australians are not willing to let us do further trials in Australia, I do not know where we would go."[9]

The Australian historian Wayne Reynolds goes further than I, arguing that Menzies' decision to host the tests "was motivated in large part by a strong desire to obtain nuclear weapons and their delivery systems."[10] But to claim that Menzies "wanted the bomb" would be to overstate the case, or at least to leave an inexact implication. The Menzies government clearly wanted to increase the credibility of the nuclear guarantees. It was not averse to – was even eager for – an active Australian role in British Commonwealth and free world nuclear defenses, from basic research to bomb trials to the acquisition of delivery systems.[11] But Menzies stopped there. Australia would be secure only by remaining part of a much larger machine, the British Commonwealth, itself working hand in hand with the US and NATO. In the Commonwealth context Australia could offer something; alone, Menzies felt, Australia would be useless.[12]

Still searching for a stronger guarantee: 1957–63

In late 1956, Menzies strongly backed the British–French Suez expedition, saying that failure to rebuff Nasser would "open the way for China to pursue similar tactics in South East Asia."[13] This stance by Menzies has often been seen as blind loyalty to Britain, but Wayne Reynolds has shown

---

[8] It is important to emphasize that for Australia, the importance of the British bomb blasts went far beyond these relatively "rationalist" concerns. The blasts were a psychological salve, helping Australians to forget for a time the "tyranny of distance": "so close" to the red-yellow peril, "so far" from mother Britain. For a complex account of the cultural aspects of the Australian nuclear experience, see Noel Sanders, "The Hot Rock in the Cold War: Uranium in the 1950s," in Ann Curthoys and John Merritt, *Better Dead than Red: Australia's First Cold War: 1945–1959*, Vol. II (Sydney: Allen & Unwin, 1986), pp. 155–169.

[9] Cited in Alice Cawte, *Atomic Australia: 1944–1990* (Kensington, NSW: NSW Press, 1992), p. 59.

[10] Wayne Reynolds, "Menzies and the Proposal for Atomic Weapons," in Frank Cain, ed., *Menzies in War and Peace* (St. Leonards, NSW: Allen & Unwin, 1997), p. 116.

[11] Jim Walsh amply documents the active Australian interest in nuclear delivery systems, which was already quite significant in the 1950s. I would simply underscore the fact that the acquisition of such systems by members of the Western alliance was hardly rare and should not be taken to imply an interest in sovereign control of the weapons themselves. Walsh, "Surprise Down Under."

[12] My critique of Reynolds is thus a critique of the implication he leaves, not of the bulk of his scholarship which shows precisely the Australian dream of integration into "Empire Defense" and the broader free world nuclear architecture. Wayne Reynolds, *Australia's Bid for the Atomic Bomb* (Melbourne: Melbourne University Press, 2000).

[13] Ibid., p. 169.

that on this occasion Menzies did exact a price for his support: a British promise to establish a permanent nuclear presence in the Far East, based in Malaya, and to integrate Australian defense forces into British nuclear planning.[14] Mere months after Menzies secured this promise, however, it lost much of its luster. At the Bermuda conference of 1957, Britain agreed to integrate its nuclear forces into NATO in exchange for the prized atomic partnership with the Americans. Australia, though an American ally, was not a member of NATO and so was not covered by these arrangements.[15] Moreover, at Bermuda it was decided, again without consulting Australia, that British nuclear tests would be moved to Nevada. Suddenly, not merely Menzies' nuclear defense arrangement but even his carefully developed nuclear testing relationship with Britain seemed hollow. Reynolds calls the Bermuda accords Britain's "great betrayal" of Australia.[16]

Despite this "great betrayal," in subsequent years Menzies did not turn away from Britain or the US. Indeed, he bent over backwards not to put the British in an awkward position with their common American partner.[17] He showed this flexibility because he quite simply had no Plan B. The Menzies government could not imagine Australia's striking out on its own, especially in the nuclear weapons field. Thus, throughout the 1950s the Menzies government consistently rejected the notion of a sovereign nuclear weapons capacity. Australian Atomic Energy Commission (AAEC) chief Philip Baxter – an oppositional nationalist about whom more later – got nowhere in his efforts to promote the accumulation of a weapons-grade plutonium stockpile. His regular proposals, first for a power reactor and later for a research reactor, fell on deaf ears. And when the Australian government did contract for a research reactor from Britain in 1954, it was not the plutonium factory that Baxter desired.[18]

[14] Ibid., pp. 169–170.

[15] The comparison with the integration of NATO countries into America's nuclear strategy constantly irked Australian leaders. Indeed, one could argue that status as well as security considerations motivated Menzies' attempts to extract an explicit nuclear weapons transfer agreement from the "great and powerful friends." See ibid., p. 215.

[16] Ibid., p. 4.

[17] Menzies understood that the British top security priority was to gain access to American nuclear secrets, and considered that British access was contingent on strict British observance of the US McMahon Act and other early "non-proliferation" measures. The caution with which the Menzies government approached Britain on the nuclear weapons issue was due to its desire to avoid forcing Britain to choose between its American and its Australian links – for the Australians knew what choice it would make. This belief was greatly encouraged by the British, whose "concerns about risking US antipathy to the passing on of any US information about nuclear matters were extreme," according to the Royal Commission. *Royal Commission*, p. 442.

[18] Roy MacLeod, "The Atom Comes to Australia: Reflections on the Australian Nuclear Programme, 1953 and 1993," *History and Technology*, Vol. 11 (1994), pp. 299–315.

Lacking a Plan B, Menzies spent the next six years making approaches to the British, and to a lesser extent the Americans, proposing Australian participation in free world nuclear defenses.[19] The most important approach came in 1961. At that time, British Prime Minister Harold Macmillan was pursuing a global nuclear test ban, and he asked Australia for its support. As Jim Walsh has documented, Menzies reacted by arming himself with a June 13 Cabinet decision authorizing him to give that support *on condition* that Australia receive "recognition now of the United Kingdom's obligation to provide Australia, if ever necessary, with a nuclear capability."[20] Although the wording of the Cabinet decision is somewhat ambiguous, what Menzies seems to have envisioned was an eventual transfer of British weapons into Australian hands in the context of a major regional or world conflict. The 1961 Menzies request, stark as it was, was still in the realm of nuclear guarantees, not in the realm of nuclear proliferation.

In his account of the 1958–61 period, Walsh suggests that bureaucratic forces pushed Menzies – against his better judgment – to make increasingly forward approaches to the British. But Walsh's bureaucratic momentum explanation does not explain why, in his words, "from September 1961 until after the Chinese nuclear test in 1964, it appears that the Australian government took no additional steps to acquire access to nuclear weapons."[21] There was even a prime opportunity to seek such access: when the British asked Australia to sign the Partial Test Ban Treaty (PTBT) of 1963. The PTBT imposed real constraints, and some states – such as de Gaulle's France and nationalist Argentina – were to refuse to join it. Yet Australia, in spite of having received none of the assurances requested in 1961, asked for nothing in return for its 1963 treaty accession.[22]

In fact, the explanation for the rise and fall of Australian interest in nailing down a "key to the cupboard" arrangement with the British lies not in bureaucratic pressures, but in changing high-level perceptions of the imminence of the Chinese nuclear threat. Before 1960, Australians saw the Chinese nuclear threat as a dangerous, but middle- to long-term

---

[19] On approaches to the Americans, see Reynolds, *Australia's Bid for the Atomic Bomb*, pp. 206–207.

[20] Cabinet Minute, Decision No. 1383 marked "Secret," June 13, 1961, "Nuclear Tests Conference: Control Posts in Australia," Series A5818/2, National Archives of Australia. Document provided by Jim Walsh.

[21] Walsh, "Surprise Down Under."

[22] Various documents including "Australian Accession to Nuclear Test Ban Treaty 1963," in folder "Correspondence between Menzies and Macmillan between July and November 1963," Series A1209/80, Item 1963/6525, National Archives of Australia. Documents provided by Jim Walsh.

possibility; hence Menzies' lackadaisical approaches to the British on the subject of nuclear transfer.[23] In 1960, by contrast, the Australian chiefs of staff for the first time requested a report on Chinese nuclear and missile development, "because of the reported growth of the military strength of China and the aggressive attitude of the Chinese government."[24] The document stated that China might be capable of "quantity production" of nuclear weapons by 1965 and could conceivably conduct a test by 1961, although it likely would not meet such an ambitious schedule. A second, much more alarming report on the subject was completed on June 6, 1961. In this report, the chiefs of staff concluded that China was likely to have a significant nuclear stockpile *at least* by 1965 – by 1962 if aided by the USSR – and could well explode a device by the end of the year.[25] Only one week after the completion of the report, on June 13, Cabinet endorsed Menzies' recommendation to seek, in exchange for Australia's support for the general test ban, firm assurances for the eventual transfer of British nuclear weapons. The link between fear of China and the 1961 Menzies approach to Macmillan therefore appears to have been quite direct.

But China did not explode a bomb at the end of 1961, and the Australians became less sure that it was about to do so. While the 1962 report on China's nuclear ambitions still sounded the alarm that the Chinese could soon become a nuclear power, for the first time the Sino-Soviet split was recognized and was considered to be a significant factor in slowing Chinese progress toward the bomb.[26] And while the chiefs had backed down somewhat from their earlier stance, the officials at the Prime Minister's Department took an even more sanguine view: "The conclusion to be

[23] "Meeting Between Mr. Macmillan and Mr. Menzies at Parliament House, Canberra on 29th January, 1958," marked "Supplementary Record for strictly limited circulation, Nuclear Weapons (top secret)," Series A7942/1, National Archives of Australia. Document provided by Jim Walsh.

[24] "Nuclear weapons and guided missiles in Communist China up to the end of 1965," Joint Intelligence Committee Report JIC (60) 28, and "Minute by Chiefs of Staff Committee at Meeting Held on Wednesday, 6th July 1960," Chiefs of Staff Meeting Agendum 41/1960, July 5, 1960, Series A7941/2, Item N12, National Archives of Australia. There had been previous reports on "Progress in the development of nuclear weapons and guided weapons in the Sino-Soviet bloc," e.g., Joint Intelligence Committee Report JIC (59) 4, but the 1960 report was the first to focus on China's independent potential.

[25] "The development or acquisition of nuclear weapons and means of delivery by Communist China up to the end of 1966," Joint Intelligence Committee Report JIC (61) 28, in Chiefs of Staff Committee Agendum No. 20/1961, June 6, 1961, Series A7941/2, Item N12, National Archives of Australia.

[26] "Advanced Weapon Development in Communist China," Joint Intelligence Committee Report JIC (62) 28, May 1962, Series A1209/134, Item 1961/845, National Archives of Australia.

reached is that you require a hell of a lot of extremely well trained scientific manpower to do the job. If China has not the Soviet Union's sympathetic support in achieving their own nuclear capability then China has quite a task ahead of her."[27] The chiefs' assessment in 1963 represented yet another step down; they reported that the Chinese were unlikely to test a device before 1964, and they even stressed, "It is unlikely that China will acquire any militarily significant advanced weapons capability, either nuclear or conventional during the period under review [1963- 68]."[28] In other words, when the Partial Test Ban Treaty came up for signature in 1963, the dominant perception in Australia was that the nuclear threat from China had receded somewhat. Thus, the Australians did not push for explicit British guarantees in 1963. A year later, they were to regret this missed opportunity when China actually did explode its first nuclear bomb.

Still no Plan B: 1964–67

From various perspectives, the mid-1960s should have represented a crucial turning point for Australian nuclear policies. From a balance of threat perspective, Australia was a country whose leadership had already demonstrated its tremendous fear of the Communists and had controlled its fear through the establishment of tight security and nuclear relation- ships, especially with the UK. Then, in 1964, the Chinese threat became much more palpable with its entry into the nuclear club, while in 1965 it became evident that Britain would be drastically reducing or elim- inating its military commitments east of Suez.[29] Given such wrench- ing changes, Australia might be expected at least to have made signifi- cant moves toward an independent nuclear weapons capacity during this period. Yet it did not.

A bureaucratic politics perspective would also expect a major nuclear weapons push from Australia in this period. The Liberal governments had long encouraged the Australian military to integrate its planning into that of the UK and the broader Free World. They had clearly indicated that Australian forces would be equipped with British or American nuclear weapons in the event of war, and they had made major investments in

---

[27] Note from A. T. Griffith to Mr. Bunting (both of the Prime Minister's Department), 16 May 1962, Series A1209/134, Item 1961/845, National Archives of Australia.

[28] "Communist China: Advanced Weapons Systems," Joint Intelligence Committee Report JIC (63) 28, July 1963, Series A1945/39, Item 100/2/21, National Archives of Australia.

[29] Millar, *Australia in Peace and War*, p. 184. Britain had already wound up its last nuclear research efforts in Australia in 1963.

nuclear-capable bombers.[30] Yet by the mid-1960s, it was becoming evident that the "great and powerful friends" were reticent about letting the Australians participate actively in their own nuclear defense. At the same time, the governments had also promised to the Australian Atomic Energy Commission (AAEC) a glorious role in the British nuclear testing program, but the program had moved to Nevada. These investments in terms of psychological and material resources should have created – and in fact did create – significant bureaucratic pressures for Australia to go it alone in the nuclear game. But these pressures, even coming on top of the objective shift in Australia's security position, did not produce a significant nuclear weapons effort in the mid-1960s.

The paltry Australian actions on the prospect of an indigenous bomb capacity during this period were as follows. In 1965, the government briefly considered the prospect of developing "an independent nuclear capability," but then it simply postponed taking any action.[31] The following year the government, now led by Menzies *protégé* Harold Holt, was reticent to accept a US request to allow International Atomic Energy Agency (IAEA) inspections of the AAEC's nuclear facilities until it determined that such inspections would not preclude an eventual nuclear weapons program.[32] But it had earlier flatly rejected a new AAEC proposal for a nuclear power plant with weapons potential.[33]

The "failure" of mid-1960s Australia to react to the Chinese test with an indigenous nuclear weapons program is a surprise from balance of threat or bureaucratic politics perspectives, but it is hardly surprising from the theoretical point of view advanced in this book. The issue of how to deal with the Chinese nuclear threat had already been thoroughly debated, and the idea of responding to it with an "Aussie bomb" had been rejected. This rejection was fundamentally the result of the dominant oppositional subaltern NIC in Canberra, which viewed a sovereign Australian nuclear weapons effort as both unrealistic and dangerous. As a 1968 note to the minister of external affairs bluntly stated:

[30] Walsh describes this history well. First there was the British Canberra in the late 1950s, then the British TSR-2 that never proved functional, then a major contract for US F-111s in 1963 that was also a somewhat unhappy episode. Walsh, "Surprise Down Under."

[31] "Minute of the Defence Committee at a Meeting on 28 October, 1965," Agendum No. 59/1965, Series A2031/14, Item 73/1965. And "Report on Overseas Visit by Defence Scientific Adviser," Series A5799/20, Item 59/1965, National Archives of Australia.

[32] Walsh, "Surprise Down Under."

[33] Don Greenless, "Options Stay Open on Nuclear Arsenal," *The Australian*, January 1, 1997, cited in Walsh, "Surprise Down Under," p. 18. Baxter had a long and continuing interest in the production of weapons-grade plutonium, as is made explicit by the AAEC Minute Paper on "Dual Purpose Magnox Reactors," marked "Confidential," July 9, 1964, Philip Baxter Papers (CN 1053) Box 15, University of New South Wales archives.

It is not possible for Australia to provide for its own security against nuclear attack. To do this it would not be sufficient to acquire nuclear weapons. It would be necessary also to have a delivery system with inter-continental range. Moreover for Australia to have a plausible deterrent it would need to be able to strike back powerfully after it had been subject to an initial nuclear attack. Apart from the economic cost which any country faces in developing this second strike capability, Australia is faced with the enormous disadvantages of its geographical position, the distance at which it would have to strike at any probable enemy, and the vulnerability of its cities and industrial complexes.[34]

In this analysis, as in so many other documents, we see the perceptual effects of an oppositional subaltern NIC. Why would Australia's geographical isolation be considered only to reduce Australian ability to reply to a nuclear attack, and not to reduce the threat of such an attack? In fact, Australia was in the process of contracting for US nuclear-capable F-111 aircraft, and it already had nuclear-capable Canberra aircraft based in the Malay peninsula. So China was much more in the range of Australian forces than vice versa, yet nonetheless the dominant viewpoint in Canberra was that Australia could not deter China.

The Australian leadership may not have reacted to its changed environment with a nuclear weapons program, but it did react. Lacking a Plan B, it continued to work on Plan A: attempting to bind Australia's "great and powerful friends" to the defense of Australia. Given the UK's retreat from east of Suez, the Menzies and Holt governments' efforts now focused more on the US umbrella. They made two important initiatives to strengthen the Australia–US tie in the mid-1960s.

First, there was a series of decisions beginning in April 1965 to send combat troops to fight alongside the Americans in Vietnam. In his official history of Australia's involvement in Southeast Asia, Peter Edwards writes:

The Government's Vietnam commitment was the product of two arguments. The first, commonly called the domino theory, rested on the assumptions that Asian communism was spreading, that it threatened Australian security, and that it would be expedient to meet the threat as early as possible and as far away as possible. The second theory, sometimes known as the insurance policy, assumed that the United States had nailed its colors to the mast in Vietnam and that Australia needed to support its great and powerful friend there to ensure that that friend would support it if it were ever threatened with attack.[35]

---

[34] Note on "Nonproliferation of Nuclear Weapons," M. R. Booker to the minister (External Affairs), March 12, 1968, archives of the Department of Foreign Affairs and Trade (DFAT).

[35] Peter Edwards, *A Nation at War: Australian Politics, Society and Diplomacy during the Vietnam War 1965–1975* (St. Leonards, NSW: Allen and Unwin in Association with the Australian War Memorial, 1997), p. 185.

The "domino theory" and the "insurance policy" were the natural out-growths of the still-dominant oppositional subaltern NIC *vis-à-vis* the Communists. In the case of the Vietnam War, these policies came at a high cost in Australian lives.

No less significant than the Vietnam commitment was the decision to host important elements of the US global nuclear defense system in Australia.[36] The Holt government agreed to the construction of "joint defense facilities" with the US on Australia's North West Cape, in Pine Gap near Alice Springs, and at Nurrungar near the British test site at Woomera.[37] The North West Cape facility was to serve as one of the two lynchpins of the US worldwide submarine communication system, while Pine Gap and Nurrungar were built as part of US satellite surveillance and early-warning systems. The establishment of these facilities likely gave Australia a place, and perhaps a significant one, on the target list for Soviet attack in the event of World War III.[38] Moreover, the new, physical US presence restricted Australia's freedom of action in foreign affairs.[39] The Holt government accepted this relatively high cost as the price of maintaining US interest in the country's survival, but it remained unsatisfied with the credibility of extended deterrence and continued to try to find ways to bind the US even more closely to the defense of Australia.

In sum, from 1964 to 1967 the Australian government's response to some major tremors in its security environment was entirely in keeping with its traditional policies. In 1967 as in 1957, there was still no Plan B. But in 1968, with a new, oppositional nationalist prime minister in power, Plan B suddenly surfaced.

A new kind of Liberal: Gorton's quest for the bomb, 1968–71

At the end of 1967, when Harold Holt died in a swimming accident, the Liberals' political fortunes were already in decline. Holt's strategy of going "all the way with LBJ" in Vietnam had proven increasingly divisive and unpopular at home.[40] Facing this crisis in popularity, the parliamentary

---

[36] For more information, see Desmond Ball, *A Suitable Piece of Real Estate: American Instal-lations in Australia* (Sydney: Hale and Iremonger, 1980).

[37] Actually the facilities were "joint" in name only, and the Australian side had only the barest information of the uses to which they were being put. For instance, during the 1973 Yom Kippur War, the three nuclear-related facilities were put on full alert without informing the Australians. Ibid., p. 16.

[38] Desmond Ball and R. H. Mathams, "The Nuclear Threat to Australia," in Michael Denborough, *Australia and Nuclear War* (Fyshwick, Australian Capital Territory: Croom Helm Australia, 1983), pp. 38–54.

[39] Ball, *A Suitable Piece of Real Estate*, p. 147.

[40] See Edwards, *A Nation at War*, esp. ch. 8.

Liberals elected a relative outsider, Senator John Gorton, to the post of prime minister. Gorton's NIC, as argued in Chapter 3, differed from that of his Liberal predecessors in that he combined a traditional Liberal oppositional mentality toward the Communists with strong Australian nationalist tendencies. Gorton's selection for the top job did not represent a mass conversion in the Liberal Party to Gorton's standpoint, which was in any case hardly a coherent doctrine. But it did reflect the desire of a party rapidly losing popularity for "something new."[41] Thus began what the journalist Alan Reid aptly termed the "Gorton experiment."[42]

Not surprisingly, given his oppositional nationalism, Gorton had long been at the extreme end of the Australian debate on nuclear weapons. As early as 1957 Gorton had made clear his reluctance to rely solely on Australia's "great and powerful friends" for protection:

I should hope that we would use our defense funds and endeavor to secure for this country some measure of atomic or hydrogen defense. I realize that a potential attacker of this country might be deterred by the possession of hydrogen bombs by the United States of America or Great Britain, but I think that we should be trusting very much indeed to the help that those great countries could give if we put our faith solely in a deterrent held by them.[43]

In office, Gorton consulted closely with the Liberal parliamentarian William Wentworth, a fanatical anti-Communist and unapologetic advocate for all things nuclear, who even developed a proposal that Australia build nuclear submarines to deliver perishables – exotic flowers, berries, oysters, and premium meats – rapidly to northern cities.[44] Gorton not surprisingly also showed far more interest than his predecessors in Australian Atomic Energy Commission (AAEC) chairman Philip Baxter's pleadings for a major atomic research and power program with clear defense implications.[45] But it was the issue of the Non-Proliferation Treaty (NPT) that really brought the nuclear question to the fore.

[41] Alan Reid, *The Gorton Experiment* (Sydney: Shakespeare Head Press, 1971), p. 27.
[42] Ibid.
[43] Speech of John G. Gorton, May 8, 1957, *Parliamentary Debates (Hansard)*, Senate, Session 1957, Second Session of the 22nd Parliament (Canberra: Government of the Commonwealth of Australia, 1957), p. 608.
[44] William Wentworth, minister for social services, letter to Philip Baxter, March 3, 1971, in Philip Baxter Papers, box 74, Archives of the University of New South Wales.
[45] It would be easy to label Baxter's pleadings as nothing more than the reflection of the AAEC's bureaucratic interest. But this is a simplistic reading, as a short biographical look at the man demonstrates. Baxter's participation in the Manhattan Project convinced him that nuclear energy in its various applications was the key to the next century. After the war, he held a position of significant responsibility and could be sure of further rapid advancement at Imperial Chemical Industries, Ltd., but he was deeply disappointed when the company withdrew from the production of nuclear energy. For Baxter, this was the last straw that convinced him that "old" Europe was tired and incapable of defending itself; only a "new" nation like Australia could potentially save European traditions, values, and genetics. As Baxter would later tell the Institution of Engineers in

The fight over the NPT

Soon after taking office, the Gorton government was faced with the question of how to deal with the recently negotiated NPT. The main traditional organs of Australian foreign and defense policy quickly recommended adhesion. In their view, Australia quite simply had no capacity to build a credible independent deterrent, and it also had an interest in lending its political support to this important objective of the American ally on whom the country relied for its nuclear protection.[46] But Gorton and his allies were not happy with that answer, so they fought for a different one.

The March 21, 1968 meeting of the Defence Committee, the highest bureaucratic organ for foreign and security policymaking, brought together representatives of External Affairs, Defence, the military, Treasury, the Prime Minister's Office, the Cabinet Office, and – unusual for this group – the Atomic Energy Commission.[47] This meeting set the tone for a raging internal battle that was destined to last for several years. The battle was between oppositional subaltern supporters of joining the NPT, and oppositional nationalist Gorton allies who rejected the NPT and promoted an independent Australian deterrent. That the division was between oppositional subalterns and oppositional nationalists is reflected in the fact that the debate turned less on the level of

Perth, the extensive training of engineers and technologists in Australia was "a fitting subject for a Crusade, the success of which will be measured by whether Australia is still a white and Christian country in the year 2,000 AD." It almost goes without saying that very quickly upon arriving in Australia, Baxter "discovered" the white race's basic enemy: Asian Communism. In the play Baxter wrote toward the end of his life, entitled *The Day the Sun Rose in the West*, Australia stands alone against the forces of the continent-wide South East Asian People's Republic, which are under the control of a scientific/engineering elite that wants, in Baxter's words, "to make the whole invasion [of Australia] a gigantic experiment in producing a new and better race." So it was much more than the desire for a bigger budget that explains Baxter's drive for a nuclear Australia: it was oppositional nationalism. Philip Gissing, "Sir Philip Baxter, Engineer: The Fabric of a Liberal-National Country Style of Thought," Ph.D. dissertation, University of New South Wales, March 1998. See also S. J. Angyal, "Sir Philip Baxter 1905–1989," *Historical Records of Australian Science*, Vol. 8, No. 3, esp. pp. 184–185.

[46] Report of the Joint Planning Committee, "An Independent Australian Nuclear Capability – Strategic Considerations," Annex to JPC Report No. 8/1968, February 2, 1968, Department of Defence File No. 67/1017, Archives of the Department of Foreign Affairs and Trade. Thanks to Jim Walsh for this document.

[47] Note on "Non-proliferation Treaty" from James Plimsoll to the minister (External Affairs), March 21, 1968, Archives of the Department of Foreign Affairs and Trade. Thanks to Jim Walsh for first unearthing this document. The fact that the AAEC was present at this high level demonstrates its institutional importance and independence. Though theoretically responsible to a minister, the Commission members held seven-year terms and could send proposals directly to Cabinet. See Clarence Hardy, *Atomic Rise and Fall: The Australian Atomic Energy Commission 1953–1987* (Peakhurst: Glen Haven Publishing, 1999), pp. 27–29.

the nuclear threat to Australia – both sides agreed that it was high – and more on whether Australia should continue to do everything in its power to keep US affection, or instead start defending itself. Most clearly taking the traditionalist position was James Plimsoll, the top civil servant at External Affairs, who argued that since a credible Australian nuclear deterrent was not on the cards, Australia's lifeline was the US nuclear deterrent. Therefore, Plimsoll argued, it would be highly unwise for Australia to start separating itself from the US diplomatically. The military and Treasury representatives, as well as the secretary of the Cabinet Office, generally seconded this point of view.[48] The two most vocal figures on the other side were the secretary of the Prime Minister's Department, C. L. S. Hewitt, and Philip Baxter, the chairman of the AAEC. Baxter and Hewitt argued that Australia actually could build a credible deterrent if it wanted to, with Baxter suggesting that the issue of delivery systems was a red herring: if necessary, he stated, "You could sneak them [nuclear bombs] into enemy cities."[49] Baxter and Hewitt also took a nationalist line on nuclear safeguards, with Hewitt rejecting "the injection of foreigners in our life as represented by inspectors of various activities at various levels."[50] The representative from the Ministry of Defence, Sir Henry Bland, also proved surprisingly hostile to the NPT, a position that was not in accord with the one expressed by his own ministry's report on the treaty one month before. Bland told the Committee:

Too many assumptions were being made that we would not be liked by the United States if we did not go along with the Treaty, and that it would have implications for ANZUS. He said this was insulting to Australia. We could not be expected to go along with the United States on everything.[51]

Plimsoll was obviously very concerned about a possible defection by Defence to the pro-bomb camp. He wrote Foreign Minister Paul Hasluck, also a traditionalist and a Gorton rival, that he heard a "disturbing tone from Bland that we ought to stand up to the Americans more."[52]

The battle lines were thus drawn. The battle was passionate and divisive within the government. Gorton was particularly dismissive of External Affairs' pro-NPT Cabinet submissions, scribbling "gobbly gook" and "this is just absolute blather while China is out of the treaty" in the margins.[53] A potential compromise slowly emerged: signature without ratification. Although such a compromise would represent a considerable success for the embattled Gorton, it was not to his liking. Gorton frankly told the British high commissioner that:

---

[48] "Note on the Non-proliferation Treaty." The military simply ignored the indigenous capability option and suggested strengthening the US guarantee to Australia.
[49] Ibid.   [50] Ibid.   [51] Ibid.   [52] Ibid.
[53] "PM's Poisoned Pen Spells the End," *Sydney Morning Herald*, January 1, 2001.

Australia was not going to sign the NPT or, if it did so, that it was not going to ratify it. [Gorton] personally thought it was stupid to sign a treaty with the intention of not ratifying it, and therefore his own preference would be for not signing . . . He expected that both governments [US and UK] would try to "twist his arm off" to get him to sign and ratify. If that pressure became too much the Australian government would resent it, and in any case would not change their decision.[54]

Gorton finally did accept the compromise of signature without ratification in February 1970. However distasteful he found the compromise, the fact is that he had succeeded in overturning the considered opinion of the bulk of the state establishment, while preserving his cherished nuclear weapons option.

Gorton and his team were against the NPT, and they were not averse to causing some diplomatic friction with Australia's "great and powerful friends" if this were the price to be paid for staying outside the new treaty. But they were also not averse to the alliance or to the US nuclear guarantee. Gorton actually tried to take a page from Menzies' playbook by inviting the US to engage in a "peaceful nuclear explosion" for engineering purposes as part of the American "Project Plowshare." In 1968, the two countries went so far as to undertake a joint feasibility study for using a nuclear explosion to create a harbor at Cape Keraudren in Northwest Australia. The Australians were ready to move forward, but the American mining company that desired the harbor backed out, and the idea fizzled out.[55] Here Gorton's thinking was clearly to make Australia useful to the American nuclear program, and to host an explosion that, "peaceful" or not, would serve as a warning to the Communists. Gorton did not see such a collaboration as a substitute for an Australian bomb; in this instance as in several others, he simply demonstrated his faith that the more deterrence, the better. As Hewitt wrote to Gorton during the NPT debate, the US guarantee was welcome but it simply could not be counted on in the crunch: "China will not be a signatory. Will the Americans come to our aid, under ANZUS, with nuclear weapons in the event of a threat to Australia by Chinese nuclear weaponry? This year; next year; in twenty-four years from now? Will they???"[56]

Interestingly, the Nixon administration actually did not actively discourage this kind of thinking. Despite Gorton's expectations, it did

---

[54] Letter marked "secret and personal" from high commissioner to Canberra, Charles Johnston, to Sir Edward Peck, Foreign Office, August 2, 1968. Attached to note marked "Secret" on "Australia and the NPT" from R. C. Hope-Jones to Lord Hood (August 23, 1968), FCO 10/124, Public Record Office, Kew, United Kingdom.

[55] Hardy, *Atomic Rise and Fall*, p. 80.

[56] Note on "The Nuclear Treaty" marked "Top Secret," C. L. Hewitt to the prime minister, April 28, 1968, Series A5619, Item C48, Part 1, National Archives of Australia.

not press Australia hard to sign the NPT.[57] Nixon took this hands-off approach to the NPT debate in Australia despite entreaties by Gorton's own External Affairs minister, William McMahon – behind Gorton's back – that he get involved.[58] Nixon's quiescence reflected the relatively low priority that his administration accorded to the NPT. Indeed, Australians took his Guam Doctrine to imply that the US might actually *favor* the acquisition of the bomb by its closest allies.[59] Even more directly, in a secret conversation in Jakarta in May, 1968, the American ambassador there suggested to his Australian counterpart that an Australian bomb could prove helpful in reassuring Suharto's Indonesia against the Communist threat.[60] These signals were encouraging to Gorton and the bomb lobby, though negative pressures probably also would have heightened their motivation to seek the bomb.

Moves toward nuclear weapons: the power reactor and uranium enrichment

As has already been made clear, the oppositional nationalist Gorton was not merely interested in staying out of the NPT; he wanted to set an actual Australian bomb program in motion. He understood that the key to such a program was to accumulate either plutonium or enriched uranium – or both. He pursued both.

In 1969, Gorton gave Baxter's AAEC what all previous prime ministers had denied it: the green light for the AAEC to contract for a large nuclear power reactor. The reactor was to be 500 MW in size and located at Jervis Bay in New South Wales.[61] Because of Gorton's shaky political position, the reactor was ostensibly designated for "civilian" purposes, but a close examination of the policymaking process clearly reveals his true motivation. For instance, a crucial determinant of utility for military purposes would be the type of reactor selected. Gorton took the "economic nationalist" position of requiring "indigenous fuel," meaning

---

[57] Briefing Book for meeting between president and Prime Minister John Gorton, National Security Files, Richard M. Nixon Presidential Materials, National Archives, College Park, Maryland.

[58] Note marked "Secret" from American Embassy, Canberra, to secretary of state, January 30, 1970; Folder "Defense Australia-US 1/1/70," Box 1688, State Department Subject-Numeric Files 1970–1973, Record Group 59, US National Archives, College Park, Maryland.

[59] Ian Bellany, *Australia in the Nuclear Age: National Defense and National Development* (Sydney: Sydney University Press, 1972).

[60] Telegram on "Indonesia and Nuclear Weapons," marked "Guard – Secret" from Australian Embassy, Djakarta, to the Department of External Affairs, May 17, 1968. Available online from National Archives of Australia RecordSearch, barcode 4171003.

[61] Cawte, *Atomic Australia*, p. 128.

that the reactor should either run on natural uranium or that the bid should include provision of uranium enrichment technology.[62] As argued in Chapter 2, this stance alone need not imply an ambition to build weapons, but Gorton's allies were actually rather frank about their true motivation. Baxter, in particular, made several statements indicating the military intent lurking behind the government's "economic nationalist" stance.[63] The military subtext was also present in Minister for National Development David Fairbairn's 1969 internal report recommending construction of the reactor, which explicitly stressed the "important long term defense implications" of the project.[64] As for the prime minister himself, after long denying any connection between the Jervis Bay project and nuclear weapons, Gorton finally admitted one when confronted with newly released archival documents at the beginning of 1999. He told the *Sydney Morning Herald*, "We were interested in this thing because it could provide electricity to everybody and it could, if you decided later on, could make an atomic bomb."[65] This "later on" decision was something Gorton had clearly already made in his own mind but had not felt powerful enough to impose on the entrenched traditionalist forces in his government and in the state.

Indeed, Gorton's attempt to sneak a nuclear weapons program into existence instead of making his purposes explicit came back to haunt him. An irony of the Jervis Bay story is that the reactor that was eventually selected could not "make an atomic bomb." Despite Gorton, Baxter, and their allies' not-so-secret motives, the scientists and engineers of the AAEC – following the call for tender to the letter – studied bids from a technical and economic but not from a military perspective. Baxter tried to promote his military agenda by being particularly strict in his interpretation of the "indigenous fuel" criterion.[66] He fought mightily on

[62] Keith Alder, *Australia's Uranium Opportunities: How Her Scientists and Engineers Tried to Bring Her into the Nuclear Age but Were Stymied by Politics* (Sydney: Pauline Alder, 1996), p. 41. This is a privately published essay by one of the Australian Atomic Energy Commission's former leading lights.

[63] Though his game plan was to focus on the economic implications of "entering the nuclear age," Baxter sometimes slipped into public declarations of military intent. In August 1969 he told the press, "The growth of this industry and the expertise and the facilities which it will create will provide a basis from which an Australian government, at any future date, feeling that nuclear weapons were essential to provide this nation's security, could move with a minimum of delay to provide such means of defense." Cited in Cawte, *Atomic Australia*, p. 127.

[64] "Submission by the minister for national development on the Establishment of a Wholly Commonwealth-Owned Nuclear Power Station," marked "Confidential for Cabinet," Submission 759, August 1969, series A5868, 1969 Cabinet papers, available online from National Archives of Australia.

[65] Pilita Clark, "PM's Story: Very much alive . . . and unfazed," *Sydney Morning Herald*, January 1, 1999.

[66] Note marked "Confidential" on "Atomic Energy: US Company Interest in Bidding on Jervis Bay Nuclear Power Station, Australia," from US Embassy, Canberra to

these grounds for the Canadian offering, a "Candu" natural uranium-heavy water reactor that would clearly have been the most useful for a nuclear weapons program. But the reactor choice was not his to make; it required the approval of the entire Atomic Energy Commission, of which Baxter was only the chairman; other members of the Commission found Baxter's strict interpretation of the "indigenous fuel" criterion untenable. In the end, the assessment by the AAEC technical team strongly recommended a British reactor offering over Baxter's preferred Candu. As for the British reactor's military potential, according to AAEC scientist Keith Alder, who was deeply involved in the technical assessment process, "No one in their right mind would try to make plutonium in that system."[67] As AAEC Executive Commissioner Maurice Timbs wrote to Baxter, in words dripping with irony, the top-to-bottom study of "technical and economic merit" had found Candu sorely lacking – but "if, *for other reasons* [than "technical and economic merit"], the government decides to negotiate for a Candu system, the Commission could have no quarrel with such a decision."[68] In other words, Timbs was saying, if your man Gorton had had the guts to come out and fight for what he really wanted, maybe we would have given him satisfaction; but since he did not, we will not. Defeated, Baxter accepted their judgment.[69] This episode shows the fallacy of the simple bureaucratic politics hypothesis that atomic bureaucracies push for the bomb.

In the end, the Jervis Bay reactor was never built at all. Before Gorton could muscle the program through Cabinet, he fell from office in 1971. His successor, William McMahon, made haste to cancel a project that he later stated was unreasonable from the point of view of economic cost and incompatible with Australia's NPT signature (the latter reason only makes sense if, as I have argued, the top decisionmakers had been viewing the reactor as part of a nuclear weapons program).[70] This stance was in keeping with McMahon's active role in soliciting American pressure on Gorton to sign the NPT in 1970, as previously noted. Thus the plutonium route to the bomb had been blocked.

Department of State, February 13, 1970, folder "Atomic Energy – Australia," Box 2867 "Science," State Department Subject-Numeric Files 1970–1973, Record Group 59, US National Archives, College Park, Maryland.

[67] Interview with Keith Alder, Australian atomic scientist (former general manager, Australian Atomic Energy Commission), Warrawee, New South Wales, October 21, 1998.
[68] Maurice Timbs, "Confidential Minute Paper re: Jervis Bay Nuclear Power Station, A.A.E.C. Commission Decision No. 3561," November 16, 1970, Philip Baxter papers (CN 1053/5), University of New South Wales archives. Italics added.
[69] Alder, *Australia's Uranium Opportunities*, p. 49, reinforced by interview with Alder.
[70] McMahon, cited in Ann Mozley Moyal, "The Australian Atomic Energy Commission: A Case Study in Australian Science and Government," *Search*, Vol. 6, No. 9 (September 1975), pp. 365–384.

Even before the cancellation of the Jervis Bay project, however, Baxter also began militating for an Australian uranium enrichment plant – another potential means of acquiring the fissile material necessary to build the bomb. Again hampered by Gorton's inability to make his bomb desires formal government policy, Baxter had to make his case on economic grounds. The economic case suddenly became solid when massive deposits of uranium in Australia's Northern Territory were discovered in 1970. It made sense to try to capture the economic "value-added" from these reserves with indigenous enrichment.[71] Australia had been devoting some resources to the technology of enrichment since 1965, but given the difficulty of the process even Baxter accepted that for a major plant they would need a big partner. Gorton gave Baxter the authority to seek such a partner. After initial discussions with the British and Americans, the Australians found a willing partner in France.[72]

The Australian–French nuclear relationship was first formalized in a cooperation agreement signed in 1969. The main potential area of cooperation was in enrichment technology: the French had it and were willing to sell it, and on the Australian side, at least the AAEC was very excited about buying it. The French clearly understood that the Australians' interest in enrichment was at least partially driven by its potential military utility. Indeed, their first relatively significant sale to the Australians, in 1971, was of a "critical facility" for the measurement of fast neutrons – something that is quite useful for research on the physical processes of nuclear explosions and for little else. But since the French did not find the prospect of an Australian bomb program troubling and indeed were not even party to the NPT, they felt no qualms about assisting the Australians' nuclear ambitions.[73] Between July 1971 and February 1972 an Australian technical team made at least three visits to the French uranium enrichment plant at Pierrelatte, which provided fissile material for military purposes.[74] Baxter's contemporaneous and later handwritten notes demonstrate his great interest not only in how much 95 percent enriched uranium such a plant could produce per year, but also – explicitly – in

---

[71] Clarence Hardy, *Enriching Experiences: Uranium Enrichment in Australia 1963–1996* (Peakhurst, NSW: Glen Haven, 1996), p. 37.

[72] Alder, *Australia's Uranium Opportunities*, pp. 52–57.

[73] Interview with Bertrand Goldschmidt, who had been the French Commissariat à l'Energie Atomique's director of international relations, Paris, September 29, 1998. Keith Alder denied that the AAEC wanted the critical facility for the reasons Goldschmidt presumed, and he remarked that in any case the machine remained a "white elephant" on the AAEC's Lucas Heights campus because the fissile material was never supplied. Interview with Alder.

[74] W. J. K. Wright, "Report on Visit to CEA, Pierrelatte on 18th February, 1972," Confidential AAEC report, March 1972, Philip Baxter papers (CN 1053/11), Archives of the University of New South Wales.

how many nuclear bombs could thus be made.[75] In November 1972, the AAEC team returned to Paris for final completion of the feasibility study for the plant. But, in December, the Australian Labor Party came to power for the first time in a generation, and the project soon ran afoul of Labor's campaign against French nuclear testing in the South Pacific (to be discussed below).[76]

In sum, the oppositional nationalist John Gorton, during his stint in power from 1968 to 1971, tried to launch an Australian nuclear weapons drive under the cover of an enhanced civilian nuclear program. After succeeding in blocking ratification of the NPT, he pursued both the plutonium and the uranium enrichment routes to the bomb. But Gorton and his allies in the bomb lobby failed to achieve their goal, in large measure because the prime minister never felt politically secure enough to take his fight for the bomb aboveboard. Parenthetically, Gorton was right about his shaky hold on power; he would eventually fall to an internal party revolt against his leadership in 1971.

Gorton tried mightily to jumpstart a nuclear weapons program while never daring to speak its name. The case of Gorton represents a partial success for the theory elaborated in Chapter 2. That Gorton avoided making a clear nuclear weapons decision is, however, a surprise for the theory, which expects oppositional nationalists to want to express their emotions by making such a decision. The Gorton episode suggests the need for further theoretical refinement, and in particular for a precise specification of just how solidly entrenched a top leader must feel before making a big decision that is likely to be unpopular among those who are needed to implement it.

The historical narrative has focused so far on the policy differences among Australian Liberals: oppositional subalterns versus oppositional nationalists. But there was a third position in the debate that was not yet represented in the corridors of power. The Australian Labor Party had been wandering in the political wilderness for over a quarter-century, but the wrenching Vietnam experience gave it the electoral opportunity for which it had been waiting. In 1972, E. Gough Whitlam and Labor swept into power and transformed the Australian nuclear debate for good.

Labor in power, 1972–75: fear no more

In December 1972, the Australian Labor Party (ALP) under Gough Whitlam came to power for the first time since 1949. The leaders of

---

[75] Handwritten notes, Philip Baxter Papers (CN 1053/11 and CN 1053/40), Archives of the University of New South Wales.
[76] Alder, *Australia's Uranium Opportunities*, p. 57.

the previous Labor governments of the 1940s had played a significant role in the formation of the United Nations, and Whitlam revived their cooperative internationalist spirit as a key element of Australian foreign policy. The twist Whitlam gave to this traditional Labor stance was to pay special attention to improving Australia's relationships within its "neighborhood": Asia. The Whitlam government's innovative Asian focus was a consequence of the searing experience of the Vietnam War, which had caused an evolution in the NIC embraced by ALP adherents.[77] In his 1966 book *Living with Asia*, the leader of the ALP left, Jim Cairns, wrote:

> There are many "ghosts" in Australia's attitude to Asia, and we ourselves have created them in the murky depths of our national consciousness which we have so little penetrated because for a century or more, standing behind Britain, we ignored Asia, and for twenty-five years since, standing behind the United States, we have only peeped out nervously at our mysterious neighbors. . . . If we believe in ghosts, no quantity or power of weapons and no locked doors can remove our fear, because ghosts are invulnerable to all weapons and can penetrate all locked doors. The only cure for fear of ghosts is to recognize that there are no ghosts.[78]

Cairns' portrayal of Australia as a country that needed to cast aside its historic, irrational fear of Asia – in a word, to cast aside its oppositional NIC – had a powerful impact on Whitlam. The NIC Whitlam carried into power remained sportsmanlike subaltern, like that of the previous Labor governments of the mid-1940s; but unlike his Labor predecessors, Whitlam focused above all on Australia's relations with its Asian neighbors. Whitlam's forceful presentation of this NIC eventually convinced not only his colleagues in the Labor Party, but also became mainstream thinking in Australian society as a whole.

After Whitlam came to power in 1972, he indeed proved determined to reject what he called "the old stultifying fears and animosities which have encumbered the national spirit for generations."[79] In line with his sportsmanlike NIC, the Whitlam government undid some of the basic traditional tenets of Australian foreign and security policy. On the diplomatic front, it extended recognition to Communist China, East Germany, and North Vietnam, among others.[80] On the security front, the government's

---

[77] The ALP had long been a stalwart supporter of the "White Australia" policy restricting immigration from Asia, and indeed it only removed that plank from its platform in 1965.

[78] J. F. Cairns, *Living with Asia* (Melbourne: Lansdowne Press, 1966), p. 5.

[79] Gough Whitlam, "Australian Foreign Policy," *Australian Foreign Affairs Record*, Vol. 44, No. 1 (January 1973), p. 32.

[80] Whitlam had visited China and had promised normalized relations before the Nixon visit. McMahon had attacked Whitlam as a Communist sympathizer for his trip; only days later, when the Nixon trip was announced, McMahon was eating humble pie. Millar, *Australia in Peace and War*, p. 218.

major defense policy address of December 1973 placed great emphasis on the idea that "Australia faces no foreseeable threat to its security for the next fifteen years," irritating the American diplomat who reported on the speech to Washington.[81] The defense minister's incantation of "no foreseeable threat" was a dramatic break from the past three decades of fear and "forward defense."

The Whitlam government indulged in some nationalist talk as well. An American diplomat wrote sneeringly, "[Whitlam] talks of asserting Australia's independence as if he had just broken shackles of slavery. He talks of a 'distinctive' Australian stance as if everything that had been done before was not distinctive."[82] But, in fact, as noted in Chapter 3, Whitlam's sometime taste for nationalist bombast was a relatively thin veneer covering basically subaltern policy inclinations *vis-à-vis* the bigger powers of Asia and the West. In particular, in contrast to the more nationalist elements in his party's base, Whitlam did not want or feel able to break with the US. He therefore never called the ANZUS treaty into question, to the great dismay of his party's left wing and even of plucky New Zealand.[83]

Whitlam's nuclear stances

In general, Whitlam's nuclear stances reflected those we would expect from a sportsmanlike subaltern NIC. First and foremost, the Whitlam government was strongly favorable to the NPT. As Shadow Labor Foreign Minister William Morrison told a US diplomat in 1971, the push in Australia to develop a nuclear weapons capability was "irresponsible . . . The ALP is opposed to this, and would in fact sign the NPT should it come to power."[84] As noted previously, the previous Liberal

---

[81] Airgram from US Embassy, Canberra, to Department of State, December 3, 1973, folder "Def Austl," box 1687, State Department Subject Numeric Files 1970–1973, Record Group 59, US National Archives, College Park, Maryland.

[82] The diplomat then admitted, "Perhaps this is partly natural . . . . During this long period of the 50s and 60s, we in the US, like many others, assumed that Australia's unfailing support of us meant that Australia had seriously considered the same questions and had independently come to the same conclusions. We were wrong." Memo from Norman B. Hannah, consul general, Sydney to the ambassador, December 17, 1973, Box 2107, State Department Subject-Numeric Files 1970–1973, Record Group 59, US National Archives, College Park, Maryland.

[83] Richard P. Broinowski, *Fact or Fission? The Truth about Australia's Nuclear Ambitions* (Melbourne: Scribe Publications, 2003).

[84] "Memo of Conversation" between William L. Morrison, shadow foreign minister (ALP) and Winthrop G. Brown, deputy assistant secretary of state for E. Asian and Pacific Affairs, May 25, 1971, folder "Pol-Austl 5/21/71," box 2105, State Department Subject-Numeric Files 1970–1973, Record Group 59, US National Archives, College Park, Maryland.

prime minister, William McMahon, was also in favor of NPT ratification, but the oppositional nationalists in his party had blocked him from doing so.[85] Once Labor came to power, NPT ratification occurred swiftly.

Whitlam's effort to collar the bomb lobby also got personal. He boldly removed two of the most active bomb proponents – the scientists Philip Baxter and Ernest Titterton – from their long-held perches of responsibility in the state.[86] Titterton even lost his position as head of the Research School of Physical Sciences at Australian National University.[87] Under the new Labor regime, these men and other supposedly strong pro-bomb bureaucratic forces were suddenly political non-entities. This is an example of how secondary bureaucratic politics is to top-level political direction in the matter of nuclear weaponry.

McMahon or another Liberal prime minister might have attempted to use NPT ratification as leverage to convince the US to increase the credibility of its nuclear guarantees to the country. This Whitlam did not do. As noted above, Whitlam – unlike his party's left wing – was in favor of keeping the American alliance. Indeed, Whitlam told Henry Kissinger in a 1973 Washington meeting that he feared the French tests in the South Pacific area (about which more below) were raising public awareness and support for a New Zealand plan for the complete denuclearization of the South Pacific. Whitlam said he did not favor this "gimmicky" policy and felt that it "would be a dead issue if the French would stop their testing."[88] But, on the other hand, he certainly saw no need to bolster America's nuclear commitment to Australia. Indeed, fearing that the American ally might involve an unknowing Australia in a war it did not want, he tried to renegotiate the terms of the so-called "joint defense facilities" to have some idea of what went on there. Whitlam also initiated these negotiations to mollify his party's nationalist left. (The changes that did result from these talks were largely cosmetic.)[89]

---

[85] Indeed, even after McMahon's coup against Gorton, Gorton was still powerful enough to take up the position of minister of defense in the new government.

[86] Baxter had retired from the AAEC chairmanship in April 1972, but he still served on the National Radiation Advisory Committee.

[87] "Top atom men to go," *Financial Review* (Australia), April 19, 1973, located in Ernest Titterton papers, Australian Academy of Sciences archives, Canberra.

[88] John A. Froebe to Henry Kissinger, "Memorandum of Your Conversation with Australian Prime Minister Whitlam on July 30, 1973," document marked "Secret/Sensitive," National Security Council Files, Box 910, Nixon Presidential Materials, College Park, Maryland. Kissinger replied to Whitlam that the French tests did not much bother the US, thus putting the lie to another popular hypothesis, at least in France – that Australia was the stalking horse for an "Anglo-Saxon" anti-French conspiracy.

[89] Millar, *Australia in Peace and War*, p. 217.

Finally, somewhat surprisingly given his subaltern NIC, Whitlam gave a budgetary boost to the post-Baxter AAEC's advanced research and development activities. In particular, Whitlam strongly supported continued AAEC research on uranium enrichment because of its potential economic benefits.[90] The goal, of course, was to produce the 3 percent enriched uranium necessary for power reactors, not the 90 percent enriched uranium that was necessary for bombs.[91] What had been an ostensible motivation for Baxter and Gorton was the real motivation for Whitlam. Australia's uranium partnership with France was to fall through because of the dispute over French weapons testing in the South Pacific, but the Whitlam government undertook negotiations with Japan to replace the French. In November 1974, Japanese–Australian cooperation in the field of enrichment was formalized.[92] The Whitlam government's interest in promoting this important and potentially lucrative technology once again shows that there is no necessary connection between nuclear technology acquisition and support for nuclear weapons – even when the technology in question is uranium enrichment.[93]

The campaign against French nuclear testing

The other major element of Whitlam's policy in the nuclear arena was his strong stance against French nuclear testing in the South Pacific. This was Whitlam's most spectacular policy stance on nuclear issues, and aspects of it incontestably smack of nationalism. Still, a close look at the case shows that Whitlam's behavior remained largely in line with his sportsmanlike subaltern inclinations. To understand Whitlam's stance, it is important to begin with the general point that leaders with sportsmanlike subaltern NICs are not necessarily willing doormats. Even though they have a keen perception of relative weakness, they also believe in the rules of the game as set forth by international institutions. Therefore, when they perceive their rights to have been violated, they appeal to those same international institutions for redress. The Whitlam government followed this script in its campaign against the French tests.

---

[90] On the other hand, he did formally cancel the Jervis Bay reactor project, which McMahon had already "deferred."

[91] Hardy, *Enriching Experiences*, p. 64.

[92] Alder, *Australia's Uranium Opportunities*, pp. 63–64.

[93] It is true, however, that the *Strategic Basis of Australian Defence Policy* in 1975 argued that Australia should make sure that it maintained enough technical capacity to be able to reopen the issue of a sovereign nuclear deterrent at a later date. Cited in Desmond Ball, "Australia and Nuclear Policy," in Desmond Ball, ed., *Strategy and Defence: Australian Essays* (Sydney: George Allen & Unwin, 1982), p. 325.

Before Whitlam, Australian governments gave France little difficulty over the harm caused by its nuclear tests in the area.[94] As late as June 1972, the McMahon government abstained from a New Zealand-sponsored resolution against the tests at the Stockholm Conference on the Environment. Indeed, the Liberals devoted most of their energy to calming the public health worries that the French tests sparked in the Australian population. Their point man on this was Ernest Titterton, a key member of the "bomb lobby."[95] The Liberals' relative lack of concern about the French tests reflected their overall positive feeling about the security benefits of nuclear testing in Australia's neighborhood – and indeed, on Australia's soil.

Labor's base, in particular in the rather nationalist trade unions, viewed the matter much differently. To many Australians, the French tests were not only a public health menace, they also served as reminders of the earlier British tests that Menzies had been so proud to host, but that Labor was gradually coming to view as nothing less than a national disgrace.[96] Labor and its union allies launched major protest demonstrations against France's testing program before and during the 1972 electoral campaign. In one pre-election message, Whitlam went so far as to label the tests "atrocities."[97]

But, in government, Whitlam's sportsmanlike subaltern NIC shone through. He did not jump at the chance to go *mano a mano* with Paris. He accepted the Department of Foreign Affairs' conclusion, made at the end of McMahon's tenure, that "Australia has major reasons of national self-interest for avoiding a confrontation with France."[98] In May 1973 France announced a new series of atmospheric tests at its South Pacific atolls, but the Whitlam government chose not to recall the Australian ambassador to Paris. It also tried, unsuccessfully, to restrain the unions from interrupting trade, mail, and other communications with France,

[94] Interview with Goldschmidt.
[95] When Titterton wrote to the Australian minister of supply about the French testing program in August 1971, he seemed more interested in the French thermonuclear bomb design than in the possible health effects for Australia. Letter from Ernest Titterton to the Hon. R. V. Garland, MP, minister for supply, August 18, 1971, marked "Confidential," Personal papers of Ernest Titterton (MS 168), Series 12/8 (National Radiation Advisory Committee), Australian Academy of Sciences Archives, Canberra.
[96] Indeed, this gradual trend toward reinterpretation would culminate in the empaneling of the 1985 Royal Commission into British Nuclear Tests in Australia, which was referred to earlier.
[97] Gough Whitlam, "Labor's Stand on the French Tests," for *The Radical*, July 11, 1972, available online from the National Archives of Australia, barcode 5024927.
[98] Department of the Prime Minister and Cabinet, "Notes on Cabinet Submission No. 17: French Nuclear Weapons Testing," January 8, 1973, available online from the National Archives of Australia RecordSearch, barcode 4986082.

since those actions went contrary to Australia's international agreements. What Whitlam did do was to join with New Zealand and other South Pacific nations in an appeal to the International Court of Justice in the Hague.[99] Moreover, Australia and New Zealand introduced a resolution in the United Nations General Assembly for a Comprehensive Test Ban Treaty (CTBT), a resolution that they would subsequently reintroduce annually over the decades.[100] In June the court ruled against France, but it proceeded to test anyway. Even then, Whitlam cautioned against "overreacting" against France, especially since China was also testing at the time and he was even more anxious to avoid a confrontation with Beijing.[101] In spite of Whitlam's caution, however, France took offense, and the two publicly froze diplomatic relations. France's late 1974 decision not to conduct further atmospheric tests in the region finally permitted a thaw.[102]

In sum, Gough Whitlam's handling of the French nuclear tests issue, like his handling of the NPT, the American nuclear guarantee, and the notion of an Australian bomb, reflected his fundamentally sportsmanlike subaltern NIC. As such, his choices bore some clear resemblances not only to those of his Labor predecessors of the 1940s, but even to those of many previous Liberal prime ministers, who also held a form of subaltern NIC. But Whitlam's policies also represented a major shift away from the traditional fear of Asia and of the "yellow–red" peril. That shift proved to be a lasting one.

After Whitlam

Although the Whitlam government fell in 1975, Whitlam's sportsmanlike subaltern reorientation of Australian foreign and security policies proved far more resilient. The 1972 electoral defeat of the Liberals appears to

---

[99] Cabinet Decision No. 598, "French Nuclear Tests" marked "confidential," May 6, 1973, available online from the National Archives of Australia RecordSearch, barcode 4986082. Australia also decided to assist a New Zealand stunt by refueling a New Zealand naval vessel that was sent to the test zone. Indeed, the Australian minister of supply himself participated in the stunt. Ironically, under the Liberals the Ministry of Supply had been one of the stronger bureaucratic voices in favor of an Australian bomb. So much for "where you stand depends on where you sit"!

[100] M. Hanson and C. J. Ungerer, "Promoting an Agenda for Nuclear Weapons Elimination: The Canberra Commission and the Dilemmas of Disarmament," *Australian Journal of Politics and History*, Vol. 44 (December 1998), p. 537.

[101] Cabinet Decision No. 840 (Foreign Affairs and Defence Committee), "French Nuclear Tests" marked "confidential," July 2, 1973 (incorrectly marked "1971"), available online from the National Archives of Australia RecordSearch, barcode 4986082.

[102] Whitlam's visit to Paris at the beginning of 1975 repaired the damage. See "Retrouvailles franco-australiennes," *Le Monde*, January 7, 1975.

have liberated them from the old orientations and prejudices.[103] The nuclear policies of the Liberal, Prime Minister Malcolm Fraser (1975–83) clearly followed Whitlam's lead. Indeed, the 1976 *Strategic Basis* report – the bottom line on Australian threat perceptions – was withering in its assessment of what it termed Australia's past "anxiety" about Asia. Because of this new assessment, not only did Fraser make no attempt to reopen the question of a nuclear weapons option; he also imposed non-proliferation safeguards "more rigorous than that adopted to date by any nuclear supplier country."[104] Under Fraser, Australia also continued to submit the call for a Comprehensive Test Ban Treaty to the UN General Assembly. Meanwhile, it continued the Whitlam policy of promoting uranium mining and maintained the Japanese tie and domestic funding levels for uranium enrichment.[105]

During the 1980s and 1990s, a series of ALP governments would further deepen the country's commitment to international efforts ending the nuclear arms race, notably appointing an ambassador for disarmament and bringing together an international commission of experts, the Canberra Commission, who called for the gradual elimination of nuclear weapons.[106] This deepening commitment to nuclear disarmament was nurtured in part by the continuing fervent, visceral public opposition to French nuclear testing.[107] The more recent Liberal governments under Prime Minister John Howard have pursued such efforts with less urgency, but the basic thrust of Australian international disarmament diplomacy remains.

The basic reason why Whitlam's nuclear policy reorientation lasted is easy to identify. Jim Cairns had been right; the cure for the fear of ghosts is simply to realize that there are no ghosts. After 1972, Australia stopped believing in ghosts.

---

[103] Alan Dupont, *Australia's Threat Perceptions: A Search for Security*, Canberra Papers on Strategy and Defence, No. 82 (Canberra: Strategic and Defence Studies Centre, Australian National University, 1991), p. 95.

[104] Quote from *Uranium – Australia's Decision* (Canberra: Australian Government Printing Service, 1977), cited in Ball, "Australia and Nuclear Policy," p. 330.

[105] The work on enrichment was finally curtailed in 1983 by Bob Hawke's Labor government. The enrichment program had become the focus of ire of the environmental movement, which in Whitlam's day was still minor. For details see Alder, *Australia's Uranium Opportunities*.

[106] Hanson and Ungerer, "Promoting an Agenda."

[107] Kim Richard Nossal and Carolynn Vivian, *A Brief Madness: Australia and the Resumption of French Nuclear Testing*, Canberra Papers on Strategy and Defence, No. 121 (Canberra: Strategic and Defence Studies Centre, Australian National University, 1997).

6   Argentina's nuclear ambition – and restraint

Introduction

According to conventional wisdom, Argentina's nuclear stances before
the 1990s – pursuit of maximum technological autonomy combined with
resistance to the non-proliferation regime – clearly indicate that it harbored a desire to build the bomb. Argentina's subsequent decisions to
curtail its nuclear program and to join the regime are therefore seen as
major successes in the struggle against proliferation.[1] But this chapter
shows that Argentina's policies were not motivated by nuclear weapons
ambitions. Indeed, it is hard to find any significant actor in the Argentine
political landscape who was motivated by such a desire. What is more,
the main consequence of non-proliferation pressures until the 1990s was
in fact to incite the Argentines further to acquire the very technologies
that the North Americans wanted to deny them.

The basic argument of this chapter is that Argentina's mix of nuclear
policies before the 1990s stemmed fundamentally from a sportsmanlike
nationalist NIC that was held by a long succession of presidents from
different parties and regime types, and that also had a wide resonance in
the Argentine state and society as a whole. It was this widely held sportsmanlike nationalist NIC that produced the country's prideful rejection of
the non-proliferation regime and the pursuit of nuclear autonomy, while
at the same time engendering the view that an Argentine bomb would be
a strategic absurdity.

---

[1] For Washington's view of the Argentine case, see Henry Sokolski, "Next Century
Nonproliferation: Victory Is Still Possible," *The Nonproliferation Review*, Vol. 4, No. 1
(Fall 1996), p. 91; Thomas Graham, Jr., "Nuclear Maturity in Argentina and Brazil,"
paper presented at SAIC Argentina and Brazil Rollback Workshop, McLean, Virginia,
October 22, 1998, http://www.lawscns.org/argbra.htm; Gary Milhollin, "Testimony of
Gary Milhollin before the Committee on Armed Services, United States Senate,
July 9, 1998," http://www.senate.gov/~armed_services/statemnt/980709gm.htm; Robert
F. Mozley, *The Politics and Technology of Nuclear Proliferation* (Seattle: University of
Washington Press, 1998), pp. 204–207.

While the evidence from Argentina generally supports the theoretical perspective adopted in this book, it represents an important anomaly for the other major theoretical perspectives on proliferation.

- Even though it found itself in a position of conventional military inferiority *vis-à-vis* its large (and increasingly nuclear-capable) neighbor Brazil, and in a position of conventional and nuclear inferiority *vis-à-vis* Great Britain, its opponent in the 1982 Falklands/Malvinas war, Argentina did not respond to these power imbalances by seeking the bomb, contrary to Realist expectations.
- The international non-proliferation regime could not restrain Argentina's nuclear weapons ambitions as institutionalists expect, because Argentina had no such ambitions in the first place. In fact, the discriminatory nature of the international regime actually proved to be a prod for Argentina's drive for nuclear autonomy. And when Argentine–Brazil nuclear tensions surfaced, rather than falling back on the existing non-proliferation structures the two chose to build a new regional institution both to settle their differences and to make common cause against the international regime.
- Bureaucratic politics models would find few countries as suited for proliferation as Argentina, a country whose military had spread its tentacles throughout the state and society – and indeed sent a steady diet of naval officers to head the national atomic energy commission. But in fact, while the Argentine military was interested in intermediate-range missiles and nuclear submarines, neither it nor any other major domestic institution ever showed any serious interest in building a nuclear arsenal.

The chapter is organized as follows. The second part explains the emergence of Argentina's stances against the non-proliferation regime and in favor of maximum national technological autonomy during the 1960s and early 1970s. The third part explores the backfiring of the tough non-proliferation pressures that the North Americans placed on Argentina beginning in 1974. The fourth part then contrasts that downward diplomatic spiral with the relatively smooth resolution of Argentine–Brazilian nuclear tensions during the same period. Finally, the reason Argentina finally abandoned its traditional nuclear policy stances and joined the international non-proliferation fold after 1989 is discussed.

Argentina's nuclear choices to 1974

During the 1960s and early 1970s, Argentina developed its basic nuclear policy stances against the non-proliferation regime and in favor of maximum national technological autonomy. This section shows that these policy choices stemmed from Argentina's widespread sportsmanlike nationalism and not from an ambition to build the bomb.

Diplomatic policies

International efforts to stem nuclear proliferation began in the early 1960s. Argentina attacked these efforts as enshrining international discrimination between the nuclear haves and have-nots. The country's principal nuclear diplomat, Ambassador Julio Carasales, labeled non-proliferation nothing more than the "disarming of the disarmed."[2] The litany of treaties that Argentina refused to sign and/or ratify is a long one: the 1963 Partial Test Ban Treaty; the 1967 Outer Space Treaty; the 1967 Tlatelolco Treaty for the Prohibition of Nuclear Weapons in Latin America; the 1968 NPT; and the 1971 Seabed Treaty.[3]

Two key pieces of evidence support the notion that Argentina's rejection of the growing non-proliferation regime reflected a sportsmanlike nationalist distaste for discrimination and not a legalistic cover for nuclear weapons ambitions. First, Argentina's diplomatic stance was considered quite comprehensible and unthreatening by Brazil, the country that had the most to lose if Argentina ended up getting the bomb. Indeed, the two supposed nuclear rivals even collaborated closely in the 1960s to oppose the discriminatory non-proliferation regime.[4] Second, it is true that one of Argentina's debating points in international fora during this time period was its desire to protect its right to utilize "peaceful nuclear explosions" (PNEs) for engineering or mining purposes.[5] But the Argentine desire to retain the *right* to PNEs did not mean that they actually ever intended to use it. Indeed, according to former Argentine Ambassador to the IAEA Antonio Carrea, around 1970 France offered to provide a PNE

---

[2] Julio Carasales, *El desarme de los desarmados: Argentina y el Tratado de no proliferación de armas nucleares* (Buenos Aires: Editorial Planear, 1987).

[3] The only exception to this litany of refusal was Argentina's ratification of the 1961 Antarctic Treaty, which contained a provision not to test nuclear weapons or stash nuclear waste on that continent. Roberto Mario Ornstein, "Contexto político internacional para los usos pacíficos de la energía nuclear," unpublished manuscript intended for publication by the *Comisión Nacional de Energía Atómica*, 1998, p. 26.

[4] See note from British Embassy, Rio de Janeiro, to Foreign and Commonwealth Office, marked "confidential," February 6, 1968. Foreign and Commonwealth Office files, 7/134, Public Record Office. Kew, UK.

[5] It is worth remembering that the nuclear powers themselves were actively promoting PNEs as a tool for economic development at the time. Optimism about the potential of PNEs would continue until at least the mid-1970s. See Theodore B. Taylor, "Commercial Nuclear Technology and Nuclear Weapon Proliferation," in Onkar Marwah and Ann Schulz, eds., *Nuclear Proliferation and the Near-Nuclear Countries* (Cambridge, MA: Ballinger Publishing Co., 1975), p. 118.

to excavate a deep-water port on the Patagonian coast.[6] But the prospect of negative diplomatic repercussions in the region, notably due to the potential radioactive contamination of fish in the southern Atlantic, led the Argentines quickly to reject the French offer.[7] This quick dismissal stands in stark contrast to the oppositional nationalist Australian Prime Minister John Gorton's eagerness for an American PNE to create a new harbor – and to scare the Communists – during the same time period (see Chapter 5).

The fact that Argentina pursued a nuclear diplomacy that privileged the goal of nationalist self-expression during the 1960s is not terribly surprising, given that the costs of such stances for its economic development objectives were still quite low. Most Northern states continued to view stemming the tide of weapons proliferation as decidedly secondary to promoting nuclear exports. The British government, for instance, hardly took Argentina's failure to ratify the Tlatelolco regional non-proliferation treaty as a reason to cease efforts to sell it a nuclear power reactor.[8] However, the relative priority that Northern states (and, in particular, the US) placed on non-proliferation and export promotion began to shift at about the time of the NPT debate. Admiral Oscar Quihillalt, head of Argentina's *Comisión Nacional de Energía Atómica* (CNEA), was especially sensitive to these changes as he had been recently serving as chairman of the IAEA's Board of Governors in Vienna.[9] Judging that continued rejection of the non-proliferation regime was putting in jeopardy the future progress of the Argentine nuclear program, Quihillalt decided in favor of Argentine adhesion to the NPT and went to see both the Argentine president and foreign minister to plead for adherence – yet another example

---

[6] Interview with Antonio Carrea, Argentine nuclear scientist and diplomat (former ambassador to the IAEA), Buenos Aires, August 17, 1999, with follow-up communication November 9, 1999.

[7] Probably because the offer was dismissed out of hand, it seems never to have made it into the diplomatic files that were scoured by Julio C. Carasales for his "Las explosions nucleares pacíficas y la actitud argentina," Consejo Argentina para las Relaciones Internacionales, Documento de trabajo no. 20, Buenos Aires, Argentina, 1997.

[8] "Note" marked "confidential" from Mr. Summerhayes, British Embassy, Buenos Aires, to Mr. Barker, American Department, Foreign Office, December 29,1967; and "Note" marked "Confidential" from A. White, Foreign Office, to Mr. Barker, American Department, Foreign Office, January 18, 1968. Folder on "Tlatelolco Treaty," Foreign and Commonwealth Office Files 10/154, Public Record Office, Kew, UK.

[9] The CNEA was until the 1980s typically run by naval officers, but this simply reflects the involvement of the Argentine military in all aspects of energy and industrial research and development. It should not be taken to reflect an extraordinary interest of the military in things nuclear. For general background, see Eduardo L. Ortiz, "Army and Science in Argentina: 1850–1950," in P. Forman and J. M. Sánchez-Ron, eds., *National Military Establishments and the Advancement of Science and Technology: Studies in 20th Century History* (Dordrecht: Kluwer Academic Publishers, 1996), pp. 153–184.

that atomic energy commissions are not inevitably "bomb lobbies."[10] Quihillalt believed he had made a strong case for the need for Argentina's diplomatic stance to adjust to the hardening attitudes of the North, but in the end he was disappointed. As Quihillalt told me, his political masters refused to accept "a diminution of our dignity."[11] This would not be the last time that Argentine leaders, given a choice between more self-expressive or more productive policy options, chose the former.

Technology policies: the first power reactor

Quihillalt's worries about the effects of staying outside the NPT reflected the fact that by the end of the 1960s Argentina had developed a vibrant, but still fragile, nuclear program. Unlike other countries that were happy to receive "turn-key" nuclear facilities from the North, sportsmanlike nationalist Argentina had a strong preference for autonomous development in the nuclear area.[12] Some within the CNEA, notably the engineer Celso Papadopoulos, interpreted this preference to mean that they should do everything in-house.[13] But the CNEA's guiding light, Jorge Sábato (a scion of an eminent Argentine family who became director of the CNEA's Metallurgy Department in 1955) understood that properly designed international partnerships would be more conducive to the ultimate goal of technological autonomy.[14] In particular, Sábato convinced his colleagues that rather than trying to design and build a nuclear power reactor from scratch, the CNEA should seek to import a nuclear power

[10] Interview with Oscar Quihillalt, Argentine nuclear scientist (former president of the *Comisión Nacional de Energía Atómica*), Buenos Aires, August 11, 1999. Quihillalt's recollection is confirmed by the note "Argentina and the NPT," Note from J. F. Wearing, British Embassy, Vienna, to R. C. Hope-Jones, Foreign Office, July 12, 1968, Foreign and Commonwealth Office Files 10/106, Public Record Office, Kew, United Kingdom.

[11] Interview with Quihillalt.

[12] Prior to the CNEA's founding, there was an odd beginning to Argentina's nuclear history, known as the "Richter affair," in which Ronald Richter, a former Nazi scientist, convinced President Juan Perón that he knew the secret to controlled fusion. Perón, greatly excited by the prospect of an unlimited source of energy, funded the project to the hilt and even at one point announced to the world that Richter had succeeded. But Richter turned out to be a fraud. For more on this story, see Mario Mariscotti, "The Bizarre Origins of Atomic Energy in Argentina," in Regis Cabral, ed., *The Nuclear Technology Debate in Latin America*, STIC No. 1 (Göteborg, Sweden: Göteborg University, 1990), pp. 16–24.

[13] Interview with Enrique Mariano and Bernardo Murmis, former CNEA scientists, Buenos Aires, August 4, 1999.

[14] Carlos A. Martínez Vidal, "Esbozo biográfico de Jorge Alberto Sábato, 1924–1983," manuscript prepared for the Asociación Argentina para el Desarrollo Tecnológico, Buenos Aires, February 1999. See also the excellent exposition of Sábato's thought in Emanuel Adler, *The Power of Ideology: The Quest for Technological Autonomy in Argentina and Brazil* (Berkeley: University of California Press, 1987).

reactor from abroad – but, he insisted, it should be fueled by natural uranium, which could potentially be developed domestically, as opposed to enriched uranium, which would have to be imported. (As noted in the Australian case, natural uranium-fueled reactors are often seen as a path toward nuclear weapons, but Sábato's motives are unimpeachable; indeed, many in the Argentine military viewed him as no less than a leftist peacenik.) Sábato's preference for natural uranium fuel quickly took root in the CNEA. Indeed, when President Arturo Illia decided to contract for a power reactor in 1964 – it was to be the first in Latin America – Quihillalt first approached France, whose reactors ran on natural uranium, in an attempt to end-run a competitive bidding process that might result in the selection of an enriched uranium option.[15] The French were ready to sell the Argentines what they wanted but only at a high price, so Quihillalt's gambit failed.[16] But in the competitive bidding the German company Siemens offered Argentina a natural uranium-fueled power reactor with spectacularly advantageous financial terms – practically a gift. Illia's successor by virtue of a coup, General Juan Carlos Onganía, soon formally accepted the German offer, and construction work began for the reactor (dubbed "Atucha I") in 1968.[17]

The second power reactor

In 1973 Argentina decided in favor of a second natural uranium-fueled reactor, this one a Canadian "Candu" design, to be built at Embalse, near Córdoba. Even more than the earlier Siemens reactor, the choice of Candu – by a military government – set off alarm bells for non-proliferation advocates.[18] In fact, however, the evidence shows that the continued Argentine preference for natural uranium reflected continued interest in technological autonomy, not a new interest in nuclear weapons.

---

[15] Note from J. Lecoq to M. le Chef du Département des Relations Extérieures, Commissariat à l'Energie Atomique, July 15, 1964. Folder "Collaboration avec l'Argentine 1953–69," Fonds Haut-Commissaire F7.27.49, archives of the Commissariat à l'Energie Atomique, Fontenay-aux-Roses, France.

[16] Note from J. Renou, Département des Relations Extérieures, "Objet: Eléments de réponse pour la note sur l'Argentine transmise par le Cabinet du Ministre," November 17, 1966. Folder "Argentine 1954–1967," Fonds Haut-Commissaire F7.27.49, archives of the Commissariat à l'Energie Atomique, Fontenay-aux-Roses, France. The French documents offer no basis to Leonard Spector's speculation that "French proliferation concerns influenced its decision to cancel the deal." Leonard S. Spector, *Nuclear Proliferation Today* (New York: Vintage Books, 1984).

[17] Daniel Poneman, "Argentina," in Jed C. Snyder and Samuel F. Wells, Jr., *Limiting Nuclear Proliferation* (Cambridge, MA: Ballinger Publishing Co., 1985), p. 98.

[18] See Spector, *Nuclear Proliferation Today*, pp. 203–204. There can be no doubt that Candu was indeed proliferation-enabling. Recall the bomb-desiring Philip Baxter's promotion of Candu for Australia that was recounted in Chapter 5.

There were three serious bids for the Embalse contract: a US (Westinghouse) bid to build an enriched uranium-fueled reactor, a mainly German (Kraftwerk Union–Siemens–Fiat) bid to build an enriched uranium-fueled reactor, and the Canadian bid to build a Candu natural uranium-fueled reactor.[19] None of the bids was made contingent on Argentine acceptance of the NPT or of full-scope safeguards.[20] Of the three, from a narrow financial perspective the Westinghouse offer was the cheapest, and the Canadian offer the most expensive.[21] Because of the cost advantages, President General Alejandro Lanusse initially leaned heavily toward approving the Westinghouse bid – which should come as a surprise to those who imagine that the military was primarily interested in the reactor as a means of obtaining plutonium for bombs.[22] But before Lanusse made his preference official, a vigorous public campaign by the CNEA– the self-appointed protector of the ideology of autonomous national development in the nuclear area – strongly criticized the enriched uranium option. In a broadly disseminated statement of purpose the CNEA's Asociación de Profesionales reminded the executive that for Argentina, nuclear power was about more than mere financial cost. They wrote,

From this decision will essentially depend whether the integration of nuclear energy in the national energy schema will constitute a positive support to the technological development of our country or will convert itself into yet another instrument of underdevelopment and political and economic dependency.[23]

The campaign succeeded in convincing Lanusse to name a commission, comprised of one representative each from the Army, Navy, Air Force,

---

[19] CNEA, "Central nuclear Córdoba: Ofertas y tipo de combustible a emplear," document marked "Secreto," sent to President Tte. General D. Alejandro Agustín Lanusse, Buenos Aires, November 23, 1972. Private archive.

[20] Each did include requirements for safeguards of varying durations on the reactor itself. The winning bid, from Canada, originally imposed safeguards only for the first fifteen years of operation (Spector, *Nuclear Proliferation Today*). The Canadians later unilaterally extended the duration of this imposition, causing a bitter dispute that will be covered in detail below.

[21] This was true both in terms of cost of construction and operating cost. As for percentage of local participation and financial terms, all offers were quite comparable. CNEA, "Central nuclear Córdoba."

[22] Etel Solingen, *Industrial Policy, Technology, and International Bargaining: Designing Nuclear Industries in Argentina and Brazil* (Stanford: Stanford University Press, 1996), p. 42. The notion that Lanusse backed the Westinghouse bid because the Westinghouse representative was a retired army colonel, Carlos Ortiz de Zárate, is incorrect. Lanusse was no friend of Ortiz de Zárate's, having essentially had him drummed out of the corps only a few years beforehand. Interview with Carlos Ortiz de Zárate, former Argentine army officer and lobbyist, Buenos Aires, August 23, 1999.

[23] APCNEA, "Asociación de Profesionales de la Comisión Nacional de Energía Atómica y la política nuclear argentina," press release, Buenos Aires, August 11, 1972. Private archive.

and the CNEA, to take a second look at the relative value of the various technologies on offer.[24]

The commission made extensive efforts to evaluate potential contribution of the three offers to national technological autonomy.[25] On this scale the Westinghouse offer came in dead last. The decision between the Canadians and Germans was trickier, however. The Canadians were offering to transfer a wide, if rather mundane set of technologies alongside their natural uranium-fueled reactor. Meanwhile, the Germans were offering the latest in ultracentrifuge uranium enrichment technology to go along with their enriched uranium-fueled reactor.[26] If Argentina had wanted the bomb, the chance to acquire the secrets of uranium enrichment would have been worth any price. But the Commission was unmoved by such temptations. The commission dismissed the German offer of an ultra-centrifuge production facility as requiring an "economy of scale" that Argentina's industrial needs could not justify. Meanwhile, it argued that the set of mundane technologies offered by the Canadians could eventually allow Argentina, if it made a "great effort," to begin designing and building power reactors on its own.[27] On the strength of the Commission's recommendation, relayed to him by the CNEA, in March 1973 President Lanusse announced the decision in favor of the Candu option on the grounds that it was a great but achievable step forward toward the goal of technological autonomy. Even the disappointed Colonel Carlos Ortiz de Zárate, who served as the chief lobbyist for the Westinghouse reactor, does not believe that the desire for nuclear weapons played a part in the final determination for Candu.[28]

In sum, ambitious but not unrealistic developmental objectives dominated the early years of Argentina's nuclear program. In spite of Quihillalt's forebodings, as late as 1973 the fact that Argentina remained outside the growing non-proliferation regime did not seriously hamper its pursuit of those developmental objectives. But a year later, the Indian "peaceful nuclear explosion" (PNE) deeply affected Northern attitudes about the export of "civilian" nuclear technology. Suddenly it became much harder for Argentina to have its cake (cost-effective nuclear development) and eat it too (a self-expressive rejection of the non-proliferation regime). As the following pages demonstrate, when forced to choose, Argentina favored the self-expressive element of its nuclear stance.

---

[24] Poneman, "Argentina."

[25] "Informes de la Comisión Interfuerzas a la Junta de Comandantes en Jefe sobre el combustible a utilizar en la central nuclear Córdoba," undated document. Private archive.

[26] CNEA, "Central nuclear Córdoba," and KWU, "Memorandum: Indigenous Uranium Enrichment in Argentina," n.d. Private archive.

[27] "Informes de la Comisión."   [28] Interview with Ortiz de Zárate.

This was a prideful reaction to heavy-handed external pressures, exactly the kind of reaction we should expect from people holding sportsmanlike nationalist NICs.

The gaucho–gringo tangle: 1974–89

The mid-1970s were a crossroads for Argentine nuclear policies. Would Argentina swallow its pride, join the non-proliferation regime and continue its productive tradition of gradually pursuing technological autonomy through close relationships with Northern nuclear suppliers? Or would it maintain its self-expressive diplomatic stance, remain outside the non-proliferation regime, and thereby hamper the progress of its nuclear program? For a time Argentina's military government leaned toward the former option of cooperation, but they changed their minds in the face of continuing North American hardball diplomacy. Indeed, nuclear relations between Argentina and North America in the 1970s entered a vicious cycle. Each new round of North American pressure would offend the Argentines' pride, leading them to renewed assertions of their independence. In turn this response would give the North Americans new "evidence" that Argentina was seeking the bomb, and the cycle continued. The fact that North American non-proliferation pressures proved so counterproductive can only be understood by taking seriously the emotional dimension of the nuclear policy choices of sportsmanlike nationalists.

Carter, Videla, and the Tlatelolco Treaty

The May 1974 Indian PNE shocked Northern nuclear suppliers and led them to begin augmenting their non-proliferation safeguards requirements. As former CNEA chief Carlos Castro Madero and Ambassador Estéban Takacs put it, "Thus began the period during which previously agreed contracts were unilaterally violated" by the Northern suppliers.[29] The first sign of trouble was a German demand that the safeguards on the Atucha I reactor, which were about to expire, be extended for the life of the plant. As Argentina had not yet fully mastered the production of natural uranium fuel elements, it had to accept the new German conditions. The pressure gradually mounted, and in December 1976 the Canadians formally announced that the recently signed nuclear technology transfer agreement would essentially be halted unless Argentina joined the NPT

---

[29] Carlos Castro Madero and Estéban A. Takacs, *Política nuclear Argentina: ¿avance o retroceso?* (Buenos Aires: El Ateneo, 1991), p. 59.

and submitted its entire nuclear program to full-scope IAEA safeguards.[30] Shortly thereafter, the new US administration of Jimmy Carter started its own effort to force the Argentines into the non-proliferation fold.

When Jimmy Carter arrived in the White House in January 1977, he launched two global diplomatic campaigns: one for non-proliferation, and the other for human rights. The Argentine military junta in power since 1976, known as the *Proceso de Reorganización Nacional*, was on the wrong side of both issues.[31] On the nuclear front, the Carter administration was demanding that Argentina at least ratify the Treaty of Tlatelolco, the regional non-proliferation treaty. From a sportsmanlike nationalist perspective Tlatelolco was less toxic than the NPT because it was less starkly discriminatory: it did not outlaw PNEs, and alongside its non-proliferation strictures it included commitments by the nuclear powers not to bring such weapons into the Latin American region. Moreover, for Tlatelolco to enter into force all states in the region, including Cuba, had to ratify it – an unlikely proposition. Argentine President General Jorge Videla was therefore willing to consider ratifying Tlatelolco, and he set up a special inter-ministerial "disarmament commission" in August 1977 to review that option.[32] By the end of the year the various organs of the state had reported back, in secret, to the commission. There were three overall patterns in their submissions. First, in yet another demonstration of the fact that Argentina's diplomatic stance was not a cover for nuclear weapons ambitions, most of the submissions were so unconcerned about the security implications of ratification that they did not bring up the issue at all.[33] Second, they all saw ratification as caving in to the US.[34] Third, nearly all contended that Argentina should only ratify if it could expect to receive a substantial technological payoff in return. The contention that Argentina should be rewarded handsomely for ratifying Tlatelolco was most clear in the submissions of most of the more powerful bureaucracies: the Army, the Air Force, the Navy, the CNEA, and

---

[30] Ibid., pp. 59–60.

[31] At the time the human rights situation in Argentina had reached catastrophic proportions. The regime unleashed a vicious campaign of torture, kidnapping, and murder against "subversives." Comisión Nacional sobre la Desaparición de Personas, *Nunca más*, 3rd ed. (Buenos Aires: Eudeba, 1997).

[32] Comisión Interministerial de Desarme, "Acta No. 1," document marked "Secreto," August 16, 1977. Document viewed at Ministerio de Relaciones Exteriores, Buenos Aires.

[33] An initial submission from the Army had implied that a delay in ratification would be desirable in order to accumulate a stockpile of plutonium, but two months later its final submission deleted that implication. Notes from Comando en Jefe del Ejercito to Ministerio de Relaciones Exteriores, October 10 and December 5, 1977. Documents viewed at Ministerio de Relaciones Exteriores, Buenos Aires.

[34] Only the Ministry of Defense considered – obliquely – the ramifications for Argentine–Brazilian relations.

the Ministry of Planning (*Planeamiento*).[35] While echoing these points, some of the weaker bureaucracies suggested a willingness to do without a concrete quid pro quo from the Americans.[36] Not surprisingly, the final decision was to negotiate for a concrete quid pro quo.

The Argentines asked the Americans for the transfer of the technology necessary for domestic production of heavy water, which after the natural uranium fuel elements was a crucial missing link in the quest for nuclear autonomy.[37] Given how flimsy the Tlatelolco regime was, it must be said that the Argentines were charging a high price for swallowing their pride. The negotiations, however, initially seemed to go well. The two sides, led by the CNEA chief Carlos Castro Madero on the one hand and by US State Department official Joseph Nye on the other, worked out a carefully worded joint communiqué in which the Argentines committed to "initiate the ratification" of Tlatelolco and the Americans committed to augment the existing bilateral accord on nuclear cooperation to include the "necessary technology and means" to satisfy the Argentine requirements in heavy water.[38] Soon thereafter, following through on the Argentine commitment, the Treaty Department of the Foreign Ministry began to "prepare the juridical instruments" for Argentine accession. But suddenly the US blocked transfer of a Canadian-built (but 15 percent US-owned) heavy water plant to Argentina, on the basis of a highly dubious legal interpretation of the joint communiqué.[39]

The American reversal made the Argentines angry. They had undertaken a public commitment to a major shift in the country's traditional

[35] Notes from Fuerza Aerea Argentina, Comando en Jefe to Ministerio de Relaciones Exteriores, December 7, 1977; Comisión Nacional de Energía Atómica to Comisión Interministerial de Desarme, Ministerio de Relaciones Exteriores, October 17, 1977; Comando en Jefe de la Armada to Ministerio de Relaciones Exteriores, November 29, 1977; Ministerio de Planeamiento de la Nación to Ministerio de Relaciones Exteriores, December 7, 1977. Documents viewed at Ministerio de Relaciones Exteriores, Buenos Aires.

[36] Notes from Consejo de Defensa, Estado de Mayor Conjunto to Comisión Interministerial de Desarme, September 14, 1977; Subsecretario de Planeamiento, Ministerio de Defensa to Ministerio de Relaciones Exteriores, September 21, 1977; Presidencia de la Nación, Secretaría de la Inteligencia del Estado to Comisión Interministerial de Desarme, November 16, 1977. Documents viewed at Ministerio de Relaciones Exteriores, Buenos Aires.

[37] Telegram marked "Secreto" from Subsecretario de Relaciones Exteriores, Ministerio de Relaciones Exteriores, to Argentine Embassy, Washington DC, February 1, 1978. Document viewed at the Ministerio de Relaciones Exteriores, Buenos Aires.

[38] Argentine–US joint communiqué, November 21, 1977, reprinted in Castro Madero and Takacs, *Política nuclear argentina*, p. 157.

[39] The argument was that the US had not agreed to allow Argentina to receive a heavy water plant, but had only agreed not to stop Argentina from acquiring the technical "means" of obtaining heavy water. Perhaps the "necessary technology" referred to in the communiqué, then, was a tanker vessel? Castro Madero and Takacs, *Política nuclear argentina*, p. 158.

diplomatic stance on non-proliferation, but suddenly they were getting nothing in return. As the then CNEA President Carlos Castro Madero and Ambassador to Canada Estéban Takacs write in their history of nuclear Argentina, "This different interpretation of a communiqué that had been long and deeply discussed, left many doubts over the good faith with which it had been drawn up . . . Our government considered itself liberated from its commitment to ratify the treaty."[40] The heavy water episode produced the strongly self-expressive turn in Argentine nuclear policies in the late 1970s.

Continuing progress in the nuclear program via the tactics of "blackmail" and "bribery"

The American reversal on the heavy water deal spurred the Argentines to pursue nuclear development with even greater energy than before. But how could they acquire the sensitive technologies that the North Americans had vowed to deny them? They found a first answer in a tactic of – to quote the later CNEA President Dan Beninson – "blackmail."[41] The core of this tactic was to begin to develop sensitive nuclear technologies domestically without any safeguards, in order to convince Northern suppliers to provide those technologies with modest safeguards. To this end, in 1978 the CNEA inaugurated a pilot plant for the production of heavy water and another pilot plant for the production of zirconium sponges – a key technology related to the production of natural-uranium fuel elements. Once Argentina had proven that in any case it had the technical capacity to go it alone, Northern offers indeed became forthcoming.[42] The "blackmail" tactic thus did meet with some success in terms of bringing Argentina closer to technological autonomy in the short term. But whereas in the early years of nuclear power the resistance to nonproliferation was relatively costless, it now was coming at a high price. This price must be measured not only in terms of dollars but also in terms of access. "Blackmail" may have succeeded in dislodging certain technologies, but it undermined the broader international links that were so important to the future of Argentina's overall nuclear development. For instance, as the Argentines built up an international reputation as a nuclear "rogue," the Canadian technology transfer relationship dried up

---

[40] Ibid.
[41] Interview with Dan Beninson, Argentine nuclear scientist (former president of the CNEA), Buenos Aires, August 9, 1999, with follow-up communication November 9, 1999.
[42] Castro Madero and Takacs, *Política nuclear argentina*, p. 97.

completely. Yet a prideful Argentina would refuse to buckle for at least another decade.[43]

In early 1979, CNEA chief Castro Madero convinced President Videla to take an even bolder leap: to announce a long-term nuclear plan involving a series of new nuclear power reactors and mastery of the entire nuclear fuel cycle, including fuel reprocessing. In nationalist terms this was the nuclear holy grail; it was also highly questionable from the perspective of the country's real economic needs.[44] But again, it would be wrong to conclude from this lack of economic justification that the *Plan Nuclear* was actually motivated by a desire to build nuclear weapons. Internal records from the ad hoc interministerial commission that was convened to evaluate the proposed *Plan Nuclear* in late 1978 reveal that the representative from the Ministry of Defense, Colonel Moreno, had to fight Castro Madero even to have the diplomatic and security consequences of the *Plan* placed on the commission's agenda.[45] When these matters were finally discussed, Moreno and the other commission representatives mainly emphasized the strategic importance of having an independent energy supply.[46]

But in the face of continuing pressure to join the non-proliferation regime, how could the Argentines hope to get their highly – even exaggeratedly – ambitious *Plan Nuclear* off the ground? The "blackmail" tactic

[43] Roberto Ornstein, the CNEA's international relations chief, finally told an Argentine Congressional committee in 1992, "We cannot remain isolated; we need international cooperation . . . The hour has come to accommodate ourselves to the new international political context so that our international cooperation can continue as fruitfully as it has up to now." These were revolutionary words, but they came several years too late to save the Argentine nuclear establishment. Roberto Ornstein, statement to *Estado y perspectivas de la Actividad Nuclear en la Argentina: Congreso organizado por las comisiones de Ciencia y Tecnología y de Energía y Combustibles de la Honorable Cámara de Diputados de la Nación, Buenos Aires, 14 al 16 de Octubre de 1992* (Buenos Aires: República Argentina, 1994), p. 261.

[44] In particular, the fuel reprocessing objective was hard to justify. Fuel reprocessing allows for the salvaging of plutonium from spent fuel elements. In theory this plutonium would then be used itself as reactor fuel in plutonium-fueled reactors, but an internal CNEA report estimated that Argentina would be in no position to utilize such fuel until the mid-1990s (CNEA, "Necesidades de reprocesamiento en la República Argentina," internal document, undated but apparently from 1980. Located in a private archive). The other standard use for plutonium, of course, would be in nuclear bombs. Note that the original public announcement of the intention to build the reprocessing plant had actually been made already in 1978. David Albright, "Bomb Potential for South America," *Bulletin of the Atomic Scientists*, Vol. 45, No. 4 (May 1989), pp. 16–20.

[45] CNEA, "Informe preparado por la Comisión Interministerial Ad-Hoc para el análisis del Plan Nuclear. Para su elevación al excelentísimo señor Presidente de la Nación," internal document prepared December 1978. Document obtained from CNEA, Buenos Aires.

[46] Interview with Antonio Federico Moreno, retired army officer and public servant (*Comisión de Defensa de la Cámara de Diputados*), Buenos Aires, August 31, 1999. Note, however, that this is the one session for which I found no rapporteur's summary.

was not up to the task: at best it could only dislodge from Northern suppliers those relatively simpler nuclear technologies that Argentina could credibly threaten to develop on its own. Instead, the tactic Castro Madero settled on might be dubbed "bribery." Northern suppliers would probably not be willing to risk the ire of the US in order to sell a single nuclear power plant to an Argentina that remained outside the NPT; but, Castro Madero reasoned, the prospect of building several plants, each with an astronomically high price tag, might help them conquer their doubts.[47] He was right.

The first step taken under the new *Plan Nuclear* was to contract for a third power reactor, to be dubbed Atucha II.[48] Unlike the first two calls for tender, in this case the Argentines specified that the reactor had to be fueled by that symbol of national autonomy, natural uranium. The natural uranium preference, which had been reasonably defensible on technical grounds ten years earlier, was by now driven purely by the goal of nationalist self-expression.[49] Moreover, only Canada continued to offer a credible natural-uranium-fueled alternative, and Canada and Argentina were deeply mired in conflict over the still-unfinished reactor at Embalse. Indeed, the Canadians' trust of the Argentines had dipped so low that they now refused to commit to serious technology transfer even if Argentina did accept full-scope safeguards.[50] This was the bitter harvest of Argentina's growing reputation as a nuclear rogue, a reputation greatly enhanced by the tactic of "blackmail." But Castro Madero's "bribery" strategy paid off – at least in terms of the self-expressive priorities that the regime had developed since the Tlatelolco agreement went sour. Under the theory that the customer is always right, the Germans (KWU-Siemens) brought their old Atucha I design out of mothballs. In addition, knowing that their reactor was technologically backward and 50 percent more expensive than the Canadian offering – which itself, at $1 billion, was no bargain – they dropped the requirement that Argentina adopt

---

[47] Note from Carlos Castro Madero, CNEA president, to President Videla, November 7, 1978. Private archive.

[48] A third power reactor had already been approved in principle in 1976, but Videla's 1979 decree authorized the CNEA to engage in "final negotiations" – in addition to putting up the money for the reactor. Poder Ejecutivo Nacional, Decreto 302.

[49] It hardly even made sense in those terms, since the US monopoly on uranium enrichment had broken down, meaning that purchase of an enriched-uranium reactor did not imply dependence on one supplier for reactor fuel. Yet even while noting these points, a March 1978 internal CNEA report still leaned toward natural uranium for the purpose of "national autonomy." Ing. Jerónimo J. C. Martínez and Cap. De Frag. (R.) Waldemar J. P. Maidana, "Uranio natural y uranio enriquecido," informe producido en el Departamento Factibilidad de Centrales Nucleares, CNEA, March 17, 1978. Private archive.

[50] Castro Madero and Takacs, *Política nuclear argentina*, p. 187.

full-scope safeguards.[51] On September 28, 1979, Argentina awarded the Atucha II contract to KWU-Siemens, along with a companion contract for an industrial-size heavy water plant to the Sulzer Brothers of Switzerland. Many more such "victories" would have bankrupted the country.

Argentina's secret uranium enrichment plant: genesis and purposes

This chapter has emphasized that Argentina's nuclear program was motivated by the desire for technological autonomy, which itself was based on a sportsmanlike nationalist NIC that was widely shared among all relevant political actors. This desire for technological autonomy also motivated the most reckless of all of the country's nuclear choices: the construction of a secret uranium enrichment plant near the village of Pilcaniyeu in the Andes mountains. Many observers have considered Pilcaniyeu to be the smoking gun that proves that Argentina under the *Proceso* was engaged in a nuclear weapons program.[52] But internal documentary evidence indicates otherwise.

The genesis of the uranium enrichment plant lay in the April 1978 passage of the US Nuclear Non-Proliferation Act (NNPA). The NNPA made it US policy to deny any provision of enriched uranium to those states that had refused to sign on to the non-proliferation regime. In the face of this US initiative, Argentina's adoption of natural uranium fuel for its power reactors suddenly looked prescient. But Argentina's smaller research reactors did require enriched uranium. Argentina's pride in its research reactors was particularly great, because it was now designing and building them itself. Moreover, the CNEA had recently won a contract to export an Argentine-built research reactor to Peru; this was to be the country's first ever significant high-technology export. The Peru reactor deal was quite modest from an economic perspective, but as the CNEA physicist and historian Mario Mariscotti told me, it was highly important as a "philosophical question . . . a question of pride."[53] For the CNEA and for the Argentines generally, the Peru reactor was a symbol of Argentina's return to the ranks of developed nations. The US cutoff of enriched uranium to Argentina suddenly put the Peru project in jeopardy.[54]

---

[51] Carlos Castro Madero, "Razones sobre las que se basó la adjudicación de la planta de agua pesada y la central nuclear Atucha II," CNEA document marked "Secreto," September 1979. Private archive. Also see Daniel Poneman, *Nuclear Power in the Developing World* (London: Allen & Unwin, 1982), p. 80.

[52] For instance, Mozley, *The Politics and Technology of Nuclear Proliferation*, p. 206; Spector, *Nuclear Proliferation Today*, pp. 220–221.

[53] Interview with Mario Mariscotti, former CNEA scientist and nuclear historian, Buenos Aires, August 4, 1999, with follow-up communication November 9, 1999.

[54] Argentina was able to acquire enriched uranium from the Soviet Union that saved the Peru deal. But the Soviet Union could not be counted on as a stable supplier, so Argentina

In response to the US cutoff, the CNEA scientist Conrado Varotto came up with a breathtakingly ambitious idea: Argentina should try to enrich its own uranium. Such a step would represent by far the most complicated technical feat that the CNEA had ever attempted. Because of the proliferation implications of enriching uranium, it would also be complicated from a diplomatic perspective. But President Videla approved the plan, though he insisted that it must remain a secret. Castro Madero agreed to undertake the project under the cover of Investigaciones Aplicadas (INVAP) S.E., a CNEA-run company.[55] This is yet another example of the backfiring of heavy-handed US non-proliferation pressures on sportsmanlike nationalist Argentina.

The first, highly secret report on the enrichment project after its launch in June 1978 mentions two policy objectives in building the plant: first, "it permits the CNEA to acquire the capacity to produce its own enriched fuel for research reactors and/or production of radioisotopes," and second, "it permits the country to acquire capacity for international negotiation in a sensitive national security area."[56] As for the technical objectives, the plant was to utilize the old-fashioned "gaseous diffusion" process to produce up to 500 kilograms of 20 percent enriched uranium per year. The estimated cost was quite small, indeed so small that the existing CNEA budget could cover it.[57] A functioning pilot plant was projected in one year's time, while the industrial-size plant was estimated to need two years for completion.[58]

It is clear from the list of policy objectives that the enrichment plant, while originally conceived of by Varotto as a means of replacing the fuel for Argentina's research reactors, had taken on additional, "national security" significance on its way to presidential approval.[59] What does the report's cryptic reference to "national security" refer to? It is quite evident that it does not refer to a nascent or even a potential nuclear weapons

needed to seek other options. See Castro Madero and Takacs, *Política nuclear argentina*, p. 80.
[55] Interview with Conrado Varotto, former head of the Argentine enrichment program, Buenos Aires, August 20, 1999. INVAP was a "state company" whose shares were held by one of Argentina's provinces, while the board was entirely controlled by the CNEA.
[56] CNEA, "Informe DDG 1/78: Informe Preliminar," document produced June 1978. Private archive. Note that the possibility of feeding some enriched-uranium fuel into the natural uranium reactors – one prominent reason the CNEA gave for the plant after its existence was revealed in 1983 – was not mentioned at the outset of the project.
[57] Castro Madero and Takacs report that the total cost was $62.5 million dollars spread out over five years. Castro Madero and Takacs, *Política nuclear argentina*, pp. 84–85.
[58] CNEA, "Informe DDG 1/78."
[59] Note that the fact that this document does mention national security shows that the *absence* of such mentions in reference to other elements of the nuclear program does not reflect some taboo about acknowledging military objectives in print, but instead reflects an actual lack of interest in such objectives.

program. In particular, there is the fact that the plant was designed to produce 20 percent enriched uranium, whereas bombs require over 90 percent enriched uranium. Some observers have opined that the plant could have eventually been reconfigured for the production of 90 percent enriched uranium, but it is hard to see why *people building a plant in total secrecy* would have chosen to make life so difficult for themselves.[60]

Rather than bombs, the most likely "national security" purpose of the enriched uranium was as fuel for an eventual fleet of nuclear submarines. Although 20 percent enrichment is insufficient for a nuclear bomb, it is more than sufficient for some types of nuclear submarine reactors. The projected amount of 20 percent enriched uranium to be produced also was sufficient to fuel submarine reactors.[61] Moreover, in contrast to the general lack of interest in nuclear weapons among Argentine elites, the idea of nuclear submarines had indeed aroused substantial interest in the Argentine Navy, the service with the closest institutional links to the CNEA.

As early as 1970, the CNEA and the Navy engaged in a joint feasibility study of nuclear propulsion, along with the Italian atomic energy authority and German and Italian firms.[62] The study had concluded that the idea was basically not feasible for Argentina. But the issue was revived in 1972–73 by the German bid for the Embalse reactor contract. In that bid, the Germans promised not only to provide uranium enrichment technology as noted earlier, but also "close collaboration also in the area of marine propulsion and compact nuclear stations for the generation of energy," e.g., reactors for the purpose of propulsion.[63] Intrigued by this possibility, in 1973 the CNEA and the Navy prepared a secret accord in which the Navy would provide funds for CNEA research in "compact power reactors, apt for naval propulsion, designed to utilize freely available national fuel."[64] This last determination – not only to study propulsion, but also to utilize "national fuel" – is crucial evidence for the link between Navy

---

[60] Leonard Spector with Jacqueline R. Smith, *Nuclear Ambitions: The Spread of Nuclear Weapons, 1989–1990* (Boulder, CO: Westview Press, 1990), p. 228.

[61] The relevant technical data can be found in Marvin M. Miller's presentation in Paul Leventhal and Sharon Tanzer, eds., *Averting a Latin American Nuclear Arms Race: New Prospects and Challenges for Argentine–Brazil Nuclear Cooperation* (New York: St. Martin's Press, 1992). It should be noted that Miller's paper is technical, not empirical in nature.

[62] CNEA, "Proyecto de propulsión naval nuclear: estudio de evaluación preliminar para la armada argentina," document marked "Reservado," dated 1971. File OP 633/1, Archives of the Escuela de Guerra Naval, Buenos Aires.

[63] CNEA, "Memorandum: Aspectos de una cooperación entre la Argentina y el grupo KWU en el área de propulsión nuclear de barcos y de unidades de pequeña capacidad de generación de energía nuclear," document dated January 3, 1973. Private archive.

[64] I cannot confirm whether or not this accord was actually given final approval, but I did find what appear to be early and final drafts. "Acta Convenio entre el Comando en Jefe de la Armada en adelante 'La Armada', representado en este acto por el señor

interest in propulsion and the uranium enrichment project. The appointment of Admiral Carlos Castro Madero, the chief of the Navy Research and Development Service (*Servicio Naval de Investigación y Desarrollo*), as CNEA president in 1976 gave even greater impetus to the country's submarine dreams.[65] In 1977 those dreams came closer to reality when the government contracted with the German company Thyssen Rheinstahl for the acquisition of a class of diesel attack submarine, the TR 1700, with operational characteristics similar to that of a nuclear submarine.[66] The deal was to construct the first two vessels in Germany and the next four in Argentina.[67] In that same year, the CNEA organized a project to build a small, enriched-uranium power reactor capable of supporting propulsion.[68] Then, in 1978, the enrichment program began.

In short, nuclear submarines, not nuclear bombs, seem to have been the "national security" interest behind the 1978 decision for the uranium enrichment plant at Pilcaniyeu.[69] Why did the Navy want nuclear submarines? Here again, the reasons lie much more in nationalist self-conceptions than in considerations of real military utility. An Argentine nuclear attack submarine might have been useful in an effort to establish control over the Falklands/Malvinas or the Beagle Channel (territorial disputes that were themselves the products of nationalist sentiments).[70] But the real advantages of nuclear submarines would be nullified unless the Navy also made less flashy but crucial overall improvements in

Comandante en Jefe de la Armada almirante Dn. Carlos Guido Natal Coda y la Comisión Nacional de Energía Atómica, en adelante la CNEA, representada por su presidente, señor Contralmirante Ingeniero Dn. Oscar Armando Quihillalt," document dated 1973. Private archive.

[65] Not only was Castro Madero a stalwart in the nuclear energy field, but he was also explicitly in favor of a nuclear submarine capability, in stark contrast to his position on nuclear weapons. See Julio C. Carasales, Carlos Castro Madero, and José M. Cohen, *Argentina y el submarino de propulsión nuclear: Posibilidades y dificultades* (Buenos Aires: Servicio de Hidrografía Naval, 1992).

[66] Interview with Carrea.

[67] Roberto L. Pertusio, *Una marina de guerra: ¿para hacer qué?* (Buenos Aires: Centro Naval, Instituto de Publicaciones Navales, 1985), pp. 219–222; John Redick, *Argentina and Brazil: An Evolving Nuclear Relationship* (Southampton: University of Southampton on behalf of the Programme for Promoting Nuclear Non-Proliferation, 1990), p. 3.

[68] This information was confirmed in interviews with former and present CNEA officials including Enrique Mariano, Dan Beninson, Roberto Ornstein, Emma Perez Ferreira, and Antonio Carrea (all during August 1999).

[69] Varotto, who headed the enrichment project, refuses to confirm a direct link, but admits that the point is "debatable." Interview with Varotto.

[70] Brazil was making noises about nuclear submarines at the time, and it is not inconceivable that the competition between the two for prestige may have played a role in fomenting this Argentine initiative.

performance, for instance in such areas as logistics and support.[71] In the end, the CNEA was to fail to miniaturize the power plant sufficiently to fit it safely in the Thyssen submarine as designed, so the Navy never actually decided in favor of building a nuclear submarine.[72] But the enrichment program did succeed, and in 1983 the military regime announced that success to a shocked world.

Summary: North America pushes, Argentina pushes back

In sum, the harder the North Americans pushed the Argentines, the harder the Argentines pushed back. While consistently steering clear of the bomb, in other respects the Argentine military regime of the late 1970s and early 1980s went on an increasingly wild binge of nationalist self-expression in the nuclear field. Such self-expression was hardly limited to its diplomatic stance. From the policy of "blackmail," to the policy of "bribery," to the utterly reckless decision to build a secret uranium enrichment plant, Argentina engaged in an orgy of nuclear technology acquisition that was both extremely costly and increasingly distant from the economy's more pressing needs. The Argentine nuclear choices in the late 1970s and early 1980s may have been increasingly unjustifiable from the standpoint of economic rationality, but they were equally increasingly emotionally satisfying in the face of heavy-handed Northern pressures. Next, I show how Argentina's spiraling diplomatic fight with the US dovetailed with its increasingly tense security relations with Brazil.

A Southern Cone nuclear arms race?

Almost all of the non-proliferation literature on Argentina has focused on Argentine–Brazilian status competition as potential kindling for a nuclear arms race. Contrary to the imaginings of Northern non-proliferation advocates, until the mid-1970s Argentina and Brazil actually viewed themselves less as rivals than as partners against unfair Northern nuclear demands. But in 1975, an Argentine–Brazilian nuclear rivalry was indeed born. This was something the Argentines had neither expected nor desired, and they soon backed away from it as best they could. The caution exhibited in Argentina's diplomacy toward Brazil stands in sharp contrast to the recklessness in Argentina's diplomacy toward the North.

---

[71] Interview with Admiral Roberto Pertusio, Buenos Aires, August 24, 1999, with follow-up communication November 10, 1999. This fact was also essentially admitted by Cohen as well in *Argentina y el submarino*, pp. 95–96.

[72] Admiral Roberto Pertusio, a submariner, was instrumental in pointing out the defects in the CNEA's design in a meeting in the early 1980s. Interview with Pertusio.

The reason for this difference is clear from the preferences of sportsman-like nationalists as outlined in Chapter 2. Argentina's leaders were willing to pursue their nationalist self-expression even at the risk of diplomatic isolation, but not at the risk of nuclear destruction.

The Argentine–Brazilian nuclear accord of 1980

The nuclear rivalry with Brazil blossomed in 1975 when Brazil and West Germany signed a gigantic, billion-dollar nuclear deal involving "the largest technology package ever to be transferred from a developed to a developing country."[73] This accord promised to help Brazil leapfrog from nuclear backwardness to the cutting edge of nuclear technology, including the highly advanced uranium enrichment process that the Germans had earlier offered Argentina. In making this deal Brazil was at least partially motivated by the desire to be able to respond quickly in case an increasingly unpredictable Argentina chose to build nuclear weapons.[74] The potential for a nuclear arms race in the Southern Cone was increased by the countries' fast-deteriorating relations over their vast shared hydro-electric resources.[75]

In 1976, the newly installed military junta appointed Oscar Camilión as ambassador to Brazil. Bilateral tensions were high, and some of the initial Argentine reactions to the German–Brazilian nuclear deal had been intemperate.[76] For Camilión, the hypothesis of an Argentine–Brazilian nuclear arms race was "not an academic problem," although he never heard any consequential Argentine official say that the country needed nuclear weapons. Camilión and his superiors felt that the Argentine–Brazilian tension was due to a limited rather than an existential conflict of interests, and therefore that a nuclear arms race was neither desirable nor inevitable. After arriving in Brazil he worked assiduously to head off such an eventuality.[77]

When in early 1977 Jimmy Carter's emissary, Warren Christopher, came to Brazil and violently attacked the German–Brazilian nuclear deal for its proliferation implications, Camilión "took the riskiest decision of

---

[73] Adler, *The Power of Ideology*, p. 281.
[74] Michael Barletta, "The Military Nuclear Program in Brazil," Center for International Security and Cooperation Working Paper, Stanford University, August 1997, p. 15.
[75] Some of the Argentine "geopolitical" school's assessments of the security implications of this other conflict are referenced and summarized in Contraalmirante Fernando A. Milia, "El pensamiento marítimo argentino," *Boletín del Centro Naval*, Vol. 111, No. 770 (April–June 1993), p. 385.
[76] Including a proposed resolution in the Argentine Congress to go nuclear – a proposal that was immediately disowned by the Argentine government and the CNEA. See Poneman, "Argentina," p. 105.
[77] Interview with Oscar Camilión, Argentine diplomat and politician who was ambassador to Brazil at the time discussed, Buenos Aires, August 17, 1999.

my diplomatic career: I told the Brazilian press that I had no doubt of the peaceful intentions of the Brazilian program."[78] Camilión says he was nearly fired for taking this initiative on his own, but cooler heads prevailed in Buenos Aires. His quick defense of Brazil against the American charges in fact became the basis for an Argentine–Brazilian nuclear *rapprochement*. Camilión recruited an eager CNEA President Castro Madero – who had made similar public comments – for informal discussions between the CNEA and its Brazilian counterpart.[79] This nuclear *rapprochement*, greatly aided by the Corpus Itaipú agreement which permitted the joint exploitation of the massive hydroelectric energy resources of the river Paraná, was formalized by an accord signed by the military presidents of Argentina and Brazil in May 1980.[80] Thus ironically, the American pressure on the non-proliferation issue "worked" in that it angered the Argentines and Brazilians so much that they patched up their differences with each other in order to form a common diplomatic front against the US.[81]

The 1980 Argentine–Brazilian nuclear *rapprochement* faced the dilemma of balancing the two conflicting imperatives of nationalism and mutual security. Neither side was any keener on accepting inspections of their facilities by fellow Latin Americans as by the IAEA. The accord that the military leaders signed in 1980 thus offered predictably weak safeguards. Instead of an inspection regime, the two sides contented themselves with verbal assurances and some limited technical cooperation between their respective atomic energy authorities.[82] That a diplomatic *entente* between Argentina and Brazil was possible on the basis of such a weak regime shows the lack of underlying enmity between the two. The agreement proved effective in defusing the immediate conflict, although in the long term the two would choose to develop a more extensive bilateral safeguards system.

Argentina's non-bomb lobby

In spite of the evidence on the sportsmanlike nationalist character of Argentine NICs that was presented in Chapter 3, the reader may still be

---

[78] Interview with Camilión.
[79] Castro Madero and Takacs, *Política nuclear argentina*, p. 232; Interview with Camilión.
[80] Julio Carasales, *De rivales a socios: El proceso de cooperación nuclear entre Argentina y Brasil* (Buenos Aires: Grupo Editor Latinoamericano, 1997), p. 62.
[81] This irony is also noted in Castro Madero and Takacs, *Política nuclear argentina*, p. 232, and in John R. Redick, Julio C. Carasales, and Paulo S. Wrobel, "Nuclear Rapprochement: Argentina, Brazil and the Nonproliferation Regime," *Washington Quarterly*, Vol. 18, No. 1 (Winter 1995), p. 118.
[82] For an analysis of the accord, see Carasales, *De rivales a socios*, pp. 62–69.

surprised at how easily the Argentines reversed course when confronted by the threat of a nuclear arms race with Brazil. How, for instance, did they beat back their internal "bomb lobby"? In fact, one of the crucial points to note about sportsmanlike nationalist Argentina is that it never had a bomb lobby. In particular, the usual suspects for such a lobby – military strategists and "geopolitical" thinkers – viewed a potential nuclear arms race with Brazil as nothing less than a "strategic absurdity."[83]

Argentina's most important defense intellectual during the 1970s was the retired general Juan Guglialmelli, editor of the highly influential *Estrategia*, an independent review of geopolitics.[84] As a good "geopolitical" thinker, Guglialmelli showed a deep and abiding concern about the Argentine–Brazilian strategic balance. But, he wrote, the need for a balance within the Southern Cone was secondary to the need for the two states to join *together* to break down the international structural obstacles to their development. As he put it in an article published in *Estrategia* in 1970, Argentina should take as its "basic thesis . . . that the national interest of both countries coincides in supporting their respective national development [efforts]. Both interests, before being contradictory, are coinciding."[85] This was a direct attack on any oppositional nationalist-type thinking. Guglialmelli would consistently maintain this basic point of view in spite of the rising Argentine–Brazilian tensions during the decade, and it led him to conclude that Argentina had little to gain and much to lose from a nuclear arms race with its neighbor.

It was in the wake of India's so-called PNE test of 1974 that Guglialmelli first brought up the question of a Southern Cone nuclear arms race in the pages of *Estrategia*.[86] In a series of articles, he wrote that for Argentina to follow India's lead would be a mistake, for whatever the prestige benefits associated with going nuclear, the "fundamental motive"

---

[83] Admiral Fernando A. Milia, "Armamento nuclear en el Cono Sur: un dislate estratégico," *Boletín del Centro Naval*, Vol. 113, No. 777 (January–March 1995), pp. 87–92.

[84] Raúl Larra, *La Batalla del General Guglialmelli* (Buenos Aires: Editorial Distal, 1995).

[85] Dirección de *Estrategia*, "Relaciones argentino-brasileñas," *Estrategia*, No. 5 (January–February 1970), p. 52.

[86] The other main military and strategic journals showed much less interest even in the general topic of nuclear weapons, let alone in the prospect of an Argentine bomb. In a review of several journals from the 1960s to the 1980s I found only one article that explicitly called for an Argentine – or, actually, for a "Latin American" bomb: Tte. Coronel Juan José Masi, "De Pearl Harbor a las fuerzas armadas nucleares latinoamericanas (la revisión del sistema interamericano de defensa)," *Revista de la Escuela Superior de Guerra*, Vol. 52, No. 414 (September–October 1974), pp. 21–34. Note that the fact that this article was published actually demonstrates that the idea of an Argentine bomb was not a taboo subject for the journals, but rather that simply very few military men were calling for one.

for going nuclear must only be "the security of the state."[87] Indeed, Guglialmelli declared that the international reaction to the Indian test had made it clear that to build even a PNE would inevitably be misperceived as a "transcendental step in another possible direction: the military use of atomic energy."[88] He called instead for bilateral Argentine–Brazilian negotiation of "concrete and reliable accords to avoid a military nuclear competition that could drift toward risky conflict situations."[89] He would repeat his call for bilateral accords after the big Brazilian nuclear deal with the Germans was announced.[90] Some years later, even in the face of what appeared to be significant Brazilian moves toward going nuclear, Guglialmelli sang the same tune and even took a stronger stance against nuclear weapons than he had in the past, using the Indian post-1974 experience as evidence that to go nuclear was not a ticket to international prestige.[91]

Nuclear policies of the Alfonsín government

Needless to say, the 1980 nuclear agreement closely reflected Guglialmelli's proposals, and it succeeded in calming Southern Cone tensions just as he predicted. But in the military regime's waning days after its defeat by Britain in the Falklands/Malvinas War, it announced the existence of the uranium enrichment plant.[92] This shocking revelation produced renewed tensions with Brazil. It was in this context that the democratically elected President Raúl Alfonsín took office. Many external observers expected that newly democratic Argentina would now join the international nuclear fold.[93] But Alfonsín – yet another sportsmanlike nationalist – was to disappoint them.

[87] Juan E. Guglialmelli, "Argentina, Brasil y la bomba atómica," *Estrategia*, No. 30 (September–October 1974), p. 13.

[88] Ibid., p. 11.

[89] Juan E. Guglialmelli, "América Latina. Venta de armas de los EEUU y eventuales implicancias de la explosión atómica de la India," *Estrategia*, No. 28 (May–June 1974), p. 65.

[90] Juan E. Guglialmelli, "¿Y si Brasil fabrica la bomba atómica? (A propósito del acuerdo brasileño-alemán)," *Estrategia*, No. 34–35 (May–August 1975), p. 14.

[91] Juan E. Guglialmelli, "¿Brasil fabrica la bomba atómica?" *Estrategia*, No. 70 (July–Sept. 1981), p. 9.

[92] There is no evidence that after the conflict with Britain the military called for an Argentine nuclear bomb, as some have suggested. The Air Force did however determine it needed intermediate-range missiles, however – a story I will discuss briefly later in this chapter.

[93] Cynthia Watson, "Will Civilians Control the Nuclear Tiger in Argentina?" in Peter Worsley and Kofi Buenor Hadjor, *On the Brink: Nuclear Proliferation and the Third World* (London: Third World Communications, 1987), pp. 209–216.

The new president did redouble efforts to build a solid bilateral nuclear regime with Brazil.[94] But after determining that the enrichment plant had in fact not been part of a secret nuclear weapons program and after calming Brazil's fears about it, Alfonsín actually ended up confirming Argentina's historic nuclear stance. Indeed, a key point to note is that as had been the case in previous decades, Argentine–Brazilian diplomatic collaboration in the 1980s was as much about opposing the global non-proliferation regime as it was about building mutual trust. The creation of a bilateral nuclear regime was hardly seen in Argentina and Brazil as the first step toward accepting the NPT and associated measures; rather, it was seen as a way of fending off pressure to join them.[95] Predictably, the two countries' joint stance against the international regime was mis-interpreted in the North and even led to fantastic assertions that the two might be planning to launch a "bi-national" bomb program.[96] (Alfonsín did make a serious proposal to work together on a nuclear submarine, which Brazil politely declined.)[97]

Alfonsín, the sportsmanlike nationalist, also maintained Argentina's vigorous efforts to achieve nuclear technological autonomy. In addition to continuing support for the uranium enrichment plant at Pilcaniyeu, he also confirmed the *Plan Nuclear*'s goal of building new nuclear power plants capable of producing a total of 700 megawatts in the coming years.[98] Moreover, during his tenure Argentina launched an aggressive nuclear export policy that succeeded in selling small nuclear research reactors (under international safeguards) to such states as Algeria and Egypt.[99]

---

[94] The breakthroughs of Southern Cone nuclear diplomacy in the 1980s have been carefully documented elsewhere, so there is no reason to detail them here. See especially Carasales, *De rivales a socios*. See also Michael Barletta, "Democratic Security and Diversionary Peace: Nuclear Confidence-Building in Argentina and Brazil," *National Security Studies Quarterly* (Summer 1999), pp. 19–38.

[95] Andrés Cisneros and Carlos Escudé, eds., *Historia general de las relaciones exteriors de la República Argentina, tomo XIV: Las relaciones políticas, 1966–1989* (Buenos Aires: Nuevohacer, Grupo Editor Latinoamericano, 2003), pp. 536–539.

[96] Such fears were expressed by North American panelists at the Montevideo conference: Leventhal and Tanzer, eds., *Averting a Latin American Nuclear Arms Race*.

[97] Interviews with Beninson and with CNEA Director of International Relations Roberto Ornstein, Buenos Aires, August 9, 1999. Here again we see Argentina's continuing interest in nuclear submarines as opposed to its lack of interest in nuclear weapons.

[98] República Argentina, Ministerio de Obras y Servicios Públicos, Secretaría de Energía, Subsecretaría de Planificación Energética, *Plan Energético Nacional 1986–2000* (Buenos Aires, República Argentina, 1986), p. 182.

[99] Tomás Buch, "La proyección comercial internacional," in Julio C. Carasales and Roberto M. Ornstein, eds., *La cooperación internacional de la Argentina en el campo nuclear* (Buenos Aires: Consejo Argentino para las Relaciones Internacionales, 1998), pp. 147–208.

The democratic transition of the 1980s had not resulted in a significant nuclear policy shift, but rather a further deepening of nationalist tendencies. By the end of Alfonsín's tenure, the diplomatic clash with the US was just as intense as it had been during the prior military regime.

The Menem nuclear policy shift

In 1989, the Peronist Carlos Menem was elected president. Menem's campaign had been old-fashioned populist in both domestic and foreign policy. His nuclear policy platform had also promised a continuation of the sportsmanlike nationalist formula that had predominated in Argentina for over three decades: resistance to the NPT, continuing progress in nuclear technology, and a disavowal of intention to build the bomb.[100] Not surprisingly, Menem's arrival in power afforded a new opportunity for Northern non-proliferation advocates to sound the alarm about a potential Argentine quest for the bomb.[101] As in previous decades, such worries turned out to be ill-founded. In fact, Menem surprised even his own supporters by bringing about a foreign and nuclear policy revolution of quite a different character. Under his guidance Argentina's external posture changed nearly overnight from the tenacious defense of its independence to what Menem's own foreign minister dubbed "carnal relations" with the United States. In the nuclear sphere, within two years of his election Menem had given in to the Americans' principal historic demands, announcing the intention to submit the nuclear program to full-scope international safeguards and then to ratify the Tlatelolco Treaty.[102] These steps – the impetus for which clearly came from the top – were approved by the Argentine Congress in 1992 and 1994, respectively. For good measure, the NPT was ratified in 1994 as well.[103] Meanwhile, deep budget cuts turned the Argentine nuclear sector into a shell of its

---

[100] Jorge Oscar Cosentino, "Política nuclear," in Partido Justicialista, Instituto Superior de Conducción Política, Consejo de Profesionales, Intelectuales y Técnicos, *Análisis, lineamientos doctrinarios y propuestas para la acción del Gobierno Justicialista* (Buenos Aires: Instituto Superior de Conducción Política del Partido Justicialista, 1989), pp. 327–344.

[101] Albright, "Bomb Potential for South America."

[102] This announcement was made jointly with the Brazilian President Fernando Collor de Mello, who had just revealed his own military's secret nuclear program. "Argentine–Brazilian Declaration of Common Nuclear Policy," International Atomic Energy Agency Information Circular INFCIRC/388, December 3, 1990, http://www.iaea.org/Publications/Documents/Infcircs/others/inf388.shtml.

[103] The reason for Argentina and Brazil's joint action in the nuclear field is often misinterpreted as a need to do everything in lockstep because of a lack of mutual confidence. In fact – as I have emphasized throughout this chapter – Argentina and Brazil worked on these issues jointly because they believed it gave them more leverage *vis-à-vis* the international community. In the early 1990s Brazil still very much wanted that leverage, while Menem had decided that it was bandwagoning with the US that gave Argentina

former self – a literal shell in the case of the Atucha II reactor, which still to this day remains uncompleted. What explains this major policy turnabout?

The typical explanation finds the source of Menem's policy shift in major geopolitical changes that were occurring contemporaneously. The fall of the Berlin Wall placed the United States in the ascendancy; this greatly reduced developing states' international margin for maneuver. Meanwhile, the hyperinflation and collapse of the Argentine economy forced it into the arms of Northern states and bankers. Whatever Menem's long-term ambitions for his country, so the argument goes, in the interest of short-term national survival he had to pawn the nuclear crown jewels. There is a ring of truth to this systemic-level hypothesis, but it cannot be the whole truth. The mere fact that a policy is no longer functional is not an adequate explanation for why a state changes it. Indeed, the productive value of Argentina's nuclear policies had been highly questionable since the mid-1970s, yet in spite of mounting economic difficulties over the years those policies had become *more* politically entrenched, not less. Moreover, many of Menem's closest advisors in the early years of his presidency were actually counseling him to persist with Argentina's traditional state-led development strategies. And as noted earlier, many foreign observers even predicted that Menem would go in the opposite direction and try to build the bomb. In short, a systemic-level hypothesis is clearly not sufficient to explain Menem's choice. To explain his choice, we need to understand his thinking.

Why, then, did he do it? The content analysis results reported in Chapter 3 closed off the most direct potential explanation, originally put forth with brio by Carlos Escudé, that (in my terminology) the external shocks led Menem to abandon his nationalist NIC in favor of a subaltern one, which in turn produced the nuclear policy shift.[104] Instead, the results clearly supported Victor Armony's alternative contention that Menem's rhetoric throughout his presidency remained squarely in the Argentine sportsmanlike nationalist tradition, albeit with a neo-liberal twist.[105] So, if Menem was indeed a sportsmanlike nationalist, how could

the most leverage. He played along with Brazil for a while, but when Brazil tarried on ratifying the NPT, Menem decided to go ahead without it. For more on the Southern Cone angle to this story, see Redick, Carasales, and Wrobel, "Nuclear Rapprochement."

[104] I myself adopted this view in my earlier effort to explain the Argentine nuclear case: see Hymans, "Of Gauchos and Gringos: why Argentina Never Wanted the Bomb, and Why the United States Thought it Did," *Security Studies*, Vol. 10, No. 3 (Spring 2001), pp. 153–185.

[105] Victor Armony, *Représenter la nation: Le discours présidentiel de la transition démocratique en Argentine 1983–1999* (Montreal: L'Univers des discours, 2000).

he have embraced the nuclear policy stance of a sportsmanlike subaltern? As Chapter 2 argued, there are limits to sportsmanlike nationalists' pursuit of national self-expression through nuclear development and rejection of international nuclear discrimination. In particular, sports-manlike nationalists will try to avoid letting these ancillary policy positions trap them into a conflict spiral that leads to the acquisition of nuclear weapons. As noted above, sportsmanlike nationalist Argentina's flexibility about these ancillary positions was clearly in evidence in its backing away from the nuclear rivalry with Brazil. I will argue that Menem's nuclear policy shift was also driven, at least at first, by international security concerns – but this time the incipient opponent was the US itself.

Menem's path to the nuclear policy shift started with a reconsideration of a different, but related policy issue. Argentina's secret Cóndor II intermediate-range missile program had been initiated in the early 1980s by the Air Force as a means of threatening the British Falklands/Malvinas.[106] European (primarily German) corporations had provided sophisticated technology for the project, and there were willing foreign buyers – notably Egypt, Iraq, and Libya. Seeing the project as a means of encouraging Argentine economic development, President Alfonsín had given it his full support.[107] Menem might have, too; in fact, many in his camp were convinced that Argentina could resolve its economic problems by pushing harder into the international military market. Even Menem himself would later become entangled in legal problems related to the illegal sale of Argentine-produced arms to Ecuador and Croatia.[108] While the US had long pressed Argentina to come clean on the missile program, internationally the pressure level was actually relatively low; Menem had been grilled about Argentina's nuclear program but *not* the missile program by the officials he met during his eye-opening European tour before the 1989 election.[109]

Menem's enthusiasm for the missile export business, however, seems to have dulled after a 1989 discussion the new president had with the Libyan leader Muammar Khadafy at the Non-Aligned Movement

---

[106] The CNEA was not involved at all in the project, as it would have had to be if the missiles were to be fitted with nuclear warheads. See Daniel Santoro, *Operación Cóndor II: La historia secreta del misil que desactivó Menem* (Buenos Aires: Ediciones Letra Buena, 1992).

[107] He also did not want to pick a fight with the Air Force. Cisneros and Escudé, eds., *Historia general de las relaciones exteriores de la República Argentina, tomo XIV*, p. 470.

[108] See the memoir of Domingo Cavallo, *El peso de la verdad: un impulse a la transparencia en la Argentina de los 90* (Buenos Aires: Planeta, 1997), esp. ch. 1.

[109] Interview with Domingo Cavallo, who accompanied Menem on the trip and would soon thereafter become his first foreign minister, Cambridge, Massachusetts, June 16, 2004.

conference in Belgrade.[110] Menem, the son of Arab immigrants, had received large campaign contributions from various Middle Eastern states, including Libya and Syria. Now that Menem had won, Khadafy wanted his reward: the Cóndor missile. Menem asked Khadafy why he was so eager to get his hands on a still-unfinished, directionless missile – a mere flying can, as his Air Force chief had put it. Khadafy told him that the real military value did not matter; what mattered was to make the Americans *believe* you have something dangerous. Khadafy's argument came as a revelation to Menem, who immediately afterward told his foreign minister, Domingo Cavallo, "If the North Americans are afraid of the Cóndor, and we now export it to this guy, we will end up being caught in the middle [of their conflict]."[111] Having thus already soured on the project, Menem became a categorical opponent of it when another of the missile's sponsors, Iraq, invaded Kuwait in August 1990 and the Americans began preparing a massive military response. In short order, Menem gave a secret order to the Air Force to cease work on the Cóndor immediately, announced in public that he was canceling the program, and moreover declared that Argentina would send troops to the Gulf to stand and, if necessary, fight alongside the Americans – something it had never done before in its history.[112] The motivation for these unprecedented actions seems evident and, in fact, consistent with the sportsmanlike nationalist Argentine tradition. Indeed, as the journalist Martín Granovsky puts it, "The Menem government convinced itself, in another demonstration of Argentine national exceptionalism . . . that it would be singled out as the principal accomplice of the Iraqi dictatorship in the entire community of nations."[113] In short, Menem the sportsmanlike nationalist might have been willing to pursue policies that *irritated* America, but in fact these policies *threatened* America. That was going too far.[114]

---

[110] Recounted in Martín Granovsky, *Misión cumplida: la presión norteamericana sobre la Argentina, de Braden a Todman* (Buenos Aires: Planeta, 1992), p. 179; Cavallo, *El peso de la verdad*, p. 20.

[111] Granovsky, *Misión cumplida*, p. 179.

[112] Menem had already given an order on July 20 suspending the program and placing it under the direct control of the chief of the Air Force (Granovsky, *Misión cumplida*, p. 200). But these actions seem to have been conceived as a prelude to a negotiation with the Americans, whereas after the Iraqi invasion of Kuwait Menem simply abandoned the notion that he could get something in return for the program's cancellation.

[113] Granovsky, *Misión cumplida*, p. 207.

[114] Indeed, one might say that changes in *American threat perceptions* mattered more to this outcome than changes in *Argentine power perceptions* (as is typically assumed). It is interesting to note that in spite of the choice for alignment, Menem did not become an automatic, unthinking supporter of US foreign policy positions. In the UN General Assembly, for instance, Argentina did not vote with the US more than 50 percent of the time. Francisco Corigliano, Leonor Machinandiarena de Devoto, and Sebastián

Menem pursued "carnal relations" with the Americans to convince them that Argentina would no longer be sleeping with the enemy. His basic choice for alignment over conflict then flowed naturally into his abandonment of Argentina's traditional nuclear policies. In November 1990, Menem made a joint declaration with Brazilian President Fernando Collor de Mello of their intention to accept full-scope IAEA safeguards and then to join the Tlatelolco treaty regime.[115] Two days after the joint declaration, Argentina signed a new bilateral nuclear accord with the US, a memorandum of understanding for technical interchange on reactor safety. A year later, at US behest Menem canceled a major nuclear technology export to Iran. He also halted the sale of research reactor components to Algeria. These actions, along with the cancellation of the Cóndor missile program, were vigorously protested by the ex-president Alfonsín and former foreign minister Dante Caputo, who complained that "no developed country threatens, with measures such as this, its own basic research and technological development."[116] This charge ignored the fact that nothing threatened Argentine development more seriously than for the Americans to lump the country together with Libya and Iraq. But, having chosen alignment as a matter of high politics, Menem also increasingly saw wisdom in the neo-liberal propositions of people like Cavallo and his subsequent foreign minister, Guido di Tella, who viewed the nuclear program as economic insanity. In one Cabinet meeting, di Tella spoke out against "investments of billions of dollars for earnings that do not reach a hundred million."[117] As Cavallo, di Tella, and other neo-liberals defeated their rivals within the administration, they began attacking the nuclear program with increasing abandon. At one point Cavallo, as minister of economy, even tried to privatize that once-proud symbol of Argentine nationalist ambition – but could find no buyers.

In spite of the adversity, the Argentine nuclear industry that had been built by successive generations of nuclear scientists and engineers somehow stumbled forward. In July 2000, the Australian government selected INVAP – formerly the cover for Argentina's secret uranium enrichment program – to construct a new, 20 megawatt (thermal) research reactor

Masana, *Las 'relaciones carnales': los vínculos políticos con las grandes potencies, 1989–2000*, Pt. 4, Vol. XV of *Historia general de las relaciones exteriors de la República Argentina*, ed. Carlos Escudé (Buenos Aires: Nuevohacer, Grupo Editor Latinoamericano, 2003), p. 226.

[115] The reasons for the Brazilian policy shift are not entirely clear, but I would not be surprised if they were found to parallel the Argentine shift. The timing of Collor de Mello's "discovery" of the secret Brazilian nuclear program, September 1990, is circumstantial evidence for this hypothesis.

[116] Corigliano *et al.*, *Las 'relaciones carnales,'* p. 34.   [117] Ibid., p. 34.

at the Lucas Heights nuclear facility near Sydney.[118] And in September 2004, INVAP also won the contract to provide the enriched uranium fuel.[119] The reactor is due to begin operation in 2005.

[118] "Contract Signed for Australia's History-Making Replacement Research Reactor," ANSTO media release, July 13, 2000, available on web at http://www.ansto.gov.au/info/press/2000_09.html.
[119] "La Argentina proveerá los combustibles del reactor nuclear australiano," INVAP press release, September 1, 2004, http://www.invap.net/news/novedades.php?id=20040109094423.

7   "We have a big bomb now": India's nuclear U-turn

Introduction

In May 1998, a newly installed Indian government led by the Hindu nationalist Atal Behari Vajpayee set off five nuclear explosions in the Rajasthan desert and declared to the world that India was now a nuclear weapons state. Why did India suddenly go for nuclear weapons after years of remaining on the other side of the threshold? This chapter finds the key reason in Vajpayee's oppositional nationalism toward Pakistan – a dramatic departure from his secularist predecessors' sportsmanlike nationalist focus on India's place in the world beyond South Asia. Surprisingly, the by now voluminous literature on the Indian tests has tended to downplay the causal importance of the distinctive NIC of Vajpayee and his Bharatiya Janata Party (BJP) in favor of a counterfactual view that sooner or later the tests would have come anyway.[1] To avoid "ahistoricism," we are asked to delve into the supposedly deeper causes of India's grasping for the bomb: the existence of a China with nuclear weapons in the region since 1964; the long-held desire of secular as well as Hindu nationalists for recognition as a world power; and the many years of bomb promotion undertaken by India's scientific-bureaucratic "strategic enclave."[2] But, in fact, what is ahistorical is to view the 1998 tests as the endpoint of a logically unfolding teleology.

---

[1] However, for an argument in favor of the "BJP hypothesis," see Praful Bidwai and Achin Vanaik, *New Nukes: India, Pakistan and Global Nuclear Disarmament* (New York: Olive Branch Press, 2000). Stephen P. Cohen, while stressing the importance of long and medium-range factors, also clearly sees the BJP's ascension to power as the crucial catalyst. Stephen P. Cohen, "Why Did India 'Go Nuclear'?" in Raju G. C. Thomas and Amit Gupta, eds., *India's Nuclear Security* (Boulder, CO: Lynne Rienner Publishers, 2000), pp. 13–36.

[2] The "objective situation" hypothesis is promoted most forcefully by Jasjit Singh, ed., *Nuclear India* (New Delhi: Knowledge World, 1998); T. V. Paul, "The Systemic Bases of India's Challenge to the Global Nuclear Order," *Nonproliferation Review*, Vol. 6, No. 1 (Fall 1998), pp. 1–11; and Ashok Kapur, "India and Multipolarity in the Asia-Pacific Regional Sub-System," paper delivered at the Annual Meeting of the American Political Science Association, September 1999. The "international prestige" hypothesis is placed in the foreground by Raj Chengappa, *Weapons of Peace: The Secret Story of India's*

This is not to deny that India was at the cusp of a nuclear weapons arsenal before 1998. Previous developments in the Indian nuclear program had clouded to the utmost the distinction between "having" and "not having" nuclear weapons. But, in the end, the case paradoxically shows how meaningful that distinction actually is. The 1998 tests, far from representing mere ratifications of a well-known, pre-existing state of affairs, in fact roiled the politics of the region in dramatic and unexpected ways – and continue to do so even to this day. As the South Asian security expert Stephen P. Cohen put it during the Indo-Pakistan crisis of 2002,

> The nuclearization of South Asia had been anticipated for decades, yet when it came, it was a surprise. Then, it was widely assumed that being nuclear weapons states, India and Pakistan could no longer go to war. Indeed, some argued that the possession of nuclear weapons by both states would eventually lead to a reconciliation of their outstanding differences. These expectations were wrong, as the two countries did become embroiled in a minor war in 1999, and despite their declared nuclear status, are again on the brink of war as they enter the sixth month of an unprecedented crisis, featuring full military mobilization and mutual nuclear threats.[3]

Of the four cases tackled in this book, the Indian one is the most complex. Not surprisingly, while it generally supports the theoretical framework introduced in Chapter 2, it does not perfectly fit that framework. In particular, Pakistan turns out to have loomed larger in the secularist Indian leaders' calculations than might have been expected given the coding results reported in Chapter 3. But the case poses even more difficult problems for the more conventional perspectives.

- First, realists generally consider the Indian bomb as a response to China's holding nuclear weapons. But the Chinese tested their bomb in 1964; yet, in spite of having long had the technical capacity, India took until 1972 to have a political decision in favor of a so-called "peaceful

---

Quest to Be a Nuclear Power (New Delhi: HarperCollins, 2000); and chapters by Amitabh Mattoo and Pramit Pal Chaudhuri in Amitabh Mattoo, ed., *India's Nuclear Deterrent: Pokhran II and Beyond* (New Delhi: Har Anand Publications Pvt., 1999). "The "strategic enclave" hypothesis is highlighted by George Perkovich, *India's Nuclear Bomb: The Impact on Global Proliferation* (Berkeley: University of California Press, 1999) and Itty Abraham, *The Making of the Indian Atomic Bomb: Science, Secrecy and the Postcolonial State* (London: Zed Books, 1998). An attempt to include all of these factors (and the BJP variable as well) is Stephen P. Cohen, "Why Did India 'Go Nuclear'?" The charge of "ahistoricism" was made by Sumit Ganguly, "Explaining the Indian Nuclear Tests of 1998," in Raju G. C. Thomas and Amit Gupta, eds., *India's Nuclear Security* (Boulder, CO: Lynne Rienner Publishers, 2000), pp. 37–66.

[3] Stephen P. Cohen, "Nuclear Weapons and Nuclear War in South Asia: An Unknowable Future," paper presented to the United Nations University Conference on South Asia, Tokyo, Japan, May 2002, http://www.brookings.edu/views/speeches/cohens/20020501.htm.

nuclear explosion" (PNE). Moreover, despite the success of the 1974 Indian PNE, the government refused to test further or to develop an actual nuclear arsenal until a quarter-century later. Clearly the Indian nuclear weapons program has not been driven by events on the other side of the Himalayas.

• Second, institutionalists generally expect decreasing interest in nuclear weapons worldwide over time, as the flip side of the rise of non-proliferation norms. But although India is hardly a "rogue state," its interest in nuclear weapons steadily increased over time, and international pressure and opprobrium even tended to solidify the Indians' resolve to go their own way.

• Third, although over the decades bureaucratic actors were able to make some progress in the shadows toward the bomb, they found that they could not achieve all they wanted without a top-down decision to go nuclear. But they could not pry that decision out of a long series of prime ministers, even quite weak ones. Indeed, all three of the major steps forward in the development of India's nuclear bomb – 1972–74, 1988, and 1998 – were taken by strong prime ministers whom the bureaucrats could hardly be said to have pushed around.

The chapter is organized as follows. The second part explains India's traditional nuclear stances as a function of the Nehruvian NIC of sportsmanlike nationalism. The third part presents an interpretation of Indira Gandhi's 1972 decision for a PNE and its immediate consequences. The fourth part explores the decisions on nuclear issues that Indian prime ministers took in the twenty-four years between the PNE and the coming to power of the BJP. Finally, BJP Prime Minister Atal Behari Vajpayee's definitive 1998 decision to go nuclear is explained.

The nuclear expression of Indian nationalism, 1947–71

From its earliest days as an independent state, India had a high international profile on nuclear issues. Despite its military weakness, India was a major player in international disarmament talks. And although it was mired in almost hopeless economic backwardness, India rapidly built a significant civilian nuclear program. Both its diplomatic and its technological ambitions – as well as its clear determination not to build the bomb – were the consequences of the NIC of sportsmanlike nationalism that was held by Jawaharlal Nehru and his successors.

Nehruvian India's nuclear diplomacy

Newly independent India took a very high profile in international disarmament negotiations, one completely out of proportion to its small military capacity. A prime example of India's diplomatic activism on the nuclear issue is Prime Minister Jawaharlal Nehru's 1954 proposal at the UN for a universal nuclear test ban. As noted in Chapter 4, only strong pressure from the US prevented French Prime Minister Pierre Mendès France from taking up Nehru's call in his own speech to the UN in November of that year. In the longer term, Nehru's proposal was a forerunner of the 1963 Partial Test Ban Treaty that banned atmospheric nuclear tests, and that India was quick to sign and ratify. In later decades, India would revive Nehru's call for a universal test ban on numerous occasions. For instance, Nehru's daughter, Prime Minister Indira Gandhi, participated in the 1983 Six-Nation Initiative for a universal test ban, and in 1988 his grandson, Prime Minister Rajiv Gandhi presented the UN with an Action Plan for the elimination of nuclear weapons by 2010, the first step of which was to be a universal test ban.[4] The vigorous and continued efforts that Nehruvian India made on this matter demonstrates not merely its strong stance against the continuing existence of nuclear weapons, but also its nationalist belief that India could make a difference on central issues of global war and peace.

India also took a high profile in the late 1960s negotiations over the NPT. Many analysts have trouble understanding why Nehruvian India could have rejected the NPT unless it at least was thinking about acquiring nuclear weapons.[5] But in fact the principle of non-discrimination mattered to Nehruvian India, and this is what kept it from supporting the NPT while promoting a universal test ban. As the British Chief Science Advisor Sir Solly Zuckerman (who had close ties with Indian statesmen and scientists) wrote in a secret 1971 report, "This refusal [of the NPT] appears to be motivated much more by a sense of injured pride and a belief that the 'haves' wish to maintain their advantage at the expense of the 'have-nots,' rather than by a determination to acquire nuclear weapons."[6] The negative Indian reaction to the uneven nature of obligations envisioned by the NPT was widespread. Even the noted nuclear dove, Indian Atomic Energy Commission (AEC) chairman Vikram Sarabhai, strongly opposed the treaty; the Indian scientist Raja Ramanna explained his position to me in this manner: "Dr. Sarabhai did not believe in nuclear

---

[4] These calls were always placed in the perspective of general nuclear disarmament, though Indian insistence on a formal linkage between the test ban and further steps to decrease the arms race waxed and waned. Dinshaw Mistry, "The Unrealized Promise of International Institutions: The Test Ban Treaty and India's Nuclear Breakout," *Security Studies*, Vol. 12, No. 4 (Summer 2003), pp. 119–160.

[5] Ganguly, "Explaining the Indian Nuclear Tests," p. 46.

[6] Draft "confidential" note from Sir Solly Zuckerman on "Visit to Indian Establishments, 7–17 March 1971," prepared by R. Press, Solly Zuckerman papers SZ/CSA/25/1, "Visit to India March 1971," University of East Anglia, Norwich, UK.

weapons, but more than that, he did not believe in signing inequitable treaties."[7] Sarabhai was not alone; a scientific poll of Indian elites at the time of the NPT negotiations found that they stood both against an Indian nuclear bomb and against the "nuclear apartheid" regime of the NPT.[8] Indeed, Indian feelings against the NPT were so strong that for any Indian leader, even Nehru's daughter, to accede would have been to "commit political suicide," as the AEC official (later chairman) Homi Sethna told an American diplomat in 1968.[9] But Indira Gandhi, a sportsmanlike nationalist herself, did not need to take a poll to determine her position on the issue.

Nehruvian India's push for nuclear development

While opposing international nuclear discrimination on the diplomatic front, Nehruvian India also devoted great efforts to building a credible civilian nuclear technology sector. It was in India's very first year of independence that Nehru created the Atomic Energy Commission, placing it directly under the authority of the prime minister in order to ensure that it did his bidding. After founding the AEC, Nehru and his chief nuclear scientist, Homi Bhabha, succeeded in importing a 40 megawatt Canadian research reactor in the mid-1950s. As a technologically backward state, India had no choice but to import the reactor, but at the same time it strongly resisted international controls and rights of inspection over it. For Nehru, if mastery of nuclear energy was part and parcel of India's newfound freedom, the maintenance of an "international" – read, Western – *droit de regard* over India's nuclear energy program represented continuing Indian enslavement.[10] The Canadians proved quite understanding of this Indian resistance, not least due to their impression of Nehru as a fundamentally honorable man, so they did not press the issue.[11] Only a few years later, India added a fuel reprocessing plant

---

[7] Written communication with Raja Ramanna, former AEC chairman, November 19, 1998.

[8] Ashis Nandy, "The Bomb, the NPT and Indian Elites," *Economic and Political Weekly*, special number, August 1972. Thanks to Stephen Cohen for this article.

[9] "Conversation with Senior GOI Nuclear Official," Department of State telegram marked "Secret," May 7, 1968, Box 2648, RG 59, Central Files "Science" 1967–69, National Archives, College Park, Maryland.

[10] There was an entire theory of history behind these points. See Jawaharlal Nehru, *The Discovery of India* (New Delhi: Oxford University Press, 1998), esp. pp. 276–80.

[11] It was "participatory internationalism" more than commercial considerations that led the Canadians to give the Indians this gift. See Iris Heidrun Lonergan, "The Negotiations Between Canada and India for the Supply of the N. R. X. Nuclear Research Reactor 1955–56: A Case Study in Participatory Internationalism," M.A. thesis, Department of History, Carleton University, Ontario, Canada, 1989.

to its nuclear infrastructure, a plant that eventually came on line in 1964. Thus a poverty-stricken, scientifically backward nation was devoting major resources to independent research and development on the most advanced technology on earth. This was the direct result of Nehru's nationalism.

With the combination of unsafeguarded reactor fuel and a fuel reprocessing plant, India had access by the mid-1960s to plutonium that it was at liberty to employ for any purpose it chose.[12] It was this combination that would eventually allow India to build a nuclear explosive device in the early 1970s. But it would be wrong to jump from this technical equation to the assertion that Nehru wanted the bomb – an assertion made today by a growing number of analysts who are determined to see a logical continuity in Indian nuclear history.[13]

One seductive argument along these lines is that of Itty Abraham, who claims that Nehru and his colleagues, as "unmitigated votaries of large-scale industrialization," were entranced with everything scientific, modern, statist, and big – and that this ideology, whatever their protestations to the contrary, made the bomb inherently attractive to them.[14] But Abraham's portrayal of Nehru as a "postcolonial" leader aping the West is in fact a substantial underestimation of the man. In fact, Nehru exhibited a remarkable level of independence from the West not only in deed but also in thought. It is well to recall that in these early years Nehru and the Congress Party he led were still fresh from the success of the highly original non-violent struggle to end British colonial rule. For the Nehruvians, nuclear weapons represented the fundamental corruption of Western modernity, which India should not merely reject itself but also teach all humanity to spurn. And Nehru did not just talk a good game; in 1957 he flatly rejected a proposal by Homi Bhabha that India start research in the area of nuclear explosives.[15] Moreover, Nehru's rejection of the bomb was *not* an anomaly in his overall stance toward technology, as Abraham would have it. It rather reflected his rejection of gigantism in all things military. Nehru was consistently at odds with the Western (mainly British) military advisors who were "helping" newly independent India to design and build a modern fighting force. These advisors were

---

[12] Exactly how much plutonium it had amassed at what moment is a matter of dispute; but the argument of this book does not hang on such technical determinations. The point here is the broader one that India had a clear path to the bomb if it so chose.

[13] The man most responsible for the evolution in perspective on Nehru is the Indian nuclear hawk K. Subrahmanyam. He now has begun to argue that Mahatma Gandhi also would have favored the Indian bomb. See Cohen, "Why Did India 'Go Nuclear'?," p. 18.

[14] The direct quote is from Abraham, *The Making of the Indian Atomic Bomb*, p. 72.

[15] Interview with T. N. Kaul, Indian diplomat (former foreign secretary), New Delhi, December 3, 1998, with follow-up letters March 7 and May 5, 1999.

trying to promote Indian investment in advanced military systems such as large bombers, rockets, and aircraft carriers. Nehru considered these grandiose schemes as likely to draw India into the international balance of power system, to ruin India's economy, to strengthen the Indian military at the expense of India's democracy, and to end in renewed Indian political dependence on the West.[16] The Nehruvian pattern of relative Indian modesty in defense procurement, both in quantitative and qualitative terms, would continue until the 1980s.[17]

Thus, Nehru's sportsmanlike nationalist vision in the area of technology was clear and his policy application of that vision remarkably consistent. In nuclear affairs, Nehru set a clear path for India: for autonomous nuclear technology, but against nuclear weapons. This position was neither ambiguous nor self-contradictory. And the proof that it rested on solid ideological and political foundations is that after Nehru died in office in 1964, his successors faithfully followed this line – even when confronted by the major challenge posed by the birth of the Chinese bomb.

India in the aftermath of China's nuclear test

In 1962, India fought and lost a disastrous border war with China. Then, in October 1964, China exploded its first nuclear bomb. It was hard not to conclude, as the US State Department did, that this one-two punch would generate an Indian bomb program.[18] Yet even though Nehru had passed away and his politically weaker successors had to confront the first serious domestic pressures for the bomb, in fact India's policy on nuclear weapons hardly budged.[19]

---

[16] "India and Defence," typed manuscript by Lord Blackett (probably 1969), Lord Blackett papers, G29 at the Royal Society, London. According to the Indian Defense Research and Development Organization chief in 1975, Blackett's 1948 report on Indian defense had served as the foundation of "modern scientific research applied to problems of India's defense and security." Sir Bernard Lovell, "P. M. S. Blackett, Baron Blackett of Chelsea," *Biographical Memoirs of Fellows of the Royal Society*, Vol. 21 (1975), p. 97.

[17] Raju G. C. Thomas, "The Growth of Indian Military Power: From Sufficient Defence to Nuclear Deterrence," in Ross Babbage and Sandy Gordon, eds., *India's Strategic Future* (Delhi: Oxford University Press, 1992), pp. 35–66.

[18] "Current status of our Bilateral Relationship with India," State Department note marked "Secret," November 5, 1965, RG 59, Lot 69 D52 Entry 5255, Box 7, National Archives, College Park, Maryland.

[19] The main supporters of matching China's bomb with an Indian reply, other than Bhabha, were the small Hindu nationalist party the Bharatiya Jana Sangh, a few young Congress MPs, and some middle-level bureaucrats including the young K. Subrahmanyam. The main opponents were Congress Party heavyweights Prime Minister Lal Bahadur Shastri, Morarji Desai (Shastri's chief rival for the post of prime minister), Defence Minister Y. B. Chavan, External Affairs Minister Swaran Singh, Nehru's Defence Minister V. C.

Two 1960s-era Indian nuclear policy shifts have been attributed to the Chinese bomb test. First, in the wake of the test Prime Minister Lal Bahadur Shastri sent diplomats to seek a nuclear guarantee from the great powers. Second, he secretly authorized the AEC to do a Study Nuclear Explosion for Peaceful Purposes. On first glance, these two acts seem significant, and Sumit Ganguly even claims that they constituted what he calls the "second phase of India's nuclear program" – a major step forward toward the bomb.[20] But, in fact, they can easily be shown to be minor variations on Nehru's basic theme.

The "quest" for a guarantee: Shastri well knew that he could secure a solid nuclear guarantee against China by choosing to ally with the United States. But the prime minister proved more interested in protecting India's non-alignment stance than in securing real protection against an eventual Chinese nuclear attack.[21] The "guarantee" Shastri and his advisors L. K. Jha and C. S. Jha sought in late 1964 and early 1965 was a joint declaration through the United Nations by the US, the UK, and the USSR not merely to protect India but *all* non-nuclear states from nuclear attack.[22] Moreover, hypersensitive to any hint of obligation on its part, India proceeded to rebuff all of the US constructive suggestions for the wording of such a resolution.[23] These were not actions of a state that felt a serious nuclear threat. Two years later, after Indira Gandhi became prime minister, L. K. Jha would again be sent to world capitals on precisely the same mission, and with precisely the same result.[24] And indeed, when India under Mrs. Gandhi finally did sign a Treaty of Friendship with the USSR in 1970, she specifically *refused* the USSR's suggestion of a nuclear guarantee for fear of compromising the hallowed

Krishna Menon, and R. K. Nehru, Nehru's brother and former secretary general of the External Affairs Ministry. Given this lineup, it is not difficult to guess who carried the day. A good summary of this episode – though he tends to overestimate Bhabha's power – is Peter Lavoy, "Learning to Live with the Bomb? India and Nuclear Weapons, 1947–1974," Ph.D. dissertation, University of California at Berkeley, 1997, pp. 345–353.

[20] Ganguly, "Explaining the Indian Nuclear Tests," p. 41.

[21] "India and Nuclear Assurances," US State Department Note marked "Secret," April 16, 1965, RG59 Central Files, Lot 69 D52 Entry 5255, Box 12, National Archives, College Park, Maryland.

[22] Interview with Dharma Vira, Cabinet secretary under Prime Minister Lal Bahadur Shastri, New Delhi, November 13, 1998 and "Record of a Private Talk between the Prime Minister and the Prime Minister of India, Mr. Shastri, at 4:15 at No. 10 Downing Street on Friday, December 4, 1964," Folder "India Dec. 1964–August 1966," PREM 13/973, Public Record Office, Kew, UK.

[23] "Your Suggestion for US Assurances to India," State Department Note from Turner C. Cameron, Jr., India Working Group to Ambassador Llewelyn Thompson, February 12, 1965, RG 59, Lot 69 D52, Entry 5255, Box 8, National Archives, College Park, Md.

[24] Letter from Indira Gandhi, prime minister of India, to Harold Wilson, UK prime minister, April 1, 1967, PREM 13/1573, Public Record Office, Kew, United Kingdom.

policy of non-alignment.[25] In sum, this so-called "quest for a nuclear guarantee" was hardly a frantic search for security that, proving fruitless, produced a decision to build nuclear weapons. Rather, it was a mere variation on Nehruvian sportsmanlike nationalist themes. Indeed, the fact that the Nehruvian NIC was not oppositional *vis-à-vis* China explains why Indian elites exhibited a fair degree of cognitive complexity overall on the issue – they saw a danger, but they did not react as if the sky were falling.

The peaceful nuclear explosion study: Of course, a nuclear guarantee would be superfluous if India had its own nuclear weapons to counter the Chinese threat. But Shastri did not want nuclear weapons. In 1965, in response to Bhabha's pressures he did secretly permit a small AEC Study [of] Nuclear Explosion for Peaceful Purposes (SNEPP): an examination of theoretical issues and general feasibility.[26] Notably, however, he instructed the AEC *not* to make contact with the Ministry of Defense laboratories, whose assistance would be necessary for the design and development of important technical aspects of any actual nuclear device. This instruction contrasts markedly with Indira Gandhi's much more significant 1972 decision for a "peaceful nuclear explosion," when the Defense labs' assistance was immediately sought.[27] In sum, the SNEPP was a minor step, implying little real high-level interest in mounting a nuclear bomb program within any reasonable time frame. Indeed, contrary to the idea that AEC chief Bhabha was a potent "nuclear mythmaker," there is even an indication that Shastri, after recovering his political balance, later punished Bhabha for his pro-bomb activities in the aftermath of the Chinese blast.[28] And, in any case, after Shastri and Bhabha's deaths in 1966, even these tentative initiatives were halted by new leader Mrs. Gandhi and her AEC chief Vikram Sarabhai.[29] In fact, Sarabhai, a vociferously anti-bomb physicist of the pacifist Jain faith, was so offended by Bhabha's explosives study that he tried to confiscate any papers written for it.[30]

---

[25] Interview with Romesh Bhandari, who at the time discussed was serving in the Indian Embassy in Moscow, New Delhi, November 25, 1998.

[26] Interviews with Homi Sethna, former AEC chairman, Bombay, December 8, 1998, and with Vira. See also Perkovich, *India's Nuclear Bomb*, p. 85.

[27] Written communication with Ramanna.

[28] "Prime Minister Shastri . . . does not seem to look to him for political advice regarding international nuclear and other scientific policy as did Prime Minister Nehru. In fact there is evidence to suggest that Bhabha, perhaps because he has had a reputation as an advocate of an Indian nuclear weapons program, has been excluded from certain high-level GOI discussions of nuclear policy matters." "Your Meeting with Dr. Homi Bhabha at 12:30 PM February 22," State Department Briefing Memorandum, marked "Secret," from Phillips Talbot to the under secretary, February 20, 1965, viewed at National Security Archive, Washington, DC.

[29] Perkovich, *India's Nuclear Bomb*, p. 114.   [30] Interview with Sethna.

Such was India's "reply" to the Chinese blast of 1964: a half-hearted search for a generic UN guarantee covering all non-nuclear states, and a few theoretical studies of nuclear explosions. What explains this feeble reply to such a major new strategic reality? The Gandhian moral impulse was certainly a factor; Shastri beat back calls for the atomic bomb at the 1964 All-India Congress conference by pointing to a huge picture of Mahatma Gandhi and saying, "I am shocked that there should be even talk of violence in his presence."[31] But probably more important was the general sense that the Chinese bomb notwithstanding, an Indian nuclear bomb effort would *decrease* Indian security. As Shastri put it to Parliament, "Impoverishing ourselves and not even defending our country is a stupid thing to do. If we spend more money on this [atom bomb] we shall not be able to spend as much on conventional weapons and the conventional army." He added, "Our neighbors will be more frightened if we begin to make the atom bomb. . . . It does not help us at all in reassuring our neighbors with whom India wants friendship."[32] Indira Gandhi was clearly coming from the same perspective when she told Parliament in 1968:

The choice before us involves not only the question of making a few atom bombs, but of engaging in an arms race with sophisticated nuclear warheads and an effective missile delivery system. Such a course, I do not think would strengthen national security. On the other hand, it may well endanger our internal security by imposing a very heavy economic burden which would be in addition to the present expenditure on defense. Nothing will better serve the interests of those who are hostile to us than for us to lose our sense of perspective and to undertake measures which would undermine the basic progress of the country. We believe that to be militarily strong, it is necessary to be economically and industrially strong. Our program of atomic energy development for peaceful purposes is related to the real needs of our economy and would be effectively geared to this end.[33]

These are undiluted Nehruvian – sportsmanlike nationalist – statements. For Shastri and Mrs. Gandhi, as for Nehru, the way to promote Indian security was through autonomous economic (including civilian nuclear) development, a foreign policy of friendship with all, not entering into military alliances which they saw as relationships of dependence with more powerful states, and avoiding bankrupting the country through unnecessarily grandiose military schemes. In short, as Indira Gandhi put it pithily

---

[31] William Bader, *The United States and the Spread of Nuclear Weapons* (New York: Pegasus, 1968), p. 63.

[32] Shastri, cited in Lavoy, "Learning to Live with the Bomb?" p. 348.

[33] Indira Gandhi in the Lok Sabha, April 24, 1968, cited in "Nuclear Weapons, a compilation prepared by the Department of Atomic Energy, July 1970," report for the Parliamentary Consultative Committee, accessed in Solly Zuckerman papers, SZ/CSA/25/2, University of East Anglia, Norwich, UK.

to one interviewer, building a nuclear arsenal would merely "bring danger where there was none before."[34] This analysis was shared not only by politicians but also by the vast majority of mainstream Indian strategic elites.[35]

In short, the sportsmanlike nationalist leaders of India did not respond in kind to the Chinese nuclear threat because they did not judge the actual or potential threat from China to be great enough to merit such a response. Their response exhibited a degree of cognitive complexity that stands in stark contrast to the fear-driven response that would have emerged if they had held an oppositional NIC. Indeed, the temperate Indian reaction can be usefully contrasted with that of the Australian Liberals, who – with their oppositional NIC – reacted to the Chinese test with mortification, though only the later Prime Minister John Gorton also proved nationalist enough to want to build an Australian bomb in reply.

India's "peaceful nuclear explosion"

In March 1971, India's nuclear weapons policy was essentially no different than it had been twenty years earlier: for nuclear power, but against nuclear weapons. A year later that traditional distinction was much less clear, as India was launched toward a "demonstration" of its nuclear explosives capacity. In this section of the chapter I argue that the decision by Indira Gandhi for a "peaceful nuclear explosion" (PNE), while a risky and intemperate power play, was not a decision to go all the way. Indeed, I argue that Mrs. Gandhi's desire *not* to have a nuclear arms race in the subcontinent actually led to her PNE decision. The decision is thus best understood as an effect, albeit a warped one, of her sportsmanlike nationalist pride. The fact that it backfired tremendously and produced a near-nuclear standoff in the South Asian subcontinent merely underscores how much the decision was driven by pride and self-righteous emotion rather than by methodical calculation.

Nuclear India as of 1971

To understand how substantial a policy shift the PNE represented, consider the status of India's nuclear weapons debate at the beginning of

[34] Indira Gandhi, interview with Rodney Jones, quoted in Perkovich, *India's Nuclear Bomb*, p. 178.
[35] For instance, George Perkovich cites similar strategic reasoning in a 1966 Adelphi Paper by Major General (ret.) Som Dutt, the first director of the Institute for Defence Studies and Analyses (IDSA), the major Indian strategic think tank. Perkovich, *India's Nuclear Bomb*, p. 129.

1971. In the public arena, the bomb lobby was spent. In a solid study of Indian nuclear politics, Ziba Moshaver finds that "from 1968 to 1974 there was no pressure from the Lok Sabha [lower house of Parliament], the bureaucracy, the media, or the public on the government to change its nuclear policy. The 1974 test thus took everyone by surprise."[36] Behind closed doors, the story was only slightly different. The British Chief Science Advisor Sir Solly Zuckerman had filed a confidential report in March 1965 that there was a significant degree of interest in nuclear weapons in India, and among elements of the military in particular.[37] But when he returned in March 1971, this interest had dimmed. The crucial message of his 1971 report to the British government was the following:

In discussions with both military and non-military people, I gained the clear impression that the Indian Government has no wish to develop nuclear weapons and is not at present planning to do so. They recognize they cannot afford to divert the necessary resources from their very pressing economic and social problems. China is their main worry and they greatly hope that somehow China can be contained in some global political arrangement, failing which they expect to come under renewed pressure to develop nuclear weapons. They appeared to regard about another two years as crucial in this respect. . . .

Neither did I find any evidence that India is seriously concerned about, or even studying, possible peaceful uses of nuclear devices, and thereby pursuing a clandestine route to the production of military nuclear weapons.[38]

Zuckerman's report accurately reflected Indian policymakers' attitudes, but behind their backs various AEC scientists had in fact been working quietly on the nuclear explosives problem. This was done in spite of Sarabhai's personal efforts to stop it.[39] One example of this work was the AEC's experimental production of polonium, an important material

---

[36] Ziba Moshaver, *Nuclear Weapons Proliferation in the Indian Subcontinent* (Basingstoke: Macmillan, 1991), p. 43.

[37] "The Impact of China and Vietnam on India's Nuclear Problem," Note by Sir Solly Zuckerman to Sir Burke Trend, dated July 7, 1966. Solly Zuckerman Papers, Folder marked "Transcripts File," Library of the University of East Anglia at Norwich. Note that in the internal hierarchy of power the Indian military was near the bottom so its opinions, while notable, were not terribly influential.

[38] Draft "confidential" note from Sir Solly Zuckerman on "Visit to Indian Establishments, 7–17 March 1971," prepared by R. Press, Solly Zuckerman papers SZ/CSA/25/1, "Visit to India March 1971," University of East Anglia, Norwich, UK. In an earlier draft of this document, Zuckerman makes clear that for the Indians, such a settlement should include admission of China to the UN. Thus Zuckerman's interlocutors were thinking more in terms of appeasement than of deterrence when they spoke of dealing with the China problem. In fact, by 1972 China was clearly being brought into the international fold, so they got their wish on that score. Manuscript note (undated, untitled) by Sir Solly Zuckerman. Solly Zuckerman Papers, Folder "Visit to India March 1971," SZ/CSA/25/1, Library of the University of East Anglia, Norwich.

[39] Interview with Sethna.

for initiating a nuclear blast. They tackled this question beginning around 1968 and, after some false starts, had success around 1971.[40] In general, however, what work the scientists could do on the bomb was greatly limited by the official policy against it, a policy that Sarabhai strictly enforced.[41] Thus, India as of 1971 cannot be said to have had a nuclear explosives program. About a year later, however, it did; and in May 1974, India's "peaceful nuclear explosion" shocked the world.

Explaining the "peaceful nuclear explosion"

To fathom why Indira Gandhi made her decision for the PNE, it is first necessary to understand that this decision was *not* a decision to acquire nuclear weapons. There are at least five separate indicators that Indira Gandhi did not want nuclear weapons for India:

- First, in public statements both prior to and after the PNE she repeatedly voiced her objections to nuclear weapons in general and for India in particular. For instance, in her 1978 interview with Rodney Jones she clearly stated, "No, we don't want nuclear weapons. They only bring danger where there was none before."[42]
- Second, if this really had been a decision for nuclear weapons, one might have expected Mrs. Gandhi to inform the military, at least after the test, of her intentions, so that it could begin thinking about the integration of the weapon into its planning. But the military, as well as the civilian Ministry of Defense, was kept in the dark both before and after the test took place.[43]
- Third, the group of top aides that she assembled in total secrecy to discuss whether or not to proceed to a test never spoke of the device as a bomb and never considered more than a single test, as would be necessary if reliable devices were envisioned.[44]

---

[40] Interview with Sethna. Other aspects of the eventual explosives program were brought in for other reasons. The Purnima critical facility, which eventually provided important information for India's first explosion, was first mooted by scientist P. K. Iyengar after his visit to a similar facility in the Soviet Union. According to Iyengar, Sarabhai approved it in 1968 as part of the move into plutonium-based fast-reactor technology for electric power. Interview with P. K. Iyengar, former AEC chairman, Bombay, December 8, 1998.

[41] Perkovich, *India's Nuclear Bomb*, p. 160.

[42] Indira Gandhi, interview with Rodney Jones, cited in Perkovich, *India's Nuclear Bomb*, p. 178.

[43] Interview with K. B. Lall, former defense secretary, New Delhi, November 16, 1999, with follow-up letters February 2 and April 14, 1999. See also Perkovich, *India's Nuclear Bomb*, pp. 174, 177.

[44] Interview with Sethna and interview with P. N. Dhar, prime minister's secretary under Indira Gandhi, Delhi, November 20, 1998 (with follow-up letter February 27, 1999). Both Sethna and Dhar were members of the small group that met with Mrs. Gandhi to discuss whether or not to have a test.

- Fourth, on the very day of the 1974 test, in the first flush of accomplishment, the scientist Raja Ramanna suggested that India plan more tests, only to find his suggestion brutally rejected by an irate Mrs. Gandhi.[45] Mrs. Gandhi's advisors T. N. Kaul and Inder Malhotra made similar suggestions and received similar dressings-down.[46] Mrs. Gandhi's opposition to further tests in fact brought the nuclear explosives work to a screeching halt.
- And fifth, Mrs. Gandhi explicitly rejected her science advisor's proposal to bend ongoing missile projects toward the development of nuclear-capable missiles: "Don't mix the two," she said.[47]

In short, the decision to explode the PNE was not a decision to build nuclear weapons. But then what was it? In the following paragraphs, I argue that the PNE is best conceptualized as a *warning shot* to the great powers and to the US in particular, meant to cause them to rethink their policy of assisting Pakistan.[48]

The 1971 war and its aftermath

In mid-1971, the crisis in East Pakistan (now Bangladesh) took on international proportions as a flood of Bengali refugees, terrorized by the Pakistani army, began crossing the Indian border. The crisis escalated, and by December India and Pakistan were at war. Within days, India was well on its way to a smashing victory that would divide Pakistan in two. In the US, the Nixon administration began to fear that India was intent not only on "liberating" East Pakistan but also on swallowing up Pakistan whole.[49] Nixon therefore ordered a "tilt" in favor of Pakistan in the form of sending a US Navy flotilla into the Bay of Bengal. The flotilla notably included the USS *Enterprise*, the country's largest and most modern aircraft carrier.[50] Mrs. Gandhi was angered by Nixon's "tilt" toward

---

[45] In Ramanna's words, Mrs. Gandhi told him, "Now that it has come let me tell you as far as I am concerned the whole program is over." Chengappa, *Weapons of Peace*, p. 202.

[46] Interview with Inder Malhotra, journalist and friend of Indira Gandhi, New Delhi, November 28, 1998, and interview with T. N. Kaul.

[47] M. G. K. Menon, quoted in Chengappa, *Weapons of Peace*, p. 214. Strangely, Chengappa writes that Menon added, "Mrs. Gandhi wasn't against doing it. But said let's not do it at the moment till we develop some capability."

[48] For a parallel interpretation, see Rajesh M. Basrur, "Nuclear Weapons and Indian Strategic Culture," *Journal of Peace Research*, Vol. 38, No. 2 (March 2001), esp. p. 186.

[49] After the war, the Nixon team convinced itself that they had prevented that. "India–Pakistan," Department of State Memorandum of Conversation marked "Secret," December 28, 1971, folder "South Asia 12/17/71–12/31/71," Box 573, National Security Council Files, Richard M. Nixon Presidential Materials Staff at College Park, Maryland.

[50] "India–Pakistan Situation," Memorandum marked "Secret" for the president from Henry A. Kissinger, December 14, 1971, folder "South Asia 12/14/71–12/16/71," Box 573, National Security Council Files, Richard M. Nixon Presidential Materials Staff at College Park, Maryland.

Pakistan, a tilt that she perceived to have existed right from the start of the crisis.[51] In an open letter to Nixon, Mrs. Gandhi came close even to blaming the US for the war.[52]

Though she felt she had both right and might on her side, in peace talks at Simla in early 1972 Mrs. Gandhi tried to appease Pakistan with soft treatment, and at first it seemed to oblige. But Indian intelligence agents soon learned that Pakistani leader Zulfiqar Ali Bhutto had "called a meeting of eminent scientists in Multan in January 1972 and announced his desire and decision to make Pakistan a nuclear weapons state."[53] Thus it became clear that Pakistan was not only unbowed by its defeat, but was in fact intending to raise the stakes in the subcontinental military competition. The fact that Mrs. Gandhi knew about the speech and was deeply concerned by it was confirmed to me by her principal secretary, P. N. Dhar, and her atomic energy chief, Homi Sethna.[54] Her decision on what to do about it came quickly; by January 1972, she was already telling her close friend Inder Malhotra that India needed to explode a nuclear device, in order to show the world that it could do it.[55] Those few others who learned of the Multan speech, like Dhar and Sethna, came to the same conclusion.[56] Those who were not privy to the information, however, did not make noises for nuclear weapons at this time.[57] For instance, the defense secretary at the time, K. B. Lall, told me that in 1972 he had seen no reason for India to acquire even a nuclear explosives capability, but that if he had seen solid intelligence that "Bhutto, smarting from a disastrous defeat, was launched on acquiring a nuclear

---

[51] But she was not fearful. The Indians basically could not imagine any scenario in which the US went to war against them, though in light of the US "tilt" they did resolve to close down military operations as quickly as possible. Interview with Lall; and see Pupul Jayakar, *Indira Gandhi, An Intimate Biography* (New York: Pantheon Books), ch. 33.

[52] Letter from prime minister of India, Indira Gandhi, to president of the United States, Richard Nixon, December 15, 1971; folder "South Asia 12/12/71–12/31/71"; Box 573, National Security Council Files, Richard M. Nixon Presidential Materials Staff at College Park, Maryland.

[53] J. N. Dixit, *Across Borders: Fifty Years of Indian Foreign Policy* (New Delhi: Picus Books, 1998), p. 437.

[54] Interviews with Dhar and Sethna.

[55] Interview with Malhotra. See also Inder Malhotra, *Indira Gandhi: A Personal and Political Biography* (Boston: Northeastern University Press, 1991).

[56] They did disagree on the details: while Sethna and eventually Gandhi felt a single test was necessary to demonstrate India's capacity, Dhar argued in their secret meetings that given the country's shaky economic position, it was not propitious to "go public" with India's capacity at that particular juncture. This nuanced position was misinterpreted, Dhar says, by Raja Ramanna in his autobiography. Ramanna was only at the last meeting, and this may have been part of the reason for the misinterpretation of Dhar's position. Interview with Dhar.

[57] Why did Mrs. Gandhi not allow this information to spread further? It is not clear. Perhaps she did not want to create a panic that would end up forcing her into a nuclear weapons program.

capability, then you would be unwise not to launch yourself on that course also."[58]

Why was the Multan speech so determinative? It was *not* because Mrs. Gandhi feared Pakistan's indigenous nuclear capacities. The cocky overall Indian attitude toward Pakistan was expressed in the post-test period by Mrs. Gandhi's chief secretary P. N. Haksar. Bhutto had declared that Pakistan would get the bomb even if such an effort required its people to "eat grass." Haksar offered this reply: "If by eating grass one can produce atom bombs, then by now cows and horses would have produced them. But, of course, the people of Pakistan under the great and charismatic leadership to which they are now exposed might produce a bomb on a diet of grass."[59] When she learned of the Multan speech, Mrs. Gandhi was slightly less dismissive than Haksar; she did ask the recently elevated AEC chief Homi Sethna to assess Pakistan's nuclear prospects. But Sethna told her not to worry: even in the worst case scenario, Pakistan could not build it for at least ten years.[60] Parenthetically, it is very significant that Sethna's AEC, when asked for its expert opinion, did not exploit this opportunity to push for an explosion – the clearest instance in the history of nuclear India in which the monopoly on technical expertise gave the scientists real power to affect political calculations. Sethna's restraint falsifies the hypothesis that bureaucratic pressures drove Mrs. Gandhi to the PNE decision.

The Multan speech had a dramatic effect not because of what it told India's leaders about Pakistan, but what it told them about Pakistan's *masters* (in their view). To Mrs. Gandhi's Nehruvian way of thinking Pakistan was quite simply not a serious competitor for India – but Pakistan was dangerous as the willing puppet of the great powers, India's real peers.[61] Thus, from the Nehruvian point of view Bhutto's Multan speech was important as a sign of what Pakistanis thought they were being allowed to do. And, in fact, Mrs. Gandhi's perception contained more than a

[58] Interview with Lall. An exception to this rule was Ambassador T. N. Kaul, who was not aware of the Multan speech but who was in favor of nuclear weaponization in order to deter China (interview with Kaul).

[59] P. N. Haksar, interview published by *Blitz* August 10, 1974, reprinted in P. N. Haksar, *India's Foreign Policy and its Problems* (New Delhi: Patriot Publishers, 1989).

[60] Interviews with Dhar and Sethna. Sethna's advice reflected a hard assessment of Pakistan's technical capacities, but it also reflected the general Indian opinion of Pakistan as a "gang that can't shoot straight" and thus would be unable to master the challenges posed by nuclear weapons development. This tendency to underestimate Pakistani capabilities stands in contrast to the definition of "oppositional nationalism," which requires an attitude of fear, not derision. See also Ashley Tellis, *India's Emerging Nuclear Posture: Between Recessed Deterrent and Ready Arsenal* (Santa Monica: RAND Corporation, 2001), pp. 50–51.

[61] This is a common theme in Indian security studies. See Stephen P. Cohen, "Perception, Influence, and Nuclear Proliferation in South Asia," ACDIS Occasional Paper, University of Illinois at Urbana-Champaign, August 1979, p. 3.

grain of truth. As a note from Henry Kissinger to Richard Nixon in 1973 made clear, the US administration was willing to help Pakistan bilaterally "in every way we can," and also to encourage China to help Pakistan in ways that Congress was preventing the US administration from doing.[62]

Pakistan's acquisition of the bomb would be a disaster, but to the Nehruvian mind this could only happen if the great powers let it (or made it) happen. What the situation called for in Mrs. Gandhi's eyes, therefore, was a strong signal to the great powers to rein in Pakistan before things got out of hand. If they were reminded that India was naturally part of the great power club, too, they would not treat it in this way. What they needed was a healthy indication both of India's potential might and of its self-restraint. The PNE – a one-shot test, not followed up by any subsequent work toward an actual arsenal – would provide this indication.

George Perkovich writes that the PNE-as-warning-shot idea might be plausible, except for the fact that, as he puts it, the PNE had the "opposite effect" on the great powers to that intended. He therefore favors a domestic politics explanation.[63] Perkovich is right that Mrs. Gandhi's gambit backfired: India was lambasted internationally as not only power-hungry but also hypocritical for its claims of "peaceful" intent. And, far from dissuading the great power supporters of Pakistan, the PNE actually made them more inclined to understand Pakistan's desire for nuclear weapons; indeed, it directly caused China to launch a major program of nuclear assistance to Pakistan.[64] But Perkovich is wrong to think that just because the PNE backfired in terms of India's international goals, these goals could not have been behind Mrs. Gandhi's motivation to do it. Governments make mistakes all the time as a result of misperception or simply the complexity of the world. The real puzzle is why Mrs. Gandhi did not *realize* that the PNE would backfire in this way.

The fundamental reason for Mrs. Gandhi's blind spot lies in her immense sportsmanlike nationalist pride, which had been inflamed even more by the 1971 war.[65] She did not anticipate the counterproductive effects of her PNE signal because of her inability to fathom how any

---

[62] Note on "Meetings with Zulfikar Ali Bhutto, Prime Minister of Pakistan" from Henry A. Kissinger to the president, September 17, 1973, p. 2, Box 935 "Pakistan: Visit of President Bhutto Sept. 18, 1973" [2 of 3], National Security Council files, Nixon Presidential Papers, National Archives, College Park, Maryland.

[63] Perkovich, *India's Nuclear Bomb*, p. 177.

[64] John W. Garver, *Protracted Contest: Sino-Indian Rivalry in the Twentieth Century* (Seattle: University of Washington Press, 2001).

[65] The great secrecy with which the PNE decision was taken, which led Mrs. Gandhi to bypass the significant analytical resources of the state, is clearly another important piece of the puzzle. For elaboration, see P. R. Chari, *Indo-Pak Nuclear Standoff: The Role of the United States* (New Delhi: Manohar, 1995), p. 52.

"unprejudiced observers" could believe that India – her country, the country of Gandhi and Nehru, a beacon of peace and non-violence throughout the world – wanted nuclear weapons.[66] Such a self-righteous attitude is one of the causes that Robert Jervis has pointed to for why state actors often wrongly assume that others will recognize their peaceful intentions.[67] Indeed, many scholars have noted that it is precisely such a clash of self-righteous attitudes that has dogged Indo-US relations since the very beginning.[68]

In sum, Indira Gandhi's decision for a PNE is paradoxically explained by her sportsmanlike desire to avoid a nuclear arms race, combined with her inflamed nationalist pride that caused her to misjudge badly the potential international reaction to such a blast. Mrs. Gandhi was counting on outsiders to see the distinction she made between the development of nuclear capacity and the weaponization of that capacity. But the outsiders, perhaps understandably, did not accept that distinction. Thus her decision, far from stopping a nascent arms race on the subcontinent, actually brought one to life.

India's nuclear stance between 1974 and 1998

In the decade after India's 1974 nuclear test, Indian policy on nuclear weapons did not budge. Indian leaders withstood significant efforts by the US Carter administration to get them to accept a regional non-proliferation agreement with Pakistan and other South Asian nations.[69] Carter's arguments did have some currency in the government of Morarji Desai, but in the end Indian resistance to "nuclear apartheid" carried the day.[70] On the other side of the coin, Indian leaders withstood significant

---

[66] The phrase "unprejudiced observers" is borrowed from Mrs. Gandhi's December 15, 1971 letter to Nixon.

[67] Robert Jervis, *Perception and Misperception in International Politics* (Princeton: Princeton University Press, 1976), p. 354.

[68] Partha S. Ghosh, "United States and India: The Reality and the Hope," ACDIS Occasional Paper, University of Illinois at Urbana-Champaign, March 1994, p. 2. See also Dennis Kux, *India and the United States: Estranged Democracies, 1941–1991* (Washington, DC: National Defense University Press, 1992).

[69] "Minutes of President Carter's Meetings with Prime Minister Desai," marked "Secret," June 13–14, 1978. Document viewed at National Security Archive, Washington, DC.

[70] The consistent Indian refusal to budge from its sportsmanlike nationalist nuclear posture even as Pakistan's nuclear program continued to grow stands in contrast to the Argentine willingness to make certain compromises to its sportsmanlike nationalist posture in the face of a growing nuclear rivalry with Brazil. The reason for this difference would be interesting to explore further. The most reasonable hypothesis would seem to be that, on the one hand, Argentine leaders respected Brazil enough to see their relationship as an actual rivalry, and indeed as one that could take on a nuclear dimension if cooler heads did not prevail. By contrast, as the withering quote from P. N. Haksar cited

pressures by some Indian atomic scientists who continued to pursue their explosive dreams. After studying how to downsize the original PNE device to a size that might actually be deliverable, the scientists pushed Mrs. Gandhi, again in power from 1980, to allow them to put their ideas into practice.[71] She hesitated, but in the end refused, telling her defense science advisor, "I am basically against weapons of mass destruction."[72]

After Mrs. Gandhi's own bodyguards assassinated her in 1984, her son Rajiv assumed the duties of prime minister. At the time, intelligence reports about Pakistan's nuclear progress were pouring in. Like his mother, Rajiv Gandhi believed that he could solve the problem by convincing the US to rein in its Pakistani client. In October 1985 he met with President Reagan, and as a result of their meeting he understood Reagan to have committed to putting a stop to the Pakistani program. Therefore, upon his return he disbanded the nuclear weapons policy group he had earlier formed and instead began a vigorous campaign for his "Action Plan for a Nuclear-Free, Non-Violent World."[73] The Action Plan was a direct descendant of Nehru's disarmament vision. Notably, the first stage in the plan was for a comprehensive test ban, to which India as well as the existing nuclear powers would subscribe. Like Nehru's disarmament proposals, however, the Action Plan did not have the immediate impact that Rajiv Gandhi had hoped it would.

The decision for "weaponization"

Rajiv Gandhi clearly was not eager to build nuclear weapons. But in spite of his meeting with Reagan, Pakistan's nuclear progress continued. Then, in the midst of a major military crisis in the subcontinent in 1987, the top

earlier demonstrates, Indian leaders at root did not respect Pakistan and saw its nuclear efforts mainly as bluff and bluster. This underestimation explains why India's leaders in the 1970s were not willing to adopt the serious confidence-building measures with Pakistan that Argentine leaders adopted with Brazil. But by the end of the 1980s, of course, the progress of the Pakistani program was undeniable, and this caused Rajiv Gandhi to attempt a number of confidence-building measures with Pakistan. Those measures, however, did not prevent Rajiv Gandhi's decision for "weaponization" that is discussed below.

[71] Perkovich, *India's Nuclear Bomb*, p. 242.
[72] Arunachalam cited in Chengappa, *Weapons of Peace*, pp. 257–260, 287. See also Perkovich, *India's Nuclear Bomb*, p. 242.
[73] K. Subrahmanyam, "Indian Nuclear Policy– 1964–98," in Jasjit Singh, ed., *Nuclear India*, pp. 40–41. The nuclear policy group had a mix of pro- and anti-bomb members. Subrahmanyam is wrong to imply that Admiral Tahiliani's report – which he admits to not having seen – argued in favor of an Indian nuclear weapons program. The report did say that a nuclear weapons program was feasible, but Admiral Tahiliani at that time saw no urgent national security need for it. Interview with Admiral R. N. Tahiliani, New Delhi, December 16, 1998.

Pakistani scientist A. Q. Khan and even President Zia himself informed journalists that their country to all intents and purposes had the bomb.[74] These statements were interpreted in India as some mix of the truth and braggadocio, but they still shook Indian elites out of their previous smugness about the Pakistani program. Therefore, in 1988 or 1989 Rajiv Gandhi gave his secret approval for work on nuclear "weaponization," and in this work Dr. P. K. Iyengar of the AEC and Dr. V. S. Arunachalam of the Defence Research and Development Organization (DRDO) were to be key players.[75] The affair was so secret that even the prime minister's closest nuclear policy advisor, the diplomat Muchkund Dubey, only guessed at the project because a scientist asked him for an estimate of how much time India would have to complete bomb assembly in a crisis, and also how many bombs it might need.[76]

This was serious work that went far beyond what had already been done for the PNE and subsequently. It involved "design, testing and production of advanced detonators, ruggedized high volt trigger systems, interface engineering, systems engineering and systems integration" as well as various "contributions in aerodynamics, arming, fusing, safety interlocks, flight trials etc."[77] In short, under Rajiv Gandhi, for the first time India had a bona fide nuclear weapons effort, albeit one whose ultimate objective was still unclear. As Rajiv Gandhi was a sportsmanlike nationalist *vis-à-vis* generic foreign "others" – one who, according to Chapter 3, refused to recognize Pakistan as a key comparison other – his choice for "weaponization" diverges from the theoretical expectations developed in this book.[78] But still, this was no straightforward decision to go nuclear. One might say instead that he was trying to make India "half-pregnant" with nuclear weapons. His decision had given the scientists not a green light but a flashing yellow one, requiring them to ask for permission for every forward step they took.[79] Given the provocations

---

[74] Sumita Kumar, "Pakistan's Nuclear Weapons Programme," in Jasjit Singh, ed., *Nuclear India*, p. 174.

[75] Interview with Iyengar.

[76] Interview with Muchkund Dubey, former foreign secretary, New Delhi, December 15, 1998.

[77] "Joint Statement by Department of Atomic Energy and Defence Research and Development Organisation," New Delhi, May 17, 1998, available at http://www.fas.org/news/india/1998/05/980500-drdo.htm. Accessed April 20, 2005.

[78] This chapter makes clear that Pakistan's nuclear progress forced the pace of Indian nuclear weapons decisionmaking from 1972 to 1998. Should this cause us to reevaluate the coding decision of Chapter 3, according to which Pakistan was not the key comparison other for the Indian secularists? In my view, it should not. The codings in Chapter 3 were – and must be – derived independently from the empirical data on India's nuclear development.

[79] Chengappa, *Weapons of Peace*, p. 335.

coming from Pakistan, what is really striking is not that Rajiv Gandhi moved toward nuclear weapons, but rather that he did not decide to go all the way. Even now, India was still reluctantly slouching toward the nuclear threshold.

After Rajiv Gandhi's tenure, his successors allowed the secret process of weaponization to continue (the top military brass, Cabinet, and most senior civil servants were out of the loop until the BJP tests of 1998).[80] But they – sportsmanlike nationalists all – also continued to agonize over whether or not to "go nuclear," which they defined as holding a series of nuclear weapons tests. And in spite of significant pressure in the 1990s to take that final step, the prime ministers before 1998 all said no. Was this reticence to test really significant, or did it just reflect a desire to have a secret nuclear weapons arsenal? In fact, in the 1990s both Indian and foreign analysts generally accepted that the subcontinent had settled into a situation of "recessed deterrence" – meaning, in essence, I won't go for a fully operational nuclear arsenal if you won't.[81] There are three separate indicators that in spite of the progress made on "weaponization," India before 1998 was still, by its own choice, a non-nuclear weapons state.

- First, since the reliability of the weapon designs had not been established, the AEC's "bombs in the basement" were potentially duds. This is why the scientists were so insistent on the need for the tests and had not built many prototype warheads.[82] Indeed, India only truly crossed

---

[80] *From Surprise to Reckoning: The Kargil Review Committee Report* (New Delhi: Sage Publishers, 2000), p. 241. It should be noted in passing that the decision for "weaponization" does reconfirm the book's focus on the prime minister as the undisputed key decision-maker in the nuclear issue area.

[81] Many have commented on the existence of this situation of "recessed deterrence," also known as "non-weaponized deterrence." Rajiv Gandhi's close advisor Arun Singh even claims that recessed deterrence tended to depress conventional military spending on both sides at a time of increasingly hostile relations. Arun Singh, "The Military Balance: 1985–1994," ACDIS Occasional Paper, University of Illinois at Urbana-Champaign, March 1997, p. 19.

[82] The AEC has now admitted that only one of the five devices tested at Pokhran in 1998 was indeed a "weapon" – and even that designation is highly questionable. Indeed, given the need for additional tests on the bomb design, before May 1998 the AEC "would have considered it foolish to make 30 warheads, not knowing if it would work or not" (interview with senior Indian nuclear engineer, name withheld on request, 2000). A recently publicized US estimate is that India even in early 2000 still had only about five warheads of dubious quality (Robert Windrem and Tammy Kupperman, "Pakistan Nukes Outstrip India's, Officials Say," MSNBC News report, June 6, 2000, available on web at http://www.msnbc.com/news/417106.asp?cp1=1, accessed April 20, 2005). By contrast, after February 2000 the Atomic Energy Regulatory Board was relieved of responsibility over weapons-related nuclear facilities. This is indicative of "round-the-clock" production of warheads since that time (interview with senior Indian nuclear engineer, name withheld on request).

the technical threshold to nuclear weapons in April 1999, with the Agni II missile test. In the months between the May 1998 nuclear tests and the April 1999 Agni test, the scientists had worked feverishly because they knew that the severe vibrations to which the warhead would be subjected in flight would *prematurely trigger the device*.[83]

- Second, a weapon is not merely a thing that goes "boom." To be at all effective, complicated modern weapons systems require the practical familiarity of those who will be asked to employ them.[84] Yet as the Kargil Review Committee put it, prior to 1998 the Indian military had been kept almost completely "in the dark about India's nuclear capability."[85] It therefore could not train with the weapons, could not integrate them into its planning, and indeed doubted their very existence. Therefore, the military could not have reasonably been expected to show any competence in employing nuclear weapons in a crisis situation.[86] As former Army Chief of Staff General V. N. Sharma told me, "There was no question of asking for or of providing the military with 'dummy warheads' for training as the military well knew that none existed. . . . It is only now in May 1998 that suitable weapon authentication tests have been carried out, and the path to weaponization has been opened up."[87]

- Third, it is true that in spite of these technical issues, in the matter of nuclear deterrence perception is often reality. Thus, even if neither side actually had nuclear weapons but if each *perceived* the other to have them, the effects on their behavior could be identical. But, in fact, the two sides' behavior toward each other changed markedly after their respective 1998 nuclear test series. Most dramatically, the new situation emboldened Pakistan to undertake the Kargil incursion, by

---

[83] Chengappa, *Weapons of Peace*, pp. 435–436. In light of these continuing technical hurdles after May 1998, it is not clear why Chengappa devotes so much attention to the 1994 "flight test" of a mock nuclear device dropped from the bomb bay of an Indian Air Force plane. Indeed, as late as 2000 the Army's former director general of military operations, V. R. Raghavan, was lamenting that India's so-called nuclear "arsenal" had "uncertain technical parameters at best" and was perhaps *still* not fully "weaponized." V. R. Raghavan, "Whither Nuclear Policy?" *The Hindu*, July 1, 2000, available at http://www.hinduonnet.com/thehindu/2000/07/01/stories/05012523.htm.

[84] See, for instance, Christopher S. Parker, "New Weapons for Old Problems: Conventional Proliferation and Military Effectiveness in Developing States," *International Security*, Vol. 23, No. 4 (1999), pp. 119–147.

[85] *From Surprise to Reckoning*, p. 241. This was the report of a government-appointed committee led by K. Subrahmanyam.

[86] This was the point of Army Chief of Staff General K. Sundarji's polemic book, *Blind Men of Hindoostan* (New Delhi: UBS Publishers, 1993).

[87] Interview with Gen. V. N. Sharma, former chief of army staff, New Delhi, December 16, 1998, with follow-up letter February 18, 1999.

far its most ambitious military move since 1971.[88] India's Kargil Review Committee concluded that Pakistan was attempting a "salami slicing" tactic that came straight out of Cold War nuclear strategy manuals.[89]

In short, the abstention from testing before 1998 had real consequences for the status of India's (and apparently also Pakistan's) nuclear weapons program. As Ashley Tellis summarizes, "The May 1998 tests, in fact, represented merely the beginnings of change."[90]

The 1995 test non-decision

I have contended that Indian prime ministers until 1998 kept India from becoming a fully fledged nuclear weapons state. That successive prime ministers considered, and then shelved, the nuclear test option is hardly evidence that India's nuclear "coming out" was bound to occur sooner or later. It is rather evidence that Atal Behari Vajpayee's ideas about nuclear weapons were profoundly different from those of his predecessors. But contrary to these points, there are some suggestions that India in fact tried to test in 1995, under the Congress Party government of P. V. Narasimha Rao, until the Americans stopped it from doing so.[91] If this were true it would indeed represent a decision to go nuclear, albeit a failed one, and it would require a change in the historical interpretation offered here. A closer examination of this episode, however, shows that in fact Rao never did decide to go nuclear.

The early years of the Rao government had originally promised a more cooperative relationship with the US on the nuclear issue. Indeed, India and the US cosponsored the UN resolution for a Comprehensive Test Ban Treaty (CTBT) in 1993. Importantly, the Rao government did not

---

[88] What was Pakistan's actual nuclear status before May 1998? K. Subrahmanyam has opined that until May 1998, "China did not allow Pakistan an entirely autonomous capability. Pakistani nuclear weapons, therefore, were strictly not military weapons capable of being used against India" (K. Subrahmanyam quoted in Major General Dipankar Banerjee, "India's Nuclear Policy – An IIC Debate," June 8, 1998, http://www.ipcs.org/newIpcsSeminars2.jsp?action=showView&kValue=413). There is some additional evidence for this hypothesis in the Kargil Review Committee report, *From Surprise to Reckoning*, p. 196, although Subrahmanyam now argues that Pakistan already had nuclear weapons before India.

[89] *From Surprise to Reckoning*, p. 242. What the committee does not mention is that on the Indian side, too, nuclear weapons were put into play in Kargil. For the first time, DRDO scientists fanned out to Indian ballistic missile sites and readied at least four missiles of both the Prithvi and Agni variety for a possible nuclear strike on Pakistan. Parenthetically, the fact that India readied an Agni for a strike on Pakistan puts to lie the idea that Agni is a "China-specific" missile.

[90] Tellis, *India's Emerging Nuclear Posture*, p. 117. See also Tellis' comments on pp. 18–19.

[91] Ganguly hammers on this point to advance his argument that to focus on the BJP's motivations to test is "ahistorical." Ganguly, "Explaining the Indian Nuclear Tests," p. 38.

condition its support for the CTBT at this time on broader movement toward worldwide disarmament.[92] This stance was in keeping with the historic Nehruvian position that a universal test ban, unlike the NPT, was not discriminatory.[93] But obviously it was in contradiction with any policy of acquiring nuclear weapons. The fact that the Rao government circa 1994 was planning to sign and ratify the CTBT is a clear indication that, even at this late date, secularist India was looking beyond Pakistan and the subcontinental nuclear rivalry to the wider world where it found its true key comparison others. But the pro-bomb BJP and its allies in the bomb lobby launched an intense campaign opposing the CTBT. Aided by the overbearing American diplomatic tactics at the CTBT and NPT Review conferences, these groups succeeded in tarring the treaty as simply another guise of "nuclear apartheid." The domestic ferment, coming during the run-up to national elections, forced the Rao government to back away from its support for the CTBT beginning in October 1995.[94] This was a major setback for India's traditional Nehruvian stance in nuclear diplomacy. Later, in June 1996, after the Rao government was succeeded by a weak United Front secularist coalition, India would abandon the CTBT negotiations entirely.

It was in the difficult political context of late 1995 that Rao considered approving a nuclear test.[95] The prime minister went so far as to ask the scientists to make initial preparations at the test site – though without allowing the explosive devices to be transferred there.[96] But after due reflection Rao chose not to proceed, and this choice predated the US discovery of the test preparations.[97] That Rao ended up deciding not to test is hardly surprising. The whole thrust of Rao's energies as prime minister had been moving in the opposite direction from a nuclear breakout. In sponsoring the CTBT the Rao government had essentially been saying that India's interests would be best served by locking in its non-nuclear weapons state status. It did not cease thinking in that way just because the BJP had forced it to abandon the CTBT. From the Rao government's point of view, there was little to be gained from a test in terms of security – after

---

[92] Mistry, "The Unrealized Promise," p. 135.

[93] Rao also had a particular interest in maintaining good Indo-American relations, as a key to the success of his project of economic opening.

[94] Mistry, "The Unrealized Promise," pp. 136–137.

[95] Andrew Koch, "Nuclear Testing in South Asia and the CTBT," *Nonproliferation Review*, Vol. 3, No. 3 (Spring–Summer 1996), pp. 98–104.

[96] Chengappa, *Weapons of Peace*, p. 395.

[97] For a strong case against the notion that the US "stopped" the tests, see Aaron Karp, "Indian Ambitions and the Limits of American Influence," *Arms Control Today*, May 1998, http://www.armscontrol.org/act/1998 05/kpmy98.asp

all, Pakistan would surely test immediately after India.[98] Meanwhile, it calculated that international sanctions could seriously disrupt India's fledgling economic opening.[99] Moreover, having seen the fleeting popularity that Indira Gandhi's 1974 PNE had given her, Rao never bought into the notion that a test would keep him in power.[100] Indeed, if the theory advanced in this book – that decisions to go nuclear arise from deep-seated emotional needs rather than from cool calculations – is correct, the very fact that Rao had to contemplate the matter long and hard after already spending four years in office itself suggests that he was not going to decide in favor of it. In sum, the 1995 Rao "non-test," far from proving that an Indian nuclear breakout was inevitable in the late 1990s, demonstrates the continuing resilience of the policy of remaining just shy of the nuclear threshold – a policy that India had already maintained for nearly a decade.

The theory advanced in this book certainly has trouble explaining India's forward creep toward nuclear weapons status in the 1990s, but it well explains why Indian decisions during that decade never went beyond nuclear ambiguity to full-fledged nuclear acquisition. Moreover, as will be demonstrated, it explains very well why a new, Hindu nationalist government in 1998 definitively ended India's ambiguous nuclear posture. Indian nuclear behavior during the decade 1988–98 may pose an empirical challenge to the theoretical framework set out in this book, but the events of 1998 offer startling empirical confirmation.

The BJP bomb

The "recessed deterrence" situation, though fraught with danger, had over the course of the 1990s proved remarkably stable. Moreover, as mentioned in the introduction to this chapter, it was expected by virtually all mainstream security analysts to endure. As a rule they did not modify their assessments even after the Hindu nationalist BJP came to power in 1998. Indeed, they had interpreted its electoral promise to "re-evaluate the country's nuclear policy and exercise the option to induct nuclear

---

[98] Interview with A. N. Varma, former principal secretary to Prime Minister Rao, New Delhi, December 2, 1998.

[99] Interview with Manmohan Singh, who at the time discussed here was minister of finance, New Delhi, December 19, 1998, and follow-up letter February 19, 1999. The evidence in Chengappa, *Weapons of Peace*, pp. 392–395 reinforces this account.

[100] One should not lose sight of the fact that for any politician to decide to go nuclear for electoral considerations would, as Rao's Principal Secretary A. N. Varma put it, be stooping so low as to be "subterranean." Interview with Varma.

weapons"[101] as a *softening* of its nuclear stance – as an indication of a new sense of responsibility on the part of a putative governing party. They were wrong.

The new government, led by the BJP in coalition with several minor party partners, was sworn in on March 19, 1998. The very next day, new Prime Minister Atal Behari Vajpayee – widely seen as a BJP "moderate" – called in AEC chief R. Chidambaram and DRDO chief A. P. J. Abdul Kalam. As one Vajpayee aide told *India Today*, "It was not a pure courtesy call."[102] Vajpayee wanted to know the technical status of the nuclear weapons program, and he also wanted to know whether tests in the form of actual explosions were technically necessary for the "induction" of nuclear weapons into India's arsenal. The scientists replied that the devices were nearly ready, but that tests would indeed be necessary. Vajpayee closed the meeting without giving them a definitive green light, but the scientists left with the knowledge "that they didn't have much persuading to do."[103] His main concern was apparently that the government would lose its first no-confidence vote in Parliament, as it had in its thirteen-day stint in power in 1996 (about which more below). The government did survive the vote on March 28. Then, on 6 April, Pakistan tested a medium-range missile, the Ghauri, which was capable of hitting India's major cities. As Vajpayee's principal secretary Brajesh Mishra recalled, "Then came the missile and all the claims from the other side of a war. And at that point, the Prime Minister said, OK, let us go ahead [with the tests]."[104] The journalist Raj Chengappa reports that in a meeting on India's security options on the very morning of the Ghauri test, Vajpayee told his aides that there was "no need for much thought. We just have to do it."[105] And so, two days later, on April 8 Vajpayee again called in Chidambaram and DRDO chief A. P. J. Abdul Kalam and asked them to proceed to the test. They said it would take them thirty days to get ready, and so he fixed the test date for May 11.[106]

---

[101] Bharatiya Janata Party, Election Manifesto 1998, "Vote BJP, Vote for a Stable Government, Vote for an Able Prime Minister," p. 31.

[102] Manoj Joshi, "Nuclear Shock Wave," *India Today*, May 25, 1998.

[103] Chengappa, *Weapons of Peace*, p. 34.

[104] "Threats of war from Pak led to Pokhran: Mishra," *The Economic Times*, November 11, 2000.

[105] Chengappa, *Weapons of Peace*, p. 49.

[106] In fact, the tests were ill-prepared not only politically but also *technically*. The scientists, for all their pleading over the years for a test, seem to have been caught by surprise by Vajpayee's determination to move forward so soon. Clearly the scientists themselves were not aware of the great influence ascribed to them by such analysts as Perkovich. The results of this haste are plain to see, especially in the fact that the May 11 tests clearly did not provide the scientists with enough information, and they had to beg Vajpayee for the second set of tests that were performed on May 13. Moreover, it is

While the test preparations went on, the government allowed domestic and foreign security experts to believe that it was being "responsible." Pakistan's Ghauri missile test had not caused a general tumult in Indian elite or mass opinion. The strategic situation was still generally perceived as remaining fundamentally stable.[107] And indeed, confirming the views of the strategic experts, on 10 April – that is, two days *after* the secret decision to test had already been made – the government announced the formation of a task force to produce recommendations for the creation of a National Security Council. The Council in turn would be tasked with carrying out a "strategic defense review" that, among other things, would evaluate the nuclear policy stance. In short, the BJP certainly *appeared* to be shuffling its electoral promise off to some undefined date far in the future. As Jasjit Singh, one of the members of the new task force and director of the prominent Institute for Defence Studies and Analyses, told *India Today* merely one week before the tests, "Their [BJP's] image was that the first thing they would do would be to test the atom bomb but they are moving with maturity and restraint."[108] But this was in fact not what was happening. Vajpayee did not need a government commission or even his own defense minister to tell him whether or not he needed the bomb. Indeed, he had already tried to make the decision to test once before, during his thirteen-day stint as prime minister in 1996, but his government had fallen on its first no-confidence vote and he thus could not set the wheels in motion.[109] Clearly, on this issue Vajpayee was a man who knew what he wanted – and he wanted it now.

On the appointed date, May 11, India conducted three tests at the Pokhran test site in the Rajasthan desert. One of the tests was of a thermonuclear device. The call from Pokhran came through at 3:45 p.m. The journalist Manoj Joshi describes the scene:

The Prime Minister's Principal Secretary Brajesh Mishra lifted the receiver hesitantly to hear an excited voice cry "Done!" Putting the caller on hold, Mishra re-entered the room. Seeing his expression, Prime Minister Vajpayee, Home Minister L. K. Advani, Defense Minister George Fernandes, Finance Minister Yashwant Sinha and Planning Commission Deputy Chairman Jaswant Singh could barely control their feelings. Advani was seen wiping away his tears. Picking

clear that more tests will eventually be needed, because the scientists had not worked in a specialist group with the military or anyone else to determine precisely what tests would be needed for what nuclear force structure. And besides that, the thermonuclear test appears to have failed. See General (ret.) V. R. Raghavan, "Dangerous nuclear uncertainties," *The Hindu*, March 13, 2000. These points were reinforced in several interviews with senior Indian military officials.

[107] See George Fernandes' comments, cited in Perkovich, *India's Nuclear Bomb*, p. 410.
[108] Ibid.   [109] Ibid., pp. 374–375.

up the receiver, Vajpayee, in an emotion-choked voice, thanked the two scientists who made it happen.[110]

Two days later, India conducted two more tests, each sub-kiloton in size. With these two test series, the decade-long subcontinental nuclear equilibrium had been destroyed.

Why Vajpayee chose to go nuclear

To reiterate, this was a decision that Vajpayee made essentially on his own, keeping even most of his Cabinet (let alone Parliament and the outside world) in the dark until it was a *fait accompli*. But why did he do it? What explains the extraordinary motivation and certitude that Vajpayee displayed in his firm decision to go nuclear immediately upon coming to power – which stands in such stark contrast to the long history of hedging on this issue by his predecessors? The answer is clear: Vajpayee, unlike his predecessors, was an oppositional nationalist *vis-à-vis* Pakistan; Pakistan's Ghauri missile test played into his preexisting tendency to experience a mixture of fear and pride; and the letting loose of those emotions proved an explosive psychological cocktail.[111] Indeed, it would be hard to find a more straightforward reflection of the theoretical expectations of Chapter 2.

The connection between Vajpayee and the BJP, their nuclear weapons ambitions and their oppositional nationalism against Pakistan is clear. The first call made by the BJP's predecessor party, the Bharatiya Jana Sangh, for nuclear weapons had actually come in a resolution of December 4, 1964, which demanded a response to China's nuclear tests.[112] But when the BJP proper was formed under Vajpayee's leadership in 1980, it no longer held that India should develop a nuclear arsenal against China or for any other reason. As late as the 1984 general election campaign, the BJP electoral manifesto did not call for building a nuclear deterrent.[113] It was only in July 1985 that the party came out

---

[110] Joshi, "Nuclear Shock Wave."

[111] Note that while the Ghauri test was causally relevant to Vajpayee's choice, this was more as an excuse than as a trigger. As Vajpayee's attempt to proceed to nuclear tests during his 1996 stint in power makes clear, he hardly needed the Ghauri to convince him of the rightness of this course.

[112] BJS, "Nuclear Deterrent Necessary," Resolution No. 13, December 4, 1964, in *BJS Party Documents 1951–1972*, Vol. III: *Resolutions on Defence and External Affairs* (New Delhi: BJS, 1973).

[113] In parliamentary statements, however, BJP stalwarts had begun to indicate that the nuclear program of Pakistan worried them gravely. For instance, in 1981, Jaswant Singh, the BJP's main spokesman on external affairs in the upper house (*Rajya Sabha*), argued that India should get nuclear weapons if Pakistan did so. Jaswant Singh in the Rajya

in favor of an Indian nuclear deterrent, naming one cause for this change of heart: Pakistan's nuclear progress. The resolution of the BJP National Executive read in part:

Reports from Pakistan indicate that the threat of a Pakistani Nuclear Bomb is real and an immediate response to this is necessary. The BJP, therefore, calls upon Government to take immediate steps to develop our own nuclear bomb.[114]

In short, the BJP had come to believe by 1985 that the Pakistani bomb either existed already or would exist very soon, and thus it demanded an urgent Indian bomb effort in response. (The resolution came at a time of escalation of Hindu–Muslim communal tensions inside India, tensions that the BJP was helping to promote.) The party ramped up its rhetoric yet further beginning in 1991, with the claim that Pakistan's nuclear status was no longer ambiguous at all but that the country was in fact "now a nuclear-weapon state."[115] These assertions continued with even more emphasis in subsequent years. True, party resolutions began also tossing in other factors, such as the China threat, as justification for an Indian bomb effort, but there could be no mistaking the wellspring of the policy. Similarly, while in the weeks following the tests, the government – in not a little disarray after taking such an ill-prepared decision – went on a public fishing expedition for arguments, after Pakistan's tests the government's line became much more focused.[116]

If the oppositional nationalists Vajpayee and the BJP were quite clear in their motivation to acquire the bomb, the sportsmanlike nationalists – most secularist parties and a good portion of the strategic elites – were quite clear in their motivation to steer clear of that choice. It has not been sufficiently noted that in the aftermath of the tests, Congress and the other secularist parties offered stern critiques of the decision. The BJP actually got into deep political trouble, and if the Pakistani reply had not come when it did the government might well have fallen.[117] This shows, parenthetically, that the BJP did not choose to test as a means of

Sabha, quoted in Madhusadan Mishra, *BJP and India's Foreign Policy* (New Delhi: Uppal Publishing House, 1997), p. 43.

[114] BJP, "Nuclear Bomb," resolution approved by the National Executive meeting at Bhopal, July 19–21, 1985, in A. Moin Zaidi, *Annual Register of Indian Political Parties 1985* (New Delhi: India Institute of Applied Political Research, 1987), pp. 431–432.

[115] BJP, "Foreign policy" resolution approved by the National Executive meeting at Thiruvananthapuram, 1991, in BJP, *Foreign Policy and Resolutions* (New Delhi: BJP, 1995).

[116] Its arguments included not only Pakistan's nuclear program and the Ghauri test, but also Pakistani activities in Kashmir, Chinese encirclement, Western hypocrisy, the rough nature of international politics, India's legitimate aspirations for great power status, etc.

[117] Dinshaw Mistry, "India and the Comprehensive Test Ban Treaty," ACDIS Research Report, Program in Arms Control, Disarmament and International Security, University of Illinois at Urbana-Champaign, September 1998.

consolidating its hold on power. In fact, it was taking a huge political risk: not only by destroying the traditional foreign policy consensus, but also by its secrecy and failure to consult Cabinet and its coalition partners. Moreover, in spite of the general popularity of the tests, the BJP got little benefit from them in regional elections later that year, which turned on the rising price of onions and potatoes.

For a complete understanding of Vajpayee's nuclear decision, however, we need to go beyond the correlation that we have established between his desire to go nuclear and oppositional nationalism. We need to explore the complex pathway by which Vajpayee's NIC impacted his nuclear decisionmaking. Here I will focus especially on the effects of fear, the difference between his emotional predisposition and that of his sportsmanlike nationalist predecessors. Vajpayee's fear led to *higher threat assessments* and to *lower cognitive complexity* on this issue than for his secularist counterparts. It also led him to *hasty decisionmaking* and a *taste for the symbolism of security and power*. All of these elements pushed him in the direction of "inducting" nuclear weapons.

Threat assessments. Fear brings about higher threat assessments. Vajpayee the oppositional nationalist clearly rejected the conventional idea that the subcontinent was in a stable situation of "recessed deterrence." As noted above, already by 1985 he and his party were claiming that the Pakistani nuclear train was unstoppable. And after the Pakistani tests of 1998, Vajpayee told Parliament, "The Pakistani tests did not come as a surprise and this vindicates our decision to test."[118] It is well to pause for a moment on this remarkable statement. Vajpayee was saying that *the Indian tests were necessary because of the Pakistani tests that the Indian tests had caused!* We would be on the other side of the looking-glass here, but for the key assumption underlying Vajpayee's statement: that Pakistan already had the bomb, while India did not. As Vajpayee also noted in his statement to the upper house (Rajya Sabha):

I would like to assure the House that Pakistan's tests do not pose any new threat to our national security because we have been monitoring Pakistan's clandestine pursuit of its nuclear programme . . . After his first tenure in office, Prime Minister Nawaz Sharif had declared in August 1994 that Pakistan possessed a nuclear bomb.[119]

---

[118] "Prime Minister's reply to the discussion in Lok Sabha on Nuclear Tests on May 29, 1998," http://www.indianembassy.org/pic/pm(ls).htm.

[119] Again, these statements were not universally accepted, and Vajpayee knew it. With the Pakistani tests, he rubbed it in: "Many honorable members have questioned the 'timing' as well as our assessment of the threat perception behind the decision to undertake the limited programme of underground nuclear tests, conducted on 11 and 13 May. One answer came yesterday in the afternoon, quite loud and clear. The action taken by the

In other words, in Vajpayee's eyes India, though testing first, was actually just evening the score with Pakistan.

Cognitive complexity. Fear brings about lower cognitive complexity and perceptual double standards. Vajpayee's lack of cognitive complexity on this issue was summarized by his disarmingly simple statement after India tested: "We have a big bomb now." As George Perkovich notes, an embarrassed government retracted Vajpayee's statement after it was printed in *India Today.*[120] Moreover, Vajpayee's view of Pakistan as "having" the bomb before 1998 *because* it had gone some way toward it, and of India as "not having" the bomb *even though* it had gone some way toward it, is a classic example of a perceptual double standard.

Haste. The fearful individual feels a great need to act as soon as possible, as much to decrease the fear as to decrease the danger. The "maturity and restraint" that secularists and mainstream strategic elites such as Jasjit Singh saw in India's "recessed deterrence" stance, the BJP saw as "drift and escapism."[121] Vajpayee was clearly not satisfied with anything less than acquiring an actual, full-blown Indian nuclear arsenal as soon as possible. As noted above, it was a mere two days after arriving in power that he summoned his scientific chiefs to discuss the test option. Then, provoked as few others were by the Ghauri test, Vajpayee told his aides that there was "no need for much thought. We just have to do it."[122] Yet this haste does not mean that Vajpayee took the issue lightly. Indeed, that Vajpayee understood his decision to be a revolutionary one is clear from the symbolic importance he ascribed to it. I now turn to that dimension of his decisionmaking process.

Symbolism. Fear leads to a frantic search for symbols of security and power, and pride leads to a desire to possess those symbols oneself. Vajpayee was very explicit about the broader symbolic dimension of his act. As he told a reporter, "The greatest meaning of these tests is that they have given India *shakti* [a Vedic concept of the liberation of energy], they have given India strength and they have given India self-confidence."[123] The 1998 tests themselves were even code-named "Operation Shakti." The liberation that Vajpayee hoped for was in large part a liberation from Pakistan. It is an old theme in Hindu nationalist rhetoric that Pakistan will cause trouble for India as long as India chooses to remain weak, but

Government of Pakistan should set at rest most queries regarding both 'timing' as well as 'threat perceptions.'" "Prime Minister's reply to the discussion in the Rajya Sabha on nuclear tests on May 29, 1998," http://www.indianembassy.org/pic/pm(rs).htm.

[120] Perkovich, *India's Nuclear Bomb*, p. 420.

[121] The quote of "drift and escapism" is from the complete BJP 1985 resolution on Pakistan and the bomb. See Zaidi, *Annual Register of Indian Political Parties 1985.*

[122] Chengappa, *Weapons of Peace*, p. 49.

[123] Atal Behari Vajpayee, interview with *India Today*, May 25, 1998.

that it will respect an India that has decided to become strong.[124] In the aftermath of the tests, Vajpayee and other BJP leaders such as Home Minister L. K. Advani (Vajpayee's number two) reiterated this theme of the tests as a symbol of their determination to put an end once and for all to the Indo-Pakistan conflict. They argued that facing a nuclear India, Pakistan could no longer mount wars, incursions, or support terrorism in Kashmir.[125] They even believed that a nuclear India could even make peace with Pakistan, finally, on its terms.[126] And if Pakistan instead tried to mount a real nuclear arms race, let it: the crushing economic burden would cause it – like the Soviet Union – to vanish altogether.[127] Meanwhile, India with the bomb would soar, taking its rightful place among the great powers. For it was "India's due," as Vajpayee told Parliament – "the right of one-sixth of humankind."[128] In these words one hears clear echoes from the French case.

But the tests did not only symbolize liberation for Vajpayee; they also – unavoidably – symbolized other, less palatable desires. Ashis Nandy cites a poem by a young Vajpayee, which apart from explicit reference to (in Nandy's words) "the victimization of the Hindus in history" at the hands of the Muslims, also offers a chilling premonition of the tests he was to order:

> This is the identity of the Hindu body, the Hindu soul and the Hindu life,
> I am that rage of Shankar, which can destroy the earth and reduce it to ashes,
> I am the devastating sound of his drum to which death dances,
> I am the unquenched thirst of the goddess of war, I am the divine laughter of Durga,
> I am the doomsday call of the god of death, the burning fire from the funeral pyre,

---

[124] For instance, in its "Principles and Policies" adopted in 1965, the BJS wrote, "By continuously fomenting anti-India feeling the rulers of Pakistan seek only to strengthen their own political position. As such, India's policy of appeasement is their biggest prop. If India were to adopt an attitude of firmness toward Pakistan, Pakistan's worked-up hostility towards India would not last long." *Bharatiya Jana Sangh Party Documents 1951–1972*, Vol. 1: *Principles and Policies, Manifestos, Constitution* (New Delhi: BJS, 1973).

[125] John F. Burns, "Visiting Nuclear Site, Indian Leader Puts Pakistan on Notice," *The New York Times*, Thursday, May 21, 1998, p. A7. Thanks to Jacques L. Hymans for this article.

[126] Thus the Lahore peace effort made by Vajpayee, seemingly so "uncharacteristic," actually stemmed just as much from the tests as the Kargil war did.

[127] This is a disturbing trend in Indian discussions of Pakistan since the early 1990s. See Stephen Cohen, *India: Emerging Power* (Washington, DC: Brookings Institution Press, 2001), ch. 7. Thanks also to Dinshaw Mistry and V. R. Raghavan for the initial insight here.

[128] "Evolution of India's Nuclear Policy," paper laid on the table of the House on May 27, 1998 by Shri Atal Behari Vajpayee, on web at http://www.indianembassy.org/pic/nuclearpolicy.htm.

If with this fire raging inside me, I burn the earth,
And the water, earth, sky, soil go up in flames on their own, do not be
    surprised.[129]

In short, the man who shattered the "recessed" nuclear equilibrium with his tests in the Rajasthan desert had not done so merely for strategic purposes; he had also done so because he – and the India of his imagination – needed the psychological reassurance of hearing that awful desert music.

Oppositional nationalism, fear, pride, haste, nuclear symbolism, all resulting in great motivation to equip the nation with nuclear weapons: the basic hypothesis of this book could hardly find greater confirmation than in the case of Atal Behari Vajpayee.

---

[129] Cited in Ashis Nandy *et al.*, "Creating a Nationality: The Ramjanmabhumi Movement and Fear of the Self" in Ashis Nandy, *Exiled at Home* (Delhi: Oxford University Press, 1998), p. 55.

8   Conclusion: lessons for policy

Identities, emotions, and the nuclear choice

The previous four chapters on France, Australia, Argentina, and India have demonstrated the explanatory utility of the theoretical framework developed in Chapter 2. In spite of the vast differences in the geographical, temporal, and political contexts of the four country cases, the theory's key variable – leaders' national identity conceptions (NICs) – did in fact systematically differentiate those who felt the need to decide for nuclear weapons from those who did not. Specifically, leaders with oppositional nationalist NICs experienced feelings of fear and pride when confronting their key comparison other, and those feelings in turn sparked strong desires to acquire the bomb. By contrast, leaders without oppositional nationalist NICs did not follow this pattern. Moreover, the desire for the bomb created a strong probability of a political decision for it; and once a political decision to acquire the bomb was in fact made, actual nuclear weapons arsenals ended up coming into existence.

Chapter 3 presented the results of the rigorous measurement strategy for leaders' NICs. Of the dozens of leaders covered in this book, it found only five who unambiguously qualified as holding oppositional nationalist NICs *vis-à-vis* some external other. Two of these, Pierre Mendès France of France and Atal Behari Vajpayee of India made the crucial decisions to endow their states with a nuclear arsenal. Another, John Gorton of Australia, tried mightily to overcome the resistance of his Cabinet and do the same, but his efforts fell short. The fourth one, Charles de Gaulle, during his brief tenure as head of government immediately after France's liberation, laid the groundwork for a military nuclear program, later strongly supported Mendès France's nuclear weapons decision, and eventually became almost indissociable from the French *force de frappe*. This leaves only the oppositional nationalist interim Argentine leader Héctor Cámpora – who was in no position to make any significant policy decisions at all.

Meanwhile, of the many leaders analyzed in this book who were not coded as oppositional nationalist, only two arguably made something resembling a decision to acquire nuclear weapons. First, France's Edgar Faure, who held an oppositional subaltern NIC toward Germany, nevertheless accepted the political determination that had been made by his immediate predecessor Pierre Mendès France and provided the funding to implement Mendès France's nuclear weapons ambitions. As argued in Chapter 4, Faure's decision cannot be understood without acknowledging the important momentum created by the prior nuclear weapons decision of Mendès France. Notably, Faure had not pushed for the bomb during his earlier time as prime minister. The case of Faure therefore does not undermine the theoretical model. Second, India's sportsmanlike nationalist Prime Minister Rajiv Gandhi allowed his scientists and engineers to proceed with nuclear "weaponization" beginning in the late 1980s. This is a more serious deviation from the book's hypotheses; but even in this case, as argued in Chapter 7, Rajiv Gandhi's decision was remarkable for its restraint and is best described as an attempt to become "half-pregnant" with the bomb. It took the oppositional nationalist Vajpayee's dramatic 1998 decision for India to come to possess a full-fledged nuclear arsenal (which, as noted in Chapter 7, only really came into existence in 1999).

Chapter 2 did more than claim that leaders with oppositional nationalist NICs should have a preference for nuclear acquisition. It also posited the causal process of how an NIC can drive a foreign policy decision, and in particular it elaborated the emotional mechanism linking identity to choice. It further suggested that there would be outward indications of those emotional drivers, for instance in a hasty and truncated process of deliberation. The case studies did indeed turn up many telltale signs of emotional decisionmaking. For instance, as noted in Chapter 7, a newly elected Vajpayee – author of a chilling poem about "this fire raging inside me" – was so intent on a detonation in 1998 that he simply waved aside the strategic considerations put forward by his aides and told them, "There [is] no need for much thought. We just have to do it."[1] Meanwhile, as noted in Chapter 4, Pierre Mendès France himself admitted to having been "dominated by that fear" of a newly reborn German *Wehrmacht* during the period when he made his nuclear choices.[2] And Mendès France, like Vajpayee, proved extraordinarily willing to cut through the

---

[1] Raj Chengappa, *Weapons of Peace: The Secret Story of India's Quest to Be a Nuclear Power* (New Delhi: Harper Collins, 2000), p. 49.

[2] Transcript of interview with Pierre Mendès France conducted by Georgette Elgey, corrected in Pierre Mendès France's own hand, October 27, 1965, fonds Elgey, Archives Nationales, Paris.

quandaries of proliferation and to make a clear decision in favor of the bomb on the day after Christmas, 1954, mere months after assuming power – a hasty decision he seems later to have come to regret. In short, the theoretical model proved useful not only for explaining *which* leaders were predisposed toward making the choice for the bomb, but also *how* they made those choices.

In sum, this book has found that leaders' choices on the bomb are the result of NIC-driven emotions that shape their information sets, their action tendencies, and indeed their very willingness to act at all on the nuclear issue. The robustness of the finding is based not just on four country cases, but in fact on many cases – dozens of individual leaders from four different countries. It is possible that investigation of other cases would point out shortcomings in the basic model developed here. However, so far the model has proven to be quite portable across space and time and notably has been applied by other scholars to the South African case.[3]

Beyond the critical question of going or not going nuclear, the leader's NIC type also proved to be a good predictor of his or her preferences on ancillary nuclear issues – the desire for nuclear technological autonomy; the willingness to join the non-proliferation regime, and the pursuit of a superpower guarantee against potential existential threats. This was the case even despite the cautions voiced in Chapter 2 about extending the model beyond the narrow nuclear weapons decision. Table 8.1 summarizes the hypothesized and actual nuclear policy preferences of the leaders covered in this book. This simplified presentation of the data cannot substitute for the empirical detail and interpretations of the case study chapters, but it does accurately reflect the successful overall performance of the theory. The hypothesized preferences from Chapter 2 for each NIC type are listed in the first column, and then specific leaders' NIC types as measured in Chapter 3 are listed in their respective country columns. Recall that the four NIC types are derived from the two identity dimensions of solidarity and status: NICs characterized by low perceived natural solidarity with the key comparison other are termed "oppositional" while the rest are termed "sportsmanlike"; NICs characterized by low perceived natural status *vis-à-vis* the key comparison other are termed "subaltern" while the rest are termed "nationalist."

Leaders' nuclear choices clearly reflect their NICs. Of course, we would not need to understand leader psychology if it were merely a reflection of deeper, more "objective" variables such as a state's international power

---

[3] Helen E. Purkitt, Stephen F. Burgess and Peter Liberman, "Correspondence: South Africa's Nuclear Decisions," *International Security*, Vol. 27, No. 1 (2002), pp. 186–194.

Table 8.1 *Summary of the theory's performance*

NIC type and specific hypotheses[a]	France (Chapter 4)	Australia (Chapter 5)	Argentina (Chapter 6)	India (Chapter 7)
A. Oppositional nationalist	**De Gaulle, Mendès France**	**Gorton**	**Cámpora**	**Vajpayee**
HA 1: Go for bomb	(✓)	(✓) (but failed)	(Interim president: no significant policy choices)	(✓)
HA 2: Pursue tech	(✓)	(✓)		(✓)
HA 3: Resist NPT	(EDC): (✓)	(✓)		X
HA 4: Seek superpower guarantee	(✓)	(✓)		
B. Oppositional subaltern	**Fourth Republic establishment**	**Traditionalist Liberals**	*(No Argentine leader fits this NIC type)*	*(No Indian leader fits this NIC type)*
HB 1: Not go for bomb	(✓) (but E. Faure)	(✓)		
HB 2: Not pursue tech	X	(✓)		
HB 3: Not resist NPT	(EDC): (✓)	(✓)		
HB 4: Seek superpower guarantee	(✓)	(✓)		
C. Sportsmanlike nationalist	*(No French leader fits this NIC type)*	*(No Australian leader fits this NIC type)*	**All except Cámpora**	**All before Vajpayee**
HC 1: Not go for bomb			(✓)	(✓) (but R. Gandhi)
HC 2: Pursue tech			(✓) (until Menem)	(✓)
HC 3: Resist NPT			(✓) (until Menem)	(✓)
HC 4: Not seek superpower guarantee			(✓)	(✓)
D. Sportsmanlike subaltern	*(No French leader fits this NIC type)*	**Whitlam**	*(No Argentine leader fits this NIC type)*	*(No Indian leader fits this NIC type)*
HD 1: Not go for bomb		(✓)		
HD 2: Not pursue tech		X		
HD 3: Not resist NPT		(✓)		
HD 4: Not seek superpower guarantee		(✓) (but did not reject either)		

[a] Correctly hypothesized preferences are marked with a check mark (✓); incorrectly hypothesized preferences are marked with an X.

position or the availability of international institutions. But in fact the case studies have shown that structural analyses cannot explain why, when, and how the leaders of these four countries dealt with the question of going nuclear. On this score, it is particularly important to reiterate this book's finding that different leaders from the same country can have very different NICs and therefore different nuclear policy preferences. The book even shows that leaders from the same political party can have very different NICs – consider, for instance, the contrast between the Australian Liberals Menzies and Gorton. The sources of these differences are in the individuals, not in the external structure. In short, if we wish to understand decisions to acquire nuclear weapons, an analysis of the psychology of individual leaders is simply unavoidable.

Such a psychological analysis could certainly go much deeper than the one attempted here. In particular, this book has offered little comment on the origins of different leaders' NICs. I made this choice for a very simple reason: those origins are quite evidently highly complex. They probably stem in part from broader cultural (or countercultural) phenomena, such as the society's collective memories of warfare. But they also probably stem in part – maybe even in large part – from leaders' personal experiences and tendencies. Further research that traces the origins of individual leaders' NICs will certainly add importantly to our understanding of international politics. But this is a task for another book. Every independent variable from one perspective can be taken as a dependent variable from another. Leaders' NICs are both complex enough in their origins and stable enough in their expression that it is not too much of a stretch to consider them as independent variables.

Puncturing common myths

"The 'domino theory' of the 21st century," said Director of Central Intelligence George Tenet to the US Senate Select Intelligence Committee in 2003, "may well be nuclear."[4] Tenet's statement was an apt one – much more so than he realized. For the original Cold War domino theory has been thoroughly discredited, and the new proliferation domino theory is based on a similar series of oversimplified claims. The new domino theory, like the old one, paints an exceedingly dark picture of world trends by lumping the truly dangerous leaders together with the merely self-assertive ones. The new domino theory, like the old one, somehow

---

[4] George Tenet statement cited in Mitchell B. Reiss, "The Nuclear Tipping Point: Prospects for a World of Many Nuclear Weapons States," in Kurt M. Campbell, Robert J. Einhorn, and Mitchell B. Reiss, eds., *The Nuclear Tipping Point: Why States Reconsider their Nuclear Choices* (Washington, DC: Brookings Institution Press, 2004), p. 4.

convinces itself that its past predictive failures only serve to underscore the danger that with just one more setback we may well reach a "tipping point" at which not just "rogue states" but the whole world defects from our side.[5] The new domino theory, like the old one, has given rise to a zero-tolerance, worldwide effort at containment that has produced some victories, much wasted effort and collateral damage, and even some self-fulfilling prophecies.

Moreover, in at least one respect the proliferation domino theory is even more alarmist than its predecessor. Since American and Western foreign policy elites never could completely fathom the attractions of communism, their anxiety about a future communist-dominated world always seemed a bit unreal, even to themselves. By contrast, they certainly can – or think they can – fathom the attractions of the bomb, for after all they clung to it throughout the Cold War, and many cling to it still. Therefore, any shred of evidence that a country is interested in nuclear technology is taken as proof positive that the country is building a "nuclear weapons capability," after which point it will be only a matter of time before it builds nuclear "weapons." But in fact, the typical assumptions that underlie the dark prognostications of "life in a nuclear-armed crowd" simply do not stand up against the empirical record. They are, in short, myths.

Myth No. 1: "States want the bomb because it is a great deterrent"

The three leaders covered in this book who clearly wanted the bomb – Pierre Mendès France of France, John Gorton of Australia, and Atal Behari Vajpayee of India – were convinced that having it would indeed be a great deterrent to their nations' foes. But the case studies also provide examples of other leaders and foreign policy elites, facing the same or at least comparable external situations, who disagreed. This book has found that the bomb is like a Rorschach test: people see in it what they want to see in it. And what they want to see in it is driven by their national identity conceptions (NICs).

For instance, take the late 1960s Australian debate over nuclear weapons. The traditionalist Australian Liberals, and notably the long-time prime minister Robert Menzies, held an oppositional subaltern NIC in contrast to Gorton's oppositional nationalism. The traditionalists, truly afraid that Australia would be the "last domino," hardly disputed Gorton's assessment of Australia's *need* for a credible nuclear deterrent against the communist enemy (the Liberals' unity on this point stood in

---

[5] Campbell, Einhorn, and Reiss, eds., *The Nuclear Tipping Point.*

contrast to the threat perceptions of others, notably those in the Australian Labor Party). What the traditionalist Liberals did dispute was Gorton's nationalism-inspired faith in Australia's *capacity* to build such a credible deterrent. For instance, the top secret 1968 report of the Defence Department's traditionalist Joint Planning Committee stated that, try as it might, "Australia can only be a lesser and not a major nuclear power."[6] Given this, "the result of an Australian nuclear attack against China even in the case of a first strike could, at best, only be relatively small. Even with thermo-nuclear weapons the percentage loss to China would be small and possibly acceptable compared with the almost total annihilation of the Australian industrial capacity and population."[7] In short, the traditionalist Liberals viewed nuclear weapons as a great deterrent, but only if a country's arsenal was of sufficient quantity and quality – and since they deemed Australia incapable of approaching those levels through its own efforts, it would be better off not trying at all but instead maintaining its dependent relationship on its great and powerful friends.

Oppositional subalterns want deterrence but don't think they can get it on their own. On the other side of the coin stand sportsmanlike nationalists, who think they can get it but don't see why they should. A good example of such an attitude comes from the long succession of Congress Party prime ministers of India. Taking their cue from Jawaharlal Nehru, they were convinced that India could build a robust and significant nuclear arsenal, but they were not convinced that India needed to do so – and indeed, they thought that such a step was likely to be strategically counterproductive. Even when the Chinese went nuclear in 1964 – a mere two years after the two nations had engaged in a shooting war – Prime Minister Lal Bahadur Shastri reacted with great restraint. As noted in Chapter 7, Shastri told Parliament, "Our neighbors will be more frightened if we begin to make the atom bomb . . . It does not help us at all in reassuring our neighbors with whom India wants friendship."[8] This desire to reassure rather than to deter extended to Shastri's refusal to seek a credible nuclear guarantee through alignment with the West. Over the decades after Shastri's passing India's stance on the bomb became increasingly complex, but in the end it took the arrival in power of the unambiguously oppositional nationalist Vajpayee – a Hindu nationalist who explicitly

---

[6] "An Independent Australian Nuclear Capability: Strategic Considerations," Annex to Joint Planning Committee Report No. 8/1968 marked "top secret," Department of Defence File No. 67/1017, p. 14. Document collected by Jim Walsh at National Archives of Australia.

[7] Ibid., p. 17.

[8] Shastri cited in Peter Lavoy, "Learning to Live with the Bomb? India and Nuclear Weapons, 1947–1974," Ph.D. dissertation, University of California at Berkeley, 1997, p. 348.

rejected the NIC promoted by Nehru – to endow the country with a full-fledged nuclear arsenal.

Myth No. 2: "States want the bomb as a ticket to international status"

Again, the three leaders covered in this book who clearly wanted the bomb – Pierre Mendès France of France, John Gorton of Australia, and Atal Behari Vajpayee of India – were convinced that having it would give them the international status they very much desired. But the case studies also provide examples of other leaders and foreign policy elites, facing the same or at least comparable external situations, who felt that the potential status benefits of acquiring the bomb were secondary or even illusory.

Not every state leader seeks to play the great power game. The French "Europeans," for instance, were not tempted by the promise that the bomb might bring their country back into the top ranks. These men were holders of an NIC that, while complex, was still identifiably oppositional subaltern toward the victors of 1940, Germany. In line with this NIC, the French "Europeans" basically saw the great power game as a losing proposition. They also wanted to impose this view on France's historic enemy before its return to full sovereignty could reignite its appetite for destruction. Therefore, as noted in Chapter 4, they inserted into the European Defense Community (EDC) treaty the stricture that the supranational EDC authorities had to approve any member state's production, importation, or exportation in one year of more than 500 grams of fissile material – far less than is necessary to produce a nuclear blast. Moreover, all fissile material produced or acquired had to be devoted to non-military purposes, and intrusive supranational inspections would verify compliance.[9] In short, when Robert Schuman signed the EDC treaty in May 1952, he was declaring an end to France's great power ambitions – a declaration that would be vigorously countered by the later oppositional nationalist prime minister Pierre Mendès France in the EDC ratification fight of late 1954. Mendès France set France on a course to become a nuclear weapons state, a status finally achieved under the presidency of Charles de Gaulle.

Even those leaders who are clearly international prestige seekers do not necessarily view the bomb as the right ticket to punch. For instance,

[9] "Note pour le Secrétaire Général, a.s. lettre du Commissariat à l'Energie atomique relative au traité instituant une Communauté européenne de defense," le jurisconsulte, Ministère des Affairs Etrangères, March 15, 1954, in Secrétariat Général, Dossier CED, 70: Dossier Général 1er janvier–18 juin 1954, Archives du Ministère des Affairs Etrangères, Paris.

for several decades Argentine leaders believed that mastery of nuclear technology would give them the international status they dearly sought. Indeed, as noted in Chapter 6, Argentina even built and operated a uranium enrichment plant. This plant was originally meant to provide the fuel for Argentina's research reactors including the one built for Peru, and it also took on the purpose of providing fuel for a planned fleet of Argentine nuclear submarines. But even though the work was being carried out in secret, the Argentines did not build the plant to produce fissile material for bombs. This was because even the military presidents in power at the time felt that the potential status benefits of a bomb project were heavily outweighed by its potential to ensnare the country in a dangerous and costly arms race with Brazil. The Indian Nehruvians analyzed in Chapter 7 went even one step further: they not only believed that the potential security costs of building the bomb outweighed the status benefits, but also that India could actually gain more international status by *abstaining* from the bomb.

Myth No. 3: "Behind the decision for the bomb stand the mean interests of those who stand to benefit personally from it"

It is certainly true that powerful state actors, and notably top nuclear energy bureaucrats, played a key supporting role in all three of this book's cases of efforts to go nuclear. In choosing for the bomb, Mendès France was telling his top nuclear administrator, Pierre Guillaumat, what Guillaumat dearly wanted to hear. Australia's chief nuclear bureaucrat, Philip Baxter, was a constant proponent of an Australian deterrent right from the start of his long tenure. And over the years India's nuclear bureaucrats also became increasingly militant for the bomb, until the advent of the BJP government under Vajpayee finally gave them the green light they had long been seeking. But the fact that certain elements of the state were gratified by the nuclear decisions of leaders does not mean that their interests and desires lay at the root of those decisions. Indeed, the case studies show the clear limits of the "Dr. Strangelove" theory of proliferation, according to which political decisionmakers are putty in the hands of brilliant, self-interested atomic scientists.

In fact, the evidence of this book suggests that nuclear bureaucrats who want to build the bomb cannot substantially move toward that end without political direction and support, and that such support is typically not forthcoming. For instance, in spite of CEA administrative chief Pierre Guillaumat's best efforts, it was not until the December 1954 decision by Pierre Mendès France that Guillaumat finally was freed from what Yves Rocard called "the hindrances that he had endured until then" and could build a bona fide nuclear weapons program.[10] The Indian nuclear weaponeers, who pushed the limits of their political mandate, were also ultimately stymied until the top leadership changed the basic policy in 1998. As noted in Chapter 7, even Rajiv Gandhi's late 1980s decision for "weaponization" was a flashing yellow light, not a green one. That the weaponeers remained frustrated through the 1990s is evident in their constant pleading to successive prime ministers for a test series, and in their tremendous gratification upon the election and decision of Atal Behari Vajpayee.

The "Dr. Strangelove" theory has deeper flaws as well. It is true that some nuclear bureaucrats are pro-bomb, but the case studies show that they are not *inherently* so. Rather, like their political masters, top nuclear bureaucrats' opinions on the bomb also appear often to be strongly influenced by their basic NICs. As noted in Chapter 5, the pro-bomb Philip Baxter was not merely a nuclear engineer; he was also the author of the play *The Day the Sun Rose in the West*, in which Australia stands alone against the forces of the South East Asian People's Republic, whose goal is "to make the whole invasion [of Australia] a gigantic experiment in producing a new and better race."[11] Baxter's nuclear dreams, however, were opposed by other, more traditionally minded members of his own Atomic Energy Commission, such as Maurice Timbs. Another example of the oversimplifications of the logic of "where you stand depends on where you sit" is the Argentine *Proceso*'s nuclear chief, Admiral Carlos Castro Madero. Castro Madero was a scientist, a military man, and above all a bureaucratic empire-builder. He parlayed his influence with President Jorge Videla into the 1979 approval of the grand, expensive *Plan Nuclear*, and also the secret uranium enrichment plant. But even though Castro Madero had enormous political clout, he consciously excluded nuclear weapons from his wish list – even to the point of trying to prevent discussion of security implications in the interministerial commission reviewing the *Plan Nuclear*.

This book has also shown that it is incorrect to ascribe nuclear weapons decisions to the mean political interests of the leaders themselves. Atal Behari Vajpayee, for instance, did not wait for his hand-picked National Security Council task force to give him political cover for deciding to "induct" nuclear weapons. He also did not consult the other parties in his governing coalition, including his own defense minister. Instead, he risked his weeks-old government – which he had toiled

---

[10] Yves Rocard, *Mémoires sans concessions* (Paris: Grasset et Fasquelle, 1988), pp. 175–176.
[11] Philip Gissing, "Sir Philip Baxter, Engineer: The Fabric of a Liberal-National Country Style of Thought," Ph.D. dissertation, University of New South Wales, March 1998.

for forty years to achieve – on one nuclear throw of the dice. And when the tests came, they produced not national unity but shock and anger from the main opposition party, which began a campaign against the government. That campaign was just beginning to draw blood when Pakistan's tests intervened to save Vajpayee's neck. In short, the Indian nuclear tests of 1998 were just as risky domestically as they were internationally. They were the product of an emotional urge, not a political calculation.

> *Myth No. 4: "The international non-proliferation regime*
> *is the finger in the dike protecting the world from a cascade*
> *of new nuclear weapons states"*

The above puncturing of myths 1, 2, and 3 undermines the typical "finger in the dike" characterization of the Non-Proliferation Treaty (NPT) and the wider non-proliferation regime. Since most state leaders find going nuclear to be less than tempting, a strong international regime is not necessary to deliver them from that temptation. But this book also provides direct empirical evidence on the utility of regime.

One of the primary asserted benefits of the international non-proliferation regime is that its existence allows states to avoid the transaction costs of independently finding a mechanism to demonstrate their abstention from nuclear weapons, thereby smoothing the way for such abstention. This point makes sense theoretically, and it certainly was easy for an Australia or an Argentina to join the NPT club once they had decided they wanted to do it. But, on the other hand, in two of the cases examined here, state leaders opposed to going nuclear were more than willing to pay the transaction costs to set up *sui generis* regional non-proliferation institutions. The French "Europeans" tried to bring about a European non-proliferation regime, first in EDC and later in the European Atomic Community (EURATOM). That these efforts failed to prevent the French nuclear weapons effort from taking off was not due to the difficulty of building a regime, but rather to the determination of the French "nationalists" to realize their nuclear ambitions. Meanwhile, beginning in the late 1970s the Argentines set up a bilateral non-proliferation regime with Brazil. As noted in Chapter 6, this regime – despite lacking the degree of transparency and rigorous inspections that are generally seen as crucial for success – produced a Southern Cone nuclear *rapprochement* so complete that it actually alarmed the North and led to fantastic assertions there that the two might be planning to launch a "bi-national" bomb program. In sum, the transaction costs of setting up non-proliferation regimes do not appear to be so high that the present international regime must be considered as a precious, irreplaceable jewel.

The more robust claims made on behalf of the international non-proliferation regime are that beyond its utility as a coordination device, it has actually generated normative pressure to change proliferation preferences. In the case studies examined here, some of those leaders who were against building nuclear weapons were indeed in favor of the NPT. But the former caused the latter, not vice versa. Those who wanted the bomb, like the Australian John Gorton or the Indian Atal Behari Vajpayee, would not let international norms stand in the way of their objective. Moreover, far from winning over doubters, the discriminatory NPT regime is perceived in many quarters as downright offensive. This book has shown how tough normative pressures on the sportsmanlike nationalist leaders of India and Argentina actually produced counterproductive results. For instance, as noted in Chapter 6, the US 1978 Nuclear Non-Proliferation Act led directly to the building of the secret Argentine uranium enrichment plant. A similar reaction by the Indians can be seen in the case of the Comprehensive Test Ban Treaty (CTBT). The Rao government had cosponsored the 1993 UN resolution for a CTBT and wanted to sign it. But, using the slogan of resistance to "nuclear apartheid" that actually applied more accurately to the NPT but seemed to fit the CTBT case because of the in-your-face posturing of US diplomacy, pro-bomb forces were able to cause the government to retreat and eventually to reverse the traditional Indian commitment to a worldwide test ban. In sum, abstention from nuclear weapons seems to come in spite of strong international non-proliferation pressures, not because of them.

Moreover, it is anachronistic to claim that the regime and the broader international anti-nuclear movement have depressed interest in the bomb by educating otherwise benighted politicians about its horror. If anything, as memories of Hiroshima and Nagasaki fade, recognition of the bomb's horror is much less today than it was at the start of the nuclear age. As noted in Chapter 4, in a November 1954 meeting – long before many of today's anti-nuclear activists were born – Pierre Mendès France and his closest associates agonized over the choice for the bomb.[12] They were particularly concerned by the arguments of the biologist Jean Rostand that use of the bomb would affect the human gene pool and thereby extinguish the human race. But Mendès France, oppositional nationalist that he was, soon became impatient with the indecision of some, for instance his Minister of Defense Emmanuel Temple. That is why we

---

[12] Interviews with Henri Caillavet, secretary of the navy under Prime Minister Mendès France, January 28 and 30, 1998, May 15, 1999, and letter dated May 11, 1999.

are here, he told Temple, to choose and to take responsibility for the consequences of our choice. Similarly, Atal Behari Vajpayee is the author of a moving poem in tribute to the victims of Hiroshima. But he, too, cut through the Gordian knot of the secularists' hesitation and decided to "have a big bomb now."[13]

In sum, the common idea that the non-proliferation regime is the most successful arms control treaty in history is based on a basic misunderstanding of the dynamics of proliferation. The non-proliferation regime has had great utility in monitoring the pace of nuclear technological diffusion, but it has not been the proverbial finger in the dike blocking a flood of new nuclear weapons states. Tough non-proliferation policies are unlikely to change the minds of those who really want the bomb, while they are likely to anger and offend many of those who do not. As I will argue below, this is not a reason to abandon the NPT regime, but it is a reason to second-guess the continual urge to "strengthen" it with ever-heavier supply-side controls.

Lessons for intelligence analysis

In May 1998, India's nuclear test series surprised and shocked Western politicians and intelligence experts. The West of course had long understood that India had the technology to test – indeed, it had done so nearly a quarter-century before – but when the tests actually came, they caught the West napping. A review panel led by retired Admiral David Jeremiah harshly criticized the US intelligence community's inability to, in Jeremiah's words, "think through how the other guy thought."[14] Six years later, in January 2004, chief US Iraq weapons hunter David Kay again arrived at Jeremiah's conclusion. Kay told a US Senate hearing that the intelligence overestimates of Iraq's nuclear capabilities had been due in part to an erroneous understanding of Saddam Hussein. "The real challenge for intelligence," Kay opined, "is going to be getting to our political leadership not just judgments about capabilities, but judgments about real intentions. And that is tough."

In short, top-ranking US officials have ascribed two of the biggest intelligence failures of the last decade to their failures to comprehend the nuclear intentions of foreign leaders. To those knowledgeable about the workings of the intelligence community in the US, these analyses come as no surprise. On one level, the failures reflect the more general

---

[13] George Perkovich, *India's Nuclear Bomb: The Impact on Global Proliferation* (Berkeley: University of California Press, 1999), p. 420.

[14] Tim Weiner, "Report Finds Basic Flaws in US Intelligence Operations," *New York Times*, June 3, 1998.

phenomenon of America's "engineering approach" in foreign policy: our tendency to try to boil down political problems to technical ones.[15] But, for various motives, the US intelligence community has proven particularly susceptible to favoring technical intelligence about nuclear capabilities over strategic intelligence about leaders' nuclear intentions. With the consolidation of the "Bush doctrine" of preventive war, the preexisting tendencies to focus on the "supply side" of the proliferation equation are likely to be exacerbated further.[16] They must be reversed. This book points the way toward better "demand side" intelligence.

"Learn to read." This was Senator Daniel Patrick Moynihan's incisive suggestion about how the intelligence community could do better analysis in the wake of the Indian tests.[17] And indeed, the oppositional nationalist BJP had been anything but coy about its nuclear intentions over the previous decade. Similarly, as early as 1957 John Gorton had declared his nuclear ambitions – indeed, for a hydrogen bomb – on the floor of the Australian Senate. In addition, this book has shown that the protestations of peaceful nuclear intentions by the Indian governments before 1998 and by the Argentines from the 1960s onward were also basically true. In short, the evidence of this book therefore suggests that declaratory nuclear policy is indeed a very good place to start for understanding nuclear intentions. Nevertheless, it would be wrong to give a free pass to every state that simply declares peaceful intentions. Pierre Mendès France, for instance, kept his nuclear weapons ambitions out of public view, and the French government only announced its weapons program beginning in 1956. Meanwhile, the Argentine uranium enrichment plant, though not aiming at producing weapons-grade fissile material, was also successfully kept under wraps until the *Proceso* decided to declare it in the waning days of its military rule. In short, leaders can lie. How, then, can we evaluate their real intentions?

This book has argued that the tendency to use the growth of nuclear capabilities, stances toward the non-proliferation regime, and general "roguishness" of the state as proxies for nuclear weapons intentions is likely to lead the analyst astray. According to these measures, for instance, the Argentine *Proceso* should have sought the bomb, but it did not. Instead, this book contends that we need to understand leaders' NICs.

---

[15] Stanley Hoffmann, *Gulliver's Troubles, or, The Setting of American Foreign Policy* (New York: McGraw-Hill for the Council on Foreign Relations, 1968).

[16] Greg Thielmann, "Preventive Military Intervention: The Role of Intelligence," *Ridgway Center for International Security Studies Policy Brief*, 04–1, University of Pittsburgh, October 2004.

[17] Senator Daniel Patrick Moynihan, cited in William C. Potter, "The Diffusion of Nuclear Weapons," in Emily O. Goldman and Leslie C. Eliason, eds., *The Diffusion of Military Technology and Ideas* (Stanford: Stanford University Press, 2003), p. 172.

The major hurdle for intelligence analysis, therefore, is that of NIC measurement. Chapter 3 introduced a systematic, multimethod approach for just this purpose. It showed that we do not need to despair about how to know what they are "really" thinking, and we do not need to bug every leader's telephone. Their own major public speeches, placed in the correct interpretive context, give us plenty of information for understanding their NICs, which in turn give us a good idea of their nuclear tendencies. Moynihan was right that the analysts could have read what Vajpayee said about his nuclear intentions, but where he also betrayed his desire for nuclear weapons was in his depiction of India and its key comparison others.

The job of intelligence, of course, is too important to leave to the intelligence community alone. Other actors, notably diplomats and politicians – or even academics – can also contribute to our store of knowledge about the leaders we are dealing with. Foreign leaders almost always try to explain their policies with respect to their understanding of their nations' histories. But unfortunately, to date on this issue top American envoys have shown a decided tendency to lecture rather than to listen. For instance, in the wake of the South Asian nuclear tests, Deputy Secretary of State Strobe Talbott traveled there for a series of extended "strategic dialogues." While Talbott tried to portray his missions as efforts at empathetic listening, in fact they were closer to pedagogical exercises in international socialization, with Talbott acting as the South Asians' tutor in the fine points of contemporary Washington nukespeak. As Talbott put it in *Foreign Affairs*, "If India and Pakistan are willing to move toward the international mainstream in the way they define and defend their interests – even if they remain for the foreseeable future outside the NPT – their relations with the United States and other members of the international community could improve substantially."[18] Talbott got what he asked for but not what he wanted. The South Asians learned to speak our nuclear language, and then surprised us again by refusing to sign on to the Comprehensive Test Ban Treaty or the rest of the US nuclear diplomatic agenda. Surely we can do better.

The potential value of this book for analyzing the nuclear intentions of current and future state leaders is clear, but perhaps an even bigger nightmare for many today is nuclear terrorism. While most non-state actors still today could not hope to engage in nuclear terrorism, the novelty is

[18] Strobe Talbott, "Dealing with the Bomb in South Asia," *Foreign Affairs*, Vol. 78, No. 2 (March–April 1999), pp. 119–20. I commented on the international pressures for India's nuclear socialization in "Inside a Bomb Shell," *The Hindustan Times* (India), April 16, 2001.

that some can.[19] The theory and methods developed here also have great potential applicability to the question of nuclear terrorism. This is rather rare, for most explanations of nuclear weapons acquisition are inextricably tied to the level of states or state institutions. By contrast, the theory advanced in this book is pitched at the level of the individual. Anyone, from a state leader to a rebel, can hold an oppositional nationalist NIC. And if they do, in this new era of increasingly accessible technologies of mass destruction, the theorized linkages from identity to emotions to policy choice should hold true for them, too.[20]

Lessons for international policy

Better intelligence about proliferation intentions is the first step toward better policies to combat proliferation. As concerns about nuclear proliferation have mounted since the end of the Cold War, policy entrepreneurs have mounted efforts in favor of a wide spectrum of international responses to it, from a stricter international non-proliferation regime, to nuclear abolition, to preventive war against proliferant states. The evidence of this book can help us to determine the likely effectiveness of these very different proposed responses.

A stricter international non-proliferation regime?

The least controversial proposed international policy response to the growing potential for more nuclear weapons states – least controversial in the US and Western Europe, that is – is to make the supply-side controls of the international non-proliferation regime much stricter. As is well known, the George W. Bush administration has favored an extreme tightening of supply-side controls, even against states that are members in good standing of the non-proliferation regime. But the idea of beefing up controls is hardly unique to the Bush administration. For instance, the 2004 report of the UN Secretary-General's High-Level Panel on Threats, Challenges and Change proposed a number of tough new steps.[21]

---

[19] Friedrich Steinhausler, "What It Takes to Become a Nuclear Terrorist," *American Behavioral Scientist*, Vol. 46, No. 6 (February 2003), pp. 782–795.

[20] There is no reason to assume that all or even most non-state terrorists hold oppositional nationalist NICs, and even less so that these NICs are directed against the West. There are, of course, many terrorists whose concerns and objectives are primarily local or domestic. Meanwhile, even many Islamic fundamentalist terrorists are likely to be found to be oppositional subaltern toward the US and the West, for terrorism, as has often been noted, is a weapon of the weak.

[21] Secretary-General's High-Level Panel on Threats, Challenges and Change, *A More Secure World: Our Shared Responsibility* (New York: United Nations, 2004), pp. 43–46.

Primary among these was to declare the Model Additional Protocol to the NPT, a very stringent set of inspection rules which only a third of the NPT member states have so far ratified, as the new international standard. It further proposed that the Security Council be prepared to act in cases of serious concern over non-compliance with that standard. It also notably called for a moratorium on the construction of new enrichment or reprocessing facilities, for the IAEA to become the guarantor for the supply of fissile material for civilian purposes contingent on compliance with safeguard and inspection procedures, for international participation in the Bush administration's Proliferation Security Initiative and Global Threat Reduction Initiative against the illicit trade in nuclear materials, and for a verifiable fissile material cutoff treaty that ends the production of highly enriched uranium for any purpose.

Is an increasingly strict international supply-side control regime likely to dissuade further proliferation? Such a strict regime may well create technical difficulties for states attempting to build unsafeguarded nuclear programs. For instance, it would be much harder to pull off the Argentines' late 1970s trick of overcoming North American export controls by turning to European alternatives. However, it should be noted that the trend in the regime has long been toward increasing strictness, yet concerns about proliferation today are higher than ever before. Given the widespread diffusion of nuclear capacities, supply-side control measures against potential proliferant states are clearly of declining utility. Moreover, a stricter regime will likely do nothing to change proliferation intentions. It is highly unlikely that more stringent controls will dissuade oppositional nationalist leaders from seeking the bomb, and in today's freewheeling global market they probably will be able to obtain the materials they need to build it, albeit perhaps more slowly and with difficulty. More problematically, it is highly unlikely that more stringent controls will dissuade sportsmanlike nationalist leaders from resisting the non-proliferation regime. Indeed, the harsher the regime becomes, the more likely that both types of nationalists will resent and resist it. There is a real danger that further attempts to "strengthen" the regime will actually cost it the support of important nuclear-abstaining states – as happened, for instance, in the case of mid-1990s India's abandonment of its longtime support for a comprehensive test ban. As a result, we will see more unwarranted accusations of nuclear weapons ambitions, and a vicious cycle of suspicion and recrimination. In short, the construction of ever-higher supply-side hurdles to civilian nuclear development, far from "strengthening" the non-proliferation regime, is in fact likely to leave the regime even weaker than it is today.

Indeed, on balance the evidence of this book suggests that the non-proliferation regime needs to become *more* flexible, not less. It is fine to request complete international transparency, but nuclear arms races can often be averted with much less than that. The initially very flimsy regional non-proliferation regime of the Southern Cone, for instance, quelled the mutual Argentine and Brazilian suspicions that conceivably could have boiled over into nuclear weapons drives. The fact that international inspectors were not privy to the two countries' nuclear secrets was irrelevant to the basic goal of avoiding the birth of Latin American nuclear arsenals. Rather than demanding a one-size-fits-all package of international safeguards and inspections, therefore, it makes sense to return to the traditional practice of allowing states to design their own bilateral or regional non-proliferation initiatives, or to join the international regime at the level of commitment with which they and their neighbors feel most comfortable. Besides, the fundamentalist approach, according to which even the smallest materials accounting flaw is a threat to regime stability, plays into the hands of those who claim that the regime is of no use at all and therefore must be discarded.

Nuclear abolition?

If supply-side controls are not enough, then the question becomes how to depress the demand for nuclear weapons. Some policy entrepreneurs believe that the answer is nuclear abolition. The longtime abolitionist Jonathan Schell, for instance, has seized on proliferation as the ultimate proof of the "folly of arms control."[22] But even traditional arms controllers have become increasingly sensitive to the NPT's double standard of grandfathering in the first five nuclear weapons states. The primary demand-side focus of the Secretary-General's High-Level Panel, for instance, was its insistence that the nuclear weapons states make much more serious efforts toward disarmament and resist the temptation to threaten nuclear attack against non-nuclear weapons states, as they promised to do in Article VI and again at the NPT review conference in 2000. These measures, it claimed, would "further diminish the perceived value of nuclear weapons, and secure robust international cooperation to staunch proliferation."[23]

If it somehow became politically feasible, nuclear disarmament by the existing nuclear powers would probably make the world a safer place.

[22] Jonathan Schell, "The Folly of Arms Control," *Foreign Affairs*, Vol. 79, No. 5 (September–October 2000), pp. 22–46.
[23] Secretary-General's High-Level Panel, *A More Secure World*, p. 42.

But would it dissuade further proliferation? The key to answering this question is to return to Chapter 1's basic insight that state leaders are fully aware of the dramatic, multidimensional and unpredictable consequences of going nuclear. They understand, in short, that to go nuclear is a revolutionary decision. Therefore, they are not going to decide to build the bomb simply because they notice that some big states in the system also happen to have it. For instance, even an intense preference for international status was simply not enough to motivate either the Indian or the Argentine sportsmanlike nationalists to go for nuclear weapons. Meanwhile, those oppositional nationalist leaders who do want the bomb are unlikely to be dissuaded from getting it because the Americans and the Russians got rid of theirs. Emotions of fear and pride, not of sportsmanlike fair play, drive the oppositional nationalist's nuclear ambitions. Now, it is true that the oppositional nationalist desire for nuclear weapons is largely the result of the bomb's symbolic significance as a totem of power, and this significance is somewhat reinforced by big-state possession of it. But the basic reason for the bomb's totemic significance is its truly awesome destructive consequences, and the knowledge of these consequences is unfortunately our common human heritage. Indeed, whether or not the nuclear weapons states disarm, this knowledge will almost certainly be reflected in an intense, continuing effort for non-proliferation. Paradoxically, the intense international non-proliferation efforts probably reinforce the totemic significance of the bomb as much as the great powers' possession of it does. In short, it is hard to imagine any future scenario – short of the bomb's replacement by even more horrible instruments of destruction – in which oppositional nationalist leaders become indifferent to it.

What, then, of the proposal that nuclear weapons states could encourage non-proliferation by at least desisting from threatening non-nuclear weapons states with nuclear attack? Unquestionably, the cumulative effect of such threats, whatever their short-term deterrent value, is to introduce greater instability into the international system. Moreover, this book's Indian case study showed that Lal Bahadur Shastri and Indira Gandhi, under some domestic pressure to go nuclear, sought to defuse that pressure via a worldwide guarantee similar to the one being proposed now. It would have been well to heed their pleas. But the causal link between nuclear threats and actual decisions to go nuclear is at best unclear. Sometimes they can actually work to dissuade such decisions, as the following pages will argue. But on a deeper level, threat perception, as this book has repeatedly shown, is in the eye of the beholder. It is not necessary for threats to be issued in order for threats to be perceived. For instance, the oppositional nationalist Atal Behari Vajpayee hardly needed prompting from Pakistan in order to conclude that Pakistan had to be deterred. By contrast, the sportsmanlike nationalist Indira Gandhi did not interpret the entry of the USS *Enterprise* into the Bay of Bengal as a military threat *per se*. The response she sent to Nixon was thus one of pride and self-righteous anger, rather than the explosive psychological cocktail of fear mixed with pride.[24] In sum, if the nuclear weapons states exercise restraint or even seriously pursue disarmament, such actions are unlikely to achieve the non-proliferation objectives that their advocates claim.

Preventive war?

The third oft-promoted option for dealing with the threat of proliferation is the idea of preventive military intervention against regimes whose leaders harbor nuclear weapons ambitions. The George W. Bush administration has embraced a unilateralist form of the preventive war option, first as a matter of declaratory policy in its 2002 *National Security Strategy of the United States* and then in its war against Iraq. But as Lee Feinstein and Anne-Marie Slaughter have pointed out, there is no inherent linkage between unilateralism and preventive war. Indeed, Feinstein and Slaughter propose a collective international duty to prevent proliferation – a parallel to the increasingly recognized international responsibility to protect individual citizens from rapacious governments. They view this duty as extending all the way up to forcible regime change when necessary.[25] Here I will try to assess the effects of *any* credible preventive war policy, whether it is unilateral or multilateral in its implementation.

First, it must be noted that the preventive war option presents tremendous ethical dilemmas, not the least of which is the stark question of whether the *possibility* of nuclear destruction is worse than the *actuality* of conventional warfare. This question in turn raises the well-debated issue of whether or not nuclear proliferation in fact makes the world more dangerous.[26] The academic claim that "more may be better" rests on the daring assumption that nuclear arsenals are managed by coolly rational leaders. Though the matter clearly requires further study, the implication of this book is that nothing could be further from the truth. Thus, the threat that nuclear proliferation will indeed lead to nuclear use seems

---

[24] Chapter 7 explained that the "peaceful nuclear explosion" program that commenced shortly after the war was in response to Prime Minister Bhutto's secret nuclear weapons speech at Multan, not the voyage of the USS *Enterprise*.

[25] Lee Feinstein and Anne-Marie Slaughter, "A Duty to Prevent," *Foreign Affairs*, Vol. 83, No. 1 (January–February 2004), pp. 136–150.

[26] Scott D. Sagan and Kenneth Waltz, *The Spread of Nuclear Weapons: A Debate* (New York: W. W. Norton, 2003).

highly plausible, certainly enough to merit a consideration of the utility of preventive military measures.

Could the credible threat of preventive war prevent further proliferation? To some degree, it might. There is a possible extension here from Chapter 2's theoretical expectation about oppositional nationalists' pursuit of superpower guarantees against potential existential threats. In Chapter 2 I argued that oppositional nationalist leaders, driven by fear of the enemy, will probably seek a superpower guarantee to lessen their short-term security problems until they can acquire the bomb, although there is ambiguity here since the nationalist desire for autonomy cuts in the other direction. The extension to this hypothesis is that the super-power might be able to use the credible threat of withdrawing the guar-antee to cause a halt to an incipient bomb program. The evidence from the four case studies in this book is insufficient to judge the validity of that idea. But Henry Kissinger did use the tactic successfully with South Korean President Park Chung Hee in 1975. Park seriously downshifted his nuclear weapons drive when Kissinger told him that the consequence of persisting would be the US cancellation of its security commitments against bellicose North Korea.[27] In other words, Park's short-term desire to avoid military disaster overcame his desire to pursue long-term nuclear self-expression. In that case Kissinger used the North Korean threat as leverage instead of issuing a direct threat himself, but the effect of a direct threat against South Korea would probably have been the same. My con-clusion is that it is plausible at least to explore the idea that a credible threat of regime change by the US or the international community could cause oppositional nationalists to think twice about pursuing a nuclear weapons program. Indeed, when the dust settles, it may turn out that the looming threat of US military action kept Saddam Hussein's nuclear weapons ambitions in check during the 1990s.

But even if this hypothesis were proven true, the case for adopting the "duty to prevent" would still not be a slam dunk. It is simply impractical to apply such a "duty" universally; but this opens the door to charges of hypocrisy. Moreover, a doctrine of preventive war carries with it enor-mous intelligence requirements that are unlikely to be met in practice. As noted above, we already do a bad job at analyzing proliferation intentions; and the more the intelligence emphasis is shifted toward military target-ing, the less money, time, or care will likely be spent on analyzing those

[27] Jacques E. C. Hymans, Seung-Young Kim, and Henning Riecke, "To Go or Not to Go: South and North Korea's Nuclear Decisions in Comparative Context," *Journal of East Asian Studies*, Vol. 1, No. 1 (February 2001), p. 103.

intentions.[28] Wars of choice based on poor intelligence can greatly damage the credibility of claims to be acting on the basis of a solemn "duty to prevent," leading to speculation about more sinister motives. In the long run, therefore, if we decide to assume the "duty to prevent" we run the very serious risk of creating more oppositional nationalists than we can curb – and what is more, now the target of their oppositional nationalism would be us. It is dangerous to fight smoke with fire.

Non-proliferation today and tomorrow

None of the three broad policy prescriptions considered above would be unambiguously beneficial to the non-proliferation cause. Tougher supply-side controls could slow – but would not stop – determined nuclear proliferants' march toward the bomb, while also offending many nuclear abstainers and therefore undermining the very non-proliferation regime they are meant to strengthen. Nuclear disarmament by the established nuclear powers could reduce the overall nuclear danger, but it would not dim the ambitions of nuclear aspirants. Finally, the threat or actuality of preventive military action could beat back this or that proliferation effort, but in the long run the assumption of a general "duty to prevent" would create a large amount of collateral damage and may actually turn out to be a formula for more proliferation, not less.

It is important to recognize that despite their differences, the three above-mentioned policy prescriptions share a set of common assumptions. All three assume that in the current international context, nuclear weapons are highly attractive to many states. This is why non-proliferation policies' counterproductive effects on nuclear abstainers are consistently ignored. All three assume the proliferation domino theory. This is what instills the proliferation policy debate with such an unnecessarily grave sense of urgency. And all three assume that the ultimate solution to the proliferation puzzle lies in some sort of fundamental change to the international system, be it sovereignty-crashing inspections, universal disarmament, or a wholesale revision of the laws of war. This is what leads many observers to end up tilling the barren terrain of despair.

By contrast, this book has argued that those common assumptions are mistaken. It has argued that most state leaders are not highly attracted to the bomb. Moreover, it has argued that leaders' preferences are actually not highly contingent on what other states decide. Therefore, proliferation tomorrow will probably remain as rare as proliferation today, with no

[28] Thielmann, "Preventive Military Intervention."

single instance of proliferation causing a cascade of new nuclear weapons states. But, on the flip side, whatever fundamental changes may come at the level of the international system, proliferation will continue – certainly by states, and possibly also by non-state groups. The determined few will simply not be dissuaded from trying to turn their nuclear dreams into reality. And where there's a will, there's a way.

Recognition of the existence of the *determined few* – both of those words are equally important – is essential and will result in more reasonable non-proliferation policy goals. It makes no sense for the US or any other country to mortgage all other legitimate foreign policy interests in pursuit of a doomed zero-tolerance policy. Being reasonable, however, need not mean being resigned. It is possible to conceive of a better non-proliferation policy for the international community than the current menu of export controls and saber-rattling. The consequences of the spread of nuclear weapons are simply too important for the United States and other world powers to become mere spectators in the matter. So what should they do? The traditional strategies of export controls, regime-building, and even saber-rattling do have a place; but they must take a back seat to policies that are more sensitive to the demand side of the proliferation equation. Here I offer four novel, demand-centric non-proliferation policy ideas. The basic intuition behind these ideas is simple: if oppositional nationalists are the problem, then those who are not oppositional nationalists are the solution.

First, as noted above, we need to stop chastising and start supporting the agendas of sportsmanlike nationalist leaders. Yes, they have nuclear ambitions, but those ambitions have limits. Failure to understand this leads to tragic missteps, like the Clinton administration's attempt to force Indian Prime Minister Narasimha Rao to commit too quickly to a comprehensive test ban that he actually wanted to sign. The US pressure played right into the hands of Rao's oppositional nationalist opponents. There is a parallel here with the US self-defeating attacks on "pink" social reformist leaders during the Cold War. We need finally to recognize that half a loaf is better than none.

Second, we need to encourage domestic institutional reform to broaden the circle of decisionmaking power over the nuclear issue. The success of the theory of this book depends on the assumption that top leaders are uniquely important in the nuclear decision. As noted in the empirical chapters, this assumption is generally empirically justified; the institutions of atomic policymaking in most countries have been designed specifically in order to maximize the top leader's control. But in the case of Australia, in spite of the institutionalized importance of the prime minister in atomic policy matters, the strong countervailing tradition of Cabinet government actually did restrain Prime Minister John Gorton – barely – from formal-izing a decision to go nuclear. The case of Gorton's nuclear policy defeat raises the possibility that the design of domestic political institutions, which properly has played little role in the empirical analysis of this book, might well represent a crucial, underused lever for non-proliferation pol-icy. The "dual-key" system has worked well enough to prevent a lone soldier from launching a nuclear weapon. A metaphorical "dual-key" system might also work to prevent a lone leader from launching a nuclear weapons program. Since dramatically different NICs often exist simulta-neously in the same society, expanding the number of veto points in the nuclear issue area could make it tougher for oppositional nationalists to have their way. Of course, the impetus for these changes probably has to come largely from the domestic society, but the international community can encourage such movements.

Third, we need to prod domestic political actors to keep oppositional nationalists out of the nuclear decisionmaking loop altogether. When an oppositional nationalist becomes the top leader, it may be too early to declare defeat (or war), but the handwriting is clearly on the wall. It is a better idea to block their ascension to power in the first place. In part this objective can be pursued by strengthening the hand of sportsman-like nationalist leaders, as recommended above. But in addition, making domestic and international actors aware of the linkage between opposi-tional nationalism and the bomb would provide them with an important additional incentive to fight hard against rising oppositional nationalists. The BJP's rise to power in India, for instance, would have been much more difficult if Indian elites had actually believed its campaign rhetoric about nuclear weapons.

Finally, in an even longer-term perspective, it is critically important to try to stamp out the general propagation and diffusion of oppositional nationalist NICs in a society. To do this is actually not as difficult as it may appear. Identities may be extremely durable at the level of individ-uals, but they are actually rather plastic at the level of societies. Each generation has the opportunity to remake the nation anew.[29] As noted above, more research is needed to understand the precise causal chain that links societal-level cultural trends and individual-level adoption of one or another NIC. But it would be foolish to ignore the possibility that future leaders (and the citizens who support them) will develop their NICs while in school. Educational curricula, schoolbooks, and classroom

---

[29] I elaborate on this idea in Jacques E. C. Hymans, "The Changing Color of Money: Euro-pean Currency Iconography and Collective Identity," *European Journal of International Relations*, Vol. 10, No. 1 (March 2004), pp. 5–31.

assignments in disciplines such as history are often explicitly intended to impact students' basic understandings of what the nation naturally stands for, and of how high the nation naturally stands.[30] The schools can help to spread oppositional nationalism, or they can help to spread a different national identity conception. Oppositional nationalism is not inevitable; it is a choice. And so, too, are the nuclear weapons it has spawned.

[30] See Jacques E. C. Hymans, "What Counts as History and How Much Does History Count? The Case of French Secondary Education," in Hanna Schissler and Yasemin Soysal, eds., *The Nation, Europe, the World: Curricula and Textbooks in Transition* (New York: Berghahn Books, 2005).

Appendix   Coding rules and results

I   Coding rules

A.   General rules for all codings

1. The basic unit of measurement is the paragraph.
2. The coding of one paragraph should not impact the coding of subsequent paragraphs.
3. The coding must be based on the explicit language of the text.
4. Statements in past, present, and future tense are coded equivalently. However, in the case of tension between statements about the long term and statements about the current state of affairs, the former are given priority.

B.   Coding for references to external actors

1. We are looking for references to external actors. An external actor is defined as any human community (or set of communities) that is not *primarily based* inside the territory we claim as our national boundaries. [Examples of such human communities would include states or peoples seeking a state (e.g., "France," "the Palestinians"), collections of states (e.g., "The Free World," "the Third World," "baseball-playing nations"), wider geographical entities (e.g., "Asia," "the Pacific Rim")' wider cultural or civilizational entities (e.g., "The Arab World," "Christendom"), and humanity as a whole (e.g., "the world," "the international community"). In addition, we also count references to the scourge of "international terrorism." Note that communities that are in part based in our territory are counted, e.g., if an American makes reference to "NATO." More coding precisions are offered below.]
2. The question being asked here is *which* external actors are referred to in *how many* paragraphs. Therefore, for each paragraph, the coder produces a list of all external actors that are referred to at least once

in that paragraph. Even if an actor is referred to more than once in the paragraph, it is only counted once. N.B. when these coding rules refer the number of "references," the reader should recall that this means "the number of paragraphs in which at least one such reference was made." [The identification of external actors should at first be reported according to the exact words in the text. At a second stage, a qualitative judgment may be made that different names refer in fact to the same external actor.]

Precisions to basic coding rules

a. The most obvious cases of references to external actors are explicit references to the communities themselves, either by proper name or pronoun ("they"). However, there are a number of other ways in which external actors may be referenced:

  i. References to individuals, organizations, or locations that can be easily identified as based in some external actor are coded as references to that external actor (e.g., "Winston Churchill," "Rolls Royce," or "Birmingham" can be coded as references to the UK).

  ii. Words or phrases associated with a definite historical conflict (e.g., America's "9/11," France's "Great War," India's "freedom struggle") are counted as references to the principal external actor with whom we engaged in the conflict.

b. There are a number of ways in which the world community as a whole may be referenced. They include the following:

  i. References to the "world," "global," "earth," "humanity," "man," and often (though not always) "international," "interdependence," "universal," "peace," "modernity," "contemporary reality," etc. One exception here is if the reference to the "world" is just part of a generic foreign other reference (e.g., "the largest milk producer in the world").

  ii. References to the "United Nations" and other broad-based international organizations (e.g., the "World Bank," the "International Atomic Energy Agency"), unless our country is not a member of these. Also, references to "all nations," "everyone," etc.

  iii. References to the category of a "normal," "ordinary," or simply generic "country," assuming we are implied to belong to this category.

c. References to the world as a whole must not be confused with references to generic foreign others. References to generic foreign others include the following:

i. General references to "foreign," "abroad," "overseas," "outside," "exterior," "external," etc. Note, however, that mere mentions of our nation's "foreign policy" need not be counted.

ii. References to our national "independence," "sovereignty," "self-determination," "freedom," "autonomy," etc., unless such references are clearly signaling a specific historic conflict with a particular foreign other. In such cases the reference is coded as a reference to that particular other.

iii. References to bilateral relations, negotiations, and conferences with generic foreign others (e.g., "a bigger army will give us more power when we negotiate. . ."), unless such references are clearly to the world as a whole (e.g., "we seek friendly relations with all nations" – see the coding rules in point b above) or, again, unless such references are clearly signaling a relationship with a particular foreign other.

iv. References to our international ranking (e.g., "We are the third largest producer of steel in the world"), or some particular characteristic that differentiates us from others ("We are a unique civilization"). Note that for the purposes of clarity of results, references to various traits we have or aspire to have can be coded either as references to unspecified generic foreign others or as references to an identifiable collection of states with similar traits. This will require judgment calls based on common sense. For instance, the declaration "we will be a successful country" would probably be coded as a reference to generic others, while the declaration "we will be an industrialized country" would probably be coded as a reference to the industrialized world. See Rule e below.

v. Simple references to "imports," "exports," "immigrants," and "emigrants," since they may be thought of as individual rather than national activities, are not counted as references to generic foreign others.

d. The rules for coding "world community" *vs.* for coding non-specific "generic foreign others" should be applied to a smaller scale, for instance in coding for "the Western community" *vs.* coding for non-specific Western others.

e. There are a number of wider categories – 1st world, 3rd world, Free World, and so forth – that may be referred to not only explicitly but also indirectly, as in for 1st world, statements about the "rich countries," "the developed countries," and even "we want to be a rich country." Of special note is the coding for references to the great powers. References to national ambitions to be "great," "big," "first rank," "top level," "a power," "hold our heads high in the world," etc., are taken as assertions of natural membership in the "Great Power community."

C.   *Moving from the list of external actors to assessment of national identity conceptions*

1. The basic list of external actors compiled above is the crucial start for the assessment of NICs.
2. It is necessary, however, to differentiate two different categories of external actors in the list: (a) "wider communities," i.e., external actors of which we are members (e.g., the "world community") and (b) "truly foreign others," i.e., external actors of which we are not members (e.g., "generic foreign others," "Brazil"). As stated in the text, to identify key comparison others, we only consider the top scorer(s) in the *latter* category.
3. The process of separating the "wider community" references from the "truly foreign other" references is generally a mechanical one. For instance, the US is a member of "NATO" but not of the "Warsaw Pact"; it is part of the "Western Hemisphere" but not "Europe"; and so forth. Occasionally there is an interpretive dimension to these codings, however; for instance, whether to consider Mexico as part of "North America." Any possibly questionable judgments about this that could make a difference to the overall results should be noted in the text.
4. Again, recall that some grouping of references to actors (e.g., grouping references to the individual Communist nations with references to the overall Communist bloc) may be legitimate here, but when it occurs it must always be explicitly defended.
5. Having identified the most-referenced other(s), to identify the level of *oppositional* NIC on the part of the speaker, take the total number of references to the other, divided by that number plus the total number of references to collective entities that include *both* our nation *and* the other. [Thus, for instance, if a US president's top other is Mexico with 5 references, and the president makes 10 references to "the Americas" and 10 references to "the world," then compute $5/(5 + 20) = 0.20$. This 0.20 is the score for the president's level of opposition *vis-à-vis* Mexico.]
6. Then, to identify the level of nationalist NIC on the part of the speaker, take the proportion of the number of references to the other, versus the number of paragraphs *making reference to the other* that also

include references to wider entities in which we, but not necessarily the other, take part. [Thus, for instance, if a US president's top other is Mexico with 5 references, and the president makes references to the "1st World" and/or to "North America" in 4 of the 5 total paragraphs where references to Mexico appear, then compute $(5 - 4)/5 = 0.20$. This 0.20 is the score for the president's level of nationalism *vis-à-vis* Mexico.]

7. Finally, we take 95 percent confidence intervals around these proportions, according to the standard formula. The justification for doing this is that we are assuming that the materials coded represent a representative sample of the speaker's total thinking.

Tabular data

Table A1 *Australia: key comparison other (KCO) codings (by individual prime ministers)*

PM, Year + Other	No. KCO refs.	Level of opposition	95% conf. interval	Level of nationalism	95% conf. interval
Chifley, 1945–49 vs. Great powers	96	0.45	0.07	0.16	0.1
Menzies, 1949–66 vs. Communists	122	0.73	0.07	0.27	0.09
Holt, 1966–67 vs. Communists	41	0.76	0.11	0.4	0.18
Gorton, 1968–71 vs. Communists	113	0.81	0.06	0.81	0.08
McMahon, 1971–72 vs. Communists	33	0.73	0.13	0.88	0.13
Whitlam, 1972–75 vs. Asian states	104	0.34	0.05	0.4	0.11

Table A2 *Argentina: key comparison other (KCO) codings (by individual and grouped presidents)*

PM, Year + Other	No. KCO refs.	Level of opposition	95% conf. interval	Level of nationalism	95% conf. interval
Rev. Arg., 1966–73 vs. Generic foreign others	56	0.45	0.09	0.7	0.12
Cámpora, 1973 vs. 1st World	94	0.57	0.08	0.64	0.1
J. Perón, 1973–74 vs. 1st World	22	0.38	0.12	0.27	0.2
I. Perón, 1975 vs. Generic foreign others	15	0.38	0.15	0.67	0.26
Proceso, 1976–83 vs. Generic foreign others	296	0.35	0.03	0.58	0.06
Alfonsín, 1983–89 vs. Generic foreign others	134	0.41	0.05	0.54	0.08
Menem, 1989–99 vs. Generic foreign others	143	0.37	0.05	0.59	0.08
Post-Menem, 1999–2004 vs. Generic foreign others	114	0.44	0.06	0.49	0.09

Table A3 *India: key comparison other (KCO) codings (by individual and grouped prime ministers)*

PM, Year + Other	No. KCO refs.	Level of opposition	95% conf. interval	Level of nationalism	95% conf. interval
PMs, 1947–89 vs. Generic foreign others	105	0.4	0.06	0.69	0.09
PMs, 1990–98 vs. Generic foreign others	51	0.53	0.1	0.71	0.13
Vajpayee, 1998–2003 vs. Pakistan	85	0.56	0.08	0.85	0.08

Table A4 *France: key comparison other (KCO) codings (by individual and grouped prime ministers)*

PM, Year + Other	No. KCO refs.	Level of opposition	95% conf. interval	Level of nationalism	95% conf. interval
De Gaulle, 1944–46 *vs.* Germany	55	0.65	0.11	0.6	0.14
Establishment 1946–49 *vs.* Germany	47	0.5	0.1	0.77	0.12
Establishment 1950–54 *vs.* Germany	109	0.25	0.04	0.41	0.09
Mendès France, 1954–55 *vs.* Germany	427	0.44	0.03	0.56	0.05

Bibliography

INTERVIEWS

Alder, Keith. Australian nuclear scientist (former General Manager, Australian Atomic Energy Commission). Warrawee, New South Wales, October 21, 1998.

Beninson, Dan. Argentine nuclear scientist (President of the *Comisión Nacional de Energía Atómica*). Buenos Aires, August 9, 1999. Follow-up communication November 9, 1999.

Bhandari, Romesh. Indian diplomat and politician. New Delhi, November 25, 1998.

Boegner, Jean-Marc. French diplomat (former head of the *Service des Pactes du Ministère des Affaires Etrangères*). Paris, January 27, 1998, January 30, 1998.

Caillavet, Henri. French politician (former Secretary of the Navy). Paris, January 28, 1998, January 30, 1998, May 15, 1999. Follow-up letter May 11, 1999.

Camilión, Oscar. Argentine diplomat and politician (former Minister of Defense). Buenos Aires, August 17, 1999.

Carrea, Antonio. Argentine nuclear scientist and diplomat (former Ambassador to the IAEA). Buenos Aires, August 17, 1999. Follow-up communication November 9, 1999.

Cavallo, Domingo. Argentine politician (former Minister of Foreign Affairs and Minister of the Economy). Cambridge, Massachusetts, June 16, 2004.

Dhar, P. N. Indian diplomat and civil servant (former Secretary, Prime Minister's Office). Delhi, November 20, 1998. Follow-up letter February 27, 1999.

Dubey, Muchkund. Indian diplomat (former Foreign Secretary). New Delhi, December 15, 1998.

Goldschmidt, Bertrand. French nuclear scientist and diplomat (original member and former head of international relations, *Commissariat à l'Energie Atomique*). Paris, September 29, 1998.

Iyengar, P. K. Indian nuclear scientist (former Chairman of the Atomic Energy Commission). Bombay, December 8, 1998.

Kaul, T. N. Indian diplomat (former Foreign Secretary). New Delhi, December 3, 1998. Follow-up letters March 7 and May 5, 1999.

Lall, K. B. Indian civil servant (former Defence Secretary). New Delhi, November 16, 1998. Follow-up letters February 2 and April 14, 1999.

Malhotra, Inder. Indian journalist (friend of Indira Gandhi). New Delhi, November 28, 1998.

Mariano, Enrique. Argentine nuclear scientist (formerly of the *Comisión Nacional de Energía Atómica*). Buenos Aires, August 4, 1999.

Mariscotti, Mario. Argentine nuclear scientist and historian (formerly of the *Comisión Nacional de Energía Atómica*). Buenos Aires, August 4, 1999. Follow-up communication November 9, 1999.

Moreno, Antonio Federico. Argentine army officer and public servant (*Comisión de Defensa de la Cámara de Diputados*). Buenos Aires, August 31, 1999.

Murmis, Bernardo. Argentine nuclear scientist (formerly of the *Comisión Nacional de Energía Atómica*). Buenos Aires, August 4, 1999.

Ornstein, Roberto. Argentine nuclear scientist and diplomat (director of international relations, *Comisión Nacional de Energía Atómica*). Buenos Aires, August 9, 1999.

Ortiz de Zárate, Carlos. Argentine army officer and lobbyist. Buenos Aires, August 23, 1999.

Pérez Ferreira, Emma. Argentine nuclear scientist (former President of the *Comisión Nacional de Energía Atómica*). Buenos Aires, August 11, 1999. Follow-up communication November 12, 1999.

Pertusio, Roberto. Argentine navy officer (Admiral, ret.). Buenos Aires, August 24, 1999. Follow-up communication November 10, 1999.

Quihillalt, Oscar. Argentine nuclear scientist (former President of the *Comisión Nacional de Energía Atómica*). Buenos Aires, August 11, 1999.

Ramanna, Raja. Indian nuclear scientist and politician (former Chairman of the Atomic Energy Commission). Written communication, November 19, 1998.

Senior Indian nuclear engineer (name withheld upon request). 2000.

Sethna, Homi. Indian nuclear scientist (former Chairman of Atomic Energy Commission). Bombay, December 8, 1998.

Sharma, V. N. Indian army officer (former Chief of Army Staff). New Delhi, December 16, 1998. Follow-up letter February 18, 1999.

Singh, Manmohan. Indian politician (former Finance Minister, currently Prime Minister of India). New Delhi, December 19, 1998. Follow-up letter February 19, 1999.

Tahiliani, R. N. Indian naval officer (Admiral, ret.). New Delhi, December 16, 1998.

Varma, A. N. Indian civil servant (former Principal Secretary to Prime Minister P. V. Narasimha Rao). New Delhi, December 2, 1998.

Varotto, Conrado. Argentine nuclear scientist (formerly of the *Comisión Nacional de Energía Atómica*, later President of the *Comisión Nacional de Actividades Espaciales*). Buenos Aires, August 20, 1999.

Vira, Dharma. Indian civil servant (Cabinet Secretary under Lal Bahadur Shastri). New Delhi, November 13, 1998.

ARCHIVAL SOURCES

Baxter papers, University of New South Wales archives, Sydney, Australia.
Bidault papers, Archives Nationales, Paris, France.

Blackett papers, Royal Society archives, London, United Kingdom.

Blanc papers, Service des Archives Privées, Service Historique de l'Armée de Terre, Château de Vincennes, Vincennes, France.

Bonnet papers, Ministère des Affaires Etrangères archives, Paris, France.

Comisión Nacional de Energía Atómica archives, Buenos Aires, Argentina.

Commissariat à l'Energie Atomique archives, Fontenay-aux-Roses, France.

Department of Foreign Affairs and Trade archives, Canberra, Australia.

Elgey papers, Service des Archives Privées, Archives Nationales, Paris, France.

Escuela de Guerra Naval archives, Buenos Aires, Argentina.

Juin papers, Service des Archives Privées, Service Historique de l'Armée de Terre, Château de Vincennes, Vincennes, France.

Juridical Service archives, Comisión Nacional de Energía Atómica, Buenos Aires, Argentina.

Liddell Hart Centre for Military Archives, King's College, London, United Kingdom.

Mendès France papers, Institut Pierre Mendès France archives, Paris, France.

Ministère des Affaires Etrangères archives, Brussels, Belgium.

Ministère des Affaires Etrangères archives, Paris, France.

Ministerio de Relaciones Exteriores archives, Buenos Aires, Argentina.

National Archives of Australia, Canberra, Australia.

National Archives and Records Administration, College Park, Maryland.

National Security Archive, George Washington University, Washington, DC.

Nixon Presidential Materials, at the National Archives, College Park, Maryland.

Parodi papers, Achives d'Histoire Contemporaine, Institut d'Etudes Politiques, Paris, France.

Public Record Office, Kew, United Kingdom.

Titterton papers, Australian Academy of Sciences archives, Canberra, Australia.

Wormser papers, Ministère des Affaires Etrangères archives, Paris, France.

Zuckerman papers, Library of the University of East Anglia at Norwich, United Kingdom.

Also various private archives.

SECONDARY AND PUBLISHED PRIMARY SOURCES CITED

Abdelal, Rawi, Yoshiko M. Herrera, Alastair Iain Johnston, and Rose McDermott, "Identity as a Variable." Paper presented to the conference on "The Measurement of Identity," Harvard University, December 2004.

Abraham, Itty. The Making of the Indian Atomic Bomb: Science, Secrecy and the Postcolonial State. London: Zed Books, 1998.

Adler, Emanuel. The Power of Ideology: The Quest for Technological Autonomy in Argentina and Brazil. Berkeley: University of California Press, 1987.

Ailleret, Charles. L'aventure atomique française. Paris: Grasset, 1968.

Albright, David, "Bomb Potential for South America." Bulletin of the Atomic Scientists 45, 4 (May 1989): 16–20.

Alder, Keith. Australia's Uranium Opportunities: How Her Scientists and Engineers Tried to Bring Her into the Nuclear Age but Were Stymied by Politics. Sydney: Pauline Alder, 1996.

Allison, Graham T., *et al. Avoiding Nuclear Anarchy: Containing the Threat of Loose Russian Nuclear Weapons and Fissile Material.* Cambridge, MA: MIT Press, 1996.

Andersen, Peter A. and Laura K. Guerrero, eds. *Handbook of Communication and Emotion: Research, Theory, Applications, and Contexts.* San Diego: Academic Press, 1998.

Anderson, Benedict R. O'G. *Imagined Communities: Reflections on the Origin and Spread of Nationalism.* London: Verso, 1991.

Angyal, S. J., "Sir Philip Baxter 1905–1989." *Historical Records of Australian Science* 8, 3 (1991): 183–197.

"Argentine-Brazilian Declaration of Common Nuclear Policy." International Atomic Energy Agency Information Circular INFCIRC/388, 3 December 1990, available at http://www.iaea.org/Publications/Documents/Infcircs/. Accessed April 20, 2005.

Arkin, William M. "The Sky-Is-Still-Falling Profession." *Bulletin of Atomic Scientists* 50, 2 (March/April 1994): 64.

Armony, Victor. *Représenter la nation. Le discours présidentiel de la transition démocratique en Argentine 1983–1999.* Montreal: L'Univers des discours, 2000.

Aron, Raymond. "Historical Sketch of the Great Debate." In Raymond Aron and Daniel Lerner, eds., *France Defeats EDC.* New York: Frederick A. Praeger, 1957: 2–23.

Aron, Raymond and Daniel Lerner, eds. *France Defeats EDC.* New York: Frederick A. Praeger, 1957.

Arregui, Juan José Hernández. *La formación de la conciencia nacional, 1930–1960.* Buenos Aires: Ediciones Hachea, 1970.

Axelrod, Robert M., ed. *Structure of Decision.* Princeton: Princeton University Press, 1976.

Babbage, Ross and Sandy Gordon, eds. *India's Strategic Future.* Delhi: Oxford University Press, 1992.

Bader, William. *The United States and the Spread of Nuclear Weapons.* New York: Pegasus, 1968.

Badic, Bertrand and Marc Sadoun, eds. *L'autre: Etudes réunies pour Alfred Grosser.* Paris: Presses de la Fondation des Sciences Politiques, 1996.

Baldwin, David A. "Power Analysis and World Politics: New Trends versus Old Tendencies." *World Politics* 31, 2 (January 1979): 161–194.

Ball, Desmond. *A Suitable Piece of Real Estate: American Installations in Australia.* Sydney: Hale and Iremonger, 1980.

Ball, Desmond, ed. *Strategy and Defence: Australian Essays.* Sydney: George Allen & Unwin, 1982.

Ball, Desmond and R. H. Mathams. "The Nuclear Threat to Australia." In Michael Denborough, ed. *Australia and Nuclear War.* Fyshwick, Australian Capital Territory: Croom Helm Australia, 1983: 38–54.

Bandura, Albert. "Exercise of Personal Agency Through the Self-Efficacy Mechanism." In Ralf Schwarzer, ed., *Self-Efficacy: Thought Control of Action.* Washington, DC: Hemisphere Publishing Corp., 1992: 3–38.

Banerjee, Dipankar. "India's Nuclear Policy – An IIC Debate," 8 June 1998, available at http://www.ipcs.org/newIpcsSeminars2.jsp?action=showView&k Value=413. Accessed April 20, 2005.

Barbier, Colette. "Les négociations franco-germano-italiennes en vue de l'établissement d'une coopération militaire nucléaire au cours des années 1956–1958." *Revue d'Histoire Diplomatique* 104, 1–2 (1990): 81–113.

Bariéty, Jacques. "La décision de réarmer l'Allemagne, l'échec de la Communauté Européenne de Défense et les accords de Paris du 23 octobre 1954 vus du côté français." *Revue Belge de Philologie et d'Histoire* 71, 2 (1993): 354–383.

Barletta, Michael. "Democratic Security and Diversionary Peace: Nuclear Confidence-Building in Argentina and Brazil." *National Security Studies Quarterly* (Summer 1999): 19–38.

"The Military Nuclear Program in Brazil." Center for International Security and Cooperation Working Paper, Stanford University (August 1997).

Barnaby, Frank. *How Nuclear Weapons Spread: Nuclear Weapon Proliferation in the 1990s*. London: Routledge, 1994.

Basrur, Rajesh M. "Nuclear Weapons and Indian Strategic Culture." *Journal of Peace Research* 38, 2 (March 2001): 181–198.

Bauer, Martin W. "Classical Content Analysis: A Review." In Martin W. Bauer and George Gaskell, eds., *Qualitative Researching with Text, Image, and Sound: A Practical Handbook*. Thousand Oaks, CA: SAGE Publications, 2000:19–37.

Bauer, Martin W. and George Gaskell, eds. *Qualitative Researching With Text, Image, and Sound: A Practical Handbook*. Thousand Oaks, CA: SAGE Publications, 2000.

Beaton, Leonard and John Maddox. *The Spread of Nuclear Weapons*. New York: Frederick A. Praeger, 1962.

Bellany, Ian. *Australia in the Nuclear Age: National Defense and National Development*. Sydney: Sydney University Press, 1972.

Bernstein, Barton J. "Understanding Decisionmaking, US Foreign Policy, and the Cuban Missile Crisis: A Review Essay." *International Security* 25, 1 (Summer 2000): 134–164.

Betts, Richard K. "Paranoids, Pygmies, Pariahs and Non-Proliferation Revisited." *Security Studies* 2, 3–4 (Spring/Summer 1993): 100–123.

Bharatiya Jana Sangh Party. *BJS Party Documents 1951–1972, v. 1: Principles and Policies, Manifestos, Constitution*. New Delhi: BJS, 1973.

BJS Party Documents 1951–1972, v. 3: Resolutions on Defence and External Affairs. New Delhi: BJS, 1973.

Bharatiya Janata Party. *Foreign Policy and Resolutions*. New Delhi: BJP, 1995.

Bidwai, Praful and Achin Vanaik. *New Nukes: India, Pakistan and Global Nuclear Disarmament*. New York: Olive Branch Press, 2000.

Bracken, Paul J. *Fire in the East: the Rise of Asian Military Power and the Second Nuclear Age*. New York: HarperCollins, 1999.

Brader, Ted A. "Campaigning for Hearts and Minds: How Campaign Ads Use Emotion and Information to Sway the Electorate." Ph.D. dissertation, Harvard University, 1999.

Broad, William J. "Chain Reaction: Facing a Second Nuclear Age." *New York Times*, August 3, 2003, "Week in Review p." p. 1.

Broinowski, Richard P. *Fact or Fission? The Truth about Australia's Nuclear Ambitions.* Melbourne: Scribe Publications, 2003.

Brown, Roger. *Social Psychology,* 2nd ed. New York: The Free Press, 1985.

Buch, Tomás. "La proyección comercial internacional." In Julio C. Carasales and Roberto M. Ornstein, eds., *La cooperación internacional de la Argentina en el campo nuclear.* Buenos Aires: Consejo Argentino para las Relaciones Internacionales, 1998: 147–208.

Buchalet, Albert. "Les premières étapes (1955–1960)." In Colloque organisé par l'Université de Franche-Comté et l'Institut Charles de Gaulle, *L'Aventure de la bombe: De Gaulle et la dissuasion nucléaire 1958–1969.* Paris: Plon, 1985.

Burns, John F. "Visiting Nuclear Site, Indian Leader Puts Pakistan on Notice." *New York Times,* May 21, 1998, p. A7.

Bush, George W. "Remarks by the President on Weapons of Mass Destruction Proliferation." Washington, DC: National Defense University, February 11, 2004. Available at http://www.whitehouse.gov/news/releases/2004/02/20040211-4.html

Butler, Richard. *The Greatest Threat: Iraq, Weapons of Mass Destruction, and the Growing Crisis of Global Security.* New York: Public Affairs, 2000.

Buzan, Barry. *People, States, and Fear: The National Security Problem in International Relations.* Brighton: Wheatsheaf, 1983.

Cabral, Regis. "The Interaction of Science and Diplomacy: The United States, Latin America and Nuclear Energy, 1945–1955." Ph.D. dissertation, University of Chicago, 1986.

Cabral, Regis, ed. *The Nuclear Technology Debate in Latin America.* Göteborg, Sweden: Göteborg University, 1990.

Cain, Frank, ed. *Menzies in War and Peace.* St. Leonards, New South Wales: Allen & Unwin, 1997.

Cairns, James F. *Living with Asia.* Melbourne: Lansdowne Press, 1966.

Campbell, Kurt M., Robert J. Einhorn, and Mitchell B. Reiss, eds. *The Nuclear Tipping Point: Why States Reconsider their Nuclear Choices.* Washington, DC: Brookings Institution Press, 2004.

Cámpora, Héctor. Speech before opening of Congress (Sesión de Asamblea Mayo 25 de 1973). In Congreso de la Nación, Cámara de Diputados, *Diario de Sesiones.* Buenos Aires: República Argentina, 1974: 27–63.

Carasales, Julio C. *El desarme de los desarmados: Argentina y el Tratado de no proliferación de armas nucleares.* Buenos Aires: Editorial Planear, 1987.

De Rivales a Socios: El proceso de cooperación nuclear entre Argentina y Brasil. Buenos Aires: Grupo Editor Latinoamericano, 1997.

"Las explosions nucleares pacíficas y la actitud argentina." Consejo Argentina para las Relaciones Internacionales Documento de trabajo no. 20, Buenos Aires, Argentina, 1997.

Carasales, Julio C., Carlos Castro Madero, and José M. Cohen. *Argentina y el submarino de propulsión nuclear – posibilidades y dificultades.* Buenos Aires: Servicio de Hidrografía Naval, 1992.

Carasales, Julio C. and Roberto M. Ornstein, eds. *La cooperación internacional de la Argentina en el campo nuclear.* Buenos Aires: Consejo Argentino para las Relaciones Internacionales, 1998.

Castro Madero, Carlos and Estéban A. Takacs. *Política nuclear argentina: avance o retroceso?* Buenos Aires: El Ateneo, 1991.

Cavallo, Domingo F. *El peso de la verdad: un impulse a la transparencia en la Argentina de los 90.* Buenos Aires: Planeta, 1997.

Cawte, Alice. *Atomic Australia: 1944–1990.* Kensington, New South Wales: NSW Press, 1992.

Cha, Victor D. "The Second Nuclear Age: Proliferation Pessimism versus Sober Optimism in South Asia and East Asia." *Journal of Strategic Studies* 24, 4 (December 2001): 79–120.

Chari, P. R. *Indo-Pak Nuclear Standoff: The Role of the United States.* New Delhi: Manohar, 1995.

Chengappa, Raj. *Weapons of Peace: The Secret Story of India's Quest to Be a Nuclear Power.* New Delhi: HarperCollins, 2000.

Child, Jack. *Geopolitics and Conflict in South America: Quarrels Among Neighbors.* New York: Praeger, 1985.

Child, John. "Geopolitical Thinking in Latin America." *Latin American Research Review* 14, 2 (Summer 1979): 89–111.

Chong, Dennis. *Rational Lives: Norms and Values in Politics and Society.* Chicago: University of Chicago Press, 2000.

Cisneros, Andrés and Carlos Escudé, eds. *Historia general de las relaciones exteriors de la República Argentina, tomo XIV: Las relaciones políticas, 1966–1989.* Buenos Aires: Nuevohacer, Grupo Editor Latinoamericano, 2003.

Clark, Gregory. *In Fear of China.* Melbourne: Lansdowne, 1967.

Clark, Pilita. "PM's Story: Very much alive . . . and unfazed." *Sydney Morning Herald*, January 1, 1999.

Cocks, Joan. *The Oppositional Imagination: Feminism, Critique and Political Theory.* London: Routledge, 1989.

Cohen, Avner. *Israel and the Bomb.* New York: Columbia University Press, 1998.

Cohen, Avner and Benjamin Frankel. "Opaque Nuclear Proliferation." In Benjamin Frankel, ed., *Opaque Nuclear Proliferation: Methodological and Policy Implications.* London: Frank Cass, 1991: 14–44.

Cohen, Raymond. "Threat Perception in International Crisis." *Political Science Quarterly* 93, 1 (Spring 1978): 93–107.

Cohen, Stephen P. *India: Emerging Power.* Washington, DC: Brookings Institution Press, 2002.

"Nuclear Weapons and Nuclear War in South Asia: An Unknowable Future." Paper presented to the United Nations University Conference on South Asia, Tokyo, Japan, May 2002, http://www.brookings.edu/views/speeches/cohens/20020501.htm.

"Perception, Influence, and Nuclear Proliferation in South Asia." ACDIS Occasional Paper, University of Illinois at Urbana-Champaign, August 1979.

"South Asia: The Origins of War and the Conditions for Peace." *South Asian Survey* 4, 1 (1997): 25–46.

"Why Did India 'Go Nuclear'?" In Raju G. C. Thomas and Amit Gupta, ed., *India's Nuclear Security.* Boulder, CO: Lynne Rienner Publishers, 2000: 13–36.

Colloque organisé par l'Université de Franche-Comté et l'Institut Charles de Gaulle. *L'Aventure de la bombe: De Gaulle et la dissuasion nucléaire 1958–1969*. Paris: Plon, 1985.

Comisión Nacional sobre la Desaparición de Personas. *Nunca más*, 3rd ed. Buenos Aires: Eudeba, 1997.

Congreso de la Nación (Argentina). *Estado y perspectivas de la Actividad Nuclear en la Argentina. Congreso organizado por las comisiones de Ciencia y Tecnología y de Energía y Combustibles de la Honorable Cámara de Diputados de la Nación, Buenos Aires, 14 al 16 de Octubre de 1992*. Buenos Aires: República Argentina, 1994.

"Contract Signed for Australia's History-Making Replacement Research Reactor." Australian National Science and Technology Organisation (ANSTO), Media Release, July 13, 2000, available at http://www.ansto.gov.au/info/press/2000_09.html. Accessed April 20, 2005.

Corbridge, Stuart and John Harriss. *Reinventing India: Liberalization, Hindu Nationalism and Popular Democracy*. Cambridge: Polity Press, 2000.

Corigliano, Francisco, Leonor Machinandiarena de Devoto, and Sebastián Masana. *Las 'relaciones carnales': los vínculos politicos con las grandes potencies, 1989–2000*, vol. XV of Carlos Escudé, ed., *Historia general de las relaciones exteriores de la República Argentina*. Buenos Aires: Nuevohacer, Grupo Editor Latinoamericano, 2003.

Coronil, Fernando. "Listening to the Subaltern: Postcolonial Studies and the Poetics of Neocolonial States." In Laura Chrisman and Benita Parry, eds., *Postcolonial Theory and Criticism*. Cambridge: D. S. Brewer, 2000: 37–55.

Cosentino, Jorge Oscar. "Política nuclear." In Partido Justicialista, Instituto Superior de Conducción Política, Consejo de Profesionales, Intelectuales y Técnicos, *Análisis, lineamientos doctrinarios y propuestas para la acción del Gobierno Justicialista*. Buenos Aires: Instituto Superior de Conducción Política del Partido Justicialista, 1989: 327–344.

Cottam, Richard W. *Foreign Policy Motivation: A General Theory and a Case Study*. Pittsburgh: University of Pittsburgh Press, 1977.

Coutrot, Aline. "La politique atomique sous le gouvernement de Mendès France." In François Bédarida and Jean-Pierre Rioux, eds., *Pierre Mendès France et le Mendésisme: L'expérience gouvernementale (1954–1955) et sa postérité*. Paris: Fayard, 1985: 309–316.

Crawford, Neta C. "The Passion of World Politics: Propositions on Emotion and Emotional Relationships." *International Security* 24, 4 (Spring 2000): 116–156.

Argument and Change in World Politics: Ethics, Decolonization, and Humanitarian Intervention. Cambridge: Cambridge University Press, 2002.

Crépin, Jean. "Histoire du Comité des Explosifs Nucléaires." In Actes du colloque organisé par l'Université de Franche-Comté et l'Institut Charles de Gaulle, *L'Aventure de la bombe: De Gaulle et la dissuasion nucléaire 1958–1969*. Paris: Plon, 1985.

Creswell, Michael and Marc Trachtenberg. "France and the German Question, 1945–1955." *Journal of Cold War Studies* 5, 3 (Summer 2003): 5–28.

Curthoys, Ann and John Merritt, eds. *Better Dead than Red: Australia's First Cold War: 1945–1959*, vol. II. Sydney: Allen and Unwin, 1986.

Dai, Xinyuan. "Information Systems in Treaty Regimes." *World Politics* 54, 4 (July 2002): 405–436.

Damasio, Antonio. *Descartes' Error: Emotion, Reason, and the Human Brain.* New York: G. P. Putnam, 1994.

Davis, Zachary S. "The Realist Nuclear Regime." *Security Studies* 2, 3–4 (Spring/Summer 1993): 79–99.

Debré, Michel. *Trois Républiques pour une France: Mémoires, 1946–1958 "Agir."* Paris: Albin Michel, 1988.

De Gaulle, Charles. "Discours à l'assemblée consultative sur le programme de la reconstruction française" (2 March 1945). In André Siegfried, ed., *L'Année politique 1945.* Paris: Editions du Grand Siècle, 1946: 442–451.

War Memoirs, Vol. 1: The Call to Honour 1940–1942, trans. Jonathan Griffin. New York: The Viking Press, 1955.

De la Malène, Christian and Constantin Melnik. "Attitudes of the French Parliament and Government toward Atomic Weapons." RAND Research Memorandum RM-2170-RC, Santa Monica, 1958.

Delumeau, Jean. *Rassurer et protéger: Le sentiment de sécurité dans l'Occident d'autrefois.* Paris: Fayard, 1989.

Denborough, Michael, ed. *Australia and Nuclear War.* Fyshwick, Australian Capital Territory: Croom Helm Australia, 1983.

Digeon, Claude. *La crise allemande de la pensée française 1870–1914.* Paris: Presses Universitaires de France, 1959.

Dirección de Estrategia. "Relaciones argentino-brasileñas." *Estrategia* 5 (January–February 1970): 48–57.

Dixit, J. N. *Across Borders: Fifty Years of Indian Foreign Policy.* New Delhi: Picus Books, 1998.

Donovan, John C. *The Cold Warriors: A Policy-Making Elite.* Lexington, MA: D. C. Heath, 1974.

Douglass, Frederick. "What the Black Man Wants: Speech at the Annual Meeting of the Massachusetts Anti-Slavery Society at Boston (April 1865)." In Carlos E. Cortés, Arlin I. Ginsburg, Alan W. F. Green, and James A. Joseph, eds., *Three Perspectives on Ethnicity: Blacks, Chicanos, and Native Americans.* New York: G. P. Putnam's Sons, 1976: 93.

Downs, George W., David M. Rocke, and Peter N. Barsoom. "Is the Good News About Compliance Good News About Cooperation?" *International Organization* 50, 3 (Summer 1996): 379–406.

Duchêne, François. *Jean Monnet: The First Statesman of Interdependence.* New York: W. W. Norton and Co., 1994.

Dumoulin, Michel, Pierre Guillen, and Maurice Vaïsse, eds. *L'Energie nucléaire en Europe: Des origins à Euratom.* Bern: Peter Lang, 1994.

Dupont, Alan. *Australia's Threat Perceptions: A Search for Security* (Canberra Papers on Strategy and Defence, 82). Canberra: Strategic and Defence Studies Centre, Australian National University, 1991.

Duroselle, Jean-Baptiste. "Les changements dans la politique extérieure de la France depuis 1945." In Stanley Hoffmann, ed., *A la recherche de la France.* Paris: Editions du Seuil, 1963: 347–400.

Duval, Marcel and Dominique Mongin. *Histoire des forces nucléaires françaises depuis 1945*. Paris: Presses Universitaires de France, 1993.

Edwardes, Michael. "Illusion and Reality in India's Foreign Policy." *International Affairs* 41, 1 (January 1965): 48–58.

Edwards, Peter G. *A Nation at War: Australian Politics, Society and Diplomacy during the Vietnam War 1965–1975*. St. Leonards, NSW: Allen and Unwin in Association with the Australian War Memorial, 1997.

Edwards. Peter G. with Gregory Pemberton. *Crises and Commitments: The Politics and Diplomacy of Australia's Involvement in Southeast Asian Conflicts, 1948–1965*. North Sydney: Allen & Unwin in association with the Australian War Memorial, 1992.

Elgey, Georgette, with Marie Caroline Boussard. *Histoire de la quatrième république, v. 3: La république des tourmentes (1954–1959)*. Paris: Fayard, 1992.

Elster, Jon. *Strong Feelings: Emotion, Addiction, and Human Behavior*. Cambridge, MA: MIT Press, 1999.

Escudé, Carlos. *Patología del nacionalismo: el caso argentino*. Buenos Aires: Editorial Tesis, 1987.

El realismo de los Estados débiles: la política exterior del primer Gobierno Menem frente a la teoría de las relaciones internacionales. Buenos Aires: Grupo Editor Latinoamericano, 1995.

Escudé, Carlos, ed. *Historia general de las relaciones exteriores de la República Argentina*. Buenos Aires: Nuevohacer, Grupo Editor Latinoamericano, 2003.

Evatt, Herbert V. *Australia in World Affairs*. Sydney: Angus and Robertson, 1946.

Falkowski, Lawrence S., ed. *Psychological Models in International Politics*. Boulder, CO: Westview Press, 1979.

Faure, Edgar. "Discours d'Edgar Faure, président du Conseil, prononcé devant l'Assemblée Nationale au cours du débat sur l'armée européenne" (13 February 1952). In André Siegfried, ed., *L'Année Politique 1952*. Paris: Editions du Grand Siècle: 482–488.

"Témoignage." In Colloque organisé par l'Université de Franche-Comté et l'Institut Charles de Gaulle, *L'Aventure de la bombe: De Gaulle et la dissuasion nucléaire 1958–1969*. Paris: Plon, 1985.

Feinstein, Lee and Anne-Marie Slaughter. "A Duty to Prevent." *Foreign Affairs* 83, 1 (January–February 2004): 136–150.

Fischerkeller, Michael P. "David versus Goliath: Cultural Judgments in Asymmetric Wars." *Security Studies* 7, 4 (Summer 1998): 1–43.

Forman, Paul and José M. Sánchez-Ron, eds. *National Military Establishments and the Advancement of Science and Technology: Studies in 20th Century History*. Dordrecht: Kluwer Academic Publishers, 1996.

Fortmann, Michel. "The Other Side of Midnight: Opaque Proliferation Revisited." *International Journal* 48 (Winter 1992–93): 151–75.

Frankel, Benjamin, ed. *Opaque Nuclear Proliferation: Methodological and Policy Implications*. London: Frank Cass, 1991.

Friese, Kai. "Hijacking India's History." *New York Times*, December 30, 2002, p. A17.

Gandhi, Rajiv. "Forty Years of Independence" (speech given at the Red Fort in Delhi, August 15, 1987). In *Rajiv Gandhi: Selected Speeches and Writings*, vol. II. Delhi: Ministry of Information and Broadcasting, 1988: 66–77.

Ganguly, Sumit. "Explaining the Indian Nuclear Tests of 1998." In Raju G. C. Thomas and Amit Gupta, eds., *India's Nuclear Security*. Boulder, CO: Lynne Rienner, 2000.

"India's Foreign Policy Grows Up." *World Policy Journal* 20, 4 (Winter 2003–4): 41–47.

Garver, John W. *Protracted Contest: Sino-Indian Rivalry in the Twentieth Century*. Seattle: University of Washington Press, 2001.

George, Alexander L. "The 'Operational Code': A Neglected Approach to the Study of Political Leaders and Decision Making." *International Studies Quarterly* 13, 2 (June 1969):190–222.

"The Causal Nexus between Cognitive Beliefs and Decision-Making Behavior: the 'Operational Code' Belief System." In Lawrence S. Falkowski, ed., *Psychological Models in International Politics*. Boulder, CO: Westview Press, 1979: 95–124.

Gerbet, Pierre. *Le relèvement 1944–1949*. Paris: Imprimerie Nationale, 1991.

Ghosh, Partha S. "United States and India: The Reality and the Hope." ACDIS Occasional Paper, University of Illinois at Urbana-Champaign, March 1994.

Gissing, Philip. "Sir Philip Baxter, Engineer: The Fabric of a Liberal-National Country Style of Thought." Ph.D. dissertation, University of New South Wales, March 1998.

Gokhale, Balkrishna Govind. "Nehru and History." *History and Theory* 17, 3 (October 1978): 311–322.

Goldman, Emily O. and Leslie C. Eliason, eds. *The Diffusion of Military Technology and Ideas*. Stanford: Stanford University Press, 2003.

Goldschmidt, Bertrand. *The Atomic Complex: A Worldwide Political History of Nuclear Energy*. La Grange Park, IL: American Nuclear Society, 1982.

"La genèse et l'héritage." In Colloque organisé par l'Université de Franche-Comté et l'Institut Charles de Gaulle, *L'Aventure de la bombe. De Gaulle et la dissuasion nucléaire 1958–1969*. Paris: Plon, 1985: 23–38.

Pionniers de l'atome. Paris: Stock, 1987.

Atomic Rivals: A Candid Memoir of Rivalries among the Allies over the Bomb, trans. Georges M. Temmer. New Brunswick, NJ: Rutgers University Press, 1990.

"Débats." In Georges-Henri Soutou and Alain Beltran, eds., *Pierre Guillaumat: la passion des grands projets industriels*. Paris: Editions Rive Droite, 1995: 71.

Goldstein, Avery. *Deterrence and Security in the 21st Century: China, Britain, France, and the Enduring Legacy of the Nuclear Revolution*. Stanford, CA.: Stanford University Press, 2000.

Gorton, John G. "Address to the Australia Club in London," *Current Notes on International Affairs* 40, 1 (January 1969): 25–28.

Speech of 8 May 1957. In *Parliamentary Debates* (Hansard), Senate, Session 1957, Second Session of the 22nd Parliament. Canberra: Government of the Commonwealth of Australia, 1957: 608.

Gowing, Margaret. *Independence and Deterrence: Britain and Atomic Energy, 1945–1952*. London: Macmillan, 1974.

Graham, Thomas Jr. "Nuclear Maturity in Argentina and Brazil." Paper presented at SAIC Argentina and Brazil Rollback Workshop, McLean, Virginia, October 22, 1998, http://www.lawscns.org/argbra.htm.

Graham, Thomas Jr., and Douglas B. Shaw. "Nearing a Fork in the Road: Proliferation or Nuclear Reversal?" *The Nonproliferation Review* 6, 1 (Fall 1998): 70–76.

Granovsky, Martín. *Misión cumplida: la presión norteamericana sobre la Argentina, de Braden a Todman*. Buenos Aires: Planeta, 1992.

Gray, Colin S. *The Second Nuclear Age*. Boulder, CO: Lynne Rienner, 1999.

Greenfeld, Liah. *The Spirit of Capitalism: Nationalism and Economic Growth*. Cambridge, MA: Harvard University Press, 2001.

Grondona, Mariano. *Argentina en el tiempo y en el mundo*. Buenos Aires: Editorial Primera Plana, 1967.

La Argentina como vocación. Buenos Aires: Planeta, 1995.

Grosser, Alfred. "France and Germany in the Atlantic Community." *International Organization* 17, 3 (Summer, 1963): 550–573.

Guglialmelli, Juan E. "América Latina: Venta de armas de los EEUU y eventuales implicancias de la explosión atómica de la India." *Estrategia* 28 (May–June 1974): 65.

"Argentina, Brasil y la bomba atómica." *Estrategia* 30 (September–October 1974): 1–15.

"¿Y si Brasil fabrica la bomba atómica? (A propósito del acuerdo brasileño-alemán)." *Estrategia* 34–35 (May–August 1975): 5–21.

"¿Brasil fabrica la bomba atómica?" *Estrategia* 70 (July–September 1981): 1–9.

Guillen, Pierre. "La France et la négociation du traité d'Euratom." In Michel Dumoulin, Pierre Guillen, and Maurice Vaïsse, eds., *L'Energie nucléaire en Europe: Des origins à Euratom*. Bern: Peter Lang, 1994: 111–127.

Haksar, P. N. *India's Foreign Policy and its Problems*. New Delhi: Patriot Publishers, 1989.

Hall, Peter A. "Aligning Ontology and Methodology in Comparative Research." In James Mahoney and Dietrich Rueschemeyer, eds., *Comparative Historical Analysis in the Social Sciences*. Cambridge: Cambridge University Press, 2003: 373–404.

Hancock, Ian. *John Gorton: He Did it His Way*. Sydney: Hodder, 2002.

Hanson, Marianne and Carl J. Ungerer. "Promoting an Agenda for Nuclear Weapons Elimination: The Canberra Commission and the Dilemmas of Disarmament." *Australian Journal of Politics and History* 44 (December 1998): 533–551.

Hardy, Clarence. *Enriching Experiences: Uranium Enrichment in Australia 1963–1996*. Peakhurst, NSW: Glen Haven, 1996.

Atomic Rise and Fall: The Australian Atomic Energy Commission 1953–1987. Peakhurst, NSW: Glen Haven, 1999.

Harrison, Lawrence E. and Samuel P. Huntington, eds. *Culture Matters: How Values Shape Human Progress*. New York: Basic Books, 2000.

Hecht, Gabrielle. *The Radiance of France: Nuclear Power and National Identity after World War II*. Cambridge, MA: MIT Press, 1998.

Hermann, Charles F., Robert S. Billings, and Robert Litchfield. "Escalation or Modification: Responding to Negative Feedback in Sequential Decision Making." Paper presented to the Fifth National Conference on Public Management Research, George Bush School of Government and Public Service,

December 3–4, 1999, http://www-bushschool.tamu.edu/pubman/papers/1999/Hermann99.pdf.

Herrera, Yoshiko M. and Bear Braumoeller, eds. "Symposium: Discourse and Content Analysis." *Qualitative Methods* 2, 1 (Spring 2004): 15–39.

Herring, George C. and Richard H. Immerman. "Eisenhower, Dulles, and Dienbienphu: 'The Day We Didn't Go to War' Revisited." *Journal of American History* 71, 2 (September 1984): 343–363.

Herrmann, Richard K. *Perceptions and Behavior in Soviet Foreign Policy*. Pittsburgh: University of Pittsburgh Press, 1985.

Herrmann, Richard K. and Michael P. Fischerkeller. "Beyond the Enemy Image and Spiral Model: Cognitive-Strategic Research After the Cold War." *International Organization* 49, 3 (1995): 415–450.

Heuser, Beatrice. *Nuclear Mentalities? Strategies and Beliefs in Britain, France, and the FRG*. London: Macmillan, 1998.

Hewitson, Patricia. "Nonproliferation and Reduction of Nuclear Weapons: Risks of Weakening the Multilateral Nuclear Nonproliferation Norm." *Berkeley Journal of International Law* 21, 3 (2003): 405–494.

Hirschman, Albert O. *A Bias for Hope: Essays on Development and Latin America*. Boulder: Westview Press, 1985.

Hitchcock, William I. *France Restored: Cold War Diplomacy and the Quest for Leadership in Europe, 1944–1954*. Chapel Hill: University of North Carolina Press, 1998.

Hodge, Bob and Vijay Mishra. *Dark Side of the Dream: Australian Literature and the Postcolonial Mind*. Sydney: Allen and Unwin, 1991.

Hoffmann, Stanley. *Gulliver's Troubles, or, The Setting of American Foreign Policy*. New York: McGraw-Hill for the Council on Foreign Relations, 1968.

"France: Two Obsessions for one Century." In Robert Pastor, ed., *A Century's Journey: How the Great Powers Shape the World*. New York: Basic Books, 1999.

Hofstede, Gert. *Culture's Consequences: International Differences in Work-Related Values*. Beverly Hills, CA: Sage Publications, 1980.

Holloway, David. *Stalin and the Bomb: The Soviet Union and Atomic Energy, 1939–56*. New Haven: Yale University Press, 1994.

Holsti, Kalevi J. "National Role Conceptions in the Study of Foreign Policy." *International Studies Quarterly* 14, 3 (September, 1970): 233–309.

Holsti, Ole. "Foreign Policy Formation Viewed Cognitively." In Robert Axelrod, ed., *Structure of Decision*. Princeton: Princeton University Press, 1976: 18–54.

"Crisis Decision Making." In Philip Tetlock *et al.*, eds., *Behavior, Society, and Nuclear War*, vol. I. New York: Oxford University Press, 1989: 8–84.

Hopf, Ted. *Social Construction of International Politics: Identities and Foreign Policies, Moscow, 1955 and 1999*. Ithaca: Cornell University Press, 2002.

Horowitz, Donald L. *Ethnic Groups in Conflict*. Berkeley: University of California Press, 1985.

The Deadly Ethnic Riot. Berkeley: University of California Press, 2001.

Hymans, Jacques E. C. "Isotopes and Identity: Australia and the Nuclear Weapons Option, 1945–1999." *Nonproliferation Review* 7, 1 (Spring 2000): 1–23.

"Of Gauchos and Gringos: Why Argentina Never Wanted the Bomb, and Why the United States Thought It Did." *Security Studies* 10, 3 (Spring 2001): 153–185.

"Inside a Bomb Shell." *The Hindustan Times*, April 16, 2001.

"Applying Social Identity Theory to the Study of International Politics: A Caution and an Agenda." Paper presented to the International Studies Association conference, New Orleans, Louisiana, March 2002.

"Why Do States Acquire Nuclear Weapons? Comparing the Cases of India and France." In D. R. SarDesai and Raju G. C. Thomas, eds., *Nuclear India in the Twenty-First Century*. New York: Palgrave-Macmillan, 2002: 139–160.

"The Changing Color of Money: European Currency Iconography and Collective Identity." *European Journal of International Relations* 10, 1 (March 2004): 5–31.

"What Counts as History and How Much Does History Count? The Case of French Secondary Education." In Hanna Schissler and Yasemin Soysal, eds., *The Nation, Europe, the World: Curricula and Textbooks in Transition*. New York: Berghahn Books, 2005.

Hymans, Jacques E. C., Seung-Young Kim, and Henning Riecke. "To Go or Not to Go: South and North Korea's Nuclear Decisions in Comparative Context." *Journal of East Asian Studies* 1, 1 (February 2001): 91–153.

Izard, Carroll. *The Psychology of Emotions*. New York: Plenum Press, 1991.

Jaffrelot, Christophe. *The Hindu Nationalist Movement in India*. New York: Columbia University Press, 1996.

Jayakar, Pupul. *Indira Gandhi, An Intimate Biography*. New York: Pantheon Books, 1992.

Jervis, Robert. *Perception and Misperception in International Politics*. Princeton: Princeton University Press, 1976.

The Meaning of the Nuclear Revolution: Statecraft and the Prospect of Armageddon. Ithaca: Cornell University Press, 1989.

"International Primacy: Is the Game Worth the Candle?" *International Security* 17, 4 (Spring 1993): 52–67.

System Effects: Complexity in Political and Social Life. Princeton: Princeton University Press, 1997.

Jimenez, Laura Ruiz. "Peronism and Anti-Imperialism in the Argentine Press: 'Braden or Perón' was also 'Perón is Roosevelt'." *Journal of Latin American Studies* 30, 3 (October 1998): 551–571.

Johnston, Alastair Iain. "Thinking about Strategic Culture." *International Security* 19, 4 (Spring 1995): 32–64.

"Joint Statement by Department of Atomic Energy and Defence Research and Development Organisation." Press release, New Delhi, May 17, 1998. Available at http://www.fas.org/news/india/1998/05/980500-drdo.htm. Accessed April 20, 2005.

Joshi, Manoj. "Nuclear Shock Wave." *India Today*, May 25, 1998.

Juin, Alphonse. *Mémoires*, vol. II. Paris: Fayard, 1960.

Kagan, Jerome. *Three Seductive Ideas*. Cambridge, MA: Harvard University Press, 1998.

Kapur, Ashok. "India and Multipolarity in the Asia-Pacific Regional Sub-System." Paper delivered at the Annual Meeting of the American Political Science Association, September 1999.

Kargil Review Committee. *From Surprise to Reckoning: The Kargil Review Committee Report*. New Delhi: Sage Publishers, 2000.

Karp, Aaron. "Indian Ambitions and the Limits of American Influence." *Arms Control Today* (May 1998), http://www.armscontrol.org/act/1998_05/kpmy98.asp

Kelman, Herbert. "The Interdependence of Israeli and Palestinian Identities: The Role of the Other in Existential Conflicts." *Journal of Social Issues* 55, 3 (1999): 581–600.

Kier, Elizabeth and Jonathan Mercer. "Setting Precedents in Anarchy: Military Intervention and Weapons of Mass Destruction." *International Security* 20, 4 (Spring 1996): 77–106.

Koch, Andrew. "Nuclear Testing in South Asia and the CTBT." *The Nonproliferation Review* 3, 3 (Spring–Summer 1996): 98–104.

Kumar, Sumita. "Pakistan's Nuclear Weapons Programme." In Jasjit Singh, ed., *Nuclear India*. New Delhi: Knowledge World, 1998: 157–187.

Kux, Dennis. *India and the United States: Estranged Democracies, 1941–1991*. Washington, DC: National Defense University Press, 1992.

"La Argentina proveerá los combustibles del reactor nuclear australiano." INVAP S.E. press release, September 1, 2004. Available at http://www.invap.net/news/novedades.php?id=20040109094423. Accessed April 20, 2005.

Larra, Raúl. *La batalla del General Guglialmelli*. Buenos Aires: Editorial Distal, 1995.

Larson, Deborah Welch. "The Role of Belief Systems and Schemas in Foreign Policy Making." *Political Psychology* 15, 1 (March 1994): 17–33.

Lavoy, Peter R. "Learning to Live with the Bomb? India and Nuclear Weapons, 1947–1974." Ph.D. dissertation, University of California at Berkeley, 1997.

Lawler, Edward J. and Shane R. Thye. "Bringing Emotions into Social Exchange Theory." *Annual Review of Sociology* 25 (1999): 217–244.

Lebow, Richard Ned. *Between Peace and War: The Nature of International Crisis*. Baltimore: Johns Hopkins University Press, 1981.

LeDoux, Joseph. *The Emotional Brain: The Mysterious Underpinnings of Emotional Life*. New York: Touchstone, 1998.

Lerner, Daniel. "Reflections on France in the World Arena." In Daniel Lerner and Raymond Aron, eds., *France Defeats EDC*. New York: F. A. Praeger, 1957: 198–225.

Leventhal, Paul L. "IAEA Safeguards Shortcomings: A Critique." Nuclear Control Institute Report, Washington, DC, September 12, 1994, http://www.nci.org/p/plsgrds.htm.

Leventhal, Paul L. and Sharon Tanzer, eds. *Averting a Latin American Nuclear Arms Race: New Prospects and Challenges for Argentine–Brazil Nuclear Cooperation*. New York: St. Martin's Press, 1992.

Lewis, John Wilson and Xue Litai. *China Builds the Bomb*. Stanford: Stanford University Press, 1988.

Lewis, Michael. "Self-Conscious Emotions: Pride, Shame, and Guilt." In Michael Lewis and Jeannette M. Haviland, eds., *Handbook of Emotions*. New York: Guilford, 1993: 623–636.

Lewis, Michael and Jeannette M. Haviland, eds. *Handbook of Emotions*. New York: Guilford, 1993.

Linton, Ralph. "Status and Role." In Paul Bohannon and Mark Glazer, eds., *High Points in Anthropology*, 2nd ed. New York: McGraw Hill, 1988: 186–198.

Locke, Kenneth D. "Status and Solidarity in Social Comparison: Agentic and Communal Values and Vertical and Horizontal Directions." *Journal of Personality and Social Psychology* 84, 3 (March 2003): 619–631.

Lonergan, Iris Heidrun. "The Negotiations Between Canada and India for the Supply of the N. R. X. Nuclear Research Reactor 1955–56: A Case Study in Participatory Internationalism." M.A. thesis, Department of History, Carleton University, Ontario, Canada, 1989.

Lovell, Bernard. "P.M.S. Blackett, Baron Blackett of Chelsea." *Biographical Memoirs of Fellows of the Royal Society* 21 (1975): 1–115.

Lovett, A. W. "The United States and the Schuman Plan: A Study in French Diplomacy 1950–1952." *Historical Journal* 39, 2 (June 1996): 425–455.

Lowe, David. *Menzies and the "Great World Struggle": Australia's Cold War 1948–1954*. Sydney: UNSW Press, 1999.

MacLeod, Roy. "The Atom Comes to Australia: Reflections on the Australian Nuclear Programme, 1953 and 1993." *History and Technology* 11 (1994): 299–315.

Mahoney, James and Dietrich Rueschemeyer, eds. *Comparative Historical Analysis in the Social Sciences*. Cambridge: Cambridge University Press, 2003.

Malhotra, Inder. *Indira Gandhi: A Personal and Political Biography*. Boston: Northeastern University Press, 1991.

Mansbridge, Jane J. "Complicating Oppositional Consciousness." In Jane J. Mansbridge and Aldon D. Morris, eds., *Oppositional Consciousness: The Subjective Roots of Social Protest*. Chicago: University of Chicago Press, 2001.

Mansbridge, Jane J. and Aldon D. Morris, eds. *Oppositional Consciousness: The Subjective Roots of Social Protest*. Chicago: University of Chicago Press, 2001.

Mansingh, Surjit. *India's Search for Power: Indira Gandhi's Foreign Policy, 1966–1982*. New Delhi: Sage Publications, 1984.

Mansingh, Surjit, ed. *Nehru's Foreign Policy: Fifty Years On*. Delhi: Vedams Books, 1998.

Mariscotti, Mario. "The Bizarre Origins of Atomic Energy in Argentina." In Regis Cabral, ed., *The Nuclear Technology Debate in Latin America*. Göteborg, Sweden: Göteborg University, 1990.

Martínez Vidal, Carlos A. "Esbozo biográfico de Jorge Alberto Sábato, 1924–1983." Manuscript prepared for the Asociación Argentina para el Desarrollo Tecnológico, Buenos Aires, February 1999.

Marwah, Onkar and Ann Schulz, eds. *Nuclear Proliferation and the Near-Nuclear Countries*. Cambridge, MA: Ballinger Publishing Co., 1975.

Masi, Juan José. "De Pearl Harbor a las fuerzas armadas nucleares latinoamericanas (la revisión del sistema interamericano de defensa)." *Revista de la Escuela Superior de Guerra* 52, 414 (September–October 1974): 21–34.

Mattoo, Amitabh, ed. *India's Nuclear Deterrent: Pokhran II and Beyond*. New Delhi: Har Anand Publications Pvt., 1999.

Mazarr, Michael J. *Nuclear Weapons in a Transformed World: The Challenge of Virtual Nuclear Arsenals*. New York: St. Martin's Press, 1997.

Mearsheimer, John J. "Back to the Future: Instability in Europe after the Cold War." *International Security* 15, 1 (Summer 1990): 5–56.

Mendès France, Pierre. *Dire la vérité: causeries du Samedi, juin 1954–février 1955*. Paris: René Julliard, 1955.

  Gouverner, c'est choisir, t. 2: Sept mois et dix-sept jours, juin 1954–février 1955. Paris: René Julliard, 1955.

  Speech of June 9, 1954. In *Journal Officiel de la République Française, Débats de l'Assemblée Nationale, 2e legislature, Vol. 25, session de 1954, tome IV, du 4 mai 1954 au 9 juin 1954*. Paris: Imprimerie des Journaux Officiels, 1956: 2851.

  Choisir: conversations avec Jean Bothorel. Paris: Stock, 1974.

  Oeuvres complètes, t. 4: Pour une république moderne 1955–1962. Paris: Gallimard, 1987.

Menem, Carlos. "Hacia la conquista del país soñado" (address to the Asamblea Legislativa, May 1, 1990). In *Carlos Menem: La esperanza y la acción*. Buenos Aires: Emecé Editores, 1990: 29–64. Available at http://lanic.utexas.edu/project/arl/pm/sample2/argentin/menem/.

  "Mensaje Presidencial del Doctor Carlos Saúl Menem a la Honorable Asamblea Legislativa en la Aperture del 117o Período de Sesiones Ordinarias" (March 1, 1999). Accessed October 17, 2000 at http://www.presidencia.gov.ar/2ADD5.html. (link no longer active).

Meyer, Stephen M. *The Dynamics of Nuclear Proliferation*. Chicago: University of Chicago Press, 1984.

Milenky, Edward S. "Arms Production and National Security in Argentina." *Journal of Interamerican Studies and World Affairs* 22, 3 (August 1980): 267–288.

Milhollin, Gary. "Testimony of Gary Milhollin before the Committee on Armed Services, United States Senate, July 9, 1998." Available at http://www.senate.gov/~armed_services/statemnt/980709gm.htm.

Milia, Fernando A. "El pensamiento maritimo argentino." *Boletín del Centro Naval* 111, 770 (April–June 1993): 378–392.

  "Armamento nuclear en el Cono Sur: un dislate estratégico." *Boletín del Centro Naval* 113, 777 (January–March 1995): 87–92.

Millar, T. B. *Australia in Peace and War: External Relations 1788–1977*. Canberra: Australian National University Press, 1978.

Miller, J. D. B. "Australian Foreign Policy – Constraints and Opportunities: I." *International Affairs* 50, 2 (April 1974): 229–241.

Mishra, Madhusadan. *BJP and India's Foreign Policy*. New Delhi: Uppal Publishing House, 1997.

Mistry, Dinshaw. "India and the Comprehensive Test Ban Treaty." ACDIS Research Report, Program in Arms Control, Disarmament and International Security, University of Illinois at Urbana-Champaign, September 1998.

  "The Unrealized Promise of International Institutions: The Test Ban Treaty and India's Nuclear Breakout." *Security Studies* 12, 4 (Summer 2003): 119–160.

Mongin, Dominique. *La bombe atomique française, 1945–1958*. Brussels: Bruylant, 1997.

Moshaver, Ziba. *Nuclear Weapons Proliferation in the Indian Subcontinent*. Basingstoke: Macmillan, 1991.

Moyal, Ann Mozley. "The Australian Atomic Energy Commission: A Case Study in Australian Science and Government." *Search* 6, 9 (September 1975): 365–384.

Mozley, Robert F. *The Politics and Technology of Nuclear Proliferation*. Seattle: University of Washington Press, 1998.

Mueller, John E. *Retreat from Doomsday: The Obsolescence of Major War*. New York: Basic Books, 1989.

"The Escalating Irrelevance of Nuclear Weapons." In T. V. Paul, Richard J. Harknett, and James J. Wirtz, eds., *The Absolute Weapon Revisited: Nuclear Arms and the Emerging International Order*. Ann Arbor, MI: University of Michigan Press, 1998: 73–98.

Murphy, John. *Harvest of Fear: A History of Australia's Vietnam War*. St. Leonards, NSW: Allen and Unwin, 1993.

Nadeau, Richard, Richard G. Niemi, and Timothy Amato. "Emotions, Issue Importance and Political Learning." *American Journal of Political Science* 39, 3 (August 1995): 558–574.

Nandy, Ashis. "The Bomb, the NPT and Indian Elites." *Economic and Political Weekly*, special number, August 1972.

Nandy, Ashis *et al.* "Creating a Nationality: The Ramjanmabhumi Movement and Fear of the Self." In Ashis Nandy, *Exiled at Home*. Delhi: Oxford University Press, 1998.

Nantet, Jacques. *Pierre Mendès France*. Paris: Editions du Centurion, 1967.

Nathanson, Donald L. *Shame and Pride: Affect, Sex, and the Birth of the Self*. New York: Norton, 1992.

Nehru, Jawaharlal. "The Task Ahead" (radio broadcast from New Delhi, August 15, 1948). In *Jawaharlal Nehru's Speeches*, vol. I. Delhi: Ministry of Information and Broadcasting, 1958: 79–82.

The Discovery of India. Delhi: Oxford University Press, 1998.

Neuendorf, Kimberly A. "Quantitative Content Analysis Options for the Measurement of Identity." Paper presented at the conference on "The Measurement of Identity," Harvard University, December 2004.

Nocher, Jean. In "2e séance du 30 Août 1954," *Journal Officiel de la République Française, Débats Parlementaires – Assemblée Nationale*. Paris: Imprimerie des Journaux Officiels, 1956: 4471.

Norem, Julie K. and Nancy Canto. "Cognitive Strategies, Coping, and Perceptions of Competence." In Robert J. Sternberg and John Kolligan, Jr., eds., *Competence Considered*. New Haven: Yale University Press, 1990: 190–204.

Nossal, Kim Richard and Carolynn Vivian. *A Brief Madness: Australia and the Resumption of French Nuclear Testing. Canberra Papers on Strategy and Defence*, 121. Canberra: Strategic and Defence Studies Centre, Australian National University, 1997.

Nye, Joseph S. "Maintaining the Non-Proliferation Regime." *International Organization* 35, 1 (Winter 1981): 15–38.

Ornstein, Roberto Mario. "Contexto político internacional para los usos pacíficos de la energía nuclear." Manuscript, Comisión Nacional de Energía Atómica (Argentina), 1998.

Ortiz, Eduardo L. "Army and Science in Argentina: 1850–1950." In P. Forman and J. M. Sánchez-Ron, eds., *National Military Establishments and the Advancement of Science and Technology: Studies in 20th Century History.* Dordrecht: Kluwer Academic Publishers, 1996: 153–184.

Osiel, Mark J. "Constructing Subversion in Argentina's Dirty War." *Representations* 75 (Summer 2001): 119–158.

Parker, Christopher S. "New Weapons for Old Problems: Conventional Proliferation and Military Effectiveness in Developing States." *International Security* 23, 4 (Spring 1999): 119–147.

Partido Justicialista, Instituto Superior de Conducción Política, Consejo de Profesionales, Intelectuales y Técnicos. *Análisis, lineamientos doctrinarios y propuestas para la acción del Gobierno Justicialista.* Buenos Aires: Instituto Superior de Conducción Política del Partido Justicialista, 1989.

Pascoe, Rob. *The Manufacture of Australian History.* Melbourne: Oxford University Press, 1979.

Pastor, Robert A., ed. *A Century's Journey: How the Great Powers Shape the World.* New York: Basic Books, 1999.

Paul, T. V. "Strengthening the Non-Proliferation Regime: The Role of Coercive Sanctions." *International Journal* 51, 3 (Summer 1996): 440–465.

"The Systemic Bases of India's Challenge to the Global Nuclear Order." *Nonproliferation Review* 6, 1 (Fall 1998): 1–11.

Power versus Prudence: Why States Forgo Nuclear Weapons. Montreal & Kingston: McGill/Queen's University Press, 2000.

Paul, T. V., Richard J. Harknett, and James J. Wirtz, eds. *The Absolute Weapon Revisited: Nuclear Arms and the Emerging International Order.* Ann Arbor: University of Michigan Press, 1998.

Perkovich, George. *India's Nuclear Bomb: The Impact on Global Proliferation.* Berkeley: University of California Press, 1999.

Perón, Juan D. "Discurso pronunciado ante los diputados y senadores nacionales reunidos en Asamblea Legislativa, al inaugurar el 99o período de sesiones ordinarias del Congreso nacional." In *Juan Perón 1973–1974: Todos sus discursos, mensajes, y conferencias,* vol. II. Buenos Aires: Editorial de la Reconstrucción, 1974: 184–191. Available at http://lanic.utexas.edu/project/arl/pm/sample2/

Pertusio, Roberto L. *Una marina de guerra: ¿ para hacer qué?* Buenos Aires: Centro Naval, Instituto de Publicaciones Navales, 1985.

Petersen, Roger D. *Understanding Ethnic Violence: Fear, Hatred, and Resentment in Twentieth-Century Eastern Europe.* Cambridge: Cambridge University Press, 2002.

Peyrefitte, Alain. *Le mal français.* Paris: Plon, 1976.

"PM's poisoned pen spells the end." *Sydney Morning Herald,* January 1, 2001.

Poneman, Daniel. *Nuclear Power in the Developing World.* London: Allen and Unwin, 1982.

"Argentina." In Jed C. Snyder and Samuel F. Wells, Jr., eds., *Limiting Nuclear Proliferation*. Cambridge, MA: Ballinger Publishing Co., 1985: 89–116.

Pool, Ithiel de Sola. "Trends in Content Analysis Today: A Summary." In Ithiel de Sola Pool, ed., *Trends in Content Analysis*. Urbana: University of Illinois Press, 1959 189–233.

Pool, Ithiel de Sola, ed. *Trends in Content Analysis*. Urbana: University of Illinois Press, 1959.

Posen, Barry R. *The Sources of Military Doctrine: France, Britain and Germany between the World Wars*. Ithaca: Cornell University Press, 1984.

Potter, William C. "The Diffusion of Nuclear Weapons." In Emily O. Goldman and Leslie C. Eliason, eds., *The Diffusion of Military Technology and Ideas*. Stanford, CA: Stanford University Press, 2003.

Pottier, Olivier. "Les armes nucléaires américaines en France." *Cahiers du Centre d'études d'histoire de la défense* 8 (1998): 35–60.

Purkitt, Helen E., Stephen F. Burgess, and Peter Liberman. "Correspondence: South Africa's Nuclear Decisions." *International Security* 27, 1 (2002): 186–194.

Quester, George. "The Statistical 'N' of 'Nth' Nuclear Weapons States." *Journal of Conflict Resolution* 27, 1 (March 1983): 161–179.

Raghavan, V. R. "Dangerous Nuclear Uncertainties." *The Hindu*, March 13, 2000, available at http://www.hinduonnet.com/thehindu/2000/03/13/stories/05132523.htm. Accessed April 20, 2005.

"Whither Nuclear Policy?" *The Hindu*, July 1, 2000, available at http://www.hinduonnet.com/thehindu/2000/07/01/stories/05012523.htm. Accessed April 20, 2005.

Ramadier, Paul. "Déclaration à l'Assemblée Nationale de M. Paul Ramadier, president du Conseil désigné le 21 janvier 1947." In André Siegfried, ed., *L'Année politique 1947*. Paris: Editions du Grand Siècle, 1948: 322.

Rao, P. V. Narasimha. "Prime Minister Rao Gives Independence Day Address." In *FBIS Daily Report: South Asia*, August 16, 1995: 57–63.

Redick, John R. *Argentina and Brazil: An Evolving Nuclear Relationship*. Southampton: University of Southampton on behalf of the Programme for Promoting Nuclear Non-Proliferation, 1990.

Redick, John R., Julio C. Carasales, and Paulo S. Wrobel. "Nuclear Rapprochement: Argentina, Brazil and the Nonproliferation Regime." *The Washington Quarterly* 18, 1 (Winter 1995): 107–122.

Reid, Alan. *The Gorton Experiment*. Sydney: Shakespeare Head Press, 1971.

Reiss, Mitchell B. *Without the Bomb: The Politics of Nuclear Non-Proliferation*. New York: Columbia University Press, 1988.

Bridled Ambition: Why Countries Constrain their Nuclear Weapons Capabilities. Baltimore: Johns Hopkins University Press for the Woodrow Wilson Center, 1995.

"The Nuclear Tipping Point: Prospects for a World of Many Nuclear Weapons States." In Kurt M. Campbell, Robert J. Einhorn, and Mitchell B. Reiss, eds., *The Nuclear Tipping Point: Why States Reconsider their Nuclear Choices*. Washington, DC: Brookings Institution Press, 2004: 3–17.

Renan, Ernest. "Qu'est-ce qu'une nation?" In John Hutchinson and Anthony D. Smith, eds., *Nationalism*. New York: Oxford University Press, 1994: 17–29.

Renouf, Alan. *The Frightened Country*. Melbourne: Macmillan, 1979.

República Argentina, Ministerio de Obras y Servicios Públicos, Secretaría de Energía, Subsecretaría de Planificación Energética. *Plan Energético Nacional 1986–2000*. Buenos Aires, República Argentina, 1986.

"Retrouvailles franco-australiennes." *Le Monde*, January 7, 1975.

Reynolds, Wayne. "Menzies and the Proposal for Atomic Weapons." In Frank Cain, ed., *Menzies in War and Peace*. St. Leonards, NSW: Allen & Unwin, 1997: 116–137.

Australia's Bid for the Atomic Bomb. Melbourne: Melbourne University Press, 2000.

Rhodes, Richard. *The Making of the Atomic Bomb*. New York: Touchstone, 1986.

Robertson, David. *The Routledge Dictionary of Politics*. London: Routledge, 2003.

Rocard, Yves. *Mémoires sans concessions*. Paris: Grasset et Fasquelle, 1988.

Rohter, Larry. "If Brazil Wants to Scare the World, It's Succeeding." *New York Times*, October 31, 2004, "Week in Review" section, p. 3.

Rosen, Stephen P. *War and Human Nature*. Princeton: Princeton University Press, 2005.

Roy, Srirupa. "Divided We Stand: Diversity and National Identity in India." Ph.D. dissertation, University of Pennsylvania, 1999.

Royal Commission into British Nuclear Tests in Australia. Parliamentary Paper No. 482/1985. Canberra: Australian Government Publishing Office, 1985.

Sagan, Scott D. "Why Do States Build Nuclear Weapons? Three Models in Search of a Bomb." *International Security* 21, 3 (Winter 1996/97): 54–86.

"Rethinking the Causes of Nuclear Proliferation: Three Models in Search of a Bomb." In Victor A. Utgoff, ed., *The Coming Crisis: Nuclear Proliferation, US Interests, and World Order*. Cambridge, MA: MIT Press, 2000: 17–50.

The Limits of Safety: Organizations, Accidents, and Nuclear Weapons. Princeton: Princeton University Press, 1993.

Sagan, Scott D. and Kenneth Waltz. *The Spread of Nuclear Weapons: A Debate*. New York: W. W. Norton, 2003.

Saideman, Stephen. "Thinking Theoretically about Identity and Foreign Policy." In Shibley Telhami and Michael Barnett, eds., *Identity and Foreign Policy in the Middle East*. Ithaca, NY: Cornell University Press, 2002: 169–200.

Sanders, Noel. "The Hot Rock in the Cold War: Uranium in the 1950s." In Ann Curthoys and John Merritt, eds., *Better Dead than Red: Australia's First Cold War: 1945–1959*, vol. II. Sydney: Allen and Unwin, 1986: 155–169.

Santoro, Daniel. *Operación Cóndor II: La historia secreta del mísil que desactivó Menem*. Buenos Aires: Ediciones Letra Buena, 1992.

SarDesai, D. R. and Raju G. C. Thomas, eds. *Nuclear India in the Twenty-First Century*. New York: Palgrave-Macmillan, 2002.

Sauvage, Jean-Christophe. "La perception des questions nucléaires dans les premières années de l'Institut des Hautes Etudes de Défense Nationale 1948–1955." In Maurice Vaïsse, ed., *La France et l'atome*. Brussels: Bruylant, 1994: 59–82.

Schacter, Daniel L. *Searching for Memory: The Brain, the Mind, and the Past.* New York: Basic Books, 1996.

Scheinman, Lawrence. *Atomic Energy Policy in France under the Fourth Republic.* Princeton: Princeton University Press, 1965.

"The Politics of Nationalism in Contemporary France." *International Organization* 23, 4 (Autumn, 1969): 834–858.

Schell, Jonathan. "The Folly of Arms Control." *Foreign Affairs* 79, 5 (September–October 2000): 22–46.

Scherer, Klaus R. "The Role of Culture in Emotion-Antecedent Appraisal." *Journal of Personality and Social Psychology* 73, 5 (November 1997): 902–922.

Scherer Klaus R. *et al.*, eds. *Appraisal Processes in Emotion: Theory, Methods, Research.* New York: Oxford University Press, 2001.

Schissler, Hanna and Yasemin Soysal, eds. *The Nation, Europe, the World: Curricula and Textbooks in Transition.* New York: Berghahn Books, 2005.

Schwarzer, Ralf, ed. *Self-Efficacy: Thought Control of Action.* Washington, DC: Hemisphere Publishing Corp., 1992.

Scott, James C. *Weapons of the Weak: Everyday Forms of Peasant Resistance.* New Haven: Yale University Press, 1985.

Secretary-General's High-Level Panel on Threats, Challenges and Change. *A More Secure World: Our Shared Responsibility.* New York: United Nations, 2004.

Sen, Amartya. "India and the Bomb." *Journal of Peace Economics, Peace Science and Public Policy* 6, 4 (Fall 2000): 16–34.

Servan-Schreiber, Jean-Jacques. *Passions.* Paris: Fixot, 1991.

Sheetz, Mark S. "France and the German Question: Avant-garde or Rearguard? Comment on Creswell and Trachtenberg." *Journal of Cold War Studies* 5, 3 (Summer 2003): 37–45.

Sherif, Muzafer. "Superordinate Goals in the Reduction of Intergroup Conflict." *American Journal of Sociology* 63, 4 (1958): 349–356.

Siegfried, André, ed. *L'Année politique.* Paris: Editions du Grand Siècle: annual.

Simon, Robert L. *Fair Play: The Ethics of Sport,* 2nd ed. Boulder: Westview Press, 2004.

Singh, Arun. "The Military Balance: 1985–1994." ACDIS Occasional Paper, University of Illinois at Urbana-Champaign, March 1997.

Singh, Jasjit, ed. *Nuclear India.* New Delhi: Knowledge World, 1998.

Singh, Jaswant. *Defending India.* Basingstoke: Macmillan, 1999.

Sloss, Leon. "The Current Nuclear Dialogue." *Strategic Forum* 156 (January 1999).

Smith, Anthony D. *Theories of Nationalism,* 2nd ed. New York: Holmes and Meier Publishers, 1983.

Smith, Roger K. "Explaining the Non-Proliferation Regime: Anomalies for Contemporary International Relations Theory." *International Organization* 41, 2 (Spring 1987): 253–281.

Snyder, Jed C. and Samuel F. Wells, Jr. *Limiting Nuclear Proliferation.* Cambridge, MA: Ballinger Publishing Co., 1985.

Snyder, Richard, H. W. Bruck, and Burton Sapin. *Foreign Policy Decision Making.* New York: Free Press of Glencoe, 1962.

Sokolski, Henry. "Next Century Nonproliferation: Victory Is Still Possible." *The Nonproliferation Review* 4, 1 (Fall 1996): 90–97.

Solingen, Etel. *Industrial Policy, Technology, and International Bargaining: Designing Nuclear Industries in Argentina and Brazil.* Stanford, CA: Stanford University Press, 1996.

Soutou, Georges-Henri. "La politique nucléaire de Pierre Mendès France." *Relations Internationales* 59 (Autumn 1989): 317–330.

L'Alliance incertaine: les rapports politico-stratégiques franco-allemands, 1954–1996. Paris: Fayard, 1996.

Soutou, Georges-Henri and Alain Beltran, eds. *Pierre Guillaumat: la passion des grands projets industriels.* Paris: Editions Rive Droite, 1995.

Spector, Leonard S. *Nuclear Proliferation Today.* New York: Vintage Books, 1984.

Spector, Leonard S. with Jacqueline R. Smith. *Nuclear Ambitions: The Spread of Nuclear Weapons, 1989–1990.* Boulder, CO: Westview Press, 1990.

Stein, Janice Gross. "Political Learning by Doing: Gorbachev as Uncommitted Thinker and Motivated Learner." *International Organization* 48, 2 (Spring 1994): 155–183.

Steinhausler, Friedrich. "What It Takes to Become a Nuclear Terrorist." *American Behavioral Scientist* 46, 6 (February 2003): 782–795.

Stoll, Richard. "World Proliferation of Latent Nuclear Capability," http://es.rice.edu/projects/Poli378/Nuclear/Proliferation/. Accessed April 19, 2005.

Subrahmanyam, K. "Indian Nuclear Policy – 1964–98." In Jasjit Singh, ed., *Nuclear India.* New Delhi: Knowledge World, 1998: 26–53.

Sundarji. K. *Blind Men of Hindoostan.* New Delhi: UBS Publishers, 1993.

Sylvan, Donald A. and James F. Voss, eds. *Problem Representation in Foreign Policy Decision Making.* Cambridge: Cambridge University Press, 1998.

Talbott, Strobe. "Dealing with the Bomb in South Asia." *Foreign Affairs* 78, 2 (March–April 1999): 110–122.

Tanham, George. *Indian Strategic Thought: An Interpretive Essay.* Santa Monica, CA: RAND, 1992.

Tannenwald, Nina. "The Nuclear Taboo: The United States and the Normative Basis of Nuclear Non-Use." *International Organization* 53, 3 (Summer 1999): 433–468.

Tanter, Raymond. *Rogue Regimes: Terrorism and Proliferation.* New York: St. Martin's Press, 1999.

Taylor, Theodore B. "Commercial Nuclear Technology and Nuclear Weapon Proliferation." In Onkar Marwah and Ann Schulz, eds., *Nuclear Proliferation and the Near-Nuclear Countries.* Cambridge, MA: Ballinger Publishing Co., 1975: 111–124.

Tellis, Ashley. *India's Emerging Nuclear Posture: Between Recessed Deterrent and Ready Arsenal.* Santa Monica: RAND Corporation, 2001.

Tetlock, Philip E. *et al.* eds. *Behavior, Society, and Nuclear War,* vol. I. New York: Oxford University Press, 1989.

Tharoor, Shashi. *Reasons of State: Political Development and India's Foreign Policy under Indira Gandhi, 1966–1977.* New Delhi: Vikas Publishing House, 1982.

Thielmann, Greg. "Preventive Military Intervention: The Role of Intelligence." *Ridgway Center for International Security Studies Policy Brief 04-1,* University of Pittsburgh, October 2004.

Thomas, Raju G. C. "The Growth of Indian Military Power: From Sufficient Defence to Nuclear Deterrence." In Ross Babbage and Sandy Gordon, eds., *India's Strategic Future*. Delhi: Oxford University Press, 1992: 35–66.

Thomas, Raju G. C. and Amit Gupta, eds. *India's Nuclear Security*. Boulder: Lynne Rienner, 2000.

"Top Atom Men to Go." *Financial Review* (Australia), April 19, 1973.

Tsebelis, George. *Nested Games: Rational Choice in Comparative Politics*. Berkeley: University of California Press, 1990.

Tulchin, Joseph S. *Argentina and the United States: A Conflicted Relationship*. Boston: Twayne, 1990.

Turner, John C. with Michael A. Hogg, Penelope J. Oakes, Stephen D. Reicher, and Margaret S. Wetherell. *Rediscovering the Social Group: A Self-Categorization Theory*. Oxford: Basil Blackwell, 1987.

Utgoff, Victor A., ed. *The Coming Crisis: Nuclear Proliferation, US Interests, and World Order*. Cambridge, MA: MIT Press, 2000.

Vajpayee, Atal Behari. Interview with *India Today*, May 25, 1998.

"Prime Minister's Independence Day Address to the Nation" (August 15, 1999). Available at http://www.indiagov.org/special/cabinet/Primeminister/1999ID_PM_Speech.html. Accessed April 20, 2005.

"Evolution of India's Nuclear Policy." Paper laid on the table of the House on May 27, 1998, available at http://www.indianembassy.org/pic/nuclearpolicy.htm. Accessed April 20, 2005.

"Prime Minister's reply to the discussion in Lok Sabha on Nuclear Tests on May 29, 1998." Available at http://www.indianembassy. org/pic/pm(ls).htm. Accessed April 20, 2005.

"Prime Minister's reply to the discussion in the Rajya Sabha on nuclear tests on May 29, 1998." Available at http://www.indianembassy. org/pic/pm(rs).htm. Accessed April 20, 2005.

Van Creveld, Martin L. *Nuclear Proliferation and the Future of Conflict*. New York: The Free Press, 1993.

Van der Kroef, Justus M. "The Gorton Manner: Australia, Southeast Asia, and the US." *Pacific Affairs* 42, 3 (Autumn 1969): 311–333.

Van Evera, Stephen. "Primed For Peace: Europe after the Cold War." *International Security* 15, 3 (Winter 1990–1991): 7–57.

"Hypotheses on Nationalism and War." *International Security* 18, 4 (Spring 1994): 5–39.

Varshney, Ashutosh. "India, Pakistan, and Kashmir: Antinomies of Nationalism." *Asian Survey* 31, 11 (November 1991): 997–1019.

Vertzberger, Yaacov Y. I.. "Rethinking and Reconceptualizing Risk in Foreign Policy Decision-Making: A Sociocognitive Approach." *Political Psychology* 16, 2 (1995): 347–380.

Walsh, Jim. "Surprise Down Under: The Secret History of Australia's Nuclear Ambitions." *Nonproliferation Review* 5, 1 (Fall 1997): 1–20.

Walter, James A. *The Leader: A Political Biography of Gough Whitlam*. St. Lucia: University of Queensland Press, 1980.

Watson, Cynthia. "Will Civilians Control the Nuclear Tiger in Argentina?" In Peter Worsley and Kofi Buenor Hadjor, *On the Brink: Nuclear Proliferation and the Third World*. London: Third World Communications, 1987: 209–216.

Watt, Alan. *The Evolution of Australian Foreign Policy 1938–1965.* Cambridge: Cambridge University Press, 1967.

Weiner, Tim. "Report Finds Basic Flaws in US Intelligence Operations." *New York Times*, June 3, 1998.

Welch, David A. *Justice and the Genesis of War.* Cambridge: Cambridge University Press, 1993.

White, Ralph K. ed. *Psychology and the Prevention of Nuclear War: A Book of Readings.* New York: New York University Press, 1986.

Whitlam, E. Gough. "Labor's Stand on the French Tests." *The Radical*, July 11, 1972.

——— "The Prime Minister's Press Conference." *Current Notes on International Affairs* 43, 12 (December 1972): 619.

——— "Australia's Foreign Policy." *Australian Foreign Affairs Record* 44, 1 (January 1973): 30–34.

Willis, F. Roy. *France, Germany and the New Europe 1945–1967*, rev. ed. Stanford: Stanford University Press, 1968.

Windrem, Robert and Tammy Kupperman. "Pakistan Nukes Outstrip India's, Officials Say." MSNBC News report, June 6, 2000, available at http://www.msnbc.com/news/417106.asp?cp1=1. Accessed April 20, 2005.

Witte, Kim. "Fear as Motivator, Fear as Inhibitor: Using the Extended Parallel Process Model to Explain Fear, Appeal, Successes, and Failures." In Peter A. Andersen and Laura K. Guerrero, eds., *Handbook of Communication and Emotion: Research, Theory, Applications, and Contexts.* San Diego: Academic Press, 1998.

Wohlstetter, Albert *et al. Moving Toward Life in a Nuclear Armed Crowd? Final Report to the US Arms Control and Disarmament Agency.* Los Angeles: Pan Heuristics, 1976.

Wolff, Kurt, ed. *The Sociology of Georg Simmel.* New York: Free Press, 1950.

Worsley, Peter and Kofi Buenor Hadjor, eds. *On the Brink: Nuclear Proliferation and the Third World.* London: Third World Communications, 1987.

Zaidi, A. Moin, ed. *Annual Register of Indian Political Parties 1985.* New Delhi: India Institute of Applied Political Research, 1987.

Name index

Subject index

America, *see* United States
anti-nuclear movement, *see* nuclear taboo
ANZUS, *see* Australia
Arab world, 52
Argentina (*see also* individual presidents
    and statespersons), 2, 14, 15, 41, 42,
    43, 47, 63, 141–170, 204, 207, 214,
    217, 220
  Air Force (*see also* Argentina – Military),
      147, 150, 167, 168
  Algeria and, 164, 169
  Antarctic Treaty, 143, 170
  Army (*see also* Argentina – military),
      147, 150
  Atucha I reactor, *see* Argentina – nuclear
      energy program
  Atucha II reactor, *see* Argentina –
      nuclear energy program
  Australia and, 119, 146, 169
  autonomy, *see* Argentina – nuclear
      energy program, sportsmanlike
      nationalists
  Beagle Channel, 158
  Brazil and, 15, 64, 142, 143, 150, 158,
      159–164, 165–166, 167, 169, 188,
      189, 212, 214, 221
  bureaucratic politics perspective on,
      142, 145
  Canada and, 141, 142, 146, 147, 148,
      149, 151, 152, 154, 159
  Candu, 146, 147, 148
  Cold War, 166
  Comisión Nacional de Energía Atómica
      (CNEA), 142, 144, 145–146, 147,
      148, 149, 150, 151, 152, 153, 154,
      155, 156, 157, 158, 159, 161, 165,
      167, 213
  Communists and, 64, 150
  Cóndor II, *see* Argentina – missile
      program
  Congress, 66, 153, 160, 165
  Croatia and, 167

  Cuba and, 150
  Defense Ministry, 150, 153
  democratic regimes (*see also* names of
      individual presidents and
      statespersons), 65, 66, 163
  "dirty war,", 64, 69, 150
  economic development (*see also*
      Argentina – nuclear energy program),
      143, 144, 147, 148, 153, 155, 161,
      162, 166, 167, 169
  Ecuador and, 167
  Egypt and, 164, 167
  Embalse reactor, *see* Argentina – nuclear
      energy program
  Falklands/Malvinas, 142, 158, 163, 167
  Fiat Corp., 147
  Foreign Ministry (*Cancillería*), 151
  France and, 143, 144, 146
  generic foreign "others,", 65, 67, 68, 70
  Germany and, 69, 146, 147, 148, 149,
      154, 157, 158, 160, 163, 167
  Great Britain, *see* Argentina – United
      Kingdom
  heavy water, *see* Argentina – nuclear
      energy program
  India and, 148, 149, 162–163, 188, 189
  institutionalist perspective on, 141, 142,
      159
  International Atomic Energy Agency
      (IAEA), 143, 144, 150, 161, 169
  International Monetary Fund (IMF)
      and, 69
  Investigaciones Aplicadas (INVAP), 156,
      169, 170
  Iran and, 169
  Iraq and, 167, 168, 169
  Italy and, 157
  key comparison other, 67
  Kraftwerk Union (KWU), 147, 154, 155
  Kuwait and, 168
  Latin America and, 65, 67, 146, 150,
      161, 162

264